The President's Counselor

The President's Counselor

THE RISE TO POWER OF *Alberto Gonzales*

Bill Minutaglio

An Imprint of HarperCollins*Publishers*

For Louis C., a wise man

HarperCollins books may be purchased for educational, business, or sales promotional use. For information, please write: Special Markets Department, HarperCollins Publishers, 10 East 53rd Street, New York, NY 10022.

FIRST EDITION

Designed by Jennifer Ann Daddio

Printed on acid-free paper

Library of Congress Cataloging-in-Publication Data has been applied for.

ISBN-10: 0-06-111920-2
ISBN-13-978-0-06-111920-0

06   07   08   09   10   DIX/RRD   10   9   8   7   6   5   4   3   2   1

Contents

Preface

After several months of research and more than two hundred interviews with colleagues, close friends, and fierce critics, a clear pattern was emerging: Alberto Gonzales had been crafting and processing the most secretive and controversial directives in modern U.S. history, but he had somehow managed to remain the most hidden member of the Bush family's inner circle. This work is an examination of his life up through his tenure as counselor to President George W. Bush—up until the moment he was sworn in as attorney general of the United States. A future work will address his time as head of the Department of Justice; for now, this book charts his path to power and the deliberately guarded work he did for the Bush family and inside the Bush White House.

He truly was "the president's counselor"—and all that that Faustian bargain meant and implied. He was first entrusted with long-hidden Bush family secrets and then entrusted with the blueprints for addressing the most grave matters facing twenty-first-century America. The fact that he once held the deep confidences of a man who would become president—and then became the point person for finding the means to prosecute the new war on terror—was all the more remarkable because of his background. He had only entered public service in the mid-1990s. His early years as the son of impoverished migrant workers in a place called Humble, Texas, hardly hinted at the hotly debated and clandestine work he would do . . . and the wicked, international ramifications of that work.

This book began years ago, as an outgrowth of my biography *First Son:*

George W. Bush and the Bush Family Dynasty. In one review of that book, political columnist David Broder wrote that he "could discern no evident bias—either adulatory or cynical." This biography was written with that goal again in mind. Too, as in my biography of Bush, I attempted here to recognize the way Gonzales's roots influenced his later behavior: Gonzales's story is linked to class and race in ways that separated him from Karl Rove, Karen Hughes, and other Bush family loyalists. Unlike those others, he wasn't a political junkie, he wasn't an overt political activist, he wasn't one to spar and play games with political reporters.

He was the in-house counselor—the keeper of confidences, a figure who aggressively pursued discretion. At one point, someone told me that Gonzales was like a man who always seemed to be holding something inside, like someone whose skin practically bulged with all the confidences he had accumulated. That person added that each time he envisioned Gonzales, he drew a mental picture of him leaning over and whispering to someone. That person suggested that if Gonzales ever sat for a portrait, it should be rendered in the manner of Rembrandt's *The Evangelist Matthew*—with Gonzales as the mostly hidden, gauzy figure hovering behind the more clearly depicted and important-looking man in the foreground ... and resting a few fingertips on the important man's back ... and leaning in to murmur in that man's ear.

As might be expected of the associates of someone whose life is, rightly or wrongly, defined by his discretion, many who knew Gonzales only reluctantly came to the phone for interviews. In the end, there were numerous in-depth interviews with a former Cabinet official, ex–White House staffers, next-door neighbors, high school friends, guidance counselors, teachers, corporate clients, law school classmates, former Texas state officials, high-ranking former military commanders, death penalty advocates and foes, constitutional experts, members of the clergy, law partners, and even old sports coaches. Research reached into Alaska, Washington, Texas, Colorado, Massachusetts, and New York. Thousands of documents, including Gonzales's military records and his work on dozens of death penalty cases, were obtained under the Freedom of Information Act and the Texas Open Records Act. From August 2005 until February 2006, an endless stream of questions was directed to his office at the Department of Justice—emphasizing that this book would concentrate on his life up until the time he was sworn in as attorney general. All but a handful of the most benign inquiries went unanswered. At one point, I was quietly pressed to share my work-in-progress with the attorney general, perhaps in exchange for answers to my questions. That proposal was declined.

Truth be told, I was initially surprised at the hushed proposal to share my work. But it made sense, in a way, as my work grew ever more complicated by each new revelation about Gonzales's secret memos, programs, and meetings during his tenure as Bush's counsel in both Texas and in Washington, D.C. It was, of course, his personal style and the nature of his work, and the nature of the post-9/11 environment in the White House, to barter in confidences, to move from shadow to light. His life, personally and professionally, has been defined by a series of trades and trade-offs. He has been, in the end, a political chiaroscurist.

In 2006, as I was concluding this look at his life from 1955 to early 2005, he was facing bruising, unforgiving lessons about the curses and blessings of living life as that whispering voice behind the throne. The president's counselor had been accused of corrupting cherished civil liberties and staining the reputation of America—and he had at the same time been hailed as an authentic American success story. Then on a profound and personal note, he would tell CNN in the spring of 2006 that it was "unclear" if his grandparents had come to the U.S. legally from Mexico.

He had gone far beyond Humble.

Bill Minutaglio, Austin, June 2006

I believe there are techniques of the human mind whereby, in its dark deep, problems are examined, rejected, or accepted. Such activities sometimes concern facets a man does not know he has.

—JOHN STEINBECK, *EAST OF EDEN*

ONE

Un Sueño

Monsignor Paul Procella, a priest from a small parish in Texas that happens to be named after a flame-haired harlot, is ambling down the carpeted, hushed hallways of the most important floor in the U.S. Department of Justice. It is the first Thursday in February 2005. He is on a private tour of one of the most heavily guarded buildings in America, because he knows someone who knows someone. The priest, a beloved fixture at his tight-knit church in a city named Humble, has come to Washington in the dead of winter because the son of one of his parishioners is being sworn into high office.

There is a secretary sitting at a desk in one hallway.

A sign on the desk reads "Office of the Attorney General."

Never shy, the priest approaches the secretary.

"Is it okay if we just walk around?"

She raises her head: "Oh yeah. It's open today for anyone who wants to." So the priest, who presides over Saint Mary Magdalene's Church, strides deeper into the inner sanctum of America's Justice Department, the headquarters for the nation's battles against terrorism and crime. Ahead there is a large conference room area—burnished, beautiful—and the priest decides to steer inside. The room is anchored by a large table with chairs around it. The room, and the way it is appointed, suggests a clear heaviness, an intense gravity. This is where the aching nightmares of 9/11, the bloody war on terrorism, and the toxic CIA leaks would be analyzed, pondered, debated.

And then Monsignor Procella suddenly notices that there is someone in the room. There is a small, frail, seventy-two-year-old lady sitting by herself in a chair. She is not at the big table. She is off to one side as if she wouldn't deign to take her place at the center of the room. She is quietly staring and is very much alone—the smallest figure in the U.S. Department of Justice's conference room. That day, all over Washington and on the editorial pages around the country, the elected, the appointed, and the self-anointed seers of politics and power are immersed in their versions of what they consider to be the great issues. And that day the white-hot flashpoint—The One Great Issue of The Day—concerns the old woman's son. He is *The Issue.*

Not far from where she is sitting, her first son is being accused of torturing people with the power of his pen—but also being lauded for his loyalty, his clear thinking. He is being labeled a traitor to his culture—but also as an inspiring role model for young people, for immigrants, in pursuit of the American Dream. He is being vilified for embodying the most hideous tendencies of the United States—and he is being praised for embodying this country's unparalleled, boundless opportunities. The priest looks down at the unlikely woman occupying the Department of Justice room. The emptiness and silence are even more dramatic when weighed against the fiery events and statements searing her son up and down the corridors of power in Washington.

"Maria," gently asks the priest, "what are you doing?"

The old lady, who had once been a migrant worker in Texas, who had once stooped over in hot, dusty fields and picked cotton, who had never gone beyond a sixth-grade education, realizes she is not alone. The priest and the mother of the new attorney general of the United States look at each other. It is 1,416 miles from Maria Gonzales's $35,600 wooden home on narrow Roberta Lane in Humble, Texas. And not much has changed at the house since she and her late husband helped to build it in 1958. The neighborhood still has no sidewalks, no curbs. Every front yard still has a weed-riddled ditch to carry away the scummy mosquito-infested sludge that always accumulates in that dank part of southeast Texas. Directly across the street from her home, one of the other old wooden houses in the neighborhood has literally fallen down—it looks as if it just sighed one day, gave up, and simply collapsed into a Gordian knot of beat-up boards, rusted wires, and jagged glass.

"Well, I just got tired of walking and so I just sat down," the old lady finally says to the priest. She was glad her parish priest had also come to Washington to see her son sworn in. "I'm going to sit in here and rest a while."

The priest marveled at her. He once thought he knew pretty much all that there was to know about the Gonzales family and their world on Roberta Lane. The widow Maria is beyond faithful at *Santa María Magdalena*. She is at the church three, sometimes four, times a week. She is omnipresent inside the ever-growing Mexican-American congregation: there are thirty-five hundred families in the church; about a thousand of them are Hispanic; about three hundred of those families speak mostly Spanish, and sometimes Maria is the only one they talk to. She is one of those short, calm, older Mexican-American women who seem to always, well, to always *just be there*. Maria speaks only when spoken to. She is never openly questioning—never. Her loyalty is never articulated—it is just so damned evident.

"She's involved in various groups, but she's not a leader of any of them. She would not do that. Everything she does is in a support role," the priest tells people.

Just a few weeks earlier, the priest had been leafing through some magazines at his church and he came across the news that President George W. Bush had nominated someone named Alberto Gonzales to be the next attorney general. He read deeper into the story. There was mention of the fact that Gonzales had grown up in a place called Humble and that his mother still lived there in the same wooden house that he had grown up in. The president of the United States had mentioned Humble, Texas—and he had told the world where Maria lived, back in that same small two-bedroom house.

The priest quickly called the Rosewood Funeral Home in Humble. He knew that's where Maria had worked for decades as a housekeeper. It's where Procella had gone to pray for so many of his deceased parishioners over the years. The funeral home owner picked up the call from the priest:

"Do you know we have a new attorney general named Alberto Gonzales?" asked the priest.

"Yeah, isn't that nice?" replied the funeral home owner.

"Did you know that is Maria's son?" said the priest. He had assumed the funeral home owner would know about it—the funeral home owner's brother had been a U.S. congressman for many years.

"No, she hasn't said anything about it," answered the surprised funeral home owner.

The priest hung up and called Maria at her home. She answered the phone.

"Maria, Alberto is named attorney general," the priest began.

"Yes," Maria replied. "He's a very good boy."

She was surprised that when she traveled to Washington, Alberto was there to meet her at the airport. She wasn't expecting that. When he was younger, Alberto did the interpreting for his mother and father when they would have to come visit him at high school. Alberto was the only one in the family to ever move away. He was the only one of Maria's eight children to go to college. Of course, he had stopped speaking much Spanish a long time ago. Both of his wives were *Norte Americanos*—white women. He had a mustache for a while when he came to Washington, but some people said the mustache made him seem *very* Mexican. Now it is gone. In Texas, he had been Catholic, of course— the family had been wedded to the Catholic Church, to *Santa María Magdalena*. But now he worshipped at a big "evangelical" Episcopal church in Virginia. He once talked about his summers picking cotton as a small boy, and he had lived in that tiny white Texas house where Maria still lives—he lived there with nine other members of his family crammed into two bedrooms, without hot water and without a telephone. He refused to let his friends visit because he was embarrassed. But now he had just sold his sprawling home in Virginia for $700,000. He didn't bother applying to college when he was leaving high school. But he wound up graduating from Harvard Law School. He used to beg rich people to buy Cokes from him when he was a kid. But now he plays golf with Ben Crenshaw and the president of the United States.

When Maria saw Alberto standing and waiting for her at the airport, she could also see that there were four somber but wary men hovering nearby in their pressed, neat suits. She had seen this before and she did not question it: "Alberto has to have escorts. Alberto has to have someone drive him," Maria tells people. Her son has spent exactly one decade—his entire public life—affixed to, adopted by, the Bush Dynasty. Now her Alberto has bodyguards.

For ten years he has been George W. Bush's *abogado*—his lawyer, his counselor. And she knows that his enemies deride him as being no different than Tom Hagen, the Robert Duvall character in *The Godfather*—the low-key but wickedly efficient and unquestioning consigliere sent on his awful missions for the Bushes, the WASP Corleones. He is, they even say, more than the President's Counselor—he is the enabler for crimes against humanity, for war crimes, for crimes against the very things America stands for and was founded upon.

At the White House, his best friend, *Presidente Bush,* will tell anyone that Maria's son is the ultimate manifestation of the Bush family's most treasured sobriquet—he is *a good man*. When either the elder George Bush or the younger George Bush wants to admit someone into their fold, when they finally determine that someone is deemed to be an unflinching loyalist—someone worthy of steering the family's ambitions—that person is literally described as "a good man." George W. Bush simply says that Alberto Gonzales is *a good man*.

But deep inside the dizzying orbits of power and hubris, Gonzales has also somehow remained as hidden as his mother inside his conference room. For most of the twenty-first century, he has been the most politically important Hispanic in America—and yet he has managed to remain, as even his admirers say, an "enigma." He is the nation's most senior law enforcement officer. And the family priest thinks sometimes Maria's son is more like his mother than anyone realizes. "I see her at the funeral home. She usually opens up in the morning. She's a caretaker, so she cleans, and you would think that is a menial job, really, but that is her work. She's very, very pleased with that and very, very loyal. She's low-key. You would never pick her out of a crowd. She is a person who certainly does not draw attention to herself.

"She's not going to be the person that tries to take over a group or anything of that nature. But . . . she will do anything she can to help others."

Of course, her son has done almost *anything* he has been asked to do by the family he owes his public career to. It is something both his critics and his allies can agree on. He is unquestioningly loyal to the Bush Dynasty. There is a reason a large picture of the elder George Bush and the younger Bush, walking together, was hanging on a wall inside Gonzales's office at the White House.

His critics, fierce and united in their hatred of him, say the problem is that, yes, he will do *anything* for the Bushes: He will attack the Clinton White House, even though the Clintons have left. He will quickly sign off on the paperwork that allows the execution of dozens of prisoners in Texas. He will construct the legal template allowing a nation to go to war . . . a template that will ultimately reveal the fact that a handful of weak-willed American soldiers exult in torture and humiliation. He will offer his written opinion that some of the internationally recognized moral codes for how captured enemy combatants should be treated are "obsolete" and "quaint"—and human rights proponents around the world would label him a torturer. He will wield the pen and the legal muscle that will protect and shield the men who help run the Bush White House— Senior Adviser Karl Rove and Vice President Dick Cheney. He will help write the controversial Patriot Act and endorse a domestic spying program that some say violates the essential civil liberties that define America. And on an acutely narrow and coldly pragmatic level, Maria's son will have more to do with the election of George W. Bush to the presidency than many of the others affiliated with his so-called Iron Triangle of advisers: Her son will protect George W. Bush from having to reveal his criminal record—and, thus, he will ensure Bush's ascent to the Oval Office.

His allies, his friends such as the president, also say he will do *anything* for the Bush family and America: He will be the steadfast lawyer for the White House, someone whose allegiances are never driven by naked ambition. He will behave in the same way that George Bush once characterized Laura Bush—he will be the "perfect" political partner, someone who will never steal the limelight or speak out of turn. He will do the taxing work, the soul-searching work, of finding the righteous legal and moral certitude to follow the letter of the law and put human beings to death in Texas. He will fight the war on terror by monitoring and tracking possible enemies—in any way possible. Yes, he will shield Cheney and Rove—but he will shield them from blatantly partisan inquiries lodged by vindictive, bitter Democrats. And yes, in the muddled and paranoid post-9/11 world, he will offer the president and his country some fresh, sage advice on how to combat the new, shadowy terrorism. He will even set in motion a wholesale conservative revolution by scouring the country for qualified legal minds, for men and women who will strictly interpret the words of the founding fathers, men and women who he will tell the president of the United States to appoint to the highest courts in the land.

One thing is clear to his enemies and his supporters: Maria's son has already taken his chair alongside the other men and women in the pantheon of the Bush Dynasty, the men and women who have put their lives in service to the family and kept it entrenched in the highest offices in America for sixty years straight.

B ack in the Department of Justice room, Maria is still sitting and visiting with her parish priest. She had told the priest something earlier. It was something she dreaded, feared, for her boy. She knows her son has many enemies, that things are different than they were for him on Roberta Lane: "I know they are going to grill him," Maria Gonzales confessed to the priest. "I hate to see him go through that."

They were calling him the architect of torture, someone who had made an easy leap from endorsing the execution of dozens of people in Texas to affirming America's right to gather and extract information from both its enemy prisoners and its citizens in any way possible. Too, there were the supporters, the ones who were saying he would make grand American history and become the first Hispanic to be named to the U.S. Supreme Court. Sometimes it all seems as evanescent as a dream, or like something that had happened so quickly it could never be measured. In Humble, his angry, drunken father and his sweet, young brother died in separate but horrible ways. Their lives were in many ways wasted, each died with ponderous questions, and now they were buried side by side at the funeral home and cemetery where Maria still reports to work every morning to clean. Surrounded by death, she is literally with her deceased husband and son every day. Sometimes she checks on their grave markers, rearranging the flowers and tidying their simple stones.

Only one of her eight children, Alberto, ever went to college. Three never even graduated high school. Maria watched Alberto, never saying a thing, as he began to spin away from the family. No one ever left Humble and what it meant, implied, except Alberto. It was always unspoken but really not unexpected that it would somehow be Alberto. He moved with a preternatural compactness, a physical way that seemed to suggest he was always processing and weighing and measuring. It was beyond methodical, it was painstaking. And it was in solid contrast to her husband, his father, and the way that man drank and drank as if it would soften the hard edge of all the limitations he must have felt. It was *como un sueño,* like a dream, and now she was sitting in the big, heavily guarded Department of Justice building her son had come to work in. It was cold in Washington. The wind was howling outside. The room seemed immune not just to the elements but to *everything* out there.

Her son once got up in front of a large crowd, including his mother and all the family members he had left far behind, and said this: *"Like my parents before me, all of my hopes and dreams are in my children."* Her son liked the way that sounded, and her son liked that quote from Ralph Waldo Emerson, the great American transcendentalist who preached self-reliance's superiority over lockstep authority: *"What lies behind us, and what lies before us, are tiny matters compared to what lies within us."*

And when Maria came to see him in Washington, she would get up at dawn, like she had done for his hungover, ex–migrant worker father over and over again for decades. Back then, back when they spoke only Spanish to each other, Maria would be there at daybreak stuffing a paper bag with tortillas and beans so that her husband could eat something with his grime-covered hands during a break at a miserable construction site.

Now her first son would come down to the kitchen in the big house and his mother would be there in the kitchen already. She'd be up at dawn for her son, like she had been for her husband back in Humble. He knew his mother was serving him, like she had served his father. *"Only I wasn't going to a construction site. I was reporting to the White House to advise the president of the United States."*

Now in Washington with her Humble parish priest looking on, the mother gathers herself to go meet her son, the *abogado.*

Together, she and her son will go see his client—*el presidente de los Estados Unidos.*

TWO

Beyond Humble

Alberto Gonzales and his miserably alcoholic father are gingerly negotiating the narrow, soggy lanes leading away from Humble, Texas, and the sluggish San Jacinto River. The father and son are passing slumping shacks built with cedar planks salvaged from abandoned East Texas farmhouses, moving alongside work clothes taking forever to dry as they hang limply on strings of twine rescued from the Houston Ship Channel docks. From some corners, Alberto Gonzales can almost make out Houston 14 miles away. The glazed spires are erupting out of the endlessly flat landscape as if Texas had cracked wide open one day and spasmodically given birth to something instantly immense and fully grown. And when the heat presses down, those buildings can seem to twitch, as if they're vibrating from the mad hype and hustle inside the offices and could just suddenly rocket into the concrete-colored heavens rippling toward the Gulf of Mexico.

He waits until his father boards the bus that will take him to another low-dollar, blue-collar job in the dizzying city some call Bombay on the Bayou. The bus goes bumping along the dirt-caked roads until it disappears inside that broad mirage of heat waves. He turns his back and finally strolls home, walking under the miserly stands of pine trees, the humidity so thick it's as if you're walking through a stand of tall, damp reeds. He could still *feel* Houston, out of sight but never out of mind. He had felt it at daybreak as he watched his mother, Maria, hand his father a paper lunch sack filled with beans and tortillas. He felt it as he watched his mother serving the eight children the same meal in the two-bedroom house.

Every day it's the same, his old man locked into his steady march out the door again . . . six and sometimes seven days a week . . . another day of finding some way . . . in the back of a friend's crappy car, on a back seat in another bus . . . toward a summoning, demanding job somewhere out there in the greater Houston area. Some days, instead of going right away with his father, he peeks through the small windows facing out to Roberta Lane. He catches a quick glimpse of his father in his overalls, maybe this time destined for a job clambering through grimy silos thick with the sour smell of processed rice trucked from east Texas and southwest Louisiana: *"As a young boy, I begged my mother to wake me before dawn so I could share breakfast with my father before he left for work."*[1]

"We didn't have a car, and I still remember my dad walking down the street as he would go to work at this construction site to catch a bus, and we were running outside and waving my dad goodbye.[2]

After school he'd always wait patiently for his father. He'd look up from a game of two-on-two baseball or football in the street with his younger brothers Antonio, Rene, and Timmy. He'd see a stoop-shouldered man trudging from the direction of all the neighborhood streets named after women—Roberta, Martha, Shirley, and Velma—but it was someone else. Dusk would be coming on, and his father still wasn't home yet. Maybe his father had gone drinking somewhere. Maybe he had stopped by Antonio Bustamante's bar, The Laredo, on North St. Charles Street, and was ordering yet another sweating *Caballito* . . . the Little Horse . . . bottled Jax beer with a label depicting that iconic image of Andrew Jackson doffing his hat while hanging on to a rearing white horse. If you were a hard-core drunk at The Laredo in Houston, you called out for *uno mas Caballito.*[3] And if you were a regular at places like The Laredo, you might weigh the aching way the Mexican-Americans in Houston labored on the very things that created the enormous wealth, the way the Mexican-Americans literally lived in the shadows of the tall buildings, the way the American Dream was really as elusive as any other *sueño* . . . any other dream.

Pablo Gonzales couldn't stop drinking. He was a shouting alcoholic whose voice would sometimes rage out of that crappy, tiny house on Roberta Lane until the neighborhood children playing in the piles of fallen pine needles would look up wide-eyed and suddenly very alert: "My father had a terrible drinking problem. He was an alcoholic, and there were many nights when I remember him coming home, and you know, severe arguments with my mother and throwing the pillow over my head and just not trying to listen to all of that. I mean, unfortunately, those happened way too often . . . you know, in that respect, I mean there were some difficult times in my family." [4]

According to some Texas records, Pablo Medina Gonzales Jr. was born July 12, 1929, perhaps to Mexican immigrants named Maria Medina and Pablo Gonzales, in the city of Kenedy in Karnes County southeast of San Antonio—a place famous for having the first Polish colony in the United States, for living and dying by cotton and cattle, for siding with the Confederacy and being home to a secret "castle" run by the pro-slavery Knights of the Golden Circle. Kenedy was named after Mifflin Kenedy, one of the ranching legends of Texas; the Kenedy Cotton Compress was one of the most important ones in Texas. According to other records, Maria Rodriguez was born August 21, 1932, not far from San Antonio, perhaps to Mexican immigrants named Fereza Salinas and Manuel Rodriguez. [5] *"My grandparents were Mexican immigrants. I remember visiting them as a very young boy—there was no telephone, no television, no hot running water, no porcelain toilet, we went to the outhouse by the railroad tracks that ran along the back of their property,"* Gonzales remembered. [6]

Pablo and Maria met as teenaged field workers, picking cotton around the greater San Antonio and south-central Texas area. Pablo made it through second grade; Maria managed to make it to sixth grade. And they came of age in a state that offered different but similarly daunting challenges to blacks and Hispanics. Chunks of Texas were ruled by oil and agribusiness—and blacks and Hispanics went belowdeck to do the grimy, grinding jobs that kept the big wheels of farming, ranching, and the petroleum and petrochemical industries humming and efficient. Segregation, racism, and brutality were daily visitors. Children were beaten for speaking Spanish; minorities were thrown down courthouse steps if they tried to register to vote; a plague of illnesses, from tuberculosis to cholera, coursed through the minority communities like a rising tide of painful, predictable sorrows.

And in the heart of the urban areas in Texas, police briskly and often violently cordoned off the "nigger towns" and the "Spanish towns" and did anything necessary to enforce unspoken checkpoints—making sure that minorities stayed on their side of the avenue, the boulevard, and the Santa Fe Railroad tracks. In rural areas there was also an acute isolation. The lives of many families whose ancestors had filtered up from Mexico revolved around an often cruel caste system in the southern parts of Texas, going to work on massive cattle ranches or sprawling farms that were, in many ways, like modern-day plantations. The Mexican-American families were not slaves, but many of them were exiled to living on the grounds of the ranches and farms where they worked, many of them bought their supplies from the ranches and farms, and many of them were economically shackled in a modern version of indentured servitude.

By the time Pablo and Maria Gonzales married in South Texas in 1952, sectors of the farming business were becoming increasingly mechanized. The mood swings in the job market for itinerant cotton laborers like Pablo and Maria were immense and unyielding. They and thousands of other desperately poor Mexican-Americans were forced to face alternatives, and many of them were leading a surge toward jobs—any jobs— near the bigger cities of Dallas and Houston. That move was expedited by the huge, shifting political landscape in parts of Texas that were built with the blood and sweat of poorly paid Mexican immigrants.

To keep crop production rolling during World War II, the Bracero Program emerged. (A *bracero* was a legal contracted worker who labored in the fields.) The program was an attempt to allow and control the flow of Mexican farmworkers into the United States and to ensure a steady, temporary supply of cheap labor. Hundreds of thousands of Mexican entered the country as *braceros,* aiming for a guarantee of basics such as shelter and jobs paying them 30 cents an hour. And many of them eventually came to Texas, despite that state's insidious reputation as a place where the farmworkers were never given good housing, were subject to harassment, and were never offered educational opportunities. In time, many of the contracted *braceros* returned to Mexico. But many decided to stay, thus triggering the Immigration and Naturalization Service's infamous Operation Wetback, which captured and expelled hundreds of thousands of Mexicans throughout the 1950s and 1960s. In Texas, thousands and thousands of Mexican-American families lived in abject fear that they would be hounded and maybe unfairly swept into the massive Operation Wetback net. Pablo and Maria Gonzales, like thousands of other barely educated, poorly paid field workers, had no inkling of the higher political ramifications—but even without knowing the intricacies of the policies, it was clear they were in an increasingly mechanized, uncertain, and unstable world *en Tejas.*

Two years after they were married, Pablo and Maria had their first child, Angelica. A year later they had their first son: records in Bexar County show that Alberto Gonzales was born August 4, 1955, in San Antonio. Friends say he was born at the historic Santa Rosa Hospital, a fixture in the city since the 1800s. His father was a twenty-six-year-old migrant worker who could barely read or speak English. His mother was a twenty-three-year-old migrant worker who was now responsible for two children and planned to have several more. For a while, when Alberto was still a child, his parents would take him from the barrio and he would spend his summers picking cotton. "I remember summers picking cotton as a small boy, being dusty and hot. We were very poor." [7] Not long after their son was born, it was very clear that they had to do something. They decided to leave the backbreaking, unpredictable work on the farms and move closer to the biggest city in the South: "My parents met as migrant workers when they were young. Once they got married and they started having children, they had to settle down, and so they settled in Houston." [8]

Houston was heaving, hot, and crowded, but it was also where people were lining up for dangerous, abysmally low-paying jobs: molding skyscrapers in 105-degree heat; ladling toxic petrochemicals in the roaring, cavernous refineries; pouring the concrete and tar for the highways ripping through the old inner city neighborhoods; building the massive Ship Channel that would serve the refineries and the petrochemical plants. There were other jobs, too—jobs that summoned memories for the migrant workers of when they coaxed cotton, corn, and oranges from hardscrabble Texas farms. In Houston, some of them were now on their knees digging their hands into the clammy, gumbo soil and nurturing the spectacular azaleas and bougainvillea in the languid, luxurious River Oaks neighborhood . . . and, this part was new, very new, for many of them . . . peering up from the gardening work and staring at the soigné, almost slow-motion world of the wealthy Anglo oil families as they mingled, danced, and laughed at another catered backyard fete under a tent.

Those poor Mexican-American families escaping to the greater Houston area filtered in from all over the state, especially the Rio Grande Valley and south-central Texas. And by the late 1950s Houston was already choking, constricted—almost a million people were there. The Mexican-Americans were instantly exiled to zones east of downtown that followed the path of caramel-colored Buffalo Bayou as it slithered toward the Houston Ship Channel, one of the most polluted waterways on the planet, estimated at one time to be comprised of 80 percent sewage. Hispanic men went to work at the nearby shipyards or on the Santa Fe Railroad.[9] And in the tightly packed, overheated areas like Magnolia Park and the Second Ward, *Segundo Barrio,* florists, cafes, cantinas, shoe repair shops, and mom-and-pop grocery stores along Navigation Boulevard struggled to maintain a semblance of community.

By the time Pablo Gonzales decided to move his family to the area, there were at least seventy-five thousand and more likely somewhere north of one hundred thousand Hispanics—or "Spanish white" as they were often labeled on census reports—in greater Houston.[10] The numbers would surge and multiply, but for now, as the Gonzales family arrived, the documented Hispanic population of Houston was pegged at only about 7 percent. The Gonzales family would be part of a very distinct minority. There were fewer "No Mexicans Allowed" signs, but you could still plainly make out the shadowy rectangle where those signs had once hung—and you didn't need a sign to tell you that you were unwelcome in a certain bank, restaurant, or store in Houston.

Pablo Gonzales had already decided that he and his new family needed to somehow carve out a life away from the heart of the city and *Segundo Barrio.* They would strike out on their own and do what a few other Mexican-Americans were doing: look for the cheapest plots of otherwise useless land on the farthest edges of major urban areas. Places like Oak

Cliff in Dallas and far south San Antonio—places where sometimes, if you distanced yourself enough, if you put yourself out in the nearest patch of woods, out in the first acre of wide-open prairie, *somewhere just far enough away,* you could raise chickens and allow the roosters, *los gallos,* to strut in the road. You could grow vegetables and you could stretch your arms wide. It felt like something to authentically call your own; there were big yards, tall trees, and a sense of belonging, of expansive ownership. It was better to be as far away as possible, better in the woods than trapped in what passed for some grand social experiment in public housing in the *Segundo Barrio* or one of the other tightly packed, isolated neighborhoods inside the city. Better to be in a place where you could retain a modicum of independence and maybe even a modicum of dreams. It wasn't for everyone, but Gonzales decided he didn't need to be like everyone else, to follow everyone else. It was good to be far enough away from the city.

All in all, it was going to be better than stooping over on the big farms run by the white *padrones,* the white godfathers who ran their Texas cattle and agricultural operations like latter-day Southern plantations.

Pablo found a quarter-acre not far from the San Jacinto River in the old town of Humble. It was 14.86 miles from Roberta Lane to Texas Avenue in the center of downtown Houston.

"My father, at different times in his life, picked crops as a migrant, worked construction, and was part of a maintenance crew at a rice field not far from here. He had few opportunities, because he was an uneducated man. I suppose that, to some, he was just a common laborer. But to me, he was a special man who had hands that could create anything. He and two of my uncles built the house that I grew up in, near Intercontinental Airport. My mother still lives there today.

"I remember playing in the field as a small boy, as they laid the cinderblocks for the foundation. First they nailed together the two-by-fours, then the Sheetrock that would form the walls, and skillfully hammered the composition shingles on the roof of the small two-bedroom house that became our home." [11]

Humble was less complex than Houston, but like so many surprising places in Texas, it had a direct connection to something outsized, extraordinary, the kind of thunderclap that actually had an impact on every town in America and every nation in the world. Named after Pleasant Humble, a dogged San Jacinto River ferry operator, it is where the pine trees of East Texas begin to give way to the flat, barren plains that lead to the Gulf of Mexico. Toward the end of the 1800s, the only business to speak of in Humble was lumber, and in 1880 there were just sixty people—ten white and fifty black—with many of the black residents doing the heavy labor sawing pine trees at the lumber mill. That insulated world was turned on its head when a gushing oil field was uncorked in 1904. Within a few months, more oil was pumping out of Humble than anyplace in Texas. The town was instantly invaded by thousands of money-grabbers, investors, hucksters, and hopefuls. A year after the massive oil splurge, ten thousand people had staked out the boomtown. And, finally, under the direction of future governor Ross Sterling, the Humble Oil and Refining Company came into being. It would later be known as Exxon.

Fifty-four years after the oil was discovered and when the Gonzales family decided to relocate to Humble, the boom was long over. Sterling had decided that he needed to take his oil company away from tiny, isolated Humble and relocate it a few miles south in more muscular, powerful Houston. And when Pablo Gonzales bought his quarter-acre in Humble, there were only two thousand residents left in the area, a mixture of laborers and a few retirees. With his brothers, he built a small white clapboard home with a well in the yard. There were two bedrooms in the 1,000-square-foot low-slung home, and there was a ditch out front that sometimes stayed filled with lukewarm water and mosquitoes. There would be no telephone service. There would be no curbs, no sidewalks, no driveway, and no garage. There was no hot water. "I remember getting water, putting it in a pot, putting it on the stove, heating it so we could take baths." [12]

Too, there would be no *policía* for the Gonzales family to worry about as they settled in a city outside of Houston.

Humble was close to Houston, but far enough away to keep Pablo's family safe. Far enough away to keep them alive. Safe from the police. Inside Houston, poor people sometimes learned to fear the police as much as the criminals. Men were still being beaten and murdered because they were Mexican-American or black. Plenty of people in the barrio knew what had happened to Manuel Crespo, the city's crusading first Hispanic cop. The former funeral home operator and community organizer had been brought onto the force in the 1940s to "talk to the Spanish"—there were rumblings in the barrio, gangs were forming, and Anglos were becoming afraid to head down Navigation toward the Ship Channel. Crespo could talk the language; he had been active in forming sports outlets for kids, starting up a Boy Scout troop, cofounding the Mexican Chamber of Commerce. He was named a detective, with Anglo patrol officers working under him—an act that never settled well with a hard-core element in Houston. In 1946 Crespo walked to his desk at the dismal police headquarters and found that a crime had been committed inside the police station: Someone had cracked open his desk and stolen all his files. Crespo reported the theft and resigned the next day. Some people said he did it out of frustration; some people said he did it because he knew he was a marked man. He went back to work running the Crespo Funeral Home, deep in the heart of the barrio. Mexican-Americans were not equals in Houston, and sometimes that racism could turn violent.

The year Alberto was born, Sigman Byrd, one of Texas's greatest unsung writers, was among a small handful of journalists in the state regularly giving voice to the normally voiceless in Houston and chronicling sides of that city that many people would rather have forgotten:

"To us who know her well, this is the most dramatic city in time, for she changes constantly, growing at once more beautiful and more hideous each day, nightly more seductive and faithless, becoming, before our very eyes, a white-towered megalopolis of the world of tomorrow. . . . Of course, from upstairs, even flying low in the yellow ground haze, you can't see the skid rows, the slums, the heartbreak, the bloated body floating in the bayou. You see only the gleaming towers of commerce, the lucent cutstone palisades of the city." [13]

In Houston, some poor people learned to fear the police as much as the criminals. They were brutalized and thrown, sometimes by rogue police, over city bridges into the murky waters of Buffalo Bayou, the city's main artery. Buffalo Bayou was, really, a symbol for the city's wicked extremes. It was where the grand Bayou Bend mansion and some of the other fine homes were located; it was also where the city's crushing, evil secrets unfolded. It was, in so many ways, the soul and birthplace of Houston. The capricious body of water was where two entrepreneurial brothers arrived in the 1800s and began building an unlikely place named in honor of Republic of Texas hero General Sam Houston. Those Anglo city "founders" were eventually laid to rest in Founder's Cemetery, a short walk from Buffalo Bayou. And outside the gates of the cemetery was a blocky and looming oak tree that could easily withstand the weight of a body hanging from a rope. For decades, frightened Mexicans and blacks simply referred to it as the "Hanging Tree." Truth be told, there were hanging trees all over Texas—on the outskirts of tiny Mexia, in far south Dallas, and in forgotten places in the tangled woods of deep east Texas. The written lynching records, such as they are, show that fifty-five Hispanics have been hung in Texas; that figure is presumed by most historians to be woefully underestimated.

Sometimes while their children waited for them to come home, some men just vanished in Houston and other parts of Texas. They disappeared, and when they did, their names didn't need to be erased from ledgers, accounts, books—those men had never been counted to begin with. Their names didn't have to be added to the rosters of the lynched. So it was really as if nothing was amiss. As if no one had vanished at all. As if they had never existed in the first place.

In the poorest Mexican communities throughout Texas, you would sometimes hear this: *Tenemos nada...pero tenemos fé.* We have nothing...but we have faith.

And the church, as always, became the bedrock for the hopelessly disenfranchised and isolated Mexican-Americans in Humble, in Texas, in the usually ironclad caste system in this part of the United States. The church was sometimes the only touchstone, the only source of faith. The Gonzales family had "very specific Catholic beliefs," says family friend Jacob Valerio, who grew up with the Gonzales boys. "Very strong Catholics, from what I saw. Their parents were very strong Catholics" [14] Maria was the driving force in that early connection to the church, and Alberto Gonzales knew it was his mother's wish that the children stay wedded to Catholicism. "My mother was devout in her religion, gave me a Catholic upbringing, so I learned right from wrong very early." [15]

And at Saint Mary Magdalene's Church—founded in 1911—the dogged, visiting priests of the Oblates of Mary Immaculate who rotated in and out of the parish would feel as if they were ministering in another land, another country, especially when they looked in the eyes of the faithful, like Pablo and Maria Gonzales and their impressionable children, Angelica, Alberto, Antonio, Christina, Theresa, Rene, Timothy, and Paul. How to explain to them, to all the families in the parish, the story of *Santa María Magdalena*? How to convince the impoverished members of the congregation that they should take hope in her story?

For millions of young Catholics, Mary Magdalene was the harlot with flame-colored hair who slinked on the periphery of humanity until she begged for inclusion. Mary Magdalene was an outsider whose redemption and acceptance came only when she confessed her shortcomings. At *Santa María Magdalena* people knew the church was named for the classic sinner possessed by demons, by some ungodly longing. According to the gospels of Mark and Luke, it wasn't until "seven demons had gone out" that *Santa María Magdalena* had been accepted . . . it wasn't until she underwent an exorcism at the hands of Jesus Christ.

The priests gingerly tried to suggest that the stories were wrong, that the real Mary Magdalene was not an inferior human being but actually a hero, a prophet, and a woman of deep, sturdy faith. Acceptance of that message would be long in coming. For the newly arrived Mexican-Americans who knew her story, *Santa María Magdalena* was still the exile outside heaven's gate. And the story of *Santa María Magdalena* was a recognizable one for Pablo Gonzales, who labored inside Houston's gates, then retreated to a poor, hidden place called Humble.

He worked *como un perro*—like a dog—then headed back to Humble, with the rich city blocks giving way to shacks built on cinder blocks, to soupy land almost humming with insect larvae, to scowling dogs roaming and pissing wherever they pleased, to dinged-up cars abandoned next to piles of rusting appliances strewn on what passed for lawns. Pablo Gonzales, his hands callused from working in Houston, drank and then drank some more. Sometimes the children cowered from the sound of his rising voice. And on Sunday, Maria was faithful at church. Her husband had settled into his bittersweet mercies and frailties out on the distant northern edges of one of the biggest cities in America. He built the house with his brothers, and that house unquestionably revolved around him.

Alberto was the second child in the family but also the first son of Pablo Medina Gonzales. He really didn't know exactly how long his father had been drinking. There was little to say about it, nothing to really do but take solace in the fact that his father sucked it all up, even with a raging hangover, and marched out the door every goddamned single day. In the spirit of *Santa María Magdalena,* that, at least, was some shred of saving grace: "No matter how much he drank on a particular night, if it were a workday the next morning, he was always up and he was always going to provide for his family, so I learned that lesson very early on." [16]

Sometimes Alberto would wonder what people in the neighborhood thought. His mother always kept all her children close by. She didn't want them wandering. If they went outdoors, they were ordered to report back every thirty minutes. [17] On weekends or at night when people came outdoors after the heat had subsided a bit and winds had gusted up from the Gulf of Mexico, he would say hello to the mothers out on the street, the ones who looked exactly like his mother, Maria. Some mornings he saw those same mothers walking down the street alongside his father—sweat already blossoming on their white dresses as they went to where they could also catch a ride or a bus to Houston, where they could go to work cleaning the mansions in River Oaks, that lavish neighborhood rolling out along Buffalo Bayou.

Sometimes it seemed like every one of the two thousand people in Humble was being pulled to Houston. Sometimes it seemed as if everyone was in service to whatever and whoever was waiting for them in voracious Houston. Maybe all of the children, Alberto included, would become exactly what their mother and father had become. At night he would hug his parents before going to sleep. In the mornings the family would sometimes go to church together and pray.

A city of unholy sighs and bruises, Houston was increasingly rimmed with fabulous excess and wretched despair in the years after World War II. It was the industrial city of the South with a permanent, smoggy blanket as testimony to the billions of dollars churning from the oil refineries. Unlike Dallas, Austin, and some other famous cities in Texas, Houston was the most internationally diverse city, the one with the consulates and the oceangoing freighters. Houston was also the one with the Old Oil Money and just enough decaying ritual, enough vine-covered history, to have perfected a special hierarchy of exclusion. The tornado of money sucked in transplants from the Northeast—so many of them climbers and strivers and family emissaries all hell-bent on profiting in some way, any way, from the oil game. When they came, they were almost obsessed with replicating the usual trappings such as country clubs, polo matches, seats on the symphony board, and tables at the diamond-studded balls, galas, and fundraisers. Increasingly, ubiquitously, the new Mexican-American arrivals to Houston did the gardening, maintaining, cleaning, and constructing attendant to all of those trappings.

And for those who were not living above the cloud line, Houston became—at an increasingly rarefied level—the most impenetrable of all Texas cities. Wealth and power and influence in its competitive counterpart of Dallas were always far more transparent—no doubt equally unobtainable but seemingly more evident, more easy to name and identify. Everyone conceded that Houston was firmly under the command of a small group of people, but very few could adequately name them or summon them to easy description. Houston had sets and subsets, layers and sublayers, and complex, moneyed conclaves in the hushed downtown corridors.

That aching sense of utter inaccessibility helped pump the first drops of blood into community movements among Houston's Hispanics. Through the first half of the twentieth century there were nascent attempts to identify cultural rallying points and win fair treatment from the *Americanos,* especially the financiers and the police and the educators. By the time the Gonzales family moved to the area, a powerful local chapter of the League of United Latin American Citizens began to champion desegregation, better schools, and improved social services. With the emergence of national LULAC leaders such as lawyer John Herrera and restaurateur Felix Tijerina, Houston became one of the flashpoints for the Latino movement.

There is no evidence that the Gonzales family immersed itself in LULAC or other Hispanic organizations such as the American G.I. Forum or Comité Patriótico Mexicano, the Mexican Patriotic Committee, which held dances, barbecues, and gatherings to celebrate Mexican culture and serve as a kind of mutual aid society. The Gonzales family hadn't sought the greater Houston area out as a culturally empowering zone, a place where the family could either be the recipient of broader social change or where it could put its shoulder to the wheel and join the cause. There was no early political activism, no overt allegiance to any number of waves such as *Viva Kennedy,* a pro–John Kennedy movement that spurred Mexican-American Catholics to hang JFK's picture on their walls, to hail him as a man of faith and sympathy—and to register to vote. "I don't remember my parents voting, but I learned the value of self-responsibility," said Gonzales.[18]

In 1956, just as Pablo Gonzales was thinking of moving his family to Houston, there had been another galvanizing moment in the state: The commanding Henry B. Gonzales rewrote Texas history by becoming the first Mexican-American in the modern Texas Senate. In 1958, the same year Pablo and Maria decided to move to Houston, Henry B. Gonzales again stunned the state by being the first Mexican-American to launch a serious run for governor. These were profound political upheavals for Mexican-Americans but the Gonzales family members were witnesses more than participants. Like many other blue-collar families coming to Houston and either headed for the city barrios or for those outskirt towns like Humble, the Gonzales family was ultimately and simply fixed on survival. They were fixed on Pablo's blue-collar jobs and they were fixed on the steady pace of their impoverished part of Texas. They were fixed on just finding some semblance of peace, home, and community. Pablo and Maria had been migrant workers. Their focus was on settling down and establishing roots. There was a clear sense in the family that they would never move again, never stray much farther than the Humble area. It was poor, but most of all it was predictable.

"When we were growing up, there was peace and quiet. We never had any trouble with crime or any violators. When the beltway came through and the city started growing, that's when we started having crime through the neighborhood every now and then. For the most part, back then, it was pretty quiet. You could leave your windows open and your doors unlocked without anybody messing with you," says neighbor Jacob Valerio.[19]

There was something else. As a kid, Alberto Gonzales didn't even realize how poor he was until he started going to Houston—and started dwelling on the tall buildings and the enormous wealth and power just a few miles away. Gonzales would later say: "Like many people that I've talked to around the country who came from impoverished backgrounds, you really don't have an idea about how poor you are until a certain age."[20]

I t was a plan, a perfect plan in so many ways.
Houston and other large Texas cities were infamous for the particular way city leaders would coalesce and plot out what to do with the "minority problem," especially as the civil rights movement gained steam in the 1940s, 1950s, and 1960s. (In Dallas, the intimidating group that ran the city for almost the entire twentieth century was the Dallas Citizen's Council—run, in part, by the Dallas Morning News, which proudly trumpeted its segregated dining facilities. The council was dubbed the Dallas *White* Citizen's Council by some minority residents.) City leaders in Texas had a simple but effective solution to avoid the kinds of protests, riots, and "embarrassing" displays of civil rights activity that might stunt the growth of business: They would "select" and identify certain minority leaders who were deemed to be the kind of people the city fathers could "work with." Those minority leaders—a businessman, an educator, a preacher—would be allowed to come to a meeting at the normally segregated country club or would be appointed to a paying, token position on a commission or a board. This process of "inclusion" and "accommodation" was the trade-off for that minority representative keeping any unrest in the minority community under control. And into the segregated River Oaks Country Club—segregated under a long-standing gentleman's agreement—would come a Hispanic or black community leader handpicked by the city leaders.

Of course, some minority leaders refused to toe the line and risk earning the derisive label of "Uncle Tom" or "coconut" (brown-skinned on the outside but white inside). But some minority leaders went to another entirely different extreme and argued that the only way for minorities to break out of their caste system, to gain access, was to become ever more like the Anglo majority—to forcefully strip away any cultural excesses that could get in the way of economic assimilation. It was a brutal conceit: Assimilate to succeed. Abandon your heritage and move on up. Stop speaking Spanish. Stop celebrating the deep cultural reference points. Start being more like the people who really ran Houston. Stop being Mexican and start "acting" Anglo.

Several days after Alberto Gonzales was born, a black teenager named Emmett Till was murdered in Money, Mississippi, by people who thought he had whistled at a white woman. In Pittsburg, Texas, the mob of men who had castrated a black man had settled into an easy rhythm in the small city. In another twenty-two years a Hispanic man in Houston named José Campos Torres would be beaten by several policemen and thrown alive into Buffalo Bayou. The mean underbelly of Texas wasn't going to change for years, for decades. Success—through assimilation or any other means—was never a given.

Growing up in the 1960s in Humble and on the edge of Houston, home to the most millionaires in the state, that megalopolis wasn't merely distant for someone like Alberto Gonzales. Given the spidery complexities—the social labyrinth, the racism, the exclusion—it would be *un milagro* for him to find his way. It would be a miracle and he would need guides, very unlikely enablers, who would crack open an edge of the gilded tent and bring him inside. Those *compañeros* would, of course, have to be like no one else he had ever encountered growing up in Humble under the roof of alcoholic Pablo Gonzales. With these guides would come enormous trade-offs. Those *compañeros* would be like the title of novelist Larry McMurtry's classic book about Houston: *All My Friends Are Going to Be Strangers*.

Alberto Gonzales and his family had moved into the shack his drunken migrant worker father had just built with his own hands in a part of Texas seemingly locked outside of Houston. Not long after, George W. Bush and his family moved into a spectacular Houston home, custom-made and cared for by Mexican-American maids and gardeners, on 1.2 acres near the country club his millionaire father had just joined.

THREE

Very Different

Her Alberto had mastered a balance between getting what he wanted and not being an overt pain in the ass. Early on, the kids at Aldine Junior High had seen it, the same thing Maria saw at home as he jockeyed for food, clothing, and the one bathroom in the house on Roberta Lane. Unlike his father, he was never prone to emotional excess, but he was competitive; he hated to lose. Albert, as all his friends and classmates called him, sometimes seemed almost emotionally flatlined and hopelessly incurious—and to some others he seemed like a paragon of steadiness, his mind probably processing a million things at once. He was, everyone agreed, resolute. And, early on, he took on a different role than his seven brothers and sisters. He would walk Angelica to school and they'd see each other in the hallways. He would walk with her to the local school library: "I loved reading. I remember my sister and I used to walk by ourselves, about a mile and a half, to an elementary school. The libraries would be open and we'd be able to check out books. I would check out history books, books about sports. Books about animals, I really, really enjoyed, but I can't recall any that particularly inspired or motivated me."[1]

He organized competitive games of catch with Antonio, Rene, and Timothy:

"I played sports. I loved sports. Growing up as a kid, I played a lot of sports during the summer with my brothers. I like to tell the story that my memories of my youth for the summers was, we'd get up in the morning—and this is when there were four boys of comparable age—and we'd play baseball, two on two, all morning. We'd make a field in our backyard, we'd put up a backstop—we had chicken wire—and we'd play baseball, two on two, all morning, go in, have lunch, my mom would then make us lay down and take a nap, which we hated, and after that we'd play baseball all afternoon." [2]

He also helped his mother with the younger children, especially Paul. In Humble, his father didn't sign him up for Cub Scout meetings, horseback riding, or camping. Gonzales learned to be self-directed, to identify a goal and aim for it. He played sports obsessively and stuck to the sports he was good at, that he could win at. He didn't belligerently steamroll people; he wanted to either keep pace with them or pass them by. Maria would tell people her son is "not the kind to trample over someone else to get what he wants. Opportunities have simply come before him, and he has taken them." [3]

At school he was beginning to learn about the cultural separation points—the ones immersed in deep history. A special required version of Texas history was being taught, and he blinked when he heard the one-sided versions of the war between the country his grandparents had come from and the state where he was being raised. "I do have memories in Texas—you have to take state history, and a large part of the course is Mexico and the Battle of the Alamo. And I remember in class fidgeting very uncomfortably with talk about how Mexico had plotted against Davy Crockett. It made me very uncomfortable." [4]

At the age of twelve, in 1967, Gonzales signed up for a menial job helping a neighbor on Saturdays selling soda and snacks at Rice University, square in the heart of what passes for Houston's intellectual and cultural corridor. "The children started working as soon as they could work," says Monsignor Paul Procella at Saint Mary Magdalene. [5] Now Gonzales would be the one trying to find a way to a perpetually summoning Houston. Now he would be following his father's path, trying to figure out how to get to a hot, sweaty task that would pay him a few dollars a day. Not far from the Houston Museum of Art, Rice University was named in honor of its original patron: murdered financier William Marsh Rice, whose lurid death by chloroform once mesmerized America. Rice had been the second richest man in Texas, having made his fortune in cotton, railroads, liquor, and insurance—with the help of his fifteen slaves. (Rice, who died in 1900, was a member of a Texas "slave patrol"—men who hunted down fugitive slaves.) He was murdered in a New York City apartment at the age of eighty-five. The sensational trial following his death riveted the nation when it was revealed that his valet and his attorney were behind his poisoning death and had conspired to use forgeries to inherit the millionaire's estate. The ashes of the murdered former slave owner were buried under an impressive sculpture on the grounds of the university he had funded.

Sometimes known as the "Harvard of the South," Rice is the most elite educational institution in Texas, and though Rice once intended it as a place for the deserving poor, over the years it had become more exclusive, out of reach. It was perhaps exclusive not by cold, hard, orchestrated intent but by years of "tradition" and those complex, prohibitive layers of society and culture that Houston specialized in. This was not a school that Pablo and Maria Gonzales even remotely targeted as one that their children would ever attend; college wasn't even anything they had considered.

The minority student population at Rice was always in the single digits. The school existed somewhere on the other side of Houston, in the zone where the wealthy people recreated, got educated, saw private doctors, and dined at the finest restaurants in the state. It was part of some shiny social order that the Gonzales family was not part of and never would be. It was one thing to go to Houston to work on a construction site or inside the sweltering rice silos, but it was too much to press on, to move deeper into the city and toward the area around Rice University, near the Houston Museum of Art and the staggeringly, over-the-top Shamrock Hotel, built by oilman Glenn McCarthy (the inspiration for Jett Rink in the movie and book *Giant* and someone who made millions, lost millions, and created his own brand of bourbon called "Wildcatter").

The Shamrock, just down the road from Rice, defined Texas for people around the country and the world. When it was built in the 1940s, it was trumpeted as the largest hotel on Earth, and it had a gift shop proudly selling postcards showing merry women water-skiing in the gargantuan hotel pool. It was the scene of knockdown, drag-out parties, orgies, balls, fetes, and god knows what. Tricked out to look vaguely Hawaiian, vaguely uber-Texan, it was like some Xanadu on the Prairie—a precursor of the famous TV show *Dallas* and its depiction of the unending, sometimes tasteless extremes of the Caligula Cowboys in the Lone Star State.

McCarthy hosted his favored political and pop culture rainmakers, from Howard Hughes to John Wayne, and for both the low-rent and the highbrow the place simply came to symbolize the jaw-dropping, wretched excess of the nouveau-mega-riche in Texas. Going to Houston to work on another construction job really was one thing; that was like going through the front door of the homes of the powerful people in Houston and waiting in the foyer. Going to the area spreading out from Rice University, including the Shamrock, was like entering the playrooms, the living rooms, the bedrooms of the Texas rich.

In Humble, Maria wondered if she had made the right decision to let her kid sell Cokes and popcorn—he not only had plans to pitch his wares at Rice but also at the famous city symbol, the Astrodome, for Houston Oilers football games. It wasn't that she didn't trust her oldest son. With Alberto, it was like launching a steady ship. "I always told them to respect their elders and their teachers, to tell the truth and to look out for each other," she said.[6] At Rice Stadium he marched up and down the steps and peered out at the tree-lined neighborhood and the historic campus.

"I got my first job selling soft drinks at Rice football games. I was just a twelve-year-old kid, carrying those heavy trays of Cokes and Sprites up and down the upper deck of Rice Stadium. After the games, as we waited for the crowds to disperse so that we could go home, I would stare over the stadium walls and watch the Rice students stroll back to the colleges. And I wondered: What would it be like to be one of you—a Rice student?

"Growing up on Houston's North Side to a mother and father who combined only had eight years of a formal schooling, I had no realistic comprehension about a Rice education. But I understood even then, as I cheered for the mighty Owls, that I wanted to go to school there."[7]

At Douglas MacArthur Senior High School, he was no. 34, the safety on the Generals football team. He had a long shock of black hair sweeping across his forehead, and when he would spring to field a ground ball for the baseball team, it would flap out from under his cap. He was one of about 54 Hispanics out of a class of 314 students; there were about 14 African-American students at MacArthur. Schools in the greater Houston area had only just become desegregated. Families, students, teachers, and police watched how the new social experiment would unfold, especially inside a city with such a brutal, violent legacy and so much minority blood on its hands.

"He was a bright student and young man. He took the college prep courses while he was in high school and made good grades. He was punctual. I don't think he did a lot of class cutting or skipping classes, or things like that. Those were the early days of integration, and he just didn't align himself with other Hispanic students. His best friends were white students who were also in the accelerated classes and going through the college prep programs," remembers Marine Jones, his high school counselor and the first African-American hired for an academic position. She was keeping a careful watch on how the races coexisted, on whether the social upheaval that was welling up in some inner city neighborhoods in Houston was going to erupt at MacArthur.

"It was somewhat rare, because most of them had their own little groups. Even though they were in the same school and played sports together, at lunch all the Hispanics would meet at one place, all the blacks would be over here, the whites would be over there. He was one of those kids who was an all-around person. He didn't limit himself to one place. He wasn't at one table. He was at all of them. My opinion is that he had the self-confidence that told him, 'I don't have to do that. I don't have to be segregated into one place. My situation is not the same as that person. I don't have the same financial support or the same type of care, but I am as good as that person. I am an equal, anyway. I am just as good as they are.' It was somewhat unusual for best friends to be of another race. But not with Al. His best friends were of every race. That didn't seem to make a bit of difference to him. He doesn't allow himself to only be seen as a minority."[8]

His Hispanic friends remember a school that had few overt racial flare-ups, perhaps an outgrowth of the fact that a majority of the teenagers realized there were very few economic distinctions between the families and neighborhoods that fed the school—that they all existed outside the gilded parts of Houston: "I don't recall any instances of racism. It was a middle- to low-income environment. There were very few students that I recall that had wealth or their families had wealth. It wasn't a situation of the rich and the poor. The whites left us alone and we left them alone. If you dated interracially, you might get stares from both racial groups and you might face a situation where parents would not approve of that," says Jody Hernandez.[9]

There were times when Gonzales would have to ask his parents to come to school to sign some papers, to meet teachers. The cultural tugs were more than obvious, and it was readily apparent to Jones that Gonzales had taken on roles as the translator and the bridge for his family: "Whenever there was an occasion to meet the parents or something like that, they were very reluctant to speak English. He would have to translate everything we were saying to them. They weren't very verbal, as far as trying to communicate."[10]

The issue of speaking Spanish was still a touchy one in Texas, occasionally sparking controversies, heated arguments, and complaints about how to strike the right balance between English and Spanish at school, church, and work. "We didn't have openness to speaking Spanish. Families were insular, self-contained, they kept to themselves. I came up speaking Spanish, but speaking Spanish at home. In our class, in our group, we weren't allowed to speak Spanish. Maybe we would make jokes in Spanish or speak it with our families. We didn't have a podium, a platform, to speak our language. They kind of stamped that out at our school," says Hernandez, a friend and baseball teammate from MacArthur.[11]

Back home in the neighborhood, the Gonzales family simply tended to keep to themselves. The neighbors saw Pablo on his way to and from work; they saw the kids walking to school or horsing around in the yard. But even with eight children, the Gonzales family tended to avoid standing out on Roberta Lane. The ties that bound the family were tight, increasingly enforced more by Maria than Pablo. "They really kept to themselves and didn't socialize much," recalls Brenda Pond, a neighbor down the street.[12] It was only at school that the first son seemed to be more engaged, more prone to crossing boundaries and borders.

Gonzales was a member of the National Honor Society in addition to playing baseball and football. He befriended Anglo and Hispanic women, including Liz Lara, who was two years behind him. She noticed that in the middle of the 1970s there was a religious inclination, a religious absorption that stood in marked contrast to some other students and maybe even the general climate: "We just met at school. There was a sense of religion, of spirituality, back then, and it was very strong among our sports teams. Not that he walked around preaching the Bible, but they had a sense of religious spirit that I think came with the camaraderie of the team. Nobody went around saying, 'Are you Baptist?' or 'Are you Catholic?' We all believed in God."[13]

Other friends, including Jody Hernandez, remember Gonzales as being one of the school athletes involved with on-campus religious groups, talking about the Bible and maybe even toting one around. According to school officials, Gonzales was a member of the Christian Student Union, a group that fostered prayer groups and various religious seminars. Christianity deep inside the Bible Belt might have served as the great equalizer for young people coming of age in an era, in a milieu, where boundaries were shifting and changing—where blacks, whites, and Hispanics were assembled in classrooms and where even the guidance counselor, Marine Jones, was African-American.

"I think it was hard being Hispanic in a mostly white school. I don't think the school was a high-income school. It was a middle-income to lower-income community. At that time, to be a minority, whether African-American or Hispanic, it was tough. You didn't get the push of achieving or making better opportunities for yourself from teachers and counselors. I've had several conversations with people who were tied into the school those days. They themselves as teachers or counselors admitted to not having the tools to help us. They were more concerned with just letting us finish high school, and they thought that's an achievement in itself. If you had the drive and motivation to excel, you sustained it pretty much on your own. I think Al did that," says Hernandez.

"We were a small minority group. We did have a bonding and helped each other in furthering our education. There was minimal or low recruitment from universities at our school. Administrators expected you to graduate and just go get a regular job, go to a community college, or go into the military. From the environment we were in, we were just trying to get through high school. We didn't have access to guest speakers, role models, or people who would encourage you. The thinking was you're going to graduate, go find a job." [14]

But Hernandez could see like just about everyone else that Gonzales must have already had some sort of plan, some sort of methodology to what he was doing. He was deliberate *and* deliberative. He was studious to the point where he sometimes seemed to be constantly evaluating situations and people. Maybe not overtly calculating, but he appeared to be picking his friends and his spots carefully: "Al never identified himself with his neighborhood. That I remember—he didn't identify himself as 'Hey, I'm from this neighborhood,' " says Hernandez. [15]

The cheerleader he knew, Liz Lara, remembers it, too: "Albert talked a lot about wanting to do things. There was always this sense of purpose with Albert. Albert wasn't always thinking about the now. He was always thinking ahead. There was some depth to him at an early age." There was depth and perhaps there was some welling tendency to overintrospection, a sense that he could fall into dark moods—a self-admitted loneliness that ran counter to the prevailing image of Gonzales as a nimble social creature, someone who could move easily from the jock clique to the bookworm clique to the religious clique, someone who seemed to have a Zelig-like way of being everywhere, anywhere, but leaving very light footprints wherever he went. One time, in a rare display of committed-to-paper emotion, he wrote Lara an intimate note:

"I, too, am a very moody person, though I am hardly alone. Loneliness sometimes finds me and leaves me lost and bewildered." [16]

Marine Jones describes an environment in high school in Humble, Texas, in the late 1960s that was predicated on dreams. An environment not fixated on *the now* but on the realm of gauzy, imprecise possibilities: "At that time there weren't many opportunities for blacks and Hispanics to get into college or that sort of thing. We told the students, 'It doesn't seem like that door will be open right now, there isn't the money, but prepare yourself.' And so our teachers worked with them from that standpoint. The standpoint of 'you are going to be successful' and 'you will have an opportunity.' Many of the students knew that they didn't have the financial backing or that sort of thing, but they still prepared themselves in

case something happened. That was the way it all operated. People there
were very future oriented. I wanted our students to prepare for the future
even if they didn't see it right then. Prepare for the future even if you don't
see it right now." [17] Gonzales, as described by Liz Lara, seemed to be intensely averse to dwelling on the now, and he deliberately never allowed
his best friends into his world on Roberta Lane. It was his home, but it
was stagnant, and it seemed like a place burdened by impossibilities, by his
father's debilitating addictions, by the literal lack of space, of room to
move.

He didn't talk about his family; no one knew his father was an alcoholic; no one knew that he had no hot running water and that until he was
a teenager the family still had to go to the corner to make telephone calls.
His friends and girlfriends simply never went to his house. Instead, he almost always made arrangements to meet people away from Roberta Lane.
Some of them thought it was odd, and some of them wondered for a second what it was he was hiding, but then people would let it pass and never
revisit the topic. It was as if his parents and his house on Roberta Lane
didn't exist, as if a freshly scrubbed, intelligent, and pragmatic Alberto
Gonzales had sprung up out of nowhere, anywhere, and walked with the
bustling student body straight through the doors of MacArthur Senior
High. There were no after-school gatherings at his house. No friends
sleeping over, eating sandwiches in the kitchen, sitting on the stoop at
dusk, or hunting for pecans in the neighborhood yards. No one knew
what the inside of that house looked like. He wanted "as little fanfare as
possible," [18] thought his high school counselor. He mastered the art of fit-
ting in but not revealing much at all. When people talked about Alberto
Gonzales, it was as if they were describing the studied demeanor of a
commercial airline pilot—reassuring, calm, unflappable, no emotional
highs or lows.

His composure might have had something to do with being a football
player in a state where playing on your high school team is often a passport
to girls, free meals, and big-man-on-campus status. He enjoyed the perks,
but he was completely aware of his Hispanic barriers and his economic
shortcomings. "In my senior year, he sat in front of me in English class. We
cut up all the time. I used to hit him in the back of the head all the time.
He sat in front of me," says Alma Villareal Cox, who was born five days

apart from Gonzales. "See, we always called him Albert. He was real outgoing, but yet he wasn't, you know? He was with the football guys and all,
and he wasn't a loud guy. He wore jeans and a T-shirt and tennis shoes all
the time. A white T-shirt and jeans. He wasn't a radical child that I can
remember. He was just very quiet, very different.

"He was in a *Li'l Abner* play one time. I don't know why I thought that
was so funny. He was the only Hispanic in that whole *Li'l Abner* musical. I
thought: Isn't that funny? He's the only Hispanic in the whole play. It was
really funny listening to him talk all country. He just played an extra in the
play. He was just some little guy who made a comment about a fly on his
nose. It was just the way he said it that I remember." [19]

Gonzales was a three-year letterman in baseball and a two-year letterman in football. His teammates said he was intensely competitive, that he
desperately wanted to win, to be better. In his last year of high school, he
was a second-team all-district pick as a safety. And his grades, some of
them accrued in advanced classes, were good enough to land him in the
National Honor Society. He was still a member of the Christian Student
Union and the International Club. He dabbled in acting, though he left
the musical inclinations in the family to his younger brother Timmy, who
would sing and play guitar with people from the neighborhood. Another
younger brother, Tony, was destined to be a Houston cop. His sisters would
probably wind up homemakers like his mother, Maria. And he still absolutely never wanted anybody he knew from school, from outside Roberta
Lane, to visit his house. His house had only gotten telephone service when
he went to MacArthur: *"During my years in high school, I never once asked my
friends over to our home. You see, even though my father had poured his heart into
that house, I was embarrassed that ten of us lived in a cramped space with no hot
running water or telephone,"* said Gonzales one day many years later. *"If I only
knew. . . . If I only knew."* [20]

Sometimes just to get away the Gonzales boys would all go running
through the big, yawning field just a few blocks northwest of their home.
They'd gallop until they were on bended knees, sucking for air, and when
they looked up, they could see how each day there seemed to be more and
more bulldozers and cement trucks parked in ever-growing parallel lines,
as if they were part of some efficient army that was going to march two-
by-two into the chest-high, toast-colored Texas windmill grass. Houston,

continuing to burst at its seams, was building a huge airport in the late 1960s a short stroll from Alberto Gonzales's house.

A small group of Houston power brokers had pooled their money, bought 3,000 acres, then sold it back to the city to be used as the home of what would initially be called Intercontinental Airport. The airport was opened to great fanfare in 1969. Houston Congressman George Herbert Walker Bush was on hand to have his picture taken and to offer some comments. That first year it served almost five million passengers. In time it would become one of the busiest airports in the world and encompass 10,000 acres. When the airport was opened, the planes would thunder in low enough that sometimes it seemed like the kids riding their bikes in Humble could just jump and touch the metal bellies. The roar would wash over the yards and streets, and sometimes if the planes came really fast and hard, the flimsy abodes would shudder and shake. In time, the home to all those huge airplanes rattling Roberta Lane would be renamed George Bush Intercontinental Airport, in honor of the congressman who went on to become the forty-first president of the United States.

H e was real competitive. He wasn't very talkative," says high school baseball teammate Robert Trapp.[21] "He was tough. He was a little fireball. He liked doing good in sports. He never gave up, never. He liked to win, I know that." His football teammate Arthur Paul adds, "I knew he was intelligent. He caught my eye as somebody who stood out. His being good at everything he did."[22]

For some, Gonzales seemed to be the classic overachiever, someone pushing and pushing. He was not physically large like some of the other hungry football players. One of his old coaches remembers: "Albert played defensive back. We had a 'monster man' at that time. Arkansas had a defense and they had what they called a monster man in the back, but he was really just a strong safety type of player. And Albert was little and wasn't a big guy by any means, but he was real tough. At that time, MacArthur wasn't a strong football team, let's just say. We had a hard time winning. He was a competitor. You look at him now and you say, 'I don't believe he ever played football.' I always called him Albert and not Alberto. . . . They were a pretty large family, right? I think he was the only one that had the opportunity to go on to school. Kind of like me. I'm one of ten children, there are ten children in my family. I'm sure Albert was like us. My daddy was just a tractor mechanic and his daddy was just a common laborer." [23]

By senior year, 1973, he was a fair but intense football player, a fair but intense baseball player, but obviously too short to play at the college level. There would be no scholarship offers. His grades were good, mostly A's and B's, but Rice University was still out of the question. Meanwhile he had never displayed any open interest in political involvement, in pressing ahead with the various opportunities to take a stand for or against the war in Vietnam—for or against Richard Nixon. He certainly wasn't swept along by the same cultural tides, the music and the counterculture, that so many other young people were embracing. In Houston there were rumblings in *Segundo Barrio,* and some people were calling for more aggressive attempts to win social justice and basic city services. At Texas Southern University in Houston, students were organizing and confronting the police—and some of those clashes would turn bloody, deadly.

But in Humble it was as if MacArthur existed in a world of black-and-white certitudes as parts of America became increasingly colorized and even intentionally ambiguous—one of his classmates said it was like *Happy Days,* like something out of the 1950s rather than the early 1970s. Revolution was not in the air. Homecoming was in the air. Some students were wondering what job they were going to get after graduation. School pranks were more important than politics; if there was a political tilt, it stemmed from the fact that many of the seniors had breathed a collective sigh of relief as news emerged that the military draft was ending in June 1973.

And on Roberta Lane there was never really any discussion of Alberto heading off to college, even though he had performed well in the classroom: "I hung around a group of kids who all enjoyed school and did relatively well. So no, it didn't surprise me, not at all. It may have surprised my parents, but it didn't surprise me." [24] But the grades, the National Honor Society membership, didn't really matter. It was, really, a given that no one in the Gonzales family had been to college—and perhaps never would. In time, three of his eight siblings would never even finish high school. College was so far off the map that he didn't bother to take any standardized college entrance exams, even though he was one of the handful of black or Hispanic students to enroll in and succeed at the advanced college preparatory classes. "It was considered a victory just to get me graduated because my parents had not graduated from high school. All I remember is how much I enjoyed school and really feeling without much direction when I graduated . . . and not knowing what to do."[25]

His counselor knew economics was a factor. She wondered how much the family was saddled by low expectations and by a sense of resignation. "There was no money in sight of his parents being able to pay for college. It just wasn't to be," says Marine Jones. "You would think . . . he would have been class president and president of the Honor Society. But minorities didn't have that many leadership roles then. They were just there . . . doing the best that they could."[26]

Later some of his friends felt a twinge of regret for not understanding how poor the Gonzales family really was: "I could see from the way he dressed that he was a little needy," says Jody Hernandez. "I almost wish that we had been closer friends. I wish that we could have lived closer to each other. We had everything we needed. Even when we were in school, I would never have guessed he had those kinds of hardships. He would never disclose them. They had so many family members living in a two-bedroom house. They were a family and they loved each other, but I'm sure it was an inconvenience."[27]

It was a slight reminder of the days when men vanished in Houston and elsewhere in Texas. There were few obvious, immediate opportunities for the first minority students to emerge from the now desegregated school environment. Affirmative action was not a policy or even an unofficial practice. It did happen, but when it did, it was in isolated, rare moments when someone knew someone who knew someone who could arrange a job or a slot at a good school. It was personal patronage, benevolence extended from the powerful to the needy. If you were black or Hispanic in Houston, you would do well to have a friend, a sponsor, someone who could catapult you into some upper echelon—someone who would direct you to the door of opportunity and maybe even help you open it. Alberto's parents didn't apply for any public assistance. If they needed money, his father would go to one of his siblings. "He never asked for help for a handout except from his brothers and sisters," Gonzales once said.[28]

Years later he would sound almost bitter about his belief that no one was there for him, that he had entered school on the heels of desegregation, at a time when that fact, that act, was considered enough of a breakthrough for blacks and Hispanics in Houston: "MacArthur is a fine school, but a lot of blue-collar families went there, and there was not the same emphasis on going to college," Gonzales would later say in his deliberate, soft, measured way. "My parents were just proud of the fact that I had finished high school."[29] And he added, "there really wasn't much encouragement from the high school and from my family" to go to any schools of higher learning.[30]

His parents were indeed very proud, but their son really didn't have a clue what to do with his life. It was, in a way, parallel to the graduation junctures reached by George W. Bush: When Bush graduated from high school and even college, he told friends that he had no particular destinations in mind, no particular goals or ambitions other than to maybe work in the things that the family dabbled in, oil and politics. Gonzales was adrift: "All I remember is how much I enjoyed school and really feeling without much direction when I graduated . . . and not knowing what to do."[31]

His father was a role model—someone who built something from nothing, someone who drowned his melancholy in drink but still managed to get up every morning and put one foot in front of the other as he headed to backbreaking jobs. But his father, too, was obviously a model to be avoided. Some experts who study the adult children of alcoholics say they can exhibit a variety of signs, including being prone to taking themselves too seriously, to endlessly searching for approval, to becoming almost painstakingly responsible, and, finally, to becoming so slavishly loyal to some other person or principle that they sometimes regrettably press on with their loyalty even when that loyalty is simply, utterly not deserved.[32] That last characteristic would become intriguing for anyone analyzing Gonzales's eventual relationship with George W. Bush.

In 1973, just as the draft was ending, Gonzales told his parents he was going to join the military. He told people he was "inspired by the military career of a friend's father."[33] He was picking the Air Force. It was his decision: "There really wasn't any guidance. I don't know. I always seemed to have people around me at critical junctures of my life who helped me make good decisions. And I've been lucky in making some decisions.[34]

"I embarked upon a path that is something totally unexpected."[35]

Some of his friends from high school were surprised a bit, but some of them were also under the certain assumption that Gonzales had a plan, some larger plot line that he had scripted and was just now embarking upon. Not many saw him staying in the military for the rest of his life. He didn't strike many people as an intensely charismatic leader, someone people instantly raced to when he entered the room, someone who sucked all the energy and heat his way. "He wasn't one of those kinds of leaders, or leadership had not made its appearance at that time," believed his counselor, Marine Jones.[36]

He was thoughtful but not inspiring. "He was very methodical in his thinking," says his high school friend, Liz Lara.[37]

FOUR

Separation Agreement

Eighteen-year-old Alberto Gonzales enlisted in the U.S. Air Force on August 24, 1973, at the same time that George W. Bush was concluding his later, oft-investigated and controversial tenure in the Texas Air National Guard. Gonzales officially entered the military at the Armed Forces Examining and Entrance Station (AFEES) in Houston and was immediately put on a plane, his first air trip ever, to basic training at Lackland Air Force Base in San Antonio, the city where he had been born and the city that was becoming the Hispanic soul of Texas.

After the prescribed six and a half weeks of basic training, the new inductees, by then finally called airmen, had gotten the standard crash course in air force history, basic marksmanship, and survival skills. Gonzales was assigned to a technical school and transferred on October 12, 1973, to Keesler Air Force Base in Biloxi, Mississippi. Keesler was a justly famous air base, perhaps best known as a training home for some of the Tuskegee airmen, the daring African-American fliers who made history by fighting against all odds to form an all-black air unit, then by performing heroically in several important World War II battles. Midway through America's involvement in World War II, Keesler was home to as many as seven thousand black military men. By the time Gonzales arrived, Keesler was still one of the largest training bases in the air force, specializing in electronics and radar.

After eight and a half weeks of immersion in communications, "secure telephone" training, and other Cold War–inspired regimens, he received orders on January 5, 1974, to report to the distant, tiny Fort Yukon Air Station, just north of the Arctic Circle in Alaska. It was, again, his choice. When Gonzales had gone to the air force office in Houston and signed up for his four years, he was told that he would most likely have to complete at least one rotation in remote Alaska. He was offered the option of doing it straight out of basic training or simply waiting for orders to come down the road later. His first assignment out of basic training, it turned out, was to an air station in Key West, Florida, but Gonzales turned it down and opted for the Alaska assignment instead, thinking he would clear it off his plate and get it done as soon as possible. "I took that assignment, I volunteered for that assignment... and so I made the decision to bypass Key West and go to Fort Yukon because I wanted to get the hard stuff out of the way first." [1] Unspoken was the possibility that he wanted to go somewhere really far away, somewhere that could have been on the dark side of the moon compared to Humble.

For someone who had never traveled outside the continental United States, the trip to the magisterial kingdoms of distant Alaska was immense. "Founded" in the mid-nineteenth century, Fort Yukon is 145 miles northeast of Fairbanks, and the area was actually first home to the indigenous Gwich'in Indian tribes, including the Yukon Flats, Chandalar River, Birch Creek, Black River, and Porcupine River tribes, which traded with one another in the sprawling lowlands near the confluence of the Porcupine and Yukon Rivers. The daily temperatures in the winter would often be subzero. There were times when the they would stay frozen at −50 or below, and there were still old-timers who remembered the wicked days in 1947 when the temperature fell all the way to −68. Stories lingered about the way people would toss jugs of water and watch the liquid freeze before it hit the ground.

Fort Yukon was considered an important outpost in the Cold War intrigue with the Soviet Union. As superpower tensions surged, long-range radar and communications programs were ordered into operation in the 1950s to assist in reconnaissance efforts. Beginning in 1956, a network of so-called White Alice radar sites were built in remote regions of Alaska to serve as early warning systems against enemy attacks. The name was "White" because the sites were in snow-blanketed zones; "Alice" was a merger of "Alaska," "integrated," "communications," and "electronics." When Gonzales stepped off the small plane and joined the hundred or so other men working at the air station, he was greeted by a sign depicting a giant moose and the words "8 miles above the Arctic Circle." Gonzales was issued some Arctic clothing and officially given the title of ACW (aircraft control and warning) systems operator, assigned to the Alaskan Air Command—basically helping to blast huge, clear communications signals to other early warning stations from high-powered antennas set up in the rugged Alaska outback. He settled into a rhythm of monitoring the equipment, shooting the shit with the other airmen, playing pickup games of baseball, and writing letters to his family and Liz Lara, not unlike the same letters the other young men in his barracks were writing in which they talked about the loneliness, the deadly freezing weather, the utter isolation.

The nearest hint of a community was a tiny, hardy Gwich'in (the name translates into "people of the caribou") village about a mile away from the air station, where six hundred indigenous people descended from an ancient aboriginal race carved out a living. Years later, in a classic work called *Caribou Rising,* the master oilman-turned-naturalist Rick Bass would brilliantly capture the tenacious and perilous existence of the Gwich'in culture and the important lineage of Native Americans spawned from the extended Gwich'in family tree, a lineage that expanded all the way to the Southwest of the United States: "Since the time of complete and utter ice—and, who knows, perhaps longer—the Gwich'in have been here, the most native of native peoples, nearly geologic in their integrity, their endurance. Not as ancient as the oil we seek to burn in our cars, but, still, more ancient than anything of mankind left on this green earth." [2]

There are no indications that Gonzales immersed himself in mingling with or studying the profound Gwich'in, or felt any rhapsodic or literal connection with the awe-inspiring areas that would form the nearby Arctic Wildlife Refuge. He was focused on staying warm and ultimately getting the hell out of Alaska as soon as his rotation was through. "All people do here is drink and gamble—and I don't like either of those," he told a friend. [3] The abstinence from alcohol was easy to understand; even on the north side of the Arctic Circle it would be hard to forget his father's alcoholic rants. Still, there were unforeseen moments that seemed to make some sort of an impression, some things that stood a chance of becoming indelible. Again, he was unfettered, finally, from Humble and the limitations that existed or that he perceived on Roberta Lane. "It was a great adventure. I was single, eighteen years old, and I had never been out of the state of Texas. The Northern lights and playing softball at midnight, it was really a great adventure for a young kid."[4]

Being so far north, he was instantly immersed in a world that bore no similarity to crowded, heated Houston—or to Humble . . . back home, smelling the alcohol coming from his sweating father and listening to him curse in Spanish, the aroma of tamales in the kitchen, the sound of his brothers guzzling water in the yard after braving the humidity for another game of catch, the chanting of the priests surrounded by incense at church, the brief relief of a warm gust of wind pushing through the towering pine trees, the feel of the damp earth and the way the rainwater never seemed to be able to sink in. He was the only one in his family to have come this far. In Fort Yukon the newly arrived airmen were warned not to stray, to stay loyal to the group. It was vital, absolutely vital—if you strayed, you would die. If you moved "off the reservation," you would get lost in the great white beyond, you would get dizzy and disoriented and simply collapse under all the trees that all looked the same, and then you would wait for a certain death.

The area around the Arctic Circle was so perfectly ordered, seemingly barren but undeniably rich, that it could have a profound effect on anyone who had been there. It was another great equalizer: the area played no favorites and didn't discriminate between the haves and have-nots—everyone struggled to stay warm and fed. And it was as if Alberto Gonzales had to be transported 4,500 miles from the steamy, messy, subtropical Bombay on the Bayou all the way to the Arctic Circle to find a place where the color of his skin was insignificant: "When you enter a stretch of woods like this one, you are not manipulated by anyone or anything, nothing is being misrepresented or withheld, you are not being lobbied, no affection (or resentment) is being dispensed or withdrawn based on what you do or don't do; there are no demons or past history in nature's relationship to complicate yours, and, perhaps most reassuring of all, nature is largely democratic—if not quite blind to the color of your skin, or any other physical characteristics, then at least nonjudgmental, impartial."[5]

There were two older Air Force Academy graduates at Fort Yukon, and when Gonzales heard their stories about the influential military school in a nice part of Colorado, he was ready to apply. If he stayed with his four-year military commitment, he could easily see himself slipping from one remote, low-level assignment to another in the Air Force, going from one communications station to another, one bleak radar site to another. It might be someplace warmer, maybe somewhere really nice, but he would most likely be just another forgotten airman in the giant air force maze. One of Gonzales's commanding officers arranged for Gonzales to take part in a college correspondence course program in which he filled out assignments and shipped them to a university instructor in Oklahoma. That instructor was apparently impressed enough with his work that he urged the air force to consider offering Gonzales a spot at the academy.[6] "Some professor at the other end of the correspondence classes called the air base and told them: 'This kid is good. He should be going to school, not sitting [in Fort Yukon].' And that somehow ended up with Al getting one of the enlisted men's slots at the Air Force Academy. Which I think is a pretty cool story—but it never gets repeated anywhere, so Al and the Bush administration must not think it is," says his friend Paul Karch.[7]

In the end, being in Fort Yukon crystallized things for Gonzales. The academy provided free tuition, free board. The trade-off was an agreement to commit to an additional five years in the military after completing the four-year program. He was not yet twenty. He could be out of the academy by age twenty-two, out of the military by twenty-seven. He petitioned his commander, who "made special arrangements for a flight surgeon to be flown up from Elmendorf Air Force Base in Anchorage for the necessary medical examination." Then he *hopped an air force tanker plane to Fairbanks in order to take the necessary physical fitness tests.*[8] Most likely at Fort Wainwright or Eileson Air Force Base near Fairbanks, he would undergo various standardized physical and academic tests for admission to the academy. "I still remember doing the required pull-ups and sit-ups in an old Army gym. Because I had not taken the SAT or ACT, special arrangements were made for me to take the ACT alone—in a small room the Air Force had converted into a makeshift library." With just one monitor in the room, he was given the ACT college entrance exam to test his skills in math, reading, and comprehension.[9]

Years later Gonzales would remember the whole application process this way: "These were extraordinary efforts, but I had found a path to a college education, and I was prepared to do whatever was required."[10] Whether he knew it or not, there might have been some other extraordinary circumstances swirling in the military and the nation. Gonzales was applying for admission to one of the leading military schools in the world at a time when specific mandates had been issued by the air force high command to increase minority enrollment in the Air Force Academy and in the Air Force Preparatory School, a feeder program for the academy.

With antimilitary sentiment still coursing through many college campuses in the early 1970s, the high command of the air force met to discuss ways to attract new recruits. Specifically, discussion centered on how to bring in more minorities. The words *affirmative action* had not emerged, as they would later, as part of an ongoing, national, controversial debate. *Favoritism, preferential treatment, quotas*—all the flashpoint words for the debate on increasing minority participation in schools and the workplace—were not yet entirely prevalent. But it was clear that internal air force policy was now officially directed at radically, immediately admitting more minorities to the Air Force Academy: "In April 1972 General John D. Ryan, then Chief of Staff of the United States Air Force, set a new goal for minority officer representation in the Air Force. By 1980 he wanted 5.6 percent of the officers in the Air Force to be members of minority groups. This represents a 300 percent increase. . . . For the U.S. Air Force Academy, this means that it should increase the number of minority graduates from 3.4 percent in 1973 to 11 percent in 1980." (Prior to 1955, the year Alberto Gonzales was born, there had been no minority students admitted to the academy; in 1955, the first student, an Asian-American cadet, was admitted. Studies indicate that the first "Spanish surname" students arrived in 1966.)[11]

Gonzales was also applying at a time when minority recruiters were anxiously looking for recent high school graduates and new enlisted men—and pitching the academy as a quality college, not so much as the starting point for a lifetime of military service. The thinking was that students would be better sold on the school as a place that offered a superior education, comparable to most of the "better" universities in America, instead of reminding students of the obvious fact that the school hoped to have people stay in the military for decades. It was hoped that once students immersed themselves in the academy regimen, they would eventually resign themselves to a lifetime career in the military.

The sales message delivered by recruiters often boiled down to a single, compelling pitch to minorities—if you put in your four years at the academy and then put in another required five years as an officer, you would have gotten paid to go to school, gotten free tuition and board, gotten a solid college degree, and you'd also be able to leave the military with a nicely defined career path: "The recruiting pitch depicts the Air Force Academy as a four-year college that offers one of the best general education programs in the country. ... If qualified, some students are able to continue graduate school or professional school, such as medical and law school, upon graduation from the Academy. In addition, during the four-year term at the Academy the student gets paid, even though all his tuition, as well as room and board, are furnished by the government." [12] Some minority airmen who sought out the academy were completely sold on the idea of it being a nine-year commitment, not a lifetime job in the military. For some candidates, especially those who had the ability to map out a personal career strategy, the idea seemed incredibly, perfectly appealing. The academy could be used as a free launching pad to some life outside the military.

Gonzales has never said whether he was aware of the affirmative action plan for minorities. But it is very clear that he was enormously gung ho to take the academy entrance tests at a time when there was a mandated, historic shift to assist minorities. It was the tenor of the times in America, and the military was responding to some sociocultural demands to ensure the presence of minorities—or, at the very least, to supply the military with enough warm bodies during a conflicted time period when anti–Vietnam War sentiment was still raging.

According to his official military records furnished by the National Personnel Records Center under the Freedom of Information Act, Alberto Gonzales didn't go straight into the academy but instead attended the U.S. Air Force Preparatory School from July 28, 1974, to June 30, 1975. Located on the grounds of the Air Force Academy, the prep school is a ten-month program designed to prepare people for possible admission to the academy, including candidates who "failed" their initial application to the academy: "If a student fails the entrance requirements [to the Academy] but has a sufficiently high score to indicate a potential to pass the test, he may go to the Air Force Academy Preparatory School. The curriculum was designed to prepare deficient Academy applicants to compete eventually in Academy entrance examinations and, hopefully, to succeed as cadets at the Academy in all phases of training." [13]

The sweeping effort, ordered by the air force chief of staff, to bring more minorities into the Academy also obviously extended to the prep school and apparently resulted in minority students being admitted with lower test scores than had previously been required: "In 1972, a more concentrated effort toward recruitment of minority students to the Prep School was attempted. Students were allowed to enter with CEEB scores slightly lower than the previous requirements." [14]

There are no published interviews with Gonzales that mention any attendance at the preparatory school or that mention whether his scores on his entrance exams for the academy were deficient to the degree that he was sent to the prep school first. Most articles also simply give the impression that he entered the military, was sent to Fort Yukon for a year or two years, then moved on to the Air Force Academy. (As one example, *Texas Monthly,* in an extensive profile of Gonzales in 2003, states, "Gonzales joined the Air Force and was stationed for two years at Fort Yukon, in Alaska." [15]) But in another instance, in a lengthy interview with the Academy of Achievement, into which he was inducted in the summer of 2005, Gonzales refers to a "year" experience in Alaska this way: "I think it would have been hard for someone who had a family and kids to be away for a year. You were allowed a thirty-day leave at some point during your year, but otherwise, being away from your family would have been tough." [16]

Based on what was released to the public, the official U.S. military records clearly state that he was assigned to Fort Yukon on January 5, 1974, and that on July 28, 1974, he is listed as being at the "USAF Preparatory School." According to his military records, he could only have served at

Fort Yukon for less than seven months.[17] However, sources close to Gonzales say he says he was in Fort Yukon for a year.

Gonzales appeared extremely glad to be wrapping up his rotation at Fort Yukon. The intense cold above the Arctic Circle had pushed him to try to get out: *"With winter temperatures consistently below zero, I quickly decided I should reconsider college as an option."*[18] And he would also later say that going to Alaska was the best decision he had ever made, "because when I was stationed there, there were two Air Force Academy graduates, and I listened to them talk about their experiences at the academy, and I thought this is something I'd like to do. So I began the process of seeking an appointment to the academy and was fortunate enough to get in.[19]

"Fortunately for me, I was rewarded with orders to report to the academy, and so I happily departed the frozen tundra of Alaska to pursue a new dream of becoming a pilot."[20]

Presuming Gonzales's government records to be accurate, he would have been in a select group of 200 to 250 students at the prep school who were immersed in an often grueling program that started in midsummer 1974. According to contemporary information about the school, it zeroed in on "academic, military, athletic and character development." And, as well, "Every cadet candidate must accept the Honor Code when entering the Prep School; the Honor Code, human relations and spiritual development are all important aspects of the program; character development training starts during Basic Military Training and continues throughout the entire year." His military records show that Gonzales was finally admitted to the U.S. Air Force Academy on July 1, 1975.[21] Like all the other cadets at the academy, he would have to finish at least 187 hours of course work: 145½ hours in academics, 14½ hours in physical education or sports, 27 hours in "leadership and military training."[22] He entered an all-male environment, though that same year there was also a move afoot to break down the gender barriers in the school. In 1975 President Gerald Ford signed the paperwork mandating that women be admitted to the academy, and in 1976, during Gonzales's second year at the school, the first woman was admitted. (The role and treatment of women at the U.S. Air Force Academy would become criminally problematic over the years,

with 12 percent of women cadets saying in 2003 that they had been victims of rape or rape attempts.)

The academy was not only favorably inclined to want to admit minorities, but it was very much interested in assimilating its new minority
students: "The Minority Affairs Office is presently engaged in organizing
Spanish-speaking and other minority officers on the staff and faculty for
similar purposes. 'We have to overcome such basic problems as deciding
on a name for all Spanish-speaking people,' one officer stated. 'At present
we are called Chicanos, Spanish-descent, Spanish-speaking, Mexican
Americans, etc.' . . . Being placed in the Academy environment, completely
away from their families, these students find that they have no one to identify with. Often the student so ostracizes himself as to develop doubts
about his abilities, his confidence in himself wanes, his achievements suffer,
and he eventually resigns."[23]

Within a year it was clear that Gonzales no longer had any interest in
filling out his four-year commitment to the academy nor in completing his five-year commitment to remain in service to the military after
graduation. Gonzales began investigating ways to expedite his departure.
He later told the *Washington Post* in 2001 that he was homesick for Houston and that he wanted to be a lawyer.[24] The *Fort Worth Star-Telegram* reported that "he grew restless with science and engineering courses."[25]
Other reports indicate his eyesight was no longer good enough to be a jet
pilot. His interest in the academy was waning in direct correlation to the
difficulty of the courses. Gonzales became the freshman class council
president. He still harbored ambitions of maybe being a fighter pilot and
took a program learning to fly gliders, but he was struggling with school:
"The academy was tough for me because there's such a concentration on
engineering and physics and chemistry, and my strengths lie in English
and history and political science and law and government. And so I did
well in terms of being on the dean's list every semester, but I struggled. It
was hard. I had to work very, very hard."

Gonzales decided that he wanted to leave the military altogether: "I
started thinking things over, probably toward the end of my freshman year
or the beginning of my sophomore year. I really began wondering whether

or not I should pursue a military career," said Gonzales. "But when I was at the academy and began thinking about my future, I sort of put it in God's hands and applied to transfer to one school, and that was Rice."[26]

Years later, in a speech, Gonzales said virtually the same thing: "My first year in Colorado Springs was a good one, but I grew restless with the engineering and science curriculum, and I became interested in politics and law. I began to wonder whether I should follow a different path. Given the extraordinary effort just to secure my service academy nomination, you can understand how I agonized over this decision. Ultimately, I simply put it into God's hands by applying for a transfer to the school I'd once dreamed about attending as a boy. If accepted at Rice, I would lead and pursue a legal career."[27]

On May 20, 1977, Cadet Third Class Alberto Gonzales submitted his letter indicating that he wanted to quit the air force and his status as an Air Force Academy cadet. He had only accumulated 91.5 of the hours necessary to graduate. His "Record of Disenrollment" from the military says: *"His military performance as a cadet was average while his academic performance was above average."* Under "Reasons and Circumstances for Disenrollment," it reads: *"Cadet resigned appointment because of: a change in career goals (Insufficient desire to complete the Academy program)."*

In another section of his "separation agreement" from the academy and the military, it says this: *"Cadet Gonzales has had a change in career objectives. Cadet Gonzales has been in the Air Force almost 4 years, with 2 years enlisted service and 2 years at the Academy. He now wants to pursue a career in law. His present plans are to attend Rice University in Texas, to study Political Science, and hopefully be admitted to their law school next year. After carefully weighing all the advantages of a military career, he has now decided to pursue another career in the civilian community."*

Rice University doesn't have a school of law, and perhaps Gonzales simply told his commanding officers that he was planning to be a pre-law student. Dean Richard Stabell at Rice sent him a letter, dated May 13, 1977, indicating that he had been accepted: *"Dear Alberto: It is my pleasant privilege to inform you that your application for admission to Rice University has been approved."* Ten years earlier he had been selling Cokes in the football

stadium stands. The gulf between his world—the world of his father's alcoholic fog and the seemingly impenetrable ceiling that hovered over Roberta Lane in Humble—and the Harvard of the South seemed as wide as
the Gulf of Mexico. It took a side trip to Fort Yukon, hunkered down in
temperatures 30 degrees below zero, to bring him full circle back to a
place where he had worked when he was twelve.

It was an unlikely trip, the first of many, and he would have a long time
to do what he was increasingly prone to do—to measure, evaluate, weigh
how far he had come . . . and who, *what forces,* had brought him there. Was
it a perfect convergence of things—increased opportunities for minorities,
his own drive—that brought Gonzales back to Rice, but this time as a
member of the "holy of the holies," not just an accidental tourist or a for-
gettable kid earning pocket change and delivering drinks to well-fed students and alumni from the lily white ivory tower inside Houston? He was
going to the same school that Howard Hughes and the presidents of Tex-
aco and Exxon and Coca-Cola and Eastman Kodak had once attended—
and the lieutenant governor of Texas, the secretary of energy, and dozens
of other influential men.

His father was still reporting to the rice mill silos, leading some maintenance crews inside the dangerous towers. His mother was still living in
the little house at the far edge of the city. Planes from the airport that
would later be named the George Bush Intercontinental Airport still
thundered overhead. His brothers and sisters were still in the area, none of
them in college, none of them moving away. Tony was going to work at
the Houston Police Department and was going to become a member of
the SWAT team. His sisters were still thinking of being homemakers.
Maybe Tim, who took inventory and processed paperwork for a plumbing
company, would find that career playing his guitar—he really loved to play
his guitar. Gonzales shared his news with them and decided that he would
keep the acceptance letter from Rice University as long as possible: "This
was my prayer, and the letter from Dean Stabell was my answer—ending
the journey that began as a daydream during those Saturday afternoon
football games." [28]

On July 8, 1977, he received another letter—a notice from the air
force that *"the separation of Cadet Alberto R. Gonzales has been approved by the
Secretary of the Air Force."*

Before Gonzales quit the Air Force Academy, he met an attractive Colorado college student named Diane Clemens, who was a year younger and whom he would eventually marry at the age of twenty-three in June 1979, two years after he had returned to Houston to attend Rice. (They would be married, in fact, just as he was graduating from the school and becoming the first member of his family to earn a college degree.) Clemens, who was raised in Illinois, instantly struck some friends as the perfect partner for the subdued, measured Alberto Gonzales: "Diane was very quiet, too. They seemed fine together, but they were just both very quiet," remembers David Abbott, who would go to law school with Gonzales.[29]

Other friends remembered them lowering their heads toward each other, teasing each other, and seeming to be very much in love. They would whisper and share private moments, seemingly locked on each other in larger crowds. And some friends would remember a very different Diane Clemens occasionally stepping forward, someone who was actually being more of a social creature than Gonzales—the person who would erupt with something spontaneous, would venture an opinion that seemed to border on being edgy, and would make a big display of rolling her eyes if she had some sort of immediate reaction to something she didn't like. "She was livelier, but I wouldn't exactly call her outgoing. She would speak her mind, though," says Paul Karch, who would also get to know Alberto and Diane Gonzales in later years.

Most people who encountered Gonzales walked away with the impression that he had the demeanor of a card player—someone who revealed very little, someone completely averse to excess, someone who had willed himself to remain in an emotionally neutral gear. He was affable, courteous, mildly sarcastic, and generally aware of the issues of the day but never flamboyant in speech or dress. He sought people to play softball with, he liked to watch sports on TV, and he seemed to almost always have the slight beginnings of a small smile on his face. His hair was fashionably skewed to a slightly longer but perfectly groomed style. He sometimes seemed to linger an extra beat, as if he were studying you, when he shook your hand. He moved across the room in a somewhat slow, very self-contained manner. And Diane at times served as the exuberant outlet—

someone who almost seemed to speak for him or at least displayed an emotional dimension that he didn't care to display.

"We were all together and she was getting very excited about some political or religious issue—just really animated, enough to kind of make you want to step back. You know how they say never to discuss religion or politics in mixed company because it ruins the dinner? Well that was one of those times," remembers Karch. Even with that kind of surprising outburst, Karch decided that Diane ultimately was one of those women who "were a little more in the shadow of their husbands."

Karch and others remember that Clemens had a cool, agreeable crispness about her, a kind of clarity that led you to believe she was a straight shooter, someone who was comfortable in her own skin, someone who had the ability to make up her own mind. "She was an organized, disciplined, take-charge kind of person. Not real loud, but with a pretty firm backbone. Diane was smart—she just wasn't on the same intellectual level as Al, I think," says Karch.[30] She would be with him for the next six years and then meet a violent end.

Rice had been, as always, the unreachable place, but Gonzales had finally been admitted, able to transfer his hours from the Air Force Academy. He had taken several basic math, science, and engineering courses at the academy and was absolved from having to take them at Rice. Instead, he was able to concentrate on the things that increasingly had captured his imagination: law and politics. He moved back to Houston and found a Rice different than the one he had seen when he was twelve and selling Cokes in the football stadium: "It was a period of settling down after several events—one occurred in the mid-1960s, allowing the admission of minority students. Another was to move away from free tuition, which had been established by the founder in the original donation," says Gilbert Cuthbertson, a longtime political science professor at Rice who would become Gonzales's mentor, eventually launching Gonzales on a path that would take him to work in the White House. "When Gonzales entered Rice, that process [of minority inclusion] was just opening up and may have been one of the major considerations in his selection of Rice as a transfer school from the Air Force Academy."[31]

The question then becomes whether his admission to Rice (and his later admission to Harvard Law School—and the fact that he was eventually named the first minority partner in the history of the storied, huge Vinson & Elkins law firm) had anything to do with race. Years later he would gingerly reflect on the topic, clearly exhibiting a reluctance to address the issue of affirmative action: "I am not naïve enough to think that race has never played a role in the opportunities given me. How do you define affirmative action? If affirmative action is quotas, then I am not for it. If it means equal opportunity, then I say I support that. But to ask for special treatment because of race, that bothers me. And that may seem sort of hypocritical from someone who has probably been helped because of his race." [32]

Gonzales had entered an institution that was actively seeking ways to become more amenable for minority applicants. At the time, Rice, according to some estimates by professors, had a minority student population targeted at anywhere from 10 to 15 percent. Rice had also undergone some of the same kinds of convulsions experienced on major campuses around the country in the '60s and '70s. Abbie Hoffman, the famous countercultural provocateur, had been prevented by college officials from giving a speech on campus in the early '70s, and that incident polarized Rice. The Students for a Democratic Society occupied several buildings, part of the Rice Memorial Center was burned, and some student records were destroyed. Hoffman wound up defying the ban and speaking on campus, anyway. But like Columbia University and some other centers of on-campus political resistance and unrest, Rice was now in a less confrontational period.

"The period in which Gonzales arrived on campus was a period of settling down and returning to normal academic routine," says Cuthbertson. [33] The war in Vietnam was over, the draft was over, and the student movement had begun to fracture. Ronald Reagan was about to be elected president and Houston resident George H. W. Bush was about to become vice president. James A. Baker III, someone who had extensive ties to Rice, was about to become the extraordinarily influential White House chief of staff—the Houstonian would have an inordinate amount of influence owing to Reagan's sometimes less-than-detail-oriented approach to running the White House.

Rice, like some Ivy League schools (including Yale, where George W. Bush had gone to school from 1964 to 1968), was broken up into a system of residential dormitories called colleges. There were no fraternities or sororities. When you entered Rice, you were assigned to or "associated" with a college, even if you weren't planning on living there. Gonzales moved into Lovett College—named after Edgar Lovett, the first president of Rice—and it had about four hundred students associated with it, with about three hundred of them actually living at the college.

Nicknamed "the toaster," Lovett was an all-male college, squatty and rectangular shaped. Built in 1968, its no-nonsense design, reinforced by cement grating that surrounded the building, stemmed from the fact that the university was concerned about the student uprisings across America and wanted their newest college to be literally riot-proof. The architects designed some rooms to have dual access to outdoor hallways so that students couldn't be trapped in their rooms if a riot really did engulf Rice. Maybe in reaction to the austere, Soviet-style look, the wags who formed the college's first student governing board called themselves the Central Committee. Lovett quickly built a reputation as an occasionally reliable party house, and it was where the Rice owl mascots were sometimes housed. Drunken undergraduates would try to climb up the concrete grates and holler at anyone aiming for a path called Virgin's Walk that led to the women's residences. In 1974, an infamous, enduring tradition was spawned at Rice, and some say specifically at Lovett: called Baker 13, it featured a retinue of half-drunk, naked students smeared with shaving cream sprinting across campus while screaming for people to join them. In later years there were serious allegations that some freshmen, including women, were ordered to drink and were then tied to trees or poles and forced to watch the Baker 13 spectacle unfold.

"It [the Rice college system] was originally modeled after the Oxford system, although in the Oxford system there are academic specialties associated with each college and at Rice there are not. Students from all kinds of disciplines are mixed in together, so in that sense it's more of a social dynamic," recalls Mark Scheevel, a classmate who lived in Lovett at the same time Gonzales did. "It becomes your home away from home, essentially your new family. The house system in the *Harry Potter* series is actually not a bad analogy. When we were at Rice, there were two coed colleges, two women's colleges, and four men's colleges." [34]

Each college had a master associated with it—usually a married man with a family who lived in an adjoining house. Sometimes unmarried associate professors also lived in the college. Dr. Sidney Burrus, a professor of electrical and computer engineering, was the Lovett master, and years later he would predictably say that Alberto Gonzales hadn't made enough of an impression to share any memories of him. The students lived in dorm rooms that were usually upstairs. Downstairs were common dining and lounge areas. There were basements with a recreation area and a TV. The mood, befitting Rice's aura as an Ivy League school plunked deep in the state of Texas, was fairly regimented at times—something that barely stirred recent Air Force Academy Cadet Alberto Gonzales. Breakfast and lunch were cafeteria style; dinner was served at set times and was a seated meal with eight people to a table, with freshmen acting as the servers.

Lovett was viewed by some as the jock college, though all the colleges were designed to have a diverse student population, drawing people with varied backgrounds and interests. Each college had developed a bit of a character—just the way that George W. Bush's Davenport College had during Bush's years at Yale. (Davenport was known as a home to jocks as was the fraternity Bush joined, Delta Kappa Epsilon.) "We had a reputation for pretty good athletic prowess. We certainly weren't reserved. Weiss College was kind of the 'Animal House' of the campus; Sid Richardson College was sort of preppy; Will Rice College was a little nerdy, that sort of thing. At the time, the two coed colleges more or less kept to themselves. They were separate universes, really—it was rare that the people from the single-sex colleges knew much about people in the coed colleges," says Scheevel.[35]

Gonzales struck some classmates and teachers as shy. The ones who got to know him—including "Doc C," as he called Cuthbertson—realized he wasn't actually timid but that he was still perfecting that analytical bent that would shape his personality for years to come. If Gonzales was spending an extra beat or two seeming to measure the alien surroundings he almost had been airlifted into—just like he had been airlifted into the frozen tundra from the predictable, suffocating rhythms of Humble—it made sense. Gonzales was just twenty-two, on a fast spin from high school to Alaska to Colorado and now to the gilded circles in a part of Houston that had always seemed unattainable. The last four years of his life had moved in a blur. His tendency to deliberate was, maybe, a way of slowing things down. His personality was clearly patterned after his mother—to speak only when spoken to, to be unafraid to enter the *Norte Americano* world, but to do it with a heavy dollop of rolling analysis. All of it was sharpened by his days in Alaska, in Colorado, and now on the Rice campus. Each twist in his life seemed to reinforce his tendency toward circumspection.

Still addicted to baseball, he played on the intramural softball team as the "rover"—a position that skewed perfectly toward his personality. He was amenable to assisting, blending in, shifting. It was, in fact, like playing defensive halfback or safety on his high school football team. The teams fielded ten players and the rover was the addition, the one who roamed the short center-field area. He was fast, which was one of the reasons he was assigned to the position, and he was still extremely competitive. The team was serious, the players wanted to win, and they even screened people based on how competitive they would be. Gonzales and his teammates came up with the team name Some Girls from the recent Rolling Stones album (With the songs "Shattered," "Beast of Burden," "Some Girls," "When the Whip Comes Down," "Before They Make Me Run"). The title song on that album was infamous for the lyrics: "black girls just want to get fucked all night, I just don't have that much jam."

Like his future boss, George W. Bush, Gonzales was never known to take any identifiable, indelible stances in the overtly political venues available at Rice. Not that there were that many to begin with: "It wasn't particularly political, although it had been around the late '60s and early '70s. That was all pretty much over by the time we got there. Students were back to just studying and so forth. The social dynamic was basically split: there was one faction of people who were perpetually studying and never did anything and one faction who studied hard but liked to go party, too. Rice was pretty much apolitical at the time. Everyone watched Nixon get bounced and then were just kind of wandering around, wondering what was going to happen next."[36]

As always, Gonzales kept his family background hidden. It simply was not a topic of discussion with his friends, teammates, classmates. He struck some of them as "really sharp, focused" and "it was clear that he had a plan."[37] He had a solidity, something that suggested he was self-confident and maybe a bit perpetually wary. "He was pretty serious. But it wasn't off-putting or anything; I remember him just as confident but not boastful or brash or anything. He was reserved." [38]

In the classroom he immersed himself in political science, and Gilbert Cuthbertson began to take notice. Cuthbertson, a popular fixture on campus who had earned his doctorate from Harvard and come to Rice in 1963, was an expert in American constitutional politics and law, political theory, and Texas politics. Gonzales took Cuthbertson's American constitutional law class, and Cuthbertson also served as Gonzales's academic adviser. In 1978 Gonzales wrote a brief for Cuthbertson's class that made a deep impression on the professor: "It was a model paper not only of analytical and organizational ability but forceful argument, which certainly anticipated his abilities as an attorney to argue in court. The case that he was arguing was called the 'Speluncean Explorers.' It's a hypothetical case used at a number of law schools to illustrate some of the problems of a reversion to a fate of nature, when individuals are cut off from the rest of civilization and are allowed to take the law into their own hands.

"I keep relatively few former student papers because I don't have room for them in the office, and the fact that I kept that one . . . I'm not going to say that it's because I anticipated that Gonzales was going to move up rapidly politically, but that paper was such a forceful and distinguished work that I did keep it." [39]

Cuthbertson simply felt that Gonzales was at the top of the Rice class. Gonzales told Cuthbertson that he was increasingly interested in making a living practicing law. "Gonzales was certainly one of the best students I ever had in my forty years of teaching at Rice and one of the most promising students intended for the field of law. I remember him very well." [40] Part of Cuthbertson's memory revolves around the way Gonzales presented arguments in the moot-court cases: "His presentation was forceful and very effective. But at the same time, Gonzales was a very quiet and respectful student—one who was intelligent and eager to learn. In reference to J. Frank Dobie's book *Coronado's Children,* I always think of Gonzales as Coronado's child—one of the new generation in Texas politics, Mexican-Americans searching for a new and better life and opportunities in Texas." [41]

George W. Bush was famous for what he didn't do at Yale: He was no-ticeably absent from political debates, discussions, exchanges, organizations. Gonzales was the same at Rice. Cuthbertson, a Democrat, was also the sponsor of the College Republicans. He chalks that task up to his belief that there were very few Republican professors at Rice and he had to step into the sponsorship role. Rice, he says, has always skewed Democrat, though in the 1970s there might have been something akin to a fifty-fifty split between Democrats and Republicans. "As far as Republican politics goes, I never would have guessed that Gonzales was a Republican. I guess we're all guilty of stereotyping to some degree, and I would have thought because of Gonzales's background, I would have assumed he was a Democrat, if anything. But I don't recall his expressing himself on political issues or participating in political debates or anything." [42]

Cuthbertson, a product of Harvard, had no hesitations in writing a strong letter of recommendation for Gonzales to Harvard Law School. Cuthbertson was pleased with Gonzales; he seemed to embody some of the lost, original ideals of Rice University from the days of its founding. "He was kind of that type of student that Rice was set up for. William Marsh Rice in his request specified poor students who could obtain a quality education. Because of the educational background of a number of minority students, you have a struggle in an academically competitive atmosphere, so minority students probably didn't apply as widely at Rice." [43] Cuthbertson only remembers writing one letter of recommendation—the one to Harvard—for Gonzales, though he is certain he advised Gonzales to apply to more than one school, perhaps to the University of Texas or the University of Houston. Cuthbertson, who had himself been accepted to Harvard Law School years earlier, was hardly surprised when Gonzales received his acceptance letter in 1979. Gonzales came to him after he received his invitation to Harvard. "Yes, he did. I'm sure he was both grateful and eager to attend Harvard. Alberto rose very well to academic challenges and competition." [44]

The Gonzales family was witnessing, living, some watershed moments, including the fact that Alberto's younger brother Tony (born May 13, 1958) was sworn into the Houston Police Department in December 1978.

At Rice University, Alberto Gonzales graduated in the spring of 1979 with a B.A. in political science. He was awarded cum laude status, his Some Girls softball team walked away with the campus championship, and he wrote this for the 1979 Rice *Campanile* yearbook: "While at Rice I have had much to be thankful for. My parents have stood behind me all the way and for this I am very grateful. I thank Diane whose love and understanding were so helpful in getting me through these four years. God has been too good to me and for this I praise him." He signed his name and wrote "1979 Poli" in parentheses. At the bottom of his carefully written note in flowing cursive, he added a note to the Air Force Academy: "I salute USAFA Class of '79." [45]

At graduation it was, again, *como un sueño*—like a dream. His father, Pablo, who had done the brutal work alongside the thousands of other unfairly compensated foot soldiers who provided the muscle that made the glittering skyscrapers soar, was there with his mother, Maria. This was a place they were unaccustomed to coming to. Still in the grips of alcohol, still living in the two-bedroom house on Roberta Lane, still rising at daybreak to slave in Houston's court, his father couldn't help but marvel at his first son. Alberto posed for a graduation picture with his father, unaware that it would be the last picture ever taken of the two of them together.

That day a thought welled up in his head: *"I actually believed I knew exactly what I wanted to do with my life. Having already realized one childhood dream, I had an unwavering, almost arrogant confidence to shape my future. But since my graduation I have learned—sometimes painfully—that life cannot be scripted. We cannot anticipate all the obstacles and opportunities that lay ahead."* [46] One thing was certain that day: Alberto would be married just a few weeks after graduation.

According to some records, Alberto Gonzales and Diane Clemens married June 16, 1979, in Harris County, Texas. There is a possibility that they were married in Colorado, then moved and reported it in Harris County. His marriage to Diane Clemens would become remarkable for the fact that over the years very few of his closest friends and associates in life even knew she existed or that she later died in a car crash. She has remained virtually absent from every article written about him. (In Washington, D.C., and in Austin, Texas, some of the people who are closest to Gonzales had no clue that Diane had died until they were told by the author of this book. At the U.S. attorney general's office, the head of Gonzales's public affairs office had not heard that Clemens had died. In the fall of 2005, his close friend, the corporate lawyer and former Texas Supreme Court justice Tom Phillips, even asked the author if he planned to interview Diane Clemens. Tasia Scolinos, the head of public affairs for the attorney general, also asked the same question.)

That summer the newlyweds made plans to relocate to Cambridge, Massachusetts, and Harvard Law School. Cuthbertson had already taken to calling him "Judge Gonzales." The "judge" title was actually an honor that Cuthbertson extended to all of the students in his constitutional law class. But there was a purpose to it as well. He wanted Gonzales and the others to start thinking of themselves as future lawyers and judges. In retrospect, he thought he knew what he needed to know about Gonzales. But, like many other people, he wasn't aware that Gonzales was married shortly after graduation. Gonzales never talked about his personal life.

For many people, it ultimately was as if Gonzales had no family, no wife, as if they didn't exist. He never revealed anything about his background at all, especially if he felt there were problems in the family—including his father's drinking. Cuthbertson knew little about Gonzales's history. "No, and he never seemed to have any personal problems, although I'm sure with the background of his family that there may have been crises or burdens."[47]

FIVE

Go to His Left

At Harvard, Gonzales entered a campus atmosphere not unlike the one he encountered at Rice—mildly politically charged, with just a few lingering nods to the student protests of the late '60s and early '70s. Harvard Law School, unlike Harvard Business School (where George W. Bush had graduated in 1975), was considered by some to be a bit liberal-leaning, and a handful of the 520 students in each class would sometimes rally around a cause if sufficiently inspired. Alberto Gonzales wasn't one of them. He was a "solid, sensible, even-keeled person. . . . Not all the law students were stable and sensible. It was the late '70s; there were protests and comings and going. . . . I don't remember him being overtly political. He was judicious as a young law student when a lot of students weren't," says Howell Jackson, a first-year classmate who shared all the same courses with Gonzales, and who would go on to become a law professor at Harvard.[1] "Al gave the impression of being sensible, not radical. There were more wild liberals than wild conservatives back then, but I don't remember Al as being either one. It was mostly a liberal student body and certainly a liberal faculty back then, so liberalism would have been the dominant theme. Ronald Reagan was elected president while I was at law school, but I would guess that he wouldn't have carried our law school class."[2]

When Gonzales moved to Cambridge, it was the first time he had ever set foot on the Harvard campus and its environs. He and Diane arrived without having arranged for an apartment, and they scrambled to find a place to live. Unlike Houston, there were fewer affordable places. With school set to start in a few days, they rented a small unit in one of two high-rise buildings in a low-income, subsidized housing project near Fresh Pond. It wasn't, as one friend said, "leafy suburbia," but it wasn't bad, either. It was a place at the intersection of some highways, strip shopping centers, and malls, a kind of commercial, verging-on-industrial area close to railroad tracks and busy roads. Within two or three days of moving in, their car was stolen.[3] Gonzales had a ten-speed bike that he sometimes rode the four miles to Langdell Hall, the home of the Harvard Law School library. He was twenty-four and a little bit older than some of the other students, each of whom was assigned to a "section" of about 130 students, and he was most likely the only one at the school to have ever served in Fort Yukon.

He tried hard to fit in. He dressed in white shirts and shorts, classmate Paul Karch taught him to play squash at Hemenway Gym, he joined the recreational softball and volleyball teams, and he attended the Friday night beer busts at George's bar/restaurant—but no one can recall him actually drinking alcohol or smoking. He laughed at other people's jokes but didn't make too many of his own. He also played for three years in the Razzle Dazzle football club—an intramural program held on Saturday mornings in the fall and centered on a made-up game, kind of like soccer, in which you throw the ball and there is continuous passing up and down the field, not just the one pass across the line of scrimmage. Quickly, Gonzales became the best player, the star, the quarterback who led the constant, scampering drives downfield.

Meanwhile, many of his fellow students did not categorize or objectify Gonzales as a minority student, even though one classmate estimated that the Hispanic population in the entire law school was "pretty small . . . 2 or 3 percent, if that." If anything, his classmates simply saw him as a silent, half-smiling presence, someone who was very athletic; he wasn't simply known as one of the two or three Hispanic students in his section. Some of his classmates remember, in contrast, one student from Puerto Rico who seemed to constantly bring up his heritage and the fact that he had also gone to a prestigious Ivy League school as an undergraduate. As always, few people had any notion that Gonzales might have been the only son of migrant workers at Harvard Law: "I had no idea at all; he was just another member of the class," says Jackson.[4]

In one rare instance he was involved in a deep conversation on abortion in the library one night with a classmate named David Abbott, including mention of a groundbreaking 1965 case called *Griswold v. Connecticut,* which revolved around the role of the government in marital privacy and birth control. Abbott and Gonzales were part of a Harvard married couples crowd—a group of five married couples who tended to congregate together, sharing potluck dinners, watching TV, catching a movie, and thinking about starting families. "Al and I were in the library one night and we had a discussion about abortion. We must have been taking constitutional law at the time. As I recall, Al didn't take a particular position on the issue at the time, but he was asking me questions. I very clearly remember Al asking me whether I believed the Constitution contained a right to privacy. I said, 'Yeah, I do, and here's why'. . . basically giving him the *Griswold v. Connecticut* response. As I recall, Al had some doubts or uncertainty about it, so we did discuss abortion in that sort of context, but as I said, I don't remember him taking a position on it. I took a position on it myself, and I know I'm much more liberal than Al. I probably gave him my very strong point of view, but he didn't argue with me. It was definitely a legal discussion, not political or moral."[5] Abbott knew that Gonzales was more conservative. It was unspoken, and he wasn't exactly sure why he felt that way about Gonzales, but he did.

The classroom environment was always inherently competitive, but people who attended Harvard with the mustached Gonzales said it was hardly like the edgy scenes in the movie *The Paper Chase.* The level of competition didn't rise to debilitating arrogance or wicked conspiracies to undermine other students. "It did have its intense aspects, though. I'd been a newspaper reporter before I went to law school, and the impression I got was that it was somewhat insular at Harvard Law. Self-centered, in a way, and boring, actually. Basically all you did for three years was have your nose in a book and go to class," says David Abbott.[6] Gonzales did well but was apparently not a soaring star in the classroom during his first year; he was a "B or B-plus student during first year," says another classmate.[7]

Abbott wondered what it was like for Gonzales to be immersed in the extraordinarily exclusive world of Harvard Law. The law school was not just one of the finest in America, it was obviously among the most influential. Without knowing all the intimate details, Abbott could guess that Gonzales had little in common with the way many of the other students at Harvard had been raised and educated. Abbott had grown up in a large, modest-income family himself. "I'm sure that it was kind of an awesome thing for someone with Al's background to get to Harvard Law, especially when you look around and there aren't a lot of people who are like you. Al had to occasionally think: 'Wow, what am I doing here?' I'm sure it had its intimidating aspects, as it does to some degree for everyone—and with a disadvantaged, minority background, it was probably doubly so for Al. A lot of the [Harvard elitism] is a kind of mythology, but nonetheless, it's a reality you deal with. Maybe Al wasn't intimidated, but I'd be surprised if he wasn't, at least a little bit." [8]

During one spring break in March 1980, Gonzales and classmates Paul Fishman and Brian McGrath took a three- or four-day bike trip on Martha's Vineyard. Gonzales had helped organize the trip and brought along his ten-speed bike. They mounted the bikes atop a small car. It was cold and there were few people on the island. They stayed at a small inn and jawed about classmates, professors, and sports. Gonzales was more than a capable bike rider; many times he left Fishman in the dust. It was an unwinding trip, a break from the droning grind, and it was also a good opportunity to espouse some earnest opinions at a time when presidential politics and the race for the White House were dominating headlines. "But I don't remember him ever discussing politics," says Fishman. [9]

That lack of political engagement didn't matter to his friends. "He was a fun guy, fun to hang out with. He was easy to be with, with a good sense of humor and an easy laugh. There were lots of people whose anxiety about being at law school was palpable, but Al didn't seem at all stressed out by law school. He was doing fine; he didn't seem to be someone who felt like he had to be at the top of the class . . . there was nothing about Al that appeared as though he was awestruck about being there. He was married, and he actually seemed very grounded," says Fishman. "His outward appearance seems to be unflappable, and maybe that reflects his background—maybe he went through so much adversity as a kid that people throwing shots at him and his political colleagues don't bother him. Or, if it bothers him, he's able to hide it." [10]

The same year as his breezy trip to Martha's Vineyard, the Gonzales family faced a searing nightmare. Alberto's younger brother Rene Gonzales died in 1980, and it instantly became a hidden family moment that again is simply never mentioned, never alluded to, and certainly never outlined in the many articles and profiles that would be written about Alberto Gonzales over the years. Like his marriage to Diane Clemens— and their subsequent divorce and her eventual death—the exact circumstances of Rene's death are carefully guarded by the Gonzales family. Rene, born on August 31, 1959, had celebrated his birthday the same month as his older brother Alberto. According to neighbors and friends, Rene had been killed while walking along a highway—maybe the highway a few blocks from the house, maybe a highway closer to the coastal city of Galveston, south of Houston—and when he was struck, he had no identification papers on him. His body, says a neighbor, was simply transported to a morgue and placed in an area reserved for the unidentified dead. Meanwhile, on Roberta Lane, people wondered why Rene Gonzales had simply vanished—why he had gone missing, where he might have gone.

Had he gotten in trouble with gangs, drugs, or those rogue police who had in 1977 made national headlines for savagely beating a young man named Jose Campos Torres, and then throwing him off a bridge, into Buffalo Bayou, where he eventually drowned? Had he decided to break free from Humble in some sort of vain attempt to be like his older, golden brother at Harvard Law School? Had he decided he couldn't face another day in the house with his alcoholic father? Or had he decided he simply didn't want to be like his father and needed to drop out, vanish, and go away where no one could find him? Brenda Pond, a longtime neighbor on Roberta Lane, remembers it this way: "Well, you know one of them died. When we found out about it, the boy had been missing. One of the sketch artists at the police department went down to the morgue—in the unclaimed bodies—and drew a sketch and put it in the newspaper. And that's how they found him. He was run over not too far from the house, out there on Highway 59." [11]

The family decided to place a small grave marker laid flat on the ground at Rosewood Funeral Home not far from Roberta Lane. The marker, no doubt mined from the same Texas quarries that yielded the pink granite for the Texas State Capitol, was plainly decorated with a rendering of an open book, perhaps the Bible, bordered by eight flowers. The marker simply reads: "Son—Rene Gonzales, 1950–1980." In an interview related to his induction to the Academy of Achievement in 2005, Gonzales simply said, "I had seven siblings; one of my brothers died when he was a relatively young man." [12]

Many of Gonzales's friends at Harvard had no clue his brother had died—and maybe had died in some tragic, mysterious way . . . maybe cut short on the bold new highway that had been built near the house to expedite the connection between Houston and Humble, to improve access to what would be called George Bush Intercontinental Airport. A friend of Gonzales's named Bill Sweeney, a businessman from Texas, said that he thought Rene had perished on that different road to the south of Houston—that he "died in Galveston after possibly being hit by a car while walking down the side of the road." Either way, if his brother Rene's death lingered with him and caused him to focus even harder on keeping his distance from the limitations and the strangehold of Humble, he never let many of his friends know. If his brother's violent death caused him to recommit himself to making a path far away from the life his father and his family had led, he never confided that fact to his closest friends at Harvard.

Alberto Gonzales was "very much the kind of person who would listen more than speak. I had no idea that he had any political leanings at all until years later when I tried to visit him in Houston and he wasn't available because he was at a fund-raiser of some kind for the first President Bush," says Paul Karch. [13] He was polite and participated usually only when he needed to in the presentations, debates, and arguments in class. The demanding, sometimes unforgiving curriculum seemed to suit his habit of studying, keeping his nose in a book, then blowing off steam by playing squash, racquetball, Razzle Dazzle, softball, and volleyball. He wasn't wallpaper and he wasn't exactly a leader in the classroom. Friends don't remember him taking an active role chasing after some of the available things—competing for a treasured spot with the *Harvard Law Review,* working with the Legal Aid Bureau or other on-campus programs, including any emerging minority-themed organizations. Friends also don't recall him working part-time jobs. As at Rice, Gonzales "pieced together various forms of financial aid to pay for the pricey schools—the GI Bill, student loans, scholarships." He would eventually tell people "[his] parents didn't pay a dime" for his schooling.[14]

Karch saw Gonzales as a follower: "At Harvard Law School, at least when I was there, there weren't many leaders in class. Almost everyone was fairly passive, so it would be accurate to say Al was more of a follower than a leader in class, but out of 130 people, there might be 10 leaders and 120 followers in class." Many students at Harvard Law were also fixed on the process, the day-to-day studies and challenges in the classroom, as opposed to viewing Harvard in coldly pragmatic ways as a place to cement future relationships, to network and jockey for some good position down the road. There was a prevailing, some might say smug, sense that everything would turn out right in the end, that the sheer power of the Harvard Law degree would lead to better, bigger things in the future. In that regard, his experience at Harvard was remarkably similar to George W. Bush's tenure at Harvard Business School. No need to spend inordinate amounts of time schmoozing, cajoling, posturing, and preening for jobs and clerkships, though a certain amount of that did go on, especially for students who made *Harvard Law Review* and were thrust into a higher-octane zone.

For Gonzales and other members of his circle, there was simply an abiding sense that doors would open once people permanently left campus. "You know that movie *The Paper Chase* which depicts Harvard Law School as hypercompetitive? Well, that movie was totally over the top—all those students freaking out. People weren't nearly that competitive, and one reason was that you were pretty much assured of getting a job at a big law firm. It might not be with the best Wall Street law firms, but while you were there, if you graduated from Harvard Law School—especially if you went to any city other than New York, Boston, and Chicago—you could get a good job at a good law firm. So it wasn't like your future income was dependent on how well you did in law school. That was irrelevant, because you were going to get a job no matter what."[15]

Gonzales hung out with a bright, talented group that included Karch, McGrath, Abbott, Jack Roberts, and Jodie Einbinder—men and women who would work for the most prestigious law firms at home and abroad or take their places in executive positions in business. Karch, like all of Gonzales's friends through the years, sometimes felt as if right up to the end he was still pulling teeth to extract information about what was in Gonzales's background. The future seemed more obvious, given the open assumption that Gonzales would do anything to return to Texas and become a corporate lawyer.

"Al was very quiet. It took a lot of work to get any personal stories out of him. I had to keep asking and asking questions. Most people asked other people questions back then, like, 'Where did you grow up, and what was it like?' But I never heard much about Al's childhood, so I guess he just deflected those questions. It wouldn't be that he was avoiding that particular topic; I think it was more that he was pretty soft spoken and just preferred to let other people talk. That wasn't hard, because one thing I can say for Harvard Law students is that they love to hear themselves talk—so if you've got someone who's quiet, they're not going to have to work very hard at staying quiet, because other people will fill the gap. You know when you and your friends are sitting around, you all start telling stories about yourselves? Well, Al never did. You'd have to ask him questions. I did have a sense that he had lots of brothers and sisters, so I must have learned that by asking him a direct question. But he never mentioned that his parents had been migrant workers or anything like that." [16]

In his second and third years Gonzales was still not registering in any profound way at Harvard Law. He essentially stayed below radar, working hard, blending in, and keeping a subdued profile. He was not known as a brilliant expert on the Constitution or really in any particular field of law. "It helped that he was older than many other students, and it helped to realize that it wouldn't be the end of the world if he didn't make straight A's (which was a good thing because he didn't). He hung around with a group of students who shared his feeling of calm and feeling of good fortune, people who knew they would get great jobs, were there to learn but also to enjoy themselves. They knew the world, eventually, would come to them." [17]

He and Diane moved into married student housing. Gonzales was wearing khakis, jeans, polo shirts, and Harvard logo sweatshirts. After his second year he arranged a clerkship in Houston with Vinson & Elkins, the iconic, blueblood Texas-headquartered law firm with deep and ever-growing connections to Washington and other power centers around the world. In Cambridge he still complained about the cold, not as much as he had complained the first winter there, but when a wicked cold snap would slice the campus, he'd linger on the weather and why anyone would want to live in such a frigid place. He kept playing squash, and he had picked it up so quickly, so well, that he instantly began beating the guy who taught him the game. Paul Karch played Gonzales at least forty times over two years and never won a single game. Gonzales was still a star on the softball team, and Fishman thought Gonzales was the best third base-man he had ever played with. Two decades later, when his conservative politics were neatly spelled out, people would come to offer this joke re-membrance about the softball star at Harvard Law: "Al could go to his left better than anybody we ever saw, but apparently he hasn't done it since."[18]

With Diane, he comfortably settled deeper into that pattern of social-izing with the small group of Harvard Law married couples. Usually it was dinner at Paul and Anne Karches' house, sometimes at Brian and Beth McGraths' home, sometimes at Jack and Jan Roberts' place or Dave and Jan Abbotts'. The host couple often cooked for everyone. Sometimes they'd all plan an outing. Once someone got tickets to a Linda Ronstadt show at Boston Garden; Diane and Paul Karch were big Ronstadt fans.[19] One time Paul organized a group trip to the Harvard–Yale football game. It was snowing, the seats were terrible, and Gonzales turned to Karch and ladled on the sarcasm: "Well, *this* was a great idea, Paul. It's big time, all right." Another time Karch and his wife, Anne, organized a trip to the movies and zoomed around Cambridge picking up the other couples in their Volvo station wagon. Al and Diane wound up sitting in the third seat, facing backward and feeling the brunt of all the fast turns and stops and starts. "Paul, . . . I like the way you drive," came Gonzales's acid commen-tary from the back seat.

On one Friday Gonzales went biking with Karch in Woods Hole on Cape Cod. Diane had gotten a part-time job in an office and wasn't going to come down until Saturday. Karch and Gonzales raced each other for twenty miles on a designated path and for the first time Gonzales seized up and actually wore out before his friend.

Maybe, once in a while, the door would open at George's tavern and Gonzales would enter, join his friends, and patiently eat a cheeseburger while they knocked back beers, hollered, and played Ms. Pac-Man. As the 1982 graduation grew closer, there was talk about life, careers, after school. Gonzales told his friends that he and Diane wanted to head back to Texas, and he wanted to go to work as a business lawyer, a corporate lawyer. There was no discussion about public service or a life in politics. It was a given that he and Diane would most likely be returning to Houston; there were still, now and then, random comments about how much nicer things like the weather were back in Texas. No one saw him going anywhere else but to a high-dollar corporate law job back in his home state.

When friends were with Gonzales and Diane, they sometimes wondered what the dynamic was in their marriage, and they wondered, too, how successful it was. "They did tease each other some but not a lot. Diane would sometimes roll her eyes over what Al did or didn't know. But I always had the sense that they were pretty close. I had the impression that they'd met in Colorado and that they'd been through some challenges together and were still facing them together, but felt like they got along. I didn't see any conflict between them," says Karch. "There also was a bit of a difference in—I'm not sure how to say it—backgrounds, I guess, among the women. My wife, for instance, was Phi Beta Kappa from Harvard, so she's rigorously intellectual. And Jan Abbott, Dave's wife, was a lawyer, too, so she was more of her husband's equal. The other three wives, including Diane, were a little more in the shadow of their husbands. I think she was an executive secretary or something like that. She was an organized, disciplined, take-charge kind of person, so I remember thinking that she was probably pretty good at doing that sort of job." [20]

Just five months before he was set to graduate and two years after his brother Rene died, Gonzales got word that his father had tumbled from a silo at a Houston rice operation where he had become head of a maintenance crew. [21] After his fall he was transported to a local hospital, where he eventually died on Friday, January 22, 1982. Years later some people would wonder if his fall had anything to do with his drinking.

Pablo Medina Gonzales was fifty-two, and he had seemed to settle into his job at the rice mill. Decades earlier a moderately thriving rice industry had grown up in some parts of southeast Texas, dovetailing on the larger rice operations in Arkansas and Louisiana. People living in the Houston area, for example, grew accustomed to the overpowering smell of the steamed, or converted, rice at the 200,000-square-foot Uncle Ben's facility near the Houston Ship Channel. The company, known for its sometimes controversial logo featuring a smiling black man with a bowtie (some people said it was a depiction of a master rice farmer from Beaumont, Texas, and other people said it was actually a maître d' from Chicago), had sprung up in Houston after World War II and carved out a niche with a formula that promised to lock in rice's nutrients. As the various area rice operations grew, more and more ex-migrant workers like Pablo Gonzales had been hired.

Pablo Medina Gonzales's death hardly registered in Houston. He was "just" another laborer who had met an untimely death while doing one of the thousands of menial, tough jobs in Houston. From one end of the greater Houston area to the other, blue-collar workers would often fall victim to some sort of accident at the workplace. It could be at one of the giant factories fanning out from the Ship Channel; it could be at one of the oil refineries or one of the petrochemical plants. It could certainly be at one of the endless construction sites in a city where people had started saying "the crane" was the "city of Houston bird"—a reference to the endless number of huge construction cranes that could be found just about everywhere in the city.

The family brought Pablo's body from Houston to Humble, and a rosary was recited at 7:00 P.M. on Sunday, January 24, at Brookside Funeral Chapel. A funeral mass was celebrated at 9:00 A.M. on Monday, January 25, at Saint Mary Magdalene's Church, with Father Adam McClosky leading the service. Pablo Medina Gonzales Jr. was then buried alongside his son Rene in Rosewood Cemetery.[22] Maria chose a metal marker embedded inside a block of pink granite. The marker, like the one for Rene, was pressed into the ground; it was not a standing tombstone. He was laid to rest in an area populated by other Hispanic families; a woman named Dominica Sanchez was buried right nearby. Pablo's marker was more elaborate than his son Rene's. It read: "Beloved Husband And Father, Pablo M. Gonzales, Jr., July 12, 1929–Jan. 22, 1982." There was a quote

from Psalm 23: *"Yea, though I walk through the Valley of the Shadow of Death,
I will fear no evil; for Thou art with me; Thy rod and Thy staff they comfort me."*
To the left side of the marker was an outline of a winged angel, hovering
in clouds and seeming to clutch a tiny star above a setting sun. Toward the
top of the marker was a standing urn suitable for holding flowers.

Alberto Gonzales was twenty-six. His mother would work for years as
a cleaning lady at the same funeral home that had buried her son and her
husband. "This gives me something to wake up for in the morning. I was
taught to depend on myself and not be a burden to anyone," she would tell
people.[23] She would learn to be a better driver and she would move well
beyond a modicum of independence. The children who were still in
Humble, unlike Alberto, would have an increased sense of obligation to
their mother—to check on her more regularly, to run errands for her, to
watch her. She had been the backbone of the family in so many ways.
Pablo had fought his demons, guided the family to Houston, built a home,
and put food on the table. And his first son would regret not appreciating
the simple fact that his father really had worked *como on perro*—like a
dog—for most of his life. His son would always regret never adequately
thanking his father and not telling him enough how much he truly cared
for him:

*"If I only knew that he would die during my last semester of law school, I
would have told him more often that I loved him. If I only knew, on my graduation
day [from college], that my dad would soon be gone, I would have thanked him for
putting a roof over my head and that I was proud to be his son. If I only knew."*[24]

By graduation it was a given that Gonzales would be going back to
Houston and that he'd be offered a job with Vinson & Elkins, maybe
even an inside track to a partnership and a $500,000 income. He had done
a clerkship, and that methodical behavior, the kind his old friend Liz Lara
had seen in high school, was still there. He had carefully planned a return
to Houston, and this one would even trump his tenure at Rice University.
This time he'd be moving permanently into that gilded world that his father and mother helped serve for so many years.

Like the Air Force Academy, like Rice, like Harvard Law, Vinson &
Elkins was moving with the trend to increase minority participation,

though in the case of Vinson & Elkins it was rather plodding. New management at the firm had realizedV&E needed to shift beyond the constant cycle of hiring bright white students who had recently graduated from the elite law schools. In the past there were no Jews, women, or people of color. The first black attorney was hired in 1974, followed by the first Hispanic in 1977. But now the borders with Mexico were increasingly blurring and Hispanic lawyers were needed to take advantage of big-time business clients; Houston, Dallas, and San Antonio were increasingly important zones for Mexican, Central American, and South American oil deals, trade partnerships, international business efforts. Having a Harvard-trained Hispanic attorney atVinson & Elkins was essentially a no-brainer, it was a hedge against the future, it was a community relations asset, and, as always, if Alberto Gonzales didn't conform to expectations, he could be bounced anytime the firm's managing partners wanted.

It didn't hurt Gonzales's chances that in 1982, the same year he was hired, the firm's original Hispanic lawyer had decided to resign after just five years atV&E.[25] There already was a distinct paucity in minority hiring atV&E, and the firm certainly didn't want to risk any criticism. As that first Hispanic attorney atV&E was leaving, Gonzales was being guaranteed a spot at the firm.

Founded in 1917 in Houston by James Elkins and William Vinson, V&E, as it is universally known, was simply one of those intensely intimidating powerhouses that had used its initial, massive oil-related profits to eventually move far beyond Houston, entrenching itself on Wall Street, in Washington, and in various foreign capitals. Old man Vinson had first come to Houston from Sherman, Texas, and he eventually invited Elkins to relocate from Huntsville, Texas, and join him. Vinson was the intellectual spine of the firm; old man Elkins was the one who would "grow the firm." By deciding to float on Texas's vast sea of oil—and to become the go-to firm helping to unscramble, define, push, and shape innumerable deals involving wildcatters, multinational energy giants, mineral rights, land battles, inheritances, insurance, drilling, production facilities, shipping, petrochemical plants, and refineries—V&E eventually would have seven hundred highly compensated lawyers in eleven offices reaching into distant corners of the world. In the twenty-first century it would be widely known as the law firm that represented Enron, the infamous, doomed company that saw several of its key executives facing trial and prison in the wake of the biggest financial collapse in U.S. history.

In the early years Elkins wanted V&E to be more than just a paper-pushing law firm. He spun V&E into all manner of money-making directions, including creating Houston's largest bank, First City National. In time, though oil and gas remained the lifeblood of the firm, V&E would branch into every imaginable form of white-collar legal work, including mega-corporate restructurings, international law, real estate, venture capital, and on and on and on. Most of all, V&E developed a corporate culture of discretion. In the madcap, dangerous world of Texas oil and big business—where the level of backstabbing, treachery, illegalities, subterfuge, and deceit was unmatched except maybe in a book that combined the Bible and the collected works of Shakespeare—V&E had earned a justly famous reputation for keeping its clients protected. If you were a V&E client, high or low, and as long as your money was good, you found yourself working with a brass-knuckled firm that bent over backward to protect your privacy, to keep you out of court and jail, to keep the revenue spigot completely unclogged.

Over the years V&E would attract high-profile partners including former Texas governor and Treasury secretary John Connally and former Senate majority leader Howard Baker. Too, it became the firm that represented Enron, Halliburton, and Brown & Root, and many of the other Texas business giants. In time V&E easily helped command and shape Houston as well as state government—and it was in perfect lockstep with the political power base in Texas by running effective interference on every nettlesome matter from environmental regulations to antitrust allegations. Much of that powerful partnering needed, of course, to be done discreetly. Someone with a personality like that of Alberto Gonzales would be right at home at the legendary Vinson & Elkins offices in the heart of Houston: "He plays things close to the vest" is how his brother Tony would put it.[26]

———

He officially joined V&E in June 1982, shortly after leaving Harvard and only five months after his father died at the rice mill. At V&E his longtime predilection toward discretion and striving—of moving deeper into Houston power and society—would be honed and refined for the next thirteen years. He would pay his dues and begin the dogged climb up the corporate law ladder. Ranking partner Harry Reasoner, who would find himself front and center years later when attention turned to the billion-dollar Enron collapse, sensed that Gonzales was driven with a "fire in his belly" to overcome whatever obstacles he had faced growing up.[27]

He would cut his teeth in the "transactional" group, putting together the paperwork on mergers, acquisitions, real estate, and banking deals. At times, as he started to increasingly specialize in real estate, he would be drafting the detailed paperwork for the very kinds of construction projects that employed thousands of undereducated, underpaid blue-collar workers like his father. With friends, Gonzales never delved into that perfect irony—the fact that his signature on a piece of paper was now the instrument that would lead to minimum-wage work for so many Mexican-American laborers in and around Houston. He was twenty-seven, his father had just died, and he had gone to the other end of the Texas food chain, to the wellspring of financial clout in Houston. He was assigned to V&E's banking/real estate/energy group, which was headed by attorney Joseph Dilg, and his work would touch on a variety of famous and infamous projects—from Enron to wholesale attempts to completely reshape the face of downtown Houston.[28]

Gonzales worked hard, pushing himself, staying late, bringing home a briefcase stuffed with papers and fielding calls at all hours. He was, like many of the other partners at the firm, automatically immersed in the jockeying to earn partner status and to reel in the really big money, though he was not as blatant, overt, and annoying about it. Very early on in his career at V&E, he was developing a certain legal style and personality. It was, of course, devoid of intimidating harangues and was instead measured, deliberate, and aimed at ultimately shifting an opponent to see the utter *reasonableness* of his argument. It's not that he was a silent assassin; he was more of a facilitator and a calm presence who had begun developing a knack for delivering exactly what the client wanted, reducing the droning, complex real estate and business transactions to easy-to-digest synopses for clients.

Many people who knew Gonzales during his years at V&E would not describe him as a brilliant legal visionary; he was not instantly, universally known as a giant legal mind. But he was efficient in a way that rarely sucked the energy out of a room or in his direction. He simply was, as one attorney said, a "get-it-done" guy. And that evolving style proved effective on several elaborate business deals, including one almost hopelessly complex public offering that took lawyers from twelve states a total of six months to unravel.

Gonzales didn't piss anybody off, at least not for very long, and he was often the voice of reason: "Being the kind of gentleman that Al is, is probably the most effective way to approach the situation, because most corporate transaction projects are projects where different constituencies with different interests are working together toward a common end, and there is a lot of persuasion involved. So, if you get everybody on your team and you get everyone working in parallel, the transaction goes so much more smoothly. I think Al, with his personality, is superb at that," said Robert Baird, a V&E partner.[29] That soft but insistent approach, coupled with his utter willingness to serve his clients, was eventually noticed by the people at V&E who could move him up through the ranks.

In the growing army of V&E attorneys, he seemed to have few enemies. He was clearly not the firm's heaviest hitter, the monster rainmaker who lined the firm's coffers with the biggest paydays, but people *liked* Al Gonzales—and it was "Al" now, not "Alberto." People seemed to wish him well, like you would wish the person sitting on the other side of the classroom well—that person who didn't raise his hand at every teacher's question. He wasn't the star quarterback, he was the safety. He wasn't the starting pitcher, he was the middleman roving the outfield. He didn't really stand out among the hundreds of skilled V&E attorneys—and that was both his limitation and his attraction. "He was the kind of person you wanted to see get ahead. He worked hard and had good writing and analytical skills," said James McCartney, who served on V&E's management committee.[30]

———

Barry Hunsaker Jr. was in the same division as Gonzales, his office was next door, and the two men shared the same secretary. He would sometimes see Gonzales driving his black two-door 328 BMW. They schmoozed a bit about Rice, about how much Gonzales enjoyed his short stint there and liked it better than being in the Air Force. When they had time, they'd make a date to play racquetball. Gonzales was cutthroat on the court and liked to play as often as possible, sometimes almost every day—it got to the point where some of his friends refused to play with him anymore. He was almost beyond competitive; he wanted to win every time. "When you played Al in racquetball, it didn't make any difference whether you were a valued client. It didn't make any difference whether you were a partner deciding whether Al makes partner. He went after it—he wanted to win. You didn't get any special treatment." [31]

Gonzales and Hunsaker shared some clients, including the company that owned and leased the big Houston Center Project—a high-dollar project that aimed to resculpt sixteen prime downtown blocks into commercial property, offices, and retail businesses. That project had Gonzales devising and reviewing multi-million-dollar construction, leasing, and joint-venture contracts and had him dealing with big hoteliers like the Four Seasons while also talking to various officials about how to connect downtown buildings with tunnels or skyways. It would become one of Gonzales's watershed efforts for V&E—he was reshaping the very city he used to stare at from a distance as a kid—and it would bring him in contact with a wide variety of power players (including the Bush family and Ken Lay), community organizations, and civic boards in Houston. Gonzales and Hunsaker were essentially doing what some lawyers call "dirt and deals" work and crafting office leases, contracts, and negotiations with big real estate clients.

As he watched his friend, Hunsaker came to believe that Gonzales left clients with the impression that he had no hidden agenda of his own, that he was unswervingly loyal to the person who hired him. It was something people would later say about Gonzales's relationship with George W. Bush. "Clients loved him because he was very interested in the clients. He didn't have the big ego associated with lawyers. He was genuinely interested in the clients as opposed to a source of revenue," says Hunsaker." [32] Hunsaker noticed something else. Gonzales didn't talk about his family, except occasionally a few mentions of his wife and later his kids. He didn't mention all the other members of his large family from Humble. "Not very much. Frankly, I learned more about his family once he left the firm and people started writing about him. He was a very private guy. Outside of his very immediate family, I never met any of his other family. And he didn't talk about them."[33]

The fact that Gonzales was Hispanic and clearly one of the few minorities becoming entrenched at the firm didn't seem to register with too many of his associates. His ethnicity, his name, was something people obviously knew and recognized, but it was never openly discussed, challenged, debated, or subject to endless lawyerly nuance. "It was something you obviously knew. But at the same time it wasn't anything that he really commented on much one way or the other," says Hunsaker. Nor did Gonzales openly espouse any great ambition to take over the firm, to position himself just perfectly to vault to a top management position. He didn't seem political, though he certainly talked politics with people. "The people who tend to be firm leaders are also ones who like the political side of it. And while Al was interested in politics and making sure good people get elected and helping good people, he's not the type who likes the limelight. I'm not sure he would ever have wanted to be highly influential at the firm."[34]

One of Gonzales's clients beginning in the 1980s was Larry Dreyfuss. Gonzales helped Dreyfuss on a variety of real estate and energy deals, including office leasing, an asset sale to Coke Industries, and a $250 million pipeline transaction. The men became friends and would sometimes dine at Italian restaurants, with Dreyfuss occasionally enjoying a glass of wine while watching Gonzales having yet another Diet Coke. Dreyfuss had decided why he liked doing business with Al Gonzales: "There's no ulterior motive to anything he does."[35] He was extremely loyal to his client in a low-key way. He took complex negotiations, like the one involving Coke Industries, and boiled them down to manageable, easy-to-understand chunks. Dreyfuss, like so many others, began using the word *calm* to describe Gonzales. For some others, it teetered on the edge of boring. And for some, including the old-timers at V&E who had grown up with the kind of reserved, staid, discreet corporate culture that coursed through the firm, Gonzales had a perfectly adequate anonymity about him: "Everyone wore a coat and tie. He was just one of the coat-and-tie guys," remembers James McCartney, a former partner at V&E who started at the firm in 1952.[36]

But outside the V&E empire, including in the Hispanic community, some people were slowly beginning to notice Gonzales. It was an outgrowth of both his own personal agenda and that calculated way V&E took an interest in grooming new clients. Gonzales, after settling into V&E and learning how to practice real estate law, was ready to move on a bit—into the politics-and-high-society land of million-dollar fund-raising, citywide boards, invitation-only galas, and uber-benefits. In short, he was ready to move beyond the leasing deals and his grinding work in the transactional group into a world that exposed him to the real power players in Houston and Texas. He had bridged the gaps between Roberta Lane and downtown; bridged the gaps between MacArthur High and Harvard Law. He had gone through the front door of the Houston buildings his father was denied entry into, even though hands like his father's had constructed them. Now he was going beyond the front door, deeper into Houston and closer to the most powerful people in the world.

SIX

Sad Commentary

After six years his marriage to Diane was crumbling. They had had no children. Many of his friends, colleagues, and coworkers had no idea there was trouble. Few of them could even recall much about Diane. By 1985, as he was still jockeying at V&E, they filed for divorce in Harris County. He was twenty-nine and she was twenty-eight. His friends from Harvard, some of whom he still kept in touch with now and then, had heard that Diane had gone to work in an office somewhere in Houston during Gonzales's first few years at V&E, perhaps continuing her work as an executive secretary. In a true testimony to the way Gonzales and his family can, as his brother Tony says, keep things "close to the vest," very few of Gonzales's closest associates even knew that Diane Clemens died in a car crash after the divorce. Gonzales's friend Bill Sweeney says, "After she and Al divorced, she moved back to Illinois, where she was raised, and sometime later was killed in a car accident."[1]

(For students of the extended Bush Dynasty, the fact that Gonzales's first wife would die in a violent car crash comes as no surprise. Some Bush-aholics talk about "the curse of the Bush women" and like to point out that as a teenager First Lady Laura Bush was involved in a deadly car accident that killed a close friend of hers from high school; that President George W. Bush's grandmother was killed when a car being driven by his ultimately unharmed grandfather tumbled down a hill in upstate New York—it was a somewhat mysterious crash that led police to conduct a careful investigation; that President George W. Bush's great-grandmother also died when she was walking down a Rhode Island street one day and a car rammed into her but not her husband.)

Gonzales's parents, of course, had sometimes argued mightily about his father's drinking but they remained wedded because it was what people did; divorce was out of the question for some fiercely Catholic families. Divorce, for some ardent Catholics, not only connoted weakness, it connoted sin. Divorce was simply never an option for Pablo and Maria Gonzales. Their son, who was increasingly moving in different circles, was different. He was no longer the knee-jerk Catholic, slavishly devoted to church doctrine. In 1985, for him, it was time to move on. And the divorce coincided with his slowly becoming a more visible face in and around those select civic circles in Houston. According to some records, his divorce from Diane Clemens was finalized on July 15, 1985, twenty days before his thirtieth birthday.

For a while, friends say, he moved into a rental unit at the Four Seasons Hotel across the street from his V&E office so that he wouldn't waste time commuting. He immersed himself deeper into the Houston Center Project—that grand, controversial plan to reshape valuable downtown real estate. He did "detail" work on a billion-dollar acquisition of Baker Hughes's industrial pump and valve division."[2] He was one of fifteen V&E lawyers who represented Occidental Petroleum in a $1.25 billion acquisition of Cain Chemical Incorporated. He also did work, as did many V&E lawyers, for the energy giant Enron. Headquartered in Houston, Enron was one of the high-flying firms that once seemed the model of business probity, or, at least, efficiency. Its executives populated the right charitable organizations and it was hard to even imagine Houston without a key player like Enron. It was also hard to imagine Vinson & Elkins even being able to hire new lawyers like Alberto Gonzales without the millions of dollars pouring in from Enron. The nature of the relationship between Vinson & Elkins and Enron was enormously deep and completely driven by a ceaseless number of complex, lucrative oil and gas deals. Dozens of V&E lawyers were constantly assigned to Enron-related concerns, and there was such cross-pollination that at least twenty V&E lawyers eventually went to work for Enron full-time. People began calling the old law firm *Vinson & Enron.*

Enron became V&E's biggest, most important client, and it accounted for almost $32 million in V&E's revenue by 2001, the year that Enron bottomed out in a miasma of controversy. One of Gonzales's mentors at the firm, managing partner Dilg, who was also affiliated with Enron work, would tell *Business Week:* "Everything that the firm's lawyers who have represented Enron have done has been in a completely professional, competent and ethical manner."[3] One thing was clear: Vinson & Elkins was the law firm of record when Enron entrenched itself at the top of the billion-dollar energy mountain. Its managing partners were good friends, at work and outside work, with Ken Lay and the other soon-to-be-infamous heads of Enron. At times some of the V&E lawyers were working so closely, so intimately, with Enron, they simply set up temporary offices there.

People at V&E maintain that Gonzales's work for Enron was related to less important matters that were far apart from the inner financial workings—far from the deals that some of the bigger, better V&E experts in energy law were handling, far from the deals that would lead to indictments of Enron executives and one of the most corrosive business scandals in American history. His most important Enron work was his assignment as one of several lawyers drawing up the legal documents allowing Enron to create a master limited partnership called EOTT Energy Partners. It was a partnership that "gathered, transported and traded crude oil, refined products and natural gas liquids."[4] Of course, for years after the collapse of Enron, it would be the various partnerships that investigators and prosecutors would hone in on, attempting to find out how those deals were structured and who knew what at Enron and any of its related firms. V&E managing partner Dilg would offer this brief observation about Gonzales, whom he had taken under his wing: "I think he was pitching in and helping some other lawyers. It [Enron] clearly wasn't a major client of his." According to V&E's internal records, Gonzales would file his last billable hours for Enron-related work in May 1994, his last year at Vinson & Elkins.[5]

He still wasn't overtly political, but he had decided to become a Republican. It was easy to do in a city and state where John Connally had set the trend by easily switching parties and simply applying his social-conservative Southern Democrat roots to the GOP. Gonzales had never shared any party affiliation patter with friends at Vinson & Elkins, but it was manifestly clear that under the guidance of men like Texas Senator John Tower and then Vice President George Herbert Walker Bush, Houston had become a Republican bastion and one of the financial nerve centers for the party's long-range missions. Vinson & Elkins, always willing to work closely with its clients, was hardly ever going to be averse to any GOP inroads. It would be a natural progression to the GOP for Gonzales, one that seemed so patently obvious that any arguments from future anti-Gonzales critics about his "abandoning" his Democratic roots would be farcical. The fact is that Gonzales never had any Democratic roots, never expressed any Democratic allegiance. The environment—inside the halls of V&E and in the corridors of power where he was being dispatched to drum up more business and to serve as the firm's "Hispanic representative"—was about the most pro-GOP imaginable.

There might have been something else, some bit of what his future best friend George W. Bush would dismiss as "psychobabble." Gonzales was clearly still striving, still fixed on a rise inside Houston's legendary and mighty law firm. In that regard, he was absolutely no different than any of the other attorneys, and, of course, really no different than all the other twenty- and thirty-something lawyers at every other big shop in the state. But at the same time he was entirely unlike most of the attorneys. He had started from farther back in the pack. No private schools, no hot running water, and no telephones. And while he was growing up poor, he was also growing up in a state that was incredibly fixated on elevating some businessmen to the status of Citizen Kings—maybe best exemplified by someone like Ross Perot.

Texas is arguably the most self-congratulatory state in the nation, and it has spawned a breathless cottage industry of self-promotion often run by so-called professional Texans based on carefully created caricatures of villains and heroes, as well as a big bouquet of on-bended-knee flattery. That industry endlessly objectifies Texas by coughing up easy stereotypes about its culture, history, politicians, and power brokers and by investing want-to-be-famous folks with even more seriousness and gravity than they ever deserve. The hype, the blizzard of superlatives, and the over-the-top caricatures that come spinning out of Texas are all often predicated on calculated attempts to cash in by selling a particular image of Texas to the rest of the country—and to cash in by selling it to a rootless, shifting segment of Texas that is hungry for some sense of place, some sense of what Texas really is.

Some authentic Texas observers bristle at the whole canard, and they take umbrage at the fact that so much of the modern mythology, the false flattery, and even the creation of all-purpose bogeymen is cooked up by people who actually don't just misunderstand what "real" Texas is like— they actually dislike most of the state, or, at the very least, don't travel the back roads or inner city alleys to see what real Texas is all about. Whatever the root motivation for the caricatures—whatever the reason for that perverse reinvention of so many Texans as either profoundly evil or gloriously angelic—they have certainly been unavoidable. The state has perhaps been deliberately compartmentalized by people who *need* to have it compartmentalized—selling easy Texas stereotypes like the old TV show *Dallas* is a hell of a lot easier than acknowledging that the people, politicians, and even those power brokers are not always exactly scripted in black and white.

Growing up, coming of age, and finding his way in corporate Houston, Gonzales was as susceptible to that hype and hustle and myth-making as anyone else. Maybe at V&E he was even more susceptible, considering how alien an environment it was when he compared it to his world in Humble. That hype and hustle in Texas was like a giant blinking roadside sign. There was, in a way, a cult of power in Texas, and in Houston it would be hard to remain disinterested in it.

He was going to be a steadfast Republican in a state that the GOP had targeted for a takeover. It was a plan, a progression that had begun in West Texas when the Bush family had come to invest millions of dollars of the family's fortune in the oil fields outside of Midland and Odessa. Having made their first Texas oil fortune, the Bushes relocated to Houston in 1959, because it was where the major oil players were being headquartered and because Houston was the most comfortable place to build the state's GOP apparatus. And, in the 1980s, as political strategists fanned out across the country trying to get a sense of what new, untapped pool of voters was out there, some of them—including George W. Bush—began reporting back that there were significant numbers of Christians in places like Texas who could be wooed to the GOP. Too, as George W. Bush repeatedly told party elders, including his father, there was a gold mine of Hispanic voters who could be sold on the socially conservative agendas of the GOP. The younger Bush and his political handler, Karl Rove, were among the first to suggest to party leaders that the GOP needed to do more in Texas to convert both those Christian and Hispanic voters to the Republican Party.

Gonzales was already there: "In his mind, the Republican Party was where he wanted to be. Back before it was popular to be a Hispanic Republican, before Republicans were even courting Hispanics," said one attorney who knew him in Houston.[6] And Gonzales was already literally listening to George W. Bush's message. The younger Bush, at the direction of one of his best friends, the bad-ass political strategist Lee Atwater, had become a surrogate speaker for his father—often dispatched to friendly turf, to easy audiences that would ask few taxing questions and that would tolerate having the son instead of the father at a luncheon speech. Gonzales met the younger Bush in 1988 in Houston at one of those surrogate speeches. It wasn't a necessarily memorable encounter for either man, but Gonzales was clearly headed to the Republican fold—and, given his jockish inclinations, his love of baseball, it wasn't hard to imagine that both men, if and when they finally got to know each other, would have at least one or two things in common. They were, after all, both the first sons in their respective families. Too, Bush had wrestled with alcohol for many years in his life—he had been arrested for drunk driving—and maybe, in some way, the fact that Pablo Gonzales was an alcoholic would also bind the two men.

As Gonzales concentrated on making his way to the brass ring and the really big money as a partner at his law firm, it made perfect sense for him to do what so many other young lawyers in Houston were doing: to become a backroom stalwart of the Republican Party. But Gonzales took it a step beyond the sometimes accepted notion that some of his fellow hungry young lawyers had professed—that the Republican Party was the one that could "maximize your earnings potential." It's clear from examining the meager handful of self-reflective statements he has offered over the years that he had come to view his life as often being almost entirely self-directed—that he had put himself in the right place at the right time to break free of his miserably impoverished upbringing. He suggested he didn't have any mentors, guides, or counselors really pushing him hard to get to college. It was his decision, no one else's, to go to Fort Yukon and not Key West. He was the one who angled for the opportunities, the openings, into the Air Force Academy, Rice, Harvard, and Vinson & Elkins. It certainly wasn't anyone in his family who had sat down with him and mapped out a career strategy. He was, as always, the only one from his family who broke free and went away—and then came back to claim a place on that side of town that seemed hopelessly distant for the son of a drunk from Humble, Texas.

Gonzales was going to do something on his own again: He would join the GOP even if he thought it still wasn't the prevailing trend for Hispanics in Texas. He might do it just because he had behaved iconoclastically before, but he might also do it just because he thought the GOP was right for his personality: "I liked what I heard about some of the Republican principles about being self-reliant, hard work, and so I just gravitated to it," said Gonzales.[7] And the Republican Party was more than willing to bring someone like Alberto Gonzales into its fold. He was exactly what the elder George Bush and the younger George Bush were looking for as they mapped out their political strategy: "He was very highly thought of by Republicans even early on. He was a highly educated, talented Hispanic at an influential law firm. Who would not want someone of that profile in their party?" one lawyer in Houston said.[8]

It was clear—and Gonzales knew it—that deep inside the Bush political network he had been identified and singled out because he was Hispanic. George W. Bush, Rove, and Atwater had those long discussions in Washington and Texas about ways to position the younger Bush for a run for the governor's office in Texas in 1994. Too, they had continued those debates about how to steal away the "middle ground" from Democrats and how to lure fence-straddling Democrats, Christian voters, and minorities to the Republican Party. Rove and Atwater both agreed that the younger Bush could be sold, marketed, as a new kind of young Republican—a "compassionate conservative" who was willing to include minorities in his game plan and in his administration. The compassionate conservative phrase had been kicked around in the older Bush's administration and campaign, but it had never really rolled forward. Rove decided it would be perfect for the next generation in the Bush family, and it would suggest that Republican leaders like the younger George Bush were opening the door to voters who had traditionally tilted toward the Democrats.

In Texas, at the law firm that was representing newly elected President George Herbert Walker Bush's good friend Ken Lay and Enron, it was hard not to notice the most prominent Hispanic—Alberto Gonzales. It was hard not to notice that he was welcome and endorsed and embraced at any number of high-profile boards and fetes in town. Finally, arrangements were made for Gonzales to fly to Washington to meet with Bush administration officials. In a nod to his military background, he was considered for a high-ranking position in the Veterans Administration. And, perhaps in a nod to his cultural background, he was considered for a job with Housing and Urban Development, where both Republicans and Democrats seemed to steer minority administrators. Gonzales told people that old man Bush "was looking to identify rising minorities in America and bring them to Washington and serve in his administration." [9]

As always, he didn't openly linger on whether the color of his skin had anything to do with where he was in life—chasing those million-dollar deals, taking up the game of golf, driving his BMW, being courted by the president of the United States, eating at Italian restaurants, and living at the Four Seasons. Opportunities had to have emerged, he decided, because he was Hispanic. But how they exactly unfolded was something he chose not to measure. It was one of the few things in life that he didn't seem to be deliberating and studying. It was something that, as if it was part of an immutable societal force, had just occurred at just the right time for him. He didn't question it, didn't openly analyze it, and didn't wonder whether he was a particular beneficiary while others in similar circumstances were not. He had decided to take a Republican view of it. He convinced himself he had done most of the heavy lifting himself; he had pulled himself up by the bootstraps rather than having someone give him a hand or a handout. He had positioned himself to take advantage of opportunities. "Like most ethnic minorities, I probably have been hurt and helped by my ethnicity. And the way I look at it, hopefully those things even out in the end. Whatever the reasons I have been given an opportunity, what is more important is what I do with it." [10]

He turned the elder Bush down, declined the job offers in D.C., and decided to concentrate on becoming a full partner at Vinson & Elkins. He would have been taking a five-figure salary in Washington when there was a possibility that he could ultimately be making a million dollars as a managing partner at one of the most powerful law firms in the world. The Bushes, particularly young George Bush, took notice that Alberto Gonzales had turned down his father.[11] The fact of the matter was that the younger Bush simply did not intimately know very many minorities outside the ones who had worked as housekeepers, cooks, and drivers for his family over the years: There were Julia May Cooper and Otha Fitzgerald Taylor, the black maids who had helped raise Bush when he was growing up in west Texas. There was an African-American adolescent named Jimmy whom Bush had gotten close to in the early 1970s when Bush worked for a short time in an inner city community program called PULL in Houston. There were the Mexican-American maids and housekeepers who worked for George and Laura Bush in Midland in the 1980s; Bush seemed to occasionally be very close to one or two of the younger women in those Mexican-American families. And, of course, there was the Mexican woman the Bush family hired when they moved to the Houston area at the same time ex-migrant worker Pablo Gonzales was moving his family there. In 1959, when the Bush family settled in their large home, a woman named Paula Rendón "came up from Mexico" to work in the Bush house near the Houston Country Club. The younger George Bush remembered her this way: "She was a woman looking for a way to make some wages to support her family back in Mexico. She loved me. She chewed me out. She tried to shape me up. And I have grown to love her like a second mom." [12]

Gonzales's first few years at Vinson & Elkins had passed by unremarkably, except for the fact that clients found him unerringly loyal and circumspect. So discreet, no one knew his politics. Even as he was being sought out by Republicans in Houston, Gonzales was still doing a very good job of keeping his affiliations buried from some friends. "I never would have even guessed he was a Republican. Stereotypically, I probably would have guessed he was a Democrat," says Lynn Liberato, the former president of the State Bar of Texas.[13]

Vinson & Elkins wanted to see what kind of political and financial capital Gonzales could accrue in social settings and public arenas. He joined more of those profile-raising groups that many of the V&E foot soldiers had been steered toward—those groups that meet for power breakfasts on the top floors of the downtown skyscrapers, the air filled with the mixed, pungent aroma of aftershave and coffee, the introductions peppered with the nod-and-wink repartee favored by bureaucrats and Rotarians everywhere. He was at the United Way, the Houston Hispanic Forum, Big Brothers and Big Sisters, Catholic Charities, Leadership Houston, and the Houston Bar Association. In 1990 he became president of the Houston Hispanic Bar Association, an organization for the minority lawyers at the bigger firms in town. (The local Mexican-American Bar Association was already in existence, but it tended to be an organization serving solo practitioners and smaller firms.) One of the first moves by the HHBA was the initiation of a pledge for law firms to increase minority hiring. Liberato remembers Gonzales making the behind-the-scenes calls to push the effort. "It's making the phone calls, having the meetings, putting the people together to build the coalitions, that sort of thing. I think he's continued to work a lot behind the scenes throughout his career."[14]

In 1990 things took a dramatic, fateful turn: He was handpicked by V&E to be special legal counsel for the group—cochaired by Enron executive Ken Lay—that was hosting a jewel that President George H. W. Bush was bringing home to Houston. The International Economic Summit would fill the city with thousands of reporters, dignitaries and functionaries from around the world—and it was Bush's way of thanking the city that had provided the money to put him in office. The biggest contributors to the Bush family were in Houston, including several Enron executives such as Lay. The upcoming summit reinforced just how much influence and sway the Bush family held in the city and how embedded Republican politics had become—and, of course, how trusted Gonzales had become within the V&E and Bush family firmaments.

His work on the International Economic Summit—which was treated in Houston and Texas with that usual hyperventilating indulgence by city leaders and state officials—was considered a smashing success. The meeting essentially went off with few hitches; not even the long-haired Italian foreign minister—hanging out late at night in the bar of the Warwick Hotel with a stunning woman on his arm and regaling listeners about the quality of the disco scene in his country—dampened a solid public relations success for Bush. Gonzales was going to be rewarded for his work. Not long after the summit, he was quietly let in on the fact that bigger things were in store him at Vinson & Elkins. The firm had decided to elevate three minority lawyers to partner, including Gonzales. In January 1991 the official announcement was made.

As a practical matter, it meant that Gonzales could make a lot more money—maybe millions of dollars over the years. He was enormously proud of his promotion and sometimes would simply say that he was the "first" minority partner at the firm instead of "one of" the first. His friends said he viewed it as an incredible personal watershed—that it was the defining moment of his life, that he had felt he had ascended to a rarified level, and that he was incredibly eager to enjoy its riches. It was also news that quickly spread through Texas's Hispanic community. Republicans and Democrats both viewed his partnership as a breakthrough—a great victory—and Hispanic members of both parties (including Texas Attorney General Dan Morales and Texas Supreme Court Justice Raul Gonzalez, both powerful Democrats) thought it important enough to come to Houston to celebrate at the private party honoring his promotion. "I knew of him when I was in law school because he was the first Hispanic to become a partner in a major law firm. At that point, it was a sad commentary, but he was entrusted with that," said David Medina, who would later become a Texas Supreme Court justice.[15] Massey Villareal, one of Gonzales's fellow board members at Big Brothers and Big Sisters in Houston, put it this way: "If I were Al Gonzales, I would start up a firm. Instead of Vinson and Elkins, it would be Vinson and Gonzales. The time has come for great wealth in the Hispanic community. There is nothing wrong with being wealthy. He's a big-picture guy and he will find what will be good for his soul."[16]

Some friends in Houston wondered about the cultural tugs, the way prominent Hispanics like Gonzales probably had to straddle things, existing somewhere between their deep cultural backgrounds and the new world they had been immersed in. "You are constantly in a flux of trying to prove you are an American or Mexican. You really don't know who you are," says Tanny Berg, a Texas real estate developer and leader in Hispanic business circles. One thing was apparent to his friends: the longer Gonzales worked at Vinson & Elkins, the more Gonzales embraced the Republican Party and the more Texas GOP leaders pursued him: "Usually you see people who have made it as part of the system, they drift towards Republicanism. The Republican Party's vast majority is white Anglo-Saxon Protestant. So it is extremely important for them to herald any sort of minority leader. The Republican Party wants to show itself to be broad-based and so it seems to accentuate those leaders." [17]

He didn't advertise it too much and he told one friend that he actually hated doing it, but he spent time handing out "push cards" and campaign literature for the blustery Clayton Williams, a cowboy hat–wearing oil millionaire from Midland who was running against Ann Richards in the 1990 governor's race in Texas. Friends said that Gonzales must have done it because he knew that he had to do it, that it was what loyal Republicans did even if they weren't enamored of the candidate or the process. By 1990 he was obviously a wholehearted GOP soldier. And he moved in a circle of politically like-minded, hungry, young lawyers who were billing top dollar for top hours. One close acquaintance in Austin said that money—and the fact that he grew up with none—was always a driving force in his life. Gonzales, said his friend, simply made it clear that he wanted to make a lot of money, and that if he went into public life in some way, it would have to be something that would eventually lead to a bigger payday after he left the public arena. Gonzales, said the friend, had stared into the future and seen a lucrative life after politics—had seen a life made even more lucrative by politics.

Longtime political observers, especially Hispanic political analysts, began watching Gonzales. His embrace of the right, of Republican politics, was more than an isolated moment. Gonzales seemed to symbolize a trend in Houston and in Texas. "I think a new generation of Hispanics, educated males and females, are coming out, are looking at what point of view and who is going to help me the most. I think a lot of Hispanics feel that the

Democratic Party has taken them for granted, particularly educated Hispanics, because they look at the communities they grew up in and it looks
the same as twenty years ago," says Neftali Partida, a Houston-based political consultant. "I think that Al at an early age gravitated to that. Hispanics are starting to become a very independent vote." [18]

If there were any doubts about his inclinations, they were made very
clear in 1991 when he was the logical choice for another obviously high-
profile partisan project. The upcoming 1992 GOP Convention was coming to Houston, and the host committee for the event was also chaired by
Ken Lay from Enron. Lay's executive assistant recommended that Gonzales be part of the legal team coordinating the GOP Convention. Lay, whose
position at Enron had made him the most sought-after rainmaker for the
biggest political and social events in Houston and Texas, was essentially
running the entire walk-up to the GOP convention. That work brought
Lay and the other Houston organizers into deeper contact with the already familiar Bush family and political network. And for a while Ken Lay
was considered *"a good man"*—he had earned that treasured Bush family
title not just for running the Economic Summit and the Republican Conventions but because he was a solid financial backer of the elder Bush.

Gonzales knew both Ken Lay and his executive assistant, Nancy Mc-
Neil. "Al worked with Lay and Nancy McNeil," says Patrick Oxford, a
longtime friend of George W. Bush and a prominent Houston attorney
who also worked on the GOP Convention. "The same people who
worked on the [International Economic] Summit worked on the GOP
Convention. We started the convention work in early 1991, so Al had just
come off the Summit. We had a mutual client who suggested I bring Al on
board to help us as a sort of general counsel, which I was delighted to do.
That client was Nancy McNeil. She was the executive assistant to Ken Lay
over at Enron." The relationship between Gonzales and Lay also apparently included participation with the Houston Area Welcome Home
Committee, a corporation put together to stage celebrations for returning
Gulf War veterans in the spring of 1991. Gonzales, Lay, and David Dun-
can, the Arthur Anderson auditor who handled Enron's books, were members of the corporation. [19]

Oxford had come to know Gonzales as intense, directed, and focused.
Oxford also didn't think that Gonzales's ethnicity had anything to do with

his being tabbed to be one of the lead lawyers handling the GOP Convention for the Bush family in Houston. "No, no, no. The reason we got Al involved was because he's a great lawyer with a lot of common sense, not because of any minority status he had. In Texas you often don't think of Hispanics as minorities, because everybody in Texas is part Mexican, basically." [20]

As 1991 unfolded, Gonzales immersed himself in work on the GOP Convention. And he began growing closer to thirty-year-old divorcée Rebecca Turner. Friends of Gonzales and Turner say Turner had first met Gonzales when she was a teenager, that she had perhaps stayed in touch with Gonzales over the years, and might have known him through the same legal circles that her husband had moved in. A mother of one child, an eight-year-old boy named Jared, she struck many people as a particularly physically attractive woman with an exuberant, extroverted personality that would forever be far more memorable than that of Gonzales. According to some records, she had gotten married to a Houston attorney named Patrick Freeze at almost exactly the same time Alberto Gonzales was married to Diane Clemens in the summer of 1979, then she had gotten divorced at almost the exact same time in the summer of 1985 that Alberto Gonzales had gotten divorced. She worked for a while, said friends, in an administrative capacity at Bank One in Houston.

Friends called the tall, blond, green-eyed woman Becky and remember her as both plain-spoken and sometimes openly emotional. Unlike the steadfastly muted man she had started dating, she had a way of drawing people into conversations, into easy laughs and confidences. She didn't, friends say, put on airs. "Becky's definitely not ostentatious. She can't go out and buy a designer dress for each and every occasion," says Larry Dreyfuss. "Becky's got the overwhelming majority of the personality. Like Mrs. [Laura] Bush is the better, more personable one, so is Becky. After fifteen minutes, you'd rather be talking to Laura or Becky." [21] Friends assumed that Gonzales had found something in Turner that he lacked. In the droning world of the gray men in their gray suits immersed in the commercial real estate deals, the political deals, the backroom chess battles, Turner was a sunny, extroverted, unbridled antidote for Gonzales. "He is not necessarily an outgoing, happy-go-lucky individual," says George Donnelly, who would be head of the Houston Hispanic Chamber of Commerce. "He's not one to get out on the dance floor and that sort of thing." [22]

Turner would be the one who would lead people to the dance floor. She'd lead a group of friends to a meal at the Macaroni Grill, or she would confide in friends about raising her young son, about her favorite movies, about clothes she was buying. "Becky tells you everything, she's very vivacious," says Dreyfuss. She was also disarming and unreserved in offering opinions on people. She was, said people who had experienced it, the type of person who could instantly immerse you in her world. She was often an open book—and an open book was something that few expected Gonzales to ever become. "I always felt very, very close to Becky. It was one of those things where you meet someone and you immediately connect. That is the kind of person Becky is. She's so honest," says her close friend Kenna Ramirez, wife of former El Paso mayor Carlos Ramirez." [23]

The year 1991 was obviously a momentous one for several reasons. It began with Gonzales making partner at V&E in January. It escalated with his being assigned to work on the Republican Convention for the American president who called Houston home. And, finally, he and Turner decided to get married after his birthday. Records indicate that Alberto Gonzales married Rebecca Turner, formerly Rebecca Turner Freeze and formerly married to Patrick Freeze, on August 31. Very quietly, some Hispanic critics from Texas would offer the politically incorrect and controversial thought that Gonzales had now gotten it all: a partnership in an ivory tower firm that had once excluded minorities and a drop-dead gorgeous *Norte Americana* trophy wife who would help to validate his arrival in Houston. Those same critics said that there was only one more pragmatic bit of inclusion left in the arc of Alberto Gonzales: He needed to reconsider that decision he had made to turn down the Bush Dynasty. At the very least, he needed to do something, anything, to will himself into some higher public profile.

In December 1991, in testimony to how careful he was about his career—how he had begun to weigh where he was going in the future, how he wanted to move beyond the confines of the law firm, how he had decided to become a vastly more political player—Gonzales arranged a meeting at a Houston restaurant with Democratic political consultant Marc Campos. The consultant had worked inside the successful campaign of newly elected Mayor Robert Lanier, a Democrat who had taken office with some strong support in the Latino community. Gonzales was on a reconnaissance mission, and he wanted to find out what it would take for him to become city attorney.

Campos was surprised. Insiders, by then, had known that Gonzales had been courted and groomed by the Bushes, that he had had worked on the Economic Summit, and was hip deep in legal work for the GOP Convention. It struck Campos as a particularly bold move for a Republican like Gonzales to be seeking out a Democratic strategist and asking for work in a Democratic administration. "He had the sense enough to know that Lanier was somewhat indebted to the Latino community for the support he got. So why not a Latino for city attorney? I pushed for him. . . . I was of the opinion that hey, here's an opportunity. There weren't very many Democratic Latino lawyers that were partner at major law firms that I could offer up as city attorney. When it comes to patronage in terms of the city, they're like the key appointments. The key ones are always the high-profile ones like fire chief, police chief, and city attorney. And I was shooting for a Latino city attorney. I didn't think his political affiliation would hurt the Latino community—after all, he'd be working for Bob Lanier."

Gonzales's quiet application was taken very seriously by the Democratic kingmakers in Houston. Campos says that Gonzales was one of the finalists, but that there simply wasn't enough support for him from other mayoral advisers—especially ones who were suspicious of Gonzales's party affiliation. "Even though he was a Republican, I never saw him as one of those zealot warriors of the right," says Campos. "I even mentioned to him that there would be some Democrats that would object to him being named—some Democrats from the Latino community . . . simply because of his party affiliation. He seemed to understand that but had a difficult time accepting it. He was more willing to reach out to his counterparts on the Democratic side than Democrats were willing to reach out to him." [24]

With Gonzales's marriage to Turner, he became a stepfather to her son, Jared Freeze. Seven months and one week after their marriage, some Texas records indicate that Alberto Graham Gonzales, their first son together, was born in Houston on April 7, 1992. That year, his focus was increasingly directed not just on his growing family but also on work for the elder George Bush, Ken Lay, and the Republican National Convention. Gonzales was handling "commercial" work, helping to draw up contracts, outlining the infrastructure organization, getting goods and services for the convention—and feeling under enormous pressure to juggle all of it. He began meeting more frequently with the select group of Houston attorneys who had been handpicked by their respective firms to form the legal infrastructure for the convention—they divvied up the leasing wrangles, the delegate controversies, the copyright and trademark discussions, the negotiations with utility contractors, the discussions with city and state officials over traffic issues, the rights of protesters, and any other emergencies that seemed to pop up on a daily basis. Compared to the hours he put in on the International Economic Summit, the work for the GOP's big gathering at the Astrodome was clearly more angst-inducing. It had Gonzales in closer contact with the Bush hierarchy, with the Bush family, with the closest family insiders.

Adding to the pressure was the fact that his work was instantly truncated when he blew out an Achilles tendon, maybe playing handball, according to Patrick Oxford. It was just before the convention and at about the same time as his first wedding anniversary. "Right in the middle of preparations, he tore his Achilles tendon, so he was sort of out of commission in the run-up. I remember him and his wife coming up to our law firm's suite, which was up in the rafters at the Astrodome, and he was on crutches. Al couldn't help us because of the surgery on his injury," remembers Oxford.[25] At that point in his career—and in terms of what passed for success in the confines of V&E and Republican politics—his physical setback didn't matter. Gonzales had earned his place with the Bushes and the Republican Party, and it was presumed to be only a matter of time before he found the right entry point to even more active involvement—or before the Bush network took another run at hiring him.

If there were pressures for Gonzales, they may have stemmed from the fact that he knew he was in the presence of people who wanted him to come to Washington and who would probably insist on it again. In 1992 there was an item in the *Houston Chronicle:* "Gonzales, who said he spent many more hours working as a volunteer lawyer for the International

Economic Summit, said the GOP Convention involves more pressure because of the number of players involved."[26]

George W. Bush's campaign for Texas governor was quietly unleashed
at the same time his father was elected to the presidency in 1988, and
it roared into a level of active planning when his father was voted out of
office in 1992. The strategy sessions for his gubernatorial run against the
enormously popular Texas governor Ann Richards—someone who had
rolled into office with deep support from minorities—were held in Dallas,
Houston, and Austin under the direction of Karl Rove.

Increasingly, Rove suggested that the campaign simply try to spin the
usual dynamics, the usual assumptions, on their heads. He had a multipart
plan to win Hispanic votes, win Christian evangelical votes, and to reinvent his client, George W. Bush, as a successful big businessman. Rove
had begun the process in the late 1980s with a careful media campaign to
characterize the young Bush as a crackling, all-American CEO—the chief
executive officer who had taken the reins of the stumbling Texas Rangers
baseball team and turned the mom–and–apple pie business into a humming, customer-friendly revenue stream.

Rove had insisted that Bush be identified in news stories as the "owner"
of the Texas Rangers, though Bush owned only 1.8 percent of the team.
Rove and Bush had structured a deal with deep-pocketed Bush family
members, investors, and colleagues: if they bought the team, the younger
George Bush would go to work for them as the "public face" of the team.
It was a job that absolutely none of the real owners of the Texas Rangers
wanted. In fact, most of them abhorred the media and harbored zero ambitions to be in the paper or on TV, let alone to run for political office. The
younger Bush could raise his profile by serving the ownership group as
their paid public spokesman who was guaranteed to get his name in the
paper on a regular basis. If the team made some money, won a few games,
it was a win–win situation. The fact that Rove and Bush were unfolding
their plan in the greater Dallas area was working out perfectly: The *Dallas
Morning News,* the so-called paper of record in Texas, was writing about
George W. Bush as if he really was the owner.

As the younger Bush's campaign for governor unfolded in the 1990s,

Rove and other Bush advisers were also on the phone to the political reporters at the *Morning News*—in particular, Wayne Slater, who was eventually entrusted to cover George W. Bush's career and life for the most influential paper in the state. Slater had conversations and visits with Rove, Karen Hughes, and other Bush intimates. A picture was once taken of Rove and Slater embracing and mugging in a carefree moment on the grounds of the Bush family's Kennebunkport mansion. And, in time, the *Dallas Morning News,* which set the tone for statewide and national coverage of Bush, was criticized by at least one staffer for not delving into Bush's life and times at the first, earliest moments that Bush became a public figure in Texas.

The criticism centered around the thought that many important questions about Bush's criminal record, military history, and business dealings should have been addressed beginning in the late 1980s and certainly in the early and mid-1990s when it first became known that Bush was going to run for governor in Texas. (After biographies were written about George W. Bush in 1999 and after Nicholas Kristof of the *New York Times,* Lois Romano of the *Washington Post,* and the staffs of the *Fort Worth Star-Telegram, Houston Chronicle, San Antonio Express-News, Boston Globe, Los Angeles Times,* and *Chicago Tribune* began doing lengthy biographical sketches of Bush, the pace and depth of coverage on Bush's background progressed from 1999 to 2004.)

For Alberto Gonzales and others interested in joining the Bush network in Texas in the early 1990s, it sometimes felt like an enthusiastic, welcoming environment, and Gonzales would be easily invited aboard the runaway train known as the George W. Bush for Governor Campaign.

Bush, again, didn't know many minorities in a state where Hispanics constituted about a quarter of the population. After his father was voted out of office, there was Fred McClure, his father's old legislative liaison on Capitol Hill: The skilled African-American deal maker had come to live in Dallas and was there to lend advice and know-how to the younger Bush. There was the Dallas housing authority head, Alphonso Jackson: Bush liked Jackson's brio and he really liked the way Jackson piped up in one of the early strategy sessions in Dallas, yelping out that the Bush team needed to take on Ann Richards and "kick her ass." (Jackson would later become the Secretary of Housing and Urban Development in the younger Bush's administration.)

There were a handful of prominent, Republican-leaning, Hispanic businessmen in Houston, El Paso, and Dallas. There was a young man in South Texas, Tony Garza, who had become a Republican county judge. (Garza would later be named ambassador to Mexico in the younger Bush's administration and would go on to marry the richest woman in that country.) There was Roderick Paige from the Houston school board and a former dean at Houston's Texas Southern University. (Paige would later be named Secretary of Education in the younger Bush's administration.) There was Carlos Ramirez, the Democratic mayor of El Paso who many people believed would throw his weight behind any Bush campaign. The fact that Bush wooed these minority figures and then simply brought so many of them to high-ranking positions in his presidential administration suggests that for years he and Rove had a carefully mapped-out strategy—a strategy that really traced back to when Bush's father first identified Alberto Gonzales and offered him jobs in *his* administration.

By October 1992 Gonzales had moved with Rebecca and their two children out of their pleasant home in West University Place—the comfortable, upscale neighborhood that surrounded his alma mater, Rice University. The family relocated to the Spring area so that Gonzales could qualify as a member of the Planning & Zoning Commission in Houston—it was a body that had more to do with the fate, future, and look of Houston than its counterparts in other cities. But a month later Gonzales (who was being identified in news stories as a "real estate attorney with the law firm Vinson & Elkins") told local papers that he had decided to abandon his bid for the commission. Gonzales told reporters that there was a conflict of interest issue, that Vinson & Elkins had clients who would appear before the commission, and that "we reviewed the situation and decided this was the best way to go."[27] Gonzales, who had previously been appointed to the influential Land Use Strategies Committee by Mayor Kathy Whitmire, added that he planned to stay on another board he had been named to: the Zoning Strategies Committee.

Political soothsayers gathered at the usual Houston watering holes and tried to deconstruct all the back-and-forth maneuvering—and the easy, quick way that Gonzales would move his family into a new house just to meet the qualifying guidelines for the planning commission . . . and then just as easily decide to drop out. There was more to the story than a sudden realization that there could be a conflict of interest. Any smart lawyer who had spent a decade doing real estate law in Houston would have known about it ahead of time.

Immediately there were whispers that Gonzales was actually being groomed to become the city's first Hispanic mayor—and that his political advisers at V&E and in the GOP had decided that their original plan to raise his profile through the planning commission was not exactly the perfect path. And, suggested other political wags, maybe Gonzales had already been identified for a more valuable role inside the Bush national machine; maybe he had been picked for something that would serve the Bush Dynasty in a much bigger way than having Gonzales be the mayor of Houston.

In 1991 there had been one other barely mentioned but extremely fortuitous moment to go along with making partner, getting married, and spending time with the members of the Bush family's inner circle: Gonzales was elected to the State Bar of Texas board of directors. It paled in instant comparison to the other moments from that year. But he would hold a seat on the board for the next three years. And it was a move that would bump him out of a strictly Houston orbit and put him more regularly in touch with high-powered attorneys from every corner of the state. In particular, he would get to know Harriet Miers, a subdued, serious lawyer from Dallas who had become one of the truly close associates of Dallas-based businessman George W. Bush and who had ascended to the presidency of the State Bar of Texas in 1992.

As the son of the former president moved his gubernatorial campaign into high gear, he had grown to increasingly favor the calm, staid Miers. She would eventually become his personal lawyer, someone he counted as a deep, trusted friend.

And, meanwhile, Miers and Gonzales would begin their own friendship. They were almost hopelessly, impossibly alike in terms of their legal style and their personalities: reserved, deliberative, never really known for giving a riveting speech, detail-oriented. They were "legal process wonks"—lawyers who seemed to be easy with the endless, droning, boring complexities of drawing up briefs, writing position papers, and doing research on corporate cases. Neither of them was famous for being on the short list of the great intellectuals in Texas, or the great constitutional scholars, or the most dazzling practitioners of extemporaneous law . . . they weren't rabbits, they were turtles. They were dry as toast and generally successful in making their clients at Exxon, Enron, Walt Disney, and Microsoft very happy. That old hand at Vinson & Elkins, partner Jim McCartney, had a term for people like Miers and Gonzales: They were "suit-and-tie" lawyers—highly paid worker ants deep inside the big, gray apparatus who made their corner of the law firm hum with a tidy efficiency.

With their work, their personalities so perfectly in sync, it would only be a matter of time before they were equally bound by their enormous fascination, loyalty, and admiration for George W. Bush. Both of them would sycophantically say that they owed so much to Bush and that he was among the most brilliant and influential people they had ever met. Miers and Gonzales would become so interwoven, their careers so intertwined, that it would be hard to imagine one without the other—and it would be both their curse and blessing to be affixed to each other, and to George W. Bush, for the rest of their public lives.

SEVEN

A Good Man

In 1993 Gonzales studied the governor's race and that almost delicious mix of very clearly contrasting candidates: high-haired incumbent Ann Richards and swaggering George W. Bush.

Until Richards profoundly disappointed her base years later by going to work as a highly paid lobbyist for the tobacco industry (the online publication *Slate* once infamously labeled her one of the "Liberal Tobacco Whores") and then going to work for a public relations firm run by George W. Bush's media guru, she had achieved almost a cult status in some liberal quarters of Texas. Bush, to counter Richards's strongholds, began campaigning hard for the minority vote, but he also began targeting the ever-growing pool of affluent suburban voters who were moving into "McMansions" in gated communities outside of Dallas, Houston, and Austin. In a way, he was appealing directly to the twin inclinations of someone like Alberto Gonzales—an educated Mexican-American son of migrant workers who now increasingly had more and more in common with the white, conservative, suburban soccer moms and dads in Texas's bigger cities.

Though he was still doing real estate deals and working for Enron (again, he would file his last billable hours for Enron in 1994), Gonzales was spending even more time serving as a presence for his law firm inside the State Bar of Texas firmament. That work at bar meetings, boards, and social functions brought him into ever-increasing contact with the State Bar president Miers, who would go on to become George W. Bush's personal lawyer as well as the general counsel for the Bush campaign for Texas governor.

Since the 1970s, Bush had been involved in a wide array of complex, entangled oil and real estate ventures. Since he moved back to Texas after graduating business school in the mid-1970s, Bush had entered any number of oil partnerships and then borrowed a half-million dollars from a friend to pay for his 1.8 percent investment in the Texas Rangers. His accountant was an old friend from Midland, Bob McCleskey, and Bush grew to have enormous faith in him. Bush quickly extended the same level of faith to Miers. Obviously the stakes were high: Rove and Bush had already confided in friends that the run for governor in Texas was a way station on the way to a chase for the White House. Any legal-business problems or snafus needed to be solved now—in 1993 and 1994—before Bush won the governor's race. Miers, who had cleaved her way through infinitely hard work on behalf of her mega-clients (Microsoft and Walt Disney), was deemed to be just the right person to help inoculate George W. Bush against any future inquiries into his legal and business dealings.

Bush, of course, won the race against Richards in 1994, and he quickly asked Miers to become his "transition period" lawyer in the weeks building up to his January 1995 inauguration. She'd handle all those questions of divestiture and oversee the legal ramifications of his financial holdings and administration appointments. And she'd make recommendations to Bush for those various appointments—first and foremost someone who would serve Bush as his permanent in-house general counsel.

That recommendation was almost too easy for her. Alberto Gonzales from Vinson & Elkins was the right candidate for both practical and coldly pragmatic reasons. He was a bright, conservative, young Republican from one of the most influential law firms in the state. He was known for being a nuts-and-bolts lawyer who stayed away from the media, was slavishly loyal to his clients, and was an expert in synthesizing and boiling down complex legal matters into easy-to-understand terms. Gonzales, almost everyone at V&E said, was able to explain things in simple declarative sentences and paragraphs to his clients, not in obfuscating legalese. When you received a legal opinion from Alberto Gonzales, it was said that he would be glad to give you the synopsis first—he gave you the short answer first, and, if you wanted, he could give the longer version later.

Beyond all of the things that might make his legal style mesh with Bush, Gonzales was Hispanic. People around the state and the country were watching to see if Bush could match the way Ann Richards had dramatically increased the number of minority appointees in her administration. It was a topic—a comparison—that was on boil in Austin. Picking Gonzales as a high-profile member of the Bush inner circle was practical and politically expedient: "Al was a Republican before it was popular for the Republicans to recruit Hispanics," said one old friend of his, a fellow attorney in Houston who was familiar with Bush's recruitment of Gonzales.[1]

In the fall of '94, before Bush would be sworn into office in the winter of '95, Miers and others pushed Bush to quickly secure the services of Gonzales. Some of the most influential pushing came from the elder George Bush, who regularly recommended business and political associates to his first son. One of Gonzales's key advisers in Austin simply says that the old man had gotten to know Gonzales and his reputation in Houston and that "when Bush won governor, his father recommended Al for general counsel." The younger Bush might have easily remembered the rising Hispanic star at V&E, the one who was the special legal counsel to the committee hosting his father's Economic Summit, the one who worked hard on his father's Republican Convention, the one who had turned down his father's offers to join his administration in Washington. "So the first time I met with him in Austin, about a week or so after the election, he talked to me about what he expected, what his vision was, what his goals were as governor," said Gonzales. The thirty-nine-year-old lawyer stared at the younger Bush and asked him, simply, "Why me?" Bush told him that he had first heard about him years ago when he had turned down his father.[2]

Several days after the election there was another meeting arranged between Bush and Gonzales at the Vinson & Elkins offices in Houston. It was a measure of how powerful V&E was—the firm representing Enron, the firm that was an essential partner to the Bush family—that the younger George Bush went to see Gonzales at his place of work. Over the years

Vinson & Elkins would become the third highest corporate contributor to the Bush family's political interests. (Enron was the largest corporate contributor to the Bush campaigns.) It would be good for Bush to see Gonzales in his realm. Too, it would be good for Bush to hear what the princes and kings at V&E had to say about Gonzales, especially Joe B. Allen III, the treasurer of V&E's Political Action Committee and a Bush pioneer, a title given to anyone who has raised at least $100,000 for the family's political coffers. Allen and Ken Lay were the largest contributors to young Bush's gubernatorial race.

It was one thing to take the daring step of naming a relative unknown—a political newbie—as the governor's general counsel. It was another thing to make sure that that choice was bulletproof, unassailable, truly skilled, and not encumbered by damaging baggage. It helped that Bush had also heard a recommendation from another of Bush's old friends, Patrick Oxford, the Houston lawyer who had worked directly with Gonzales on both the Economic Summit and the GOP Convention. Bush knew and trusted Oxford, and Oxford heartily endorsed Gonzales as the right person to become the governor's general counsel.

Bush and Oxford walked to the V&E offices together and waited for Gonzales to come down from his office: "I remember going with Bush over to Vinson & Elkins to meet Al," says Oxford. "We asked Joe B. Allen to introduce them, and Al came down to a conference room to visit with us. I remember that very well. They hit it off really well, I can tell you that. The governor spoke, Al listened. Al spoke, the governor listened. It was just a very comfortable man-to-man relationship."[3]

People who heard about those postelection meetings believed that Bush had made up his mind fairly quickly. It was his way to make quick decisions—and being in the power zone at V&E, seeing the obvious endorsement from Bush pioneer and champion fund-raiser Joe B. Allen, it would make sense. Alberto Gonzales was going to work for George W. Bush. But right up until he officially tendered his resignation, some people who had spent their careers clinging to the corporate law rungs thought Alberto Gonzales from piss-poor Roberta Lane wouldn't abandon the big dollars to take on the guaranteed headaches at the State Capitol in unpredictable Austin. Not many of them would do it. Of course, not many of them would ever be singled out, the way Gonzales had been, for a job with someone already running for the presidency. "He kind of surprised all of us when he . . . resigned his partnership at the law firm to commit himself to public service. But I think Al had really sort of thought about it and deliberated over the decision," said James Daniel Thompson III, another V&E partner.[4]

Gonzales was the son of migrant workers who slaved in the court of King Cotton. Bush was the first son in a political dynasty fueled by Big Oil. They were both *of* Texas—they were both *products of* Texas. They were defined by the things that defined Texas. Gonzales was born into a house his father had literally built. Bush was born into the House of Bush, perhaps the most storied political and business dynasty in modern American history. Of course, there was that other ironic juxtaposition. There was a move afoot to rename the big airport just down the road from the clapboard houses on Roberta Lane. The jets were still zooming over the home where Gonzales had been raised in Humble, Texas. Maria still lived in that house. Every morning she still woke up and dressed for her job as a cleaning lady at a funeral parlor. That old Gonzales house still shook when the planes came too close on their way to what would become the George Bush Intercontinental Airport.

He was going to turn forty in 1995. He was still not known to take a drink. His friends said he had few recognizable passions other than his family, work, and racquetball. Like George W. Bush, he never espoused a keen interest in any particular author, musician, or artist—or in any particular genre. He was a regular churchgoer, he hung pictures of his family on his wall, he kept up with current affairs. Friends said that he seemed well read, but they couldn't identify what books or authors he preferred. He was clearly fixated on his career, friends continued, but he was not really willing to talk about his career arc in terms of ambitions or goals. He would shift the conversation, move to another topic, when other attorneys mapped out their personal strategies. And if the talk drifted into some deeper, some might say airy, realm of pseudo-intellectual discussion, he would often go silent. There was a sense that he wasn't necessarily anti-intellectual, as some suggested George W. Bush had been (the prevailing theory being that Bush had been embittered by his ostracizing experience at Yale in the 1960s, and that he had grown to loathe the intellectual community as a liberal outpost). Rather, it seemed to friends that Gonzales was simply preoccupied with his work, with staying on top of the legal chess match in front of him. He was bright, said his friends, but not interested in loftier intellectual pursuits—including applying some arching vision, some scholarly rumination, to the field of law. He was process-oriented, detail-oriented, fastidious. If he enjoyed one thing in his work, it was that mission of redaction, that pursuit of boiled-down solutions and answers for a client. He enjoyed being with, more than anyone else, other lawyers. And he was going to move to Austin, leaving what most likely was at least a half-million-dollar income at Vinson & Elkins to take a job paying somewhere closer to $90,000. Gonzales had put in a dozen years in corporate law, had become a handsomely paid partner, and had developed a taste for impeccably tailored suits.

In some way it actually wasn't entirely unusual for someone to take a few years out from the corporate grind to go to work in a powerful government slot—with the full understanding that that lawyer would simply return to the corporate world later and that he would probably return to an even more powerful position at the firm. Gonzales's work as the general counsel to the governor of Texas would be invaluable to his career and to a firm like V&E. It was a short-term financial cutback, and it certainly wasn't as if Gonzales was going to work for subsistence wages providing free legal aid to the indigent or to Mexican immigrants. He had told himself that he would put in a few years, then head back to the higher-income world of private law. "Quite frankly, I anticipated it would be a temporary move, that I would go into government for a few years and then return to private practice," said Gonzales.[5]

In Austin, Gonzales would join a key group of advisers, aides, and backroom soldiers, most of whom would stay by Bush's side for years. Rove, the GOP spin doctor who had never graduated college but had become the most powerful Republican strategist in the state, was the senior political adviser. Karen Hughes, the square-jawed daughter of the former military governor of the Panama Canal Zone and someone who had been a TV personality in Fort Worth, would oversee communications. Joe Allbaugh, nicknamed Pinky by Bush (courtesy of the fact that he had the turgid face of Dick Butkus, topped by a divot of hair on a sand trap of pink scalp), would be the blustery chief of staff. Clay Johnson, Bush's lanky friend and roommate from the exclusive Phillips Andover High School as well as Yale, would oversee appointments to various boards and commissions.

And there were, as usual, several other pallid political lifers from Austin whom Bush inherited from previous GOP administrations. There were people such as Reggie Bashur, a political adviser who had served former Texas governors including the Foghorn Leghorn-ish, harrumphing oilman Bill Clements. But compared to almost all the others who joined the new Bush administration, Gonzales was a buttoned-down political neophyte who hadn't quite grasped the real way politics in Texas could be stretched, bent, and interpreted to fit the moment. He hadn't spent his days seducing and cajoling the political reporters from the *Dallas Morning News* who were assigned to cover state politics. He hadn't mingled with the insider baseball people at the bars, restaurants, and private clubs filtering out from Congress Avenue in downtown Austin. For most of the seasoned players, Gonzales was an unknown entity, and Gonzales liked it that way. Bush *really* liked it that way.

The new governor routinely would harangue Rove or Hughes if he ever felt that either one of them was upstaging him in a public setting. He would pull them aside, his face red, and he would simply issue what the Bush family liked to call "behavior modification." He could curse like a sailor, jab a finger in a chest, and plant his jaw within an inch or two of someone's face while rocking and bobbing on his heels. Bush, friends said, sometimes resented Rove's status as a political intellectual, as the savvy Svengali who had carefully created Bush as if he was some political laboratory experiment cooked up in Rove's dreary, windowless offices in Austin. More than once, Bush would tell members of the media that a particular idea was his idea, not Karl Rove's. He would sometimes remind people that it was his press conference—not a Karen Hughes or a Karl Rove press conference—if he ever spotted his aides enjoying gab fests with reporters.

But Bush never had to worry about intercepting his new general counsel. Gonzales would rather have eaten glass than submit to an interview or an off-the-record schmooze fest. Gonzales didn't care for it, didn't care for the limelight or the perceived political capital of parrying, thrusting, feeding, and leaking tidbits—even innocuous tidbits—to the media.

Gonzales had never told his best friends in life—from high school, to college, to law school, to Vinson & Elkins—about his family in Humble, his dead brother, his dead ex-wife, his dead father. Why would he play give-and-take with the media? It was a trait—an intrinsic dimension that would simply endear him forever to George W. Bush.

Bush's need for almost abject loyalty inside his inner circle stemmed from his acute understanding of his family's political history: After the elder Bush had been voted out of office in 1992, the younger Bush and Rove reviewed what had gone horribly wrong; they were looking for clues, for problems to avoid. The more they met in Austin and Dallas, the more Rove and Bush kept circling back to the same cold, hard belief: The elder Bush had been ill-served by a series of leaks on an already disloyal ship. With the Bush administration in increasing disarray in the months leading up to the '92 presidential election, the White House had become like a sieve. The son told friends that his father had been sabotaged by disloyal staffers who were going to the media. He became, to some degree, obsessed with the notion. He began repeating his favorite political dictum: "Perception is everything in politics." For the younger Bush, the way a politician was "perceived" was paramount—and that perception had to be controlled and crafted at all times. That meant there could be no variance, no room for leaks that might alter the perception. Everyone needed to "stay on message"—and Alberto Gonzales, the younger Bush decided, would always stay on message, he would never leak information, he would be so unquestionably loyal that he would never be someone to worry about. He would be, of course, *a good man*.

Bush did what he always does: He gave Gonzales a nickname. Karl Rove was "Turd Blossom," because wherever Rove went, some shit was bound to blossom; he called Karen Hughes the "High Prophet," because her maiden name was Parfitt; he wound up calling Gonzales "Fredo." Most people said it had nothing to do with Bush seeing himself as Michael Corleone, the brother of subservient but treacherous Fredo, in *The Godfather*; most people said it had everything to do with the fact that Bush didn't linger with people's last names in any exact way…that he was calling Gonzales "Fredo" because it sounded like a shortened version of "Alberto."[6] For grins, Bush sometimes even took to calling Gonzales "Al Fredo."[7]

Of course, there was still a sharp learning curve as Gonzales was abruptly forced to think more like a politician than a by-the-book real estate attorney. Bush advisers who saw him in action in the first few weeks and months after he moved to Austin said that he was so rigid in his thinking that he hardly knew how to play the political game: "Al would say, 'This piece of legislation is unconstitutional, veto it.' He was probably absolutely right. But then it would come to me, and I was the political guy. If Al had marked veto and the reason was it was unconstitutional, I would say, 'Go ahead and sign it, Governor.' It's not up to us to say whether it's unconstitutional. That's for the Supreme Court to decide. Al, I don't think, was comfortable with that at first," said Dan Shelley, who was Governor George W. Bush's legislative director in Austin.[8]

There were other obvious changes, including ones on the home front. Gonzales was thrust into a new world inside much smaller Austin. He was removed from his comfortable cycle of friends and family in Houston, where he sometimes could check in on his mother in Humble and always find time to play racquetball with an attorney from Vinson & Elkins. Austin was not home to the same sprawling, omnipresent Hispanic community as the one in Houston. Gonzales, by 1995, didn't strike many friends as someone who was spontaneously, wildly or overtly in touch with his Hispanic heritage—he didn't speak Spanish; he didn't wax on about his roots or his informed passion for some bit of Hispanic history, food, or music. And now he was in Austin, a place that was more efficiently segregated along racial and economic lines than Houston.

In Austin the Hispanic and black communities were effectively exiled east of Interstate 35, while the prosperous Anglo communities were on the west side of the highway. It was a college town and home to one of the largest universities in the nation; it was more of a "business casual" town; it was a political insider town; and it was simply far different culturally and stylistically than the international megalopolis of Houston. In the 1960s Austin had been a Mecca for what constituted the counterculture in Texas: hippies, musicians, and iconoclasts came to Austin attracted by the University of Texas, the cheap barbecue, the live music, and the pretty swimming holes. In time it became the self-anointed liberal bastion of Texas, and it could be argued that its patron saint was Willie Nelson, who had dropped out of the Nashville country music scene and found a funky home in the hills outside of Austin where he could peacefully smoke pot, play music, and go golfing with his pals.

By the time Gonzales moved to Austin, preparing to move to the affluent west side, it was in the grips of a major expansion, with thousands of high-tech workers flocking in from California and creating a kind of Silicon Hills in Central Texas. (People who wistfully watched Old Austin fade away called it the "Californication" of Texas.) Housing prices soared. Some of the things that gave the town charm—mom-and-pop Mexican cantinas and taco shacks, famous old juke joints, and honky-tonks—dwindled with an upsurge in gentrification, urban pioneers, and citywide demolition and expansion. The laid-back lifestyle was fading fast, and Austinites complained that a glossy hip factor had settled on the city. Maybe the changes were best summed up when Doug Sahm, the legendary Texas musician who single-handedly personified the hippie sense of what Austin was all about in the '60s, announced he was leaving in the '90s. Sahm said he was fed up with the yuppies and that "you couldn't get a good enchilada" in Austin anymore. He was moving to San Antonio, where he said that city's cultural reference points, including its rich Hispanic culture, would be encouraged to flourish.

At the Gonzales household, neither Alberto nor his wife were much concerned with whether Austin had changed for the good or the bad—and about whether Austin was a good place for a man whose migrant worker parents sometimes didn't speak much English. They were fixed on the immediate reality of taking a big hit in their bank account and wondering if all the striving, career climbing, was being neglected. "It was very difficult for me to make the change to go from a partner's salary to government salary," said his wife, Rebecca. "But it never caused Al a moment of anxiety. He knew we'd be fine. He knew the door had been opened for him and sacrifices had to be made. It was an easy choice." [9] They decided that Rebecca would go back to work. In October 1996 she landed a $40,000-a-year job in the Sexual Assault Prevention and Crisis Services department inside the Texas attorney general's office. According to reports in the *Boston Globe,* performance reviews showed that she lacked "basic skills required for the job of a grants program fiscal administrator." One evaluation indicated that she needed to learn more about sexual assault work and also needed to take accounting classes; her supervisor, in other remarks, said she had increased her skills and knowledge after starting work.

If Gonzales felt under some form of pressure shifting from his predictable existence inside the velvet coffin at Vinson & Elkins where he had spent the last twelve years of his life, it was not apparent to either his new associates or his old friends. If he felt isolated as a Hispanic in wealthy West Austin, it wasn't readily apparent. It could have been related to the simple fact that he saw his work for Bush as a temporary way station. He would put in a few years, then get out, better positioned to make the really huge money at Vinson & Elkins.

He was usually the first one in the office, about 6:30 in the morning, according to attorney Stuart Bowen, whom Gonzales interviewed over a lunch meeting at the Four Seasons Hotel in Austin and then offered a job as one of his assistant counsels. Gonzales felt an instant kinship with Bowen; he had spent four years on active duty as an intelligence officer in the air force. (Bowen would go on to work with Gonzales in Washington and eventually become the Special Inspector General for Iraq Reconstruction.) Bowen and others watched how Gonzales decorated his office with a sword mounted in a case and several pictures of his family—he had one picture on his desk of Rebecca standing on a rocky cliff with some waves in the background—but never discussed that family at work. "He was fairly mum on personal details of his upbringing," said Bowen. There were other pictures in his office. "He had a lot of pictures of himself and Bush 41 [President George Herbert Walker Bush]," said another lawyer in the office.[10]

Unlike some of the attorneys who reported to him, Gonzales seemed to relish the staff meetings held every morning. Some of his staffers could actually hear him coming down the hallway—his ankles had developed a kind of creaking noise. He liked the slightly more casual meetings in the afternoons and Fridays when he and his team of lawyers would eat popcorn and drink Cokes in the outer room outside his main office.

It was clear that he was treating Bush the same way he had treated his clients in real estate or Enron circles in Houston: He was still able to reduce his legal opinions to smaller portions that almost any nonlegal mind could quickly fathom. Gonzales was entrusted to offer legal opinions on an extremely wide variety of matters: whether Indian tribes in Texas could open up casinos; whether convicts might be eligible for some form of death-row reprieve; dealing with a request from Bush's teenaged daughters for a place to go swimming and trying to figure out if they could be accommodated by Bush accepting a membership in an Austin country club; assessing the viability and legality of legislation that Bush hoped to sell to the cantankerous Texas legislature. "We were all really learning at the same time because Al didn't have any experience in most of that stuff either," said one of his staffers.[11]

The backroom players in the Texas Capitol—wags in Texas brag that the Capitol is larger than any capitol building in the nation, including the nation's capitol—began to seek Gonzales out, trying to get a read on him, trying to see how they could curry favor with him and Bush: "He was extremely discreet. You'd go by Al's office and say 'Boy, there was quite a stir in so and so's office yesterday.' This is the way we all gather information around the Capitol. But with Al you'd get nothing back. Maybe an 'Um' or a 'Really?' I never had any idea what he was telling Bush or what he knew," said former state state senator David Sibley, one of Bush's most trusted loyalists.[12]

Bush was prone to bursts of sarcasm and acidic wit—not unlike his mother—and he was surrounded by similar personalities who were usually glad to offer their own opinions in rapid-fire, stinging fashion. Allbaugh, Hughes, and Rove would strut into Bush's burnished wood office and gleefully deconstruct the day's flattering editorials in the *Dallas Morning News* or the way the weak-kneed Democrats seemed to be in the grip of some sort of welling pro-Bush aura. Bush was enjoying enormous approval ratings and there was time to gloat, but Gonzales was never a participant in the banter, the usual political bombast and bomb throwing that took place in the governor's high-ceilinged, second-floor lair with the commanding view of downtown Austin. Gonzales was there, usually to the side, usually with the tiniest hint of a smile on his face. But he was behaving the same way he had when he worked in service to his energy company clients or when he had worked for the Bush family in staging the International Economic Summit and the Republican National Convention. He didn't just work to turn the spotlight away, he avoided it like it would possibly fry him.

After a summit meeting with Bush, Rove, Hughes, and Allbaugh, Gonzales would simply retreat to his office, gather his associate counsels, and set about the process of producing a heavily boiled-down position paper that would be sent back up to Bush's desk. His assistant counsels appreciated his lack of histrionics, his nonoperatic counterpoint to Bush's occasionally volatile tendencies; they also came to see him as a steadier counterpoint to the pale and intimidating Rove or the combative Hughes or the beefy, barking Allbaugh. "One of the reasons the governor liked Al was that when he presented something, he was very concise and to the point and at the end he made a recommendation," said Bush adviser Vance McMahan.[13] "When he met with the governor, it was all business. Unlike the others—Karen, Karl, Joe—he did not give and take a lot of quips. He is not a quipper," said Bowen.[14]

The family lived in the affluent rolling hills to the west of Austin, in a community not far from the Barton Creek Country Club—the most prestigious resort in the city and a place where the elder and younger George Bush liked to play golf with Ben Crenshaw or tennis with the former president of Argentina. Their home in West Austin—in a part of town filled with dot-com millionaires, transplanted high-tech executives from California, and many of the people who had gotten rich by working for nearby billionaire Michael Dell—was also not far from where both Karl Rove and Karen Hughes kept homes.

Gonzales, as did plenty of Bush insiders, learned to like golf—but maybe not exactly the way Bush liked to play it. Bush insisted on playing "aerobic golf," trying to sprint from one hole to another, running counter to the languid elements of the game. Gonzales would never play that way. He'd develop an 18 handicap, and he'd play the way he worked: steadfast and not taking any chances by rushing the whole process. It was one of his biggest hobbies, something he began to do more often with Bush, but friends could not recall his being openly rapturous or poetic about the game. He also sometimes liked to play tennis, and he enjoyed watching NBA games, football games at the University of Texas at Austin, the Texas

Rangers, the Houston Oilers (and later, when they moved, the Tennessee Titans), and the Houston Astros. Friends said he was a minor movie buff and once confessed to having a weakness for romantic comedies. He was always ready and willing to whip anybody on the racquetball court. But many friends also said there were no easily identifiable works of music, literature, cinema, or visual art that he used as constant, reinforcing reference points in his life. When people saw him listening to music—maybe while driving with him—he had on soft rock or country music. One friend thought he had a fondness for the Beach Boys, maybe the Doobie Brothers. He didn't express a deep love for any particular kind of food. One close coworker, a judge in Texas, when asked if he could "recall any books, movies, types of food, that sort of thing" for which Gonzales had an abiding interest or affection, simply said, "My memory of this could be wrong, but I do believe Alberto had a fondness for McDonald's french fries. It seemed to me that the law clerks at the courthouse used to joke about that—they'd all cut out to go to lunch, and they'd run by McDonald's for Alberto . . . but I could be wrong."[15]

He was quite similar to his new boss, George W. Bush: Bush liked to golf and fish and watch baseball. But he didn't dwell on those activities in any rhapsodic way or in the same sense that the writer Roger Angell would imbue baseball with some sort of deep, higher purpose. Gonzales appeared to be much like Bush: Bush, through much of his personal life, seemed to enjoy the *doing*—the process of a personal activity—but rarely left friends and family with the sense that he was pondering any higher intellectual meaning, profound historical context, or spiritual underpinning to the personal activities he enjoyed. People who knew him very well have said that the way he plays golf sums it all up: He rushes through the process, doesn't linger, doesn't wax sentimental about the beauty of the natural surroundings, and doesn't surrender to the languid possibilities of the game. He cracks jokes, barnstorms, races, bull-rushes his way from the first tee to the last, often making a game of seeing who can finish first.

Gonzales was also not one to linger on anything in particular. If anything, his touchstone was simply his work as a lawyer: "He works constantly. He's always been a hard worker," says his old friend Larry Dreyfuss. The consensus among people who knew him was that if he was searching for a passion, some sort of personal poetry, it was found in confronting the

mountain of statutes, briefs, position papers, arguments, and counterargu-
ments, then beginning the very methodical climb to the top, to the conclusion. Working for twelve straight years on million-dollar real estate and
energy deals—day in and day out wrapped up in laborious negotiations
shoulder-to-shoulder with all the other crisp-looking downtown Houston attorneys—had instilled a dogged, assembly-line mentality. In the governor's office and later at the White House, it was considered gospel that
you could simply shovel the blizzard of paperwork over to Alberto Gonzales's office and he would begin to process it piece by piece by piece.

Through it all, friends said he retained an unusual ability to focus on
you in conversation; he was a very adept listener. He was certainly attuned
to contemporary affairs, as well as slowly becoming increasingly fluid in
the way social lubrication makes the quirky, sometimes dangerous, Texas
political system move. He was unflaggingly polite in his correspondence;
sometimes it was hard to tell if he was pandering to the people he sent
personal notes to on official State of Texas letterhead. In one note to
thank *Texas Monthly* publisher Mike Levy for sending him a coffee mug
adorned with pictures of horned toads, Gonzales gushes over the simple
gift that is sent out en masse every year—at one point he says it is "toadally"
cool. In another note, he writes to a dignitary he has visited in Mexico,
and offers thanks and an odd apology: *"Many thanks for your hospitality during my recent visit to Mexico. I very much appreciated your generosity and your
willingness to teach me about your people and country. I have enclosed copies of recent articles in Texas papers about Mexico. I thought you might find these stories
interesting. I am sorry that they are written in English. Please call me if you are ever
in Austin, Texas. I look forward to meeting with you again. Sincerely, Alberto Gonzales, General Counsel."*

People who have read his personal correspondence released under the
Texas Open Records Act have said he comes across as almost naive in a
wonky, nerdy kind of way—apologizing because he is sending English-
language stories about Mexico to someone in Mexico. His attempts at
humor, at establishing a bonhomie, have the faintly bittersweet tone of
someone who is trying too hard to be liked. And inside Bush's so-called
Iron Triangle he was easily, repeatedly overshadowed in the morning strategy sessions, at the power breakfasts at the Governor's mansion, and at any
of the gatherings at Karl Rove's house in west Austin.

But those sometimes fumbling attempts at collegiality in his personal correspondence stand in naked contrast to the wide variety of other official memos and papers from his desk, especially the ones that would put him at the heart of the most intense debates in Texas. Gonzales literally handled thousands of issues as the general counsel: Bush once asked him to do a favor for an old friend and check into whether Fort Worth police were conducting a "lackadaisical and inept investigation" into a murder in that city; he handled correspondence with the family of missing atheist leader Madalyn Murray O'Hair; he wrote detailed letters to a state representative who wanted to know why her spouse wasn't put on the State Board of Dental Examiners; he communicated with people organizing an official Texas trade delegation to India; when another old friend of Bush's sent a letter inquiring about the parole status of someone in El Paso, the letter was put on Gonzales's desk with a typical note from Bush's personal secretary: *"Al G.—Please look into this. Jim Paul is good friend of Gov's but as you can see it should be treated as a 'normal' req."* [16]

The volume of work was high and sometimes boundless in scope: Gonzales was dealing with correspondence from candidates for state district judge. He was shipping out copies of Bush's favorite bills that had died in the Texas Senate, such as antigambling measures that Rove wanted passed in order to curry favor with conservative Christian voters, and he was shipping them to law-and-order district attorneys in Texas with unsubtle notes that said, "I hope we can count on your support," and that "it would be helpful if you would forward your comments in writing to me at your earliest convenience." He wrote terse letters to the representatives of a group called the Republic of Texas who had sent along something called a *Common Law Summons Notice of Intent to Take Oral Deposition* of Bush. Gonzales wrote back that *"you have no jurisdiction over Governor Bush and he is not required to honor your instruction to appear under this Common Law Summons and give testimony."* [17]

Congressman Dan Miller contacted Bush and asked him to hound someone in Texas for child support payments allegedly owed to a woman in Miller's district in Florida, and the mess was shipped to Gonzales. He reviewed innumerable executive orders, creating the Governor's DWI Task Force and appointing the Municipal Advisory Council as the Texas State Information Depository. Too, he quickly dropped the hammer when Rove and Bush perceived a possible "perception problem." In one instance, when news leaked out that the state had to pay almost $90,000 to settle a lawsuit against the Texas Liquor Commission, Gonzales fired off a letter: *"I know that you and other members and employees of your agency will take appropriate steps to prevent a reoccurrence of the type of behavior that resulted in this settlement, and that all responsible persons are appropriately disciplined."* [18]

Gonzales also suffered the indignity of Bush staffers sending him office memos with his name spelled wrong—"Gonzalez" instead of "Gonzales"—and with brisk little notes, some hastily scrawled. The notes would tell him what to do and how to do it: "I'd appreciate it if you could look into this question. I'd suggest beginning with the legislation that created the Commission," or, "Al, I need to talk with you ASAP."

He also reviewed correspondence from Karl Rove about Texas not recognizing out-of-state same-sex marriages. And he learned to rapidly move on matters raised by Bush's longtime good friend and advise Doug Wead. A former Bush White House staffer who left in a swirl of controversy, Wead was an Amway salesman, an evangelical Christian, and a close associate of Jim and Tammy Faye Bakker. He routinely advised the Bush family on how to win votes from "the movement," as Wead called Christian conservatives. Wead, who would later develop a habit of secretly tapping his conversations with the younger Bush, had traveled the country with George W., written an authorized book with the Bush family, and introduced the Bushes to many of the evangelical, fundamentalist Christian conservative leaders in America. Wead did more than most to bridge the gap between the Bush family's gilded Yale–Harvard–Episcopal backbone with the "red state" world of Christian conservatism. He served as the Bush family's guide to that unfamiliar realm, bringing George W. Bush around the nation to meet Christian leaders in the 1980s.

In 1995 Wead sent Bush a note suggesting that reporters were about to dig into a story about a Texas inmate who allegedly had been the victim of abuse in prison. Part of Wead's note to his old friend said, *"Needless to say, I'm proud of you. Recently you seemed to have disappeared from the national radar screen which probably is a pretty good idea. The media hate a hot dog. Are you aware of the controversy over Texas prisoner Jan Weeks Katona? . . . My first instinct was to ignore it, but it has received so much attention that I decided you needed to be alert to the issue and have someone check it out. At least for political reasons."*

Wead's warning was sent to Gonzales, and a flurry of investigations ensued: *"Mr. Weed [sic] asked us to investigate the status of Ms. Katona, warning of a reporter who was preparing to publish an article reporting that Ms. Katona was the victim of abuse."* At Bush's insistence, Gonzales wrote a personal note to Wead thanking him for the heads-up.

And, finally, when the financial heavy-hitter friends of the Bush family, the ones from the oil business, got in touch and asked for Bush to pull some strings for them, Gonzales would also be told to review letters like this:

The Honorable Askar Akayev
President
The Kyrgyz Republic

Dear President Akayev:

    I am writing to introduce you to William C. Nixon whom I have known for over twenty years. Mr. Nixon is a personal friend of the Bush family. I understand Mr. Nixon is currently working to develop an oil refinery near Bishkek which will help the Kyrgyz Republic become more self reliant for gasoline and jet fuel. . . . In short, I know Mr. Nixon and know him to be a man of his word. I wish you and your country great success.

                    Sincerely, George W. Bush.[19]

Increasingly, as Gonzales settled in his job, there were also matters of criminal jurisprudence. They were far removed from anything he might have mastered in the big-money real estate world in Houston. He had never tried a criminal or civil case. "Al certainly didn't know any criminal stuff since he came from V&E," says Karen Greene, an attorney who worked with Gonzales once he became general counsel.[20] He was inundated with letters, petitions, and faxes from people asking for his advice on how to win someone a pardon, parole, or, most dramatically, a reprieve from the death chamber. Gonzales and Bush both knew that Texas was known in some circles as the State of Death—that it put more people to death than any other state in the nation. It struck some people as the perfect, awful irony that on the day Bush was inaugurated there was also an execution taking place at midnight in the infamous death chamber 170 miles away in Huntsville, Texas.

EIGHT

State of Death

At midnight, twelve hours before Bush was officially sworn in as the new governor of Texas in January 1995, a convicted murderer named Mario Marquez was executed despite his defenders claiming that he was mentally retarded, that he had an IQ of 65, that he had the adaptive skills of a seven-year-old—and that the evidence of his mental retardation was not allowed to be presented at his trial. Most of Bush's aides, including Gonzales, had already started working as part of the transition to a new administration in Texas. It was the first of many executions that would occur under Gonzales's watch.

For years, with his children already long asleep, Gonzales would often sit with just one other aide in his Austin office and receive phoned-in updates from the execution chamber in Huntsville as the minutes and seconds ticked down to a prisoner's death. The executions, when he first had to deal with them, were always scheduled for a minute after midnight. And 170 miles away, in Austin, the scene in his office would take on a surreal, eerie flavor. From a speakerphone would come the somber but insistent voice of an official walking Gonzales through what was happening as the doomed prisoner was led from his cell to the execution room. With the area around the State Capitol completely hushed and dark, Gonzales would slip out of his double-breasted suit jacket and listen as the prisoner was strapped to a gurney and injected with poison until prison officials told Gonzales that the inmate had been declared dead. The process was abstract and removed; it was a process Gonzales would go through over and over again.

"When we first started out, the executions were at midnight. So, we did work late obviously on those. We would be on the phone with the warden down in Huntsville. I remember the first one we did, just he and I . . . he was always present and the duties would rotate among the assistant general counsels, depending on who had researched the issues and written a memo for the governor. It was odd, simply because of the play-by-play, if you will, of an execution order over the phone while we would sit and wait until we got notice that the prisoner had expired, and then we would notify the governor, and then that would be it. That was odd," said one of his assistant counsels.[1]

And as Bush began the more aggressive posturing and positioning for the Republican presidential nomination, the death penalty turned acutely political. Rove had stumbled on the idea of painting Bush as a "compassionate conservative," the kind of person who would name a minority figure like Alberto Gonzales to be his lawyer—but how would that compassionate conservative title jibe with the constant parade of prisoners to death row and execution?

Texas has led the nation with hundreds of death row inmates and executions since the U.S. Supreme Court ruled that the executions were legal again in 1976. Increasingly complex issues emerged involving juveniles on death row, mentally retarded prisoners on death row, and, of course, the possibility that there were wrongfully convicted men and women on death row. These hotly debated questions had hardly emerged during the contentious race between Ann Richards and George W. Bush. Richards and Bush were both in favor of the death penalty. But as Bush began to think about the White House, there were provocative death row cases starting to capture national attention as questions emerged about just how much of a "compassionate conservative" Bush really was. His bombastic spokesperson, Karen Hughes, had taken to yelling at reporters: "What part don't you understand? Compassionate? Conservative?"

What was clear was that the death penalty cases wouldn't go away. Texas was always going to be the State of Death. Any connection—karmic, political, and otherwise—to the events unfolding in the death chamber were sure to stick with anyone who wanted to persist as a member of Bush's inner circle. In Austin the tension surrounding the death penalty issue began to become almost palpable as Bush insiders tried to straddle the fence, selling Bush as someone willing to put people to death while appearing to reach out to the middle-ground voter, to minorities, and to wavering Democrats, some of whom might be opposed to the death penalty. It was a moral debate trapped inside thorny political urgencies, and Gonzales found himself writing memo after memo that literally had to do with whether a human being would live or die.

In time Gonzales watchers would simply refer to them as the "clemency memos." As a body of work, those memos would barrel him straight toward something he had never anticipated or wanted. For critics, Alberto Gonzales would come to embody the cruel soul of Texas and George W. Bush. For some critics around the world, Alberto Gonzales would even come to embody the worst tendencies of America. He was about to embark on a winding, twisted path that would lead him far beyond being a well-paid "dirt and deals" real estate lawyer. As the governor of Texas's general counsel—and the man who was personally advising the governor on who should be put to death in Texas—Gonzales would review clemency petitions, then prepare his own clemency memo for fifty-seven possible executions. He was embarking on a career of compromises.

Each of those pending executions was, perhaps by definition, controversial—though, increasingly, as each one was scheduled and conducted, there was less and less attention devoted to them by the media. The executions, starting with that one on the very day Bush was inaugurated, occurred with rapidity and efficiency, one after another, until it was hard to find any mention of them on the air or on the printed page. The fact that Democrat Ann Richards had been a dogged defender of the death penalty in Texas highlighted that it was a course of retribution endorsed by the majority of voters in the state. Bush was no different than Richards in his steadfast support of the death penalty. As the cases mounted up, the executions quietly took place in the state death chamber, and little attention was paid to them. But the anonymity or even a sense of resignation began to end as Bush tested the presidential waters.

———

Stuart Bowen liked his boss Al Gonzales. They had clicked right away personality-wise. Bowen felt that Gonzales listened to him and trusted him. Most of all, Bowen thought that Gonzales was a *very* good listener. If he was unsettled by the parade of dead men walking, if he was unhinged in some way by having to listen to all those prisoners being put to death night after night while he sat in an office adorned with pictures of his children, Gonzales never showed it. He was still unflappable, still almost inscrutable. At night he would sit in his office, jacket off, tie and suspenders still on, without displaying any emotional extremes. Bowen sat with him when the death news came in from Huntsville: "He had, you know ... if it was odd for him, he didn't really show it. He's known to maintain his equanimity in virtually any situation. I've never seen him lose his temper. Yeah, there were a lot of controversial issues that we dealt with, and I never saw him lose his temper. I never heard him use curse words or use foul language, either." [2]

Karen Greene, the attorney whom Gonzales had hired on the spot not long after coming to Austin, couldn't believe how placid-seeming he could be. She would say that he was "one of these types that just was eternally calm." She took to telling a joke about him behind his back: She'd pretend she was an alarmed friend of Gonzales, someone who would race over to him while screaming, *"Al! Al! Your pants are on fire!"* And then Greene would do her perfect imitation of Gonzales simply nodding and slowly saying, "Ooookaay."

Working in a George Bush administration put everything under a magnifying glass for Gonzales—with the Bush pedigree, with the fact that Bush was going to be running for president, with the conga line of reporters snaking to Texas to do another profile of Bush. Local Democrats were still bitter about Bush's win over Ann Richards and had continued sniping at Bush; national Democratic operatives were camping out at the lobby of the Four Seasons and over beers at the Texas Chili Parlor, trying to figure out a way, any way, to embarrass or ensnare Bush. Through it all, Greene came to think that there were plenty of fires, but Gonzales never blinked. "He never raised his voice. He never seemed ruffled. And you know, perfectly, immaculately groomed. And, just never, never let us see him sweat." [3]

———

Five months into Gonzales's new job, he and Turner had their second child together in the summer of 1995. Gabriel Quinn was born June 5, according to some Texas records, in Harris County. Friends remember it as a hectic, frenzied time as the new Bush administration wrestled with fractious legislative agendas at the State Capitol. Rebecca had told Gonzales and friends that she was going to insist on having her baby delivered in Houston with her original doctor. In his office, as the pressures at the Capitol multiplied and Bush and Rove worked hard to push for tax cuts, privatizing the welfare system, and giving control of social programs to religious groups, Gonzales kept telling his staffers that "I have to be there" to see his son born. That second son was finally born right at the end of the superheated legislative session—and Gabriel joined Graham and stepbrother Jared. A friend remembers that Gonzales called Bush and told him he was a father to a new baby boy. Bush congratulated Gonzales and told him he should take one day off. Friends wondered if Gonzales would finally explode at Bush, but he didn't. "Well," Gonzales told people in his office, "we are busy right now."

He put up pictures of his kids in his office—a less-than-glamorous second-floor room that for some architecturally odd reason had windows that were partially blocked by large pink granite slabs. When Gonzales was on the phone, pigeons would mate outside the windows, cooing louder and louder. Gonzales's children would visit him at work sometimes. Their father was pushing forty; their mother was close to thirty-five. He'd let the kids eat doughnuts and drink chocolate milk at his desk.

In August, Gonzales celebrated at his fortieth birthday party, and friends who were there once again noted the fact that he refused to take a sip of alcohol even when he was being toasted. One lawyer from Houston put it this way: "You won't see him straying off course. It could be midnight and no cars on the road. If there is a stop sign, he will sit there and wait."[4] One time, some people in the counsel's office asked him why he never drank: "I've had enough of that." Some knew that he was talking about his father.

A few days after his birthday Gonzales and staff lawyer Karen Greene traveled from Austin to Huntsville to witness the scheduled execu-

tion of Vernon Lamar Sattiewhite. The convicted murderer from San Antonio was born the same year and month as Gonzales. His execution was
scheduled to take place on Tuesday, August 15, at 12:01 A.M.

On the morning of June 19, 1986, nursing student Sandra Sorrell and
her new boyfriend were walking toward the San Antonio school they
both attended. Suddenly, Sattiewhite joined them, grabbed Sorrell's arm,
put her into a headlock, pulled out a .22-caliber pistol, and began dragging
her behind a building. He had dated Sorrell in the past, and he had threatened her on an off for weeks. The new boyfriend followed them into a
parking lot, trying to talk Sattiewhite into letting her go. Sattiewhite suddenly threw Sorrell to the ground, then quickly yanked her back up and
shot her point-blank in the head two times.

"Ain't nobody else gonna have her," said Sattiewhite as he tore off his
shirt and then repeatedly placed the gun to his own head. He finally
sprinted away but was tracked down by police, who found him standing
on a riverbank. He had the gun pointed at his head again. He pulled the
trigger, the gun misfired, and Sattiewhite finally surrendered.

Sattiewhite told his interrogators he had worked as a "laborer" and that
he was raised by an aunt after his mother died when he was seven. He was
a special education student in public schools, and, according to records
from Gonzales's office, he might have been abused as a child. He dropped
out in eighth grade after getting into heavy drug use. Bexar County records indicated that he tried to kill himself at the age of twenty-one by
shooting himself in the stomach. Psychiatric records also showed that on
another occasion he was hospitalized for swallowing a mixture of Clorox
and Black Flag.

In a third suicide attempt, Sattiewhite tried to jump off a bridge at the
Six Flags amusement park. Finally, his prison records indicated that he said
he was haunted for seventeen years by his deceased grandmother's spirit
and he had been conversing with her spirit for all those years. In 1976 he
was arrested for capital murder for shooting a man in the face at a bar. After
serving three years, he was paroled. He also had two robbery convictions
on his rap sheet. Just weeks before he killed his ex-girlfriend, Sattiewhite
had again threatened Sorrell. Police records showed that he had pulled a
gun twice on Sorrell, including that case the police had investigated ten
days before her death. Sattiewhite was convicted in 1986 for kidnapping

and murdering Sorrell, and he was sent to Texas's burgeoning death row. Nine years later he learned that an execution date had finally been set.

The week before his scheduled execution, his attorney sent a final clemency petition to Bush and the Board of Pardons and Paroles. Gonzales, as usual, reviewed the case and prepared his clemency summary for Bush. In the one he brought to Bush on August 14, the day before the execution, Gonzales summarized Sattiewhite's plea for clemency:

"The basis for the request are as follows: The underlying felony of kidnapping used to establish the charge of capital murder is not sufficiently supported by the evidence. Although Sattiewhite is truly remorseful, mitigating evidence regarding Sattiewhite's unstable childhood and abuse as a child were not presented to the jury. Sattiewhite was temporarily insane at the time he committed the murder; and he is currently incompetent to be executed. These claims have been raised in state and federal habeas corpus proceedings and have been denied by the courts. The most viable claim would be Sattiewhite's competency to be executed. It is likely that he will again petition the trial court to obtain a hearing on his competency.

"In support of the claim that the underlying offense of kidnapping was not supported by sufficient evidence, the petition includes a letter from Karen Amos, a former prosecutor who was involved in Sattiewhite's prosecution. She states that a decision was made to upgrade the murder charge against Sattiewhite to capital murder even though the evidence was marginal. This letter, Sattiewhite's attorney maintains, supports the claim that the decision to prosecute Sattiewhite for capital murder was made because the District Attorney's office failed to obtain protective orders to protect Sorrell, who had complained the day before her murder of Sattiewhite's assaults on her."

In part of his five-sentence conclusion, Gonzales writes this to Bush: *"It is likely that Sattiewhite's execution will be carried out as scheduled. The only viable claim remaining is whether Sattiewhite is competent to be executed. If the courts deny this claim, then all courts would have reviewed and denied relief on all claims. For that reason it does not appear that anything would be gained by a reprieve or commutation."* [5]

It's not clear why Gonzales decided to attend Sattiewhite's execution. His clemency memo to Bush is a bit different than several others, especially in that he seems to linger longer with mitigating factors; he devotes three sentences to outlining the defense's allegation bolstered by the prosecutor that there was "marginal evidence" for a capital murder charge and that perhaps the district attorney's office had decided to seek the death penalty for Sattiewhite because it was embarrassed by not getting Sorrell a protective order that might have saved her life. Again, it's unclear whether Gonzales was stirred to attend the execution by the suggestion that a man was being executed with questions hanging over his head or whether he was simply "sent" by Bush, as Greene would later say.

By the time Gonzales and Greene flew to Huntsville, it was early in the afternoon. They met with the prison officials and the chaplain and toured the various prison units. Greene remembers Gonzales being fascinated by the cells and being surprised at how small they were. They broke for dinner and came back to continue their tour. At one point while they were walking through death row, some of the men began screaming hideously sexual vulgarities, shouting about a woman being in their presence, and taking wicked delight with Karen Greene's red hair: *"Yeah! Get that red hair down here!"* Greene was stunned; Gonzales was outwardly unfazed.

That night, just before midnight, Gonzales and Greene were escorted to a room with a two-way mirror. They were in the same room as the prison officials who were going to administer the deadly drugs to Sattiewhite—one of the seventeen people to be put to death in 1995 after Bush had been sworn in. Gonzales watched as the officials arranged the flow from intravenous units into a tube that ran through a little hole into the room where Sattiewhite was strapped down with the IV hooked to his arm. Sattiewhite offered his last statement, including mentioning a Ms. Fielder (maybe a reference to Pamela Fielder, who had become a heroine in battered women's circles): "I would like to say—I just hope Ms. Fielder is happy now. I would like to thank my lawyer, Nancy, for her help on my case and for being with me now."

Within minutes, it seemed as if Sattiewhite had drifted into a deep sleep. He was, of course, dead. Greene and Gonzales stared silently, left the room, and less than an hour later they were boarding a flight back to Austin. It was close to one in the morning. Like he had been when the prisoners screamed hideous sexual profanities at his coworker—really, like he had been his entire life—Gonzales simply didn't talk about what he had seen.

———

Years later, writer Alan Berlow would do an extraordinary analysis in the *Atlantic Monthly* of Bush's and Gonzales's roles in the Texas death penalty cases, particularly analyzing the clemency memos that Gonzales wrote and delivered to Bush on fifty-seven pending executions. Berlow's work would be different than the reporting done by the *Dallas Morning News*. The sweep and scope of Berlow's inquiry led him to his own damning conclusions. In a sense, Berlow would make a case that Gonzales was probably behaving exactly as he had throughout his legal career. He was being an incredibly efficient, loyal lawyer—for his client. He was doing what he or any other hired lawyer was paid to do, which was putting the interests of his client first and foremost. Berlow and other critics would contend that Gonzales was simply identifying an outcome that his client wanted: "Bush made it clear he wasn't interested in clemency, and Gonzales delivered. His work product is what his client, Bush, wanted. Gonzales knew that. They created a standard—that you had to have evidence of absolute innocence or incomplete access to the courts. Gonzales had to be part of creating the standard. They are defining clemency so narrowly, in a way that is virtually impossible to get clemency." [6]

Wayne Slater of the *Dallas Morning News* appeared on National Public Radio to talk about Gonzales and the clemency memos. He thought that Gonzales was both a "good guy" and "very thoughtful" and that he strived to do his work for Bush "in a reasonable way." Slater said, "He's not a showboat, he likes to work behind the scenes—very thoughtful, quiet, self-effacing, good guy." He added that if Bush had a particular request, "Gonzales would find a way—I mean, in a reasonable way—to do it." Slater was asked how he responded to the intense investigation that Berlow had launched into Gonzales in Texas: "I have to tell you, one of the things that Gonzales did—and this is neither positive nor negative or perhaps positive-negative, depending how you look at it—is he was able, he was obligated by law and constitution in Texas to deliver the . . . basically to vet these death penalty cases before an execution and to present the essence of the case to the governor in advance of the execution for the governor's judgment if he wanted to delay or pardon or offer clemency.

"And in these cases, Gonzales was very successful in putting into short order often very long, complicated cases." Later, Slater added, "The inter-

esting thing about Gonzales is you see the political left attacking Gonzales
as some kind of evil guy." [7]

Berlow, the first to extensively study Gonzales's clemency memos, contended that Gonzales simply produced cursory outlines of the death
penalty cases, emphasizing the grisly crimes, omitting the basis for any
clemency petitions, then shipping his hopelessly nugget-sized summaries
to Bush. During Bush's tenure as governor, 152 people were put to death;
Gonzales provided Bush with clemency memos on at least 57 of those
cases. And it could have been almost as simple as a perfect convergence of
an attorney's legal style meeting up with his client's managerial style: Gonzales was hired, in part, because he had the ability to reduce everything
down to short, simple memos . . . and Bush was clearly known as someone
who simply wanted the bottom line.

Berlow claims that Gonzales ultimately ignored the true purpose of a
clemency memo, which was "Bush's primary source of information in
deciding whether someone would live or die." The Gonzales memos are
indeed hauntingly brief, usually only three to seven pages long, dominated
with an outline of the crime the prisoner was accused of, a biography of
the prisoner, and a chronological review of the evolution of the case. Gonzales liked to order his with Roman numerals: "I" was called "Brief Summary of the Facts"; "II" was "Personal Background" (of the person to be
executed); "III" was "Previous Criminal History"; "IV" was "Summary of
Proceedings"; "V" was usually a one-paragraph "Conclusion."

Absent in the memos is any big-picture legal or historical backdrop—
some sweeping, contextual reference point that might help Bush decide
whether to order a thirty-day reprieve. An examination of all of Gonzales's
clemency memos, provided under the Texas Open Records Act, shows
little to no lengthy recitation of mitigating circumstances or Supreme
Court opinions including discussions about how judges were ruling on
the matter of mentally retarded and juvenile death row inmates, issues that
emerged over and over again in Texas. Berlow would charge that Gonzales
delivered these ready-to-be-rubber-stamped clemency memos—each
memo had a box titled "DENY" that awaited a check mark and signature
from Bush—and that there was at most a thirty-minute discussion be-

tween Bush and Gonzales about the merits of the inmate's plea for clemency.

The facts of these death row cases—involving prisoners who oftentimes had been on death row for several years as their cases took different twists and turns—were complex and countless. DNA testing and other forensic strides were becoming more readily available and raising questions about whether everyone on death row was certifiably, unequivocally guilty in the first place. By any estimation and well beyond the taint of partisan politics, Gonzales's memos to Bush are achingly concise and boiled down. Sattiewhite's clemency memo, as one example, is five pages long; his court files, police files, psychiatric files, and various petitions and pleas would no doubt fill hundreds, perhaps thousands, of pages. The co-counsels who worked with Gonzales have said that there was an extraordinary amount of deliberation put into the clemency memos—that what was ultimately printed in the three- to five-page memo to Bush didn't reflect the countless hours put into studying the merits of each death row case.

But it could be argued that that is the exact problem with the Gonzales clemency memos: These were the final bits of paperwork that the governor of Texas was going to look at—the final instruments he would study when deciding whether he could put his muscle into at least temporarily staying an execution. Knowing Bush's "governing style," knowing that Bush was a self-described CEO, knowing that Bush championed himself as quick in just about everything he did in life—including playing "aerobic golf"—were these clemency memos groomed to be more palatable to Bush . . . at the expense of the very grave issues at hand? At this particularly grave moment, should Gonzales have erred on the side of demanding— commanding—that Bush exercise far more deliberation than he was prone to showing on other matters that crossed his desk?

A well-recognized fact that Republicans and Democrats agree on in Texas is that the governor's office is limited in constitutional scope. The governor in Texas doesn't necessarily spend his time writing laws and bills; he spends his time willing them or cajoling them into existence. The Texas legislature only meets for a few months every other year. The governor in Texas, some observers say, has more time to deliberate, to meditate, to analyze and immerse himself in an ongoing issue, including, perhaps, each of the individual executions in Texas. And as he entered office, Bush had identified what his advisers were calling the "four major food groups" for his administration: (1) initiating tax cuts, (2) privatizing welfare, (3) improving Texas's dead-last ranking in most education studies, and (4) blocking those big-time lawsuits against corporations. Those issues dominated the in-house staff meetings and almost every public utterance by Bush or a Bush staffer. The death penalty was not an issue that was really publicly addressed, that needed to be addressed. Again, both Bush and his predecessor had clearly stated they were strong proponents of the death penalty as were a majority of voters in the state of Texas.

Bush was never one to feel as if he needed to leave some sort of soul-baring statement on paper that would attest to the mental and spiritual energy he might have devoted to one of his decisions. As always, he viewed some of that as "psychobabble"—fodder for historians and reporters looking for some deeper meaning in things that he claimed were all too obvious. Still, some of those historians and reporters hoped that his autobiography—*A Charge to Keep*—would be the one place where he would truly reveal a bit of his soul and even offer a glimpse into what he and Gonzales were thinking as he they weighed the increasing number of executions in Texas.

The death penalty is indeed addressed in his book, and the focus is on the execution of one particular inmate who had received international attention during his run for the presidency. Bush insists that he labored over that decision, like all of his decisions, and that it was a moment of personal crisis. But critics would say that whatever "soul-baring" emotion he describes in that book is not authentic, because his autobiography was written for him by his communications director Karen Hughes. It wasn't in his words; it was in her words. He didn't write his autobiography, and how could Karen Hughes adequately articulate what was really in George W. Bush's heart as he read each of the fifty-seven memos prepared by Alberto Gonzales and abruptly delivered to Bush's office just a few hours or even a few minutes before an execution?

Studying those Gonzales memos, realizing that the three- to five-page memo in one's hand was all that stood between someone living and dying, could be a profound experience for some people who obtained them. The Gonzales memos seemed, by any rationale, to cry out for days, not minutes, of review . . . for more information . . . for a curious mind. Even those at utter peace with the righteousness of the death penalty might have raised some questions. People who worked with Gonzales attested to the time, the fastidiousness, of Gonzales's work on the clemency memos. Unspoken was the thought that it also took time to reduce all that work down to three or four or five pages for Bush. The questions for some observers were beyond controversial: Was there some sin of omission by Gonzales when everything was boiled down? Did Gonzales groom his memos to serve his client rather than to serve justice and humanity?

Berlow put it this way: "I think both he and Bush, while you can't prove that they have executed an innocent person, there is also no way to know that they didn't. I think his work was unethical, immoral, and unconscionable—you could use any of those words. I don't have a clear sense of his having any convictions. What are they? I like Gonzales; he's a decent guy who has pulled himself up by the bootstraps. But his lawyer work leaves something to be desired. It is unconscionable." Berlow also seems to suggest that there are two Gonzaleses: the one who could write what Berlow and others contend are blithe and thus immoral memos on dozens of death penalty cases and the one who seems to be unassuming and well liked by friends. "There are all kinds of people who are good with their grandkids, what can I say?" says Berlow.[8]

Sister Helen Prejean, well known for her anti–death penalty stance and who was played by Susan Sarandon in the movie *Dead Man Walking* (based on Prejean's book), also developed similar feelings about Gonzales. Her argument, like Berlow's, is that you can know the reticent Gonzales by his memos. Later in life, in his career at the White House, people would say the same thing about other controversial memos he would write.

"I'm gonna tell you, I look at him through the prism of what he did with Bush [in Texas]. That says a lot about the character of a person who expedites and legitimizes a person's execution. It is a most telling thing about how his mind works and what his deepest values are," says Prejean. After reviewing the Gonzales memos, she says, "He doesn't ever include any mitigating evidence or any of the legal problems, or even issues of actual innocence. He made it so Bush wouldn't lose any sleep." Prejean says she could envision Gonzales in an elevator, maybe with Supreme

Court Justice Antonin Scalia and several people from the "inner city," and all of them would be trapped together when the elevator got stuck, each of them getting hungry and thirsty. She thinks it would be a great scene in a novel, and she thinks the best way to view Gonzales is under a microscope of class, not race.

"These are not necessarily horrible people. I'm sure that with his family, Gonzales is nice. But what happens is the perversion of good people who get mixed up and serve something that is unjust and remove themselves from the effects—that is what happened with the Holocaust. It's pressure. Social pressure. I can picture a young Alberto Gonzales, picture him growing up, doing well, and he knows where he gets kudos, and he follows that social path, and he doesn't see the effects of what he does and isn't in touch with it. It would take something really big—a Katrina in his life—to bust it open."[9]

Gonzales, maybe owing to the pace and number of executions he was handling, really was determined to emulate Bush in terms of managerial style. He had learned to move on. He was very clear about what he saw as the upside to Bush's managerial methods: "He's very good about getting information, hearing all sides . . . he gets his information, and then I'm sure he thinks about these big issues, and he makes a decision, and he moves on, and sometimes there's criticism. It doesn't matter. He's made a decision, and you move on. And so I think I'm a little bit like that. You have to be. There are too many decisions to make."[10]

At their heart, the objections to Gonzales's death penalty deliberations in Texas had everything to do with critics suggesting he was simply preparing cursory outlines for Bush—that he was not just boiling down the incredibly complex cases to meet Bush's short attention span, but he was also leaving out complicating facts that might lead any governor to clamor for the execution to be put on pause. And Bush, for sure, had developed a style reminiscent of his favorite political figure, Ronald Reagan. Bush had also always wanted to be a Great Communicator like some people said Reagan had been, and history would be the judge on whether he would succeed on that score. But he also thought it prudent to be, as Reagan had been, an expert at delegating authority.

Bush often described himself as a CEO occupying the governor's mansion. He was like a corporate head who surrounded himself with talented, driven, and loyal operating officers, managers, and department heads. It was never part of Bush's intention or interest level to micromanage. Friends and foes of Bush and Gonzales said that when it came to the death penalty, Bush was going to rely very heavily on everything Gonzales would tell him about each of the dozens of executions scheduled in Texas. He would delegate the fine points of the pending executions to one man, Alberto Gonzales, then Gonzales would instruct his assistant counsels to dig into the history of the death penalty cases and bring him a core that he could go back to Bush with.

The *Chicago Tribune* would eventually release a heavily documented examination revealing that in one-third of the death penalty cases in Texas, the lawyers for the defendants were either ultimately subject to legal sanctions or disbarment; the *Tribune's* investigation would also suggest that in at least forty instances, at the sentencing phase, the defendant's lawyers produced either zero evidence or sometimes just a single witness.[11] And in a few years there would be an exchange between Alberto Gonzales and Senator Russell Feingold, the Democrat from Wisconsin, during Senate Judiciary Committee hearings into Gonzales's nomination for attorney general. Feingold was zeroing in on Gonzales's role in the death penalty cases in Texas, and, in particular, one infamous case in which a death row inmate was seeking to have his case reviewed because his attorney had fallen asleep during his murder trial:

SEN. FEINGOLD: *"I want to now ask you about the role you had when you were counsel to then-governor Bush. You prepared what are referred to as clemency memos summarizing a particular death-row inmate's case and his plea for clemency from the governor. . . . Now, according to my staff's review of the clemency memorandum, it appears you presented these memos to the governor almost always on the day of execution. Why is that? On such a grave matter as life and death, why was the decision left until the day of execution?"*

GONZALES: *"The ultimate decision may have been left—or came close to—the time of the execution because that was the desire of the governor. However, those memos reflect a summary of discussions that often occurred between my office and the governor in connection with every execution. It was not unusual—in fact, it was quite common that I would have numerous discussions with the governor well in advance of a scheduled execution...."*

The exchange continued:

SEN. FEINGOLD: *"I guess I want to know, in this way you've just described the process worked, did you ever seek additional time in order to allow the governor adequate time to review and understand that case? In other words, after he read the memo that was presented on the day of the scheduled execution, was there even an occasion when more time was requested?"*

GONZALES: *"I don't remember an occasion when more time was requested when we presented that final memo. I do remember many occasions when I would go to the governor and talk about the facts of a particular case and the basis of clemency, and the governor would—if I expressed concerns or questions—the governor would direct me to go back and find out and to be absolutely sure, because while the governor believes in the death penalty, he believes that it deters crimes and saves lives, he also believes very firmly that it should be applied fairly and only the guilty should be punished."*

SEN. FEINGOLD: *"On that point, one of the cases involved an inmate on death row named Carl Johnson. He was executed in September 1995, during the first year that Governor Bush was in office and you were his counsel on these matters. Mr. Johnson was represented by a lawyer named Joe Cannon, who slept through the major portions of the trial, and who was apparently notorious in legal circles for this behavior. In his challenges appealing the trial conviction, Mr. Johnson argued consistently that he had had ineffective counsel, primarily based on the sleeping lawyer who represented him at trial. In your memo to the governor discussing this case and impending execution, however, you failed to make any mention whatsoever of the basis for Mr. Johnson's appeal. You go to great lengths to describe the underlying facts of the murder, but there's no mention of the fact that his lawyer slept through the major portions of the trial. I'd like you to, in a second, explain this omission. I want to know how the governor could have waived the clemency memo fully and properly, if you had failed to even indicate the basis for the clemency request."*

GONZALES: *"Senator, as I described to you, the process—those memos reflected the end of a process of educating the governor about the facts of a particular case. And the fact that it may not have been included in the memo, we may have had numerous discussions about it, he may have said, 'Has that issue been reviewed in the courts carefully and thoroughly?' and we may have gone back . . . I . . . I don't remember the facts of this particular case. But we may have gone back, our office may have gone back and seen that, yes, in fact, this question of ineffective assistance of counsel had been reviewed numerous times in our courts and had found the allegations frivolous."*

Feingold seemed incredulous at the response from Gonzales and suggested that the case, which had become a kind of poster child for anti–death penalty advocates, had simply become too infamous for Gonzales not to remember it:

SEN. FEINGOLD: *"Well, that's . . . this is a very famous case. It's hard for me to imagine that you don't know the specifics of it. And it's almost unimaginable to me that a final formal legal memo to the governor would not have included reference to the fact that this man's lawyer slept during the trial."*

At that point in the exchange, Senate Judiciary Chair Arlen Specter interrupted: *"Senator Feingold's time is up, but, Judge Gonzales, you may answer the question."*

Gonzales looked at Feingold and Specter and said, *"I don't have a response, unless there was a question."*

Feingold replied: *"It was a statement."* [12]

The debates about Gonzales's role in the ultimate form of punishment in Texas were also the ultimate harbinger of the controversies he'd face one day in Washington, especially when he was crafting memos and advising the president of the United States on what exactly it means to spy on people or torture a human being in the twenty-first century. His clem-

ency memos and the ones prepared for him by his staff attorneys clearly
are stripped-down, compressed versions of enormously complex death
penalty cases that often had taken twists and turns over several years. Gonzales and his attorneys have said they spent the right amount of time analyzing those cases and preparing those final memos for Bush; critics say
that it is simply not reasonable, feasible, for anyone to adequately summa-
rize the cases and to make artful, thoughtful recommendations of life-and-
death issues in three to five pages... and to deliver those memos to
the governor of Texas on the same day that someone is scheduled for execution.

Swirling around the controversy was another thought lodged by
Bush–Gonzales supporters—that the whole debate overestimates the role
that Bush could play in preventing someone from being executed. That
argument centers around the contention that under Texas law, Bush didn't
have a magic wand to commute a death sentence (unless he had a recommendation from a majority of members on the Texas Bureau of Pardon
and Paroles); he merely had the ability to grant a thirty-day stay of execution to allow the bureau to reconsider the case. Of course, death penalty
foes said that was all they really wanted from Bush and Gonzales—some
more time, some more thought, and some more deliberation. People who
observed Gonzales in Texas said his clemency memos—and, really, the way
they were delivered at the last moment—seemed not to be put together
by the same careful, deliberative man who painstakingly put together
lengthier real estate and mergers-and-acquisitions memos for his corporate clients.

They wondered if Bush, with his emphasis on quick, bottom-line answers—with his general inclination to view the world in black-and-white
terms and not to wallow in what he would call needless, indecisive ambiguity—had somehow moved Gonzales into a new legal style. Bush valued
certainty, firm commitment, bold decision making. Critics of Bush and
Gonzales heatedly suggested that that political style simply doesn't jibe
with having to make evaluations of who should live and die.

The executions of particular prisoners drew national attention to
Gonzales and Bush. Gonzales's three-page memo responding to Terry
Washington's thirty-page clemency centered squarely on the hideous
crime. Washington had been convicted of murdering a twenty-nine-year-

old mother of two children by stabbing her eighty-five times—stabbing her so often and so brutally that she was almost disemboweled. Gonzales's memo clearly restates the details of a horrific, staggering crime. There is very little mention of the fact that Washington was a mentally retarded thirty-three-year-old man with the communication skills of a seven-year-old, that he likely had ineffective counsel, and that there may be new mitigating evidence to consider. The extensive national debate over the execution of mentally retarded men and women was not outlined. Opponents to Washington's death said his case cried out for some mitigating circumstances to at least be mentioned in Gonzales's clemency memo. Washington's mental limitations and the fact that he and his ten siblings were regularly beaten with whips, water hoses, extension cords, wire hangers, and fan belts were never made known to the jury, although both the district attorney and Washington's trial lawyer knew about those bits of mitigating evidence. Nor did Gonzales mention that Washington's lawyer hadn't brought a mental health expert to the stand.

The David Spence case was another rallying point for Bush–Gonzales critics: Spence was put to death after being convicted of a triple murder of teenagers near a Waco lake, not far from where Bush would eventually own a ranch. His stay on death row, stretching out almost fifteen years, was punctuated by a series of subsequent investigations and revelations that pointed to the possibility of his being an innocent man. Another suspect had been identified by the police, but that news was never shared in court. That other suspect had a history of twenty-five assaults, many against teenagers, many at the same Waco lake, and he had apparently told several people that he had been involved in the murders. That other suspect eventually shot himself in the head with a gun when police came to question him about another crime. Meanwhile, the key prosecution witnesses were assailed for alleged inconsistencies in their stories. They first said that the victims were screaming, and then when it was noted to the witnesses that the victims were found gagged, the witnesses said that the victims were gagged after they had been killed.

The Spence case became for some a symbol of how jumbled, confused, and contradictory death penalty cases can become—and how Texas should do what Governor George Ryan would later do in Illinois: commute the sentences of everyone on death row, suggesting that it was the only way to rule out the possibility that an innocent person would be sent to death. In Texas, Gonzales was able to recommend that Bush grant the thirty-day stay, order the review board to uncork a special investigation, demand a new hearing, or simply even ask the review board to reverse the death sentence. None of the memos written by Gonzales indicate that he suggested those options to Bush.

B ush's closest Hispanic political intimates were Gonzales and Tony Garza, that handsome, charismatic Cameron County judge who seemed exceedingly comfortable in social settings and whom Bush had tabbed to be secretary of state. They weren't rivals, but they represented different tendencies for the Hispanic vanguard in the new Bush administration. Garza seemed easy in public, comfortable campaigning; Gonzales liked working "inside," as some of his V&E partners called it: "Gonzales had gone inside, in-house" was what they said in Houston. The politicizing of Alberto Gonzales, though, was going to take place whether he liked it or not.

In his first year in-house with Bush, Gonzales was sent by the American Council of Young Political Leaders as a member of a delegation to China; the next year he was sent on another American Council of Political Leaders trip to Mexico. Both of those trips were meant to educate Gonzales in that all-purpose world where fact-finding merged with glad-handing. Still, friends said, he came back from those political awareness trips much preferring the backroom, the brokering, and working around a hidden conference room—not giving speeches, not pressing the flesh at functions, and not giving interviews. On a side note, he also didn't relish the idea of ever seeing the inside of a courtroom. He wasn't a defense attorney and told some friends he never wanted to be one.

But in 1996, the same year he was still being pushed to pursue a hands-on political education by Bush and Rove, he found himself in a courtroom setting that touched on more than just attorney–client privilege: It touched on deep secrets that the Bush family had deliberately kept hidden for decades. They were secrets that involved that mantra George W. Bush repeated—"perception is everything in politics"—and they were secrets that arguably could have a direct effect on the presidential election.

The *Dallas Morning News*—trying to set the tone for statewide coverage on Bush's first campaign for governor, and under the supervision of editors Stu Wilk and Bob Mong—had not published any stories about Bush's criminal history. Perhaps the paper had investigated Bush's background and not unearthed anything. Perhaps the paper had not investigated his background. Either way, as it was later revealed, the acute specifics of Bush's criminal background (and military records) were reported on *after* he was elected governor, not before: Bush had been detained by the police and ordered to leave Princeton Township in New Jersey after a melee; he had been charged with disorderly conduct after stealing from a store in New Haven; he had been charged with being drunk and driving a car with his teenaged sister as a passenger in Kennebunkport, not far from the family's seaside mansion on the Maine coast.

Gonzales no doubt sometimes had to deal with V&E clients in Houston who had criminal backgrounds. Being the in-house counsel for the governor of Texas—for a governor by the name of Bush, for a man who was the son of the former president of the United States, for a man who was presumed to be running for the White House—was an entirely different matter.

It reached a breaking point, a defining moment for Gonzales, in 1996 when George Walker Bush, age fifty, residing at 1010 Colorado Street in a building more commonly known as the Governor's mansion, received an envelope containing his official Travis County jury summons. That summons would lead to Gonzales's only court appearance on behalf of Bush.

On September 30 Bush and Gonzales headed toward the impressive-looking Travis County Courthouse a block away from the Governor's mansion. Bush told the *Dallas Morning News* that he was "glad" to serve and that he considered it his duty. He described himself as an "average guy" reporting to jury duty. The three encounters with police that were in his background still had not been mentioned in stories about him.

At the courthouse Bush was assigned to a drunk driving case involving a stripper from a well-known Austin club called Sugar's. The case would be heard in County Court 3 with Judge David Crain presiding. Crain, a Democrat, was acutely interested in making sure that there were no dis-

ruptions in his courtroom and that the trains ran on time despite the obvious media hullabaloo of having the governor of Texas as a prospective
juror. Prosecutor John Lastovica was a law-and-order figure, and most
people assumed he would be happy to have a law-and-order governor like
Bush as one of the jurors. It was also a foregone conclusion that Bush
would probably wind up as the jury foreman.

Defense attorney David Wahlberg had mixed feelings. He was intrigued by the notion of asking Bush "some questions," of having Bush
"under oath where he has to answer some questions," but he was wary of
the politics involved. Wahlberg, like several people in Texas, had heard rumors about Bush having once had a terrible drinking problem and that he
had apparently just stopped one day. Wahlberg was curious and thought
some of the real stories about Bush would emerge as he was being quizzed
for possible jury duty. "Because, my sense of it was that nobody stops
drinking immediately unless there was some dramatic cause, like your
wife threatens you with divorce. Or you were in a terrible accident. Or
you got arrested. Or any one of a bunch of causes. It has been my experience in dealing with a lot of DWI [driving while intoxicated] cases that
nobody stops unless there is some serious reason. I was going to ask him
about that. There have been some stories around here about his serious
partying and stuff like that back in Midland [where Bush had lived and
waged a losing battle for Congress], and I wanted to ask him a few questions about that, so I was looking forward to having him sit there. It was
not until—it was a good while later—that the story broke that he had
actually been arrested for DWI. If he had answered truthfully under oath
or if he had answered truthfully in filling out the juror information card,
he would have had to disclose that" [13]

When filling out his juror information card, Bush didn't enter anything in a required section that asked, "Have you ever been accused, or a
complainant, or a witness in a criminal case?" He had been charged with
disorderly conduct in 1968 and drunk driving in 1976. It wasn't against
the law to leave the section blank, and years later, a spokesman for Bush
would say that the jury questionnaire had been filled out by a Bush travel
aide who didn't know the answers to eleven of the forty questions and had
left them blank. [14]

The day of the trial, Wahlberg, Lastovica, and Crain were at the bench conferring about minor preliminary issues. They looked up as Alberto Gonzales walked in the courtroom and asked for permission to approach the bench. Behind Gonzales they could see Bush in the hallway, outside the courtroom, holding an impromptu press conference and bantering with other prospective jurors. Wahlberg heard Gonzales introduce himself to Crain and say he was there on behalf of Governor Bush, and he heard Gonzales say "that they had reconsidered their position and had concluded that it would be inappropriate for a sitting governor to serve as a juror in a criminal case."

It was a curveball that no one had really expected. It seemed to fly in the face of the buildup and the prospect of positive public relations that had gone into Bush's jury duty. Bush, who had run a campaign predicated on projecting an image of himself as an "ordinary" Texan who had worked hard to get where he was, now had his lawyer arguing for him to be dismissed from the same kind of time-consuming, low-paying jury pool that hundreds, maybe thousands, of "ordinary" Texans are ordered to serve on every week.

The four men—Gonzales, the defense attorney, the prosecutor, and the judge—talked for a bit at the bench, then retreated to the judge's chambers. The defense attorney, prosecutor, and judge would remember that Gonzales then "asked to have an off-the-record conference in the judge's chambers."[15] The in-chambers meeting lasted fifteen to twenty minutes. Years later Gonzales would say he had "no recollection of requesting a meeting in chambers," but he did recall talking about a possible "conflict" with having Bush serve on a jury. Gonzales would also say he had not "requested" that Bush be removed from the jury pool.[16]

Whether Gonzales asked for a meeting in chambers or not, the other men remember meeting there. And they remember Gonzales introducing an argument that they had never heard before: that the governor of Texas shouldn't be selected as a juror because the governor would be trapped in a conflict of interest if he was ever asked to pardon the defendant. Judge Crain was stunned. There was almost zero chance that the defendant, if convicted, would ask the governor of Texas to pardon her. "In public, they were making a big show of how he was prepared to serve. In the back room, they were trying to get him off," said Judge Crain.[17]

In the end, Wahlberg, Judge Crain, and the prosecutor agreed to strike

Bush from the pool. Wahlberg especially wasn't going to object. As tempt-
ing as it was to grill a governor, he wanted to do right by his client. By
excluding Bush from the jury, he assumed he was excluding someone
who would have been a "hang 'em high" kind of Texas guy.

The defense attorney had to admire Gonzales—to a point. "I am board
certified in criminal defense. I have tried a bunch of cases. I have had a real
good success rate. And he tricked me—okay? In terms of his skill level, I
have to give him pretty high marks. He was very . . . he was very low-key
about the situation. It was not like he was coming in trying to force anything on us. He was quiet, persuasive, made his legal arguments . . . which
we all thought were bogus, but there was enough of an argument there, it
was a tolerable argument. I was basically just there and recognized that this
was a guy who knew what he was doing." After Bush was relieved of his
jury duty, Wahlberg had time to really dwell on what had just happened.

"I have some real ethical concerns about the way it all happened.
I think that there is no doubt in my mind that this whole little charade
was designed to prevent Bush from having to answer any questions under
oath and was specifically designed to avoid having to disclose his arrest
record and expose him to any questions. I can get pretty far afield on occasion, and walking into a jury selection with a lawyer who has free rein to
ask virtually any question about anything, then . . . yeah, I can see that they
were worried about that. It was clear to all of us that is exactly what happened. The charade worked."

Wahlberg wondered where Alberto Gonzales was as a lawyer—where
he had gone to in terms of his view of the law and his loyalties to his client.
Gonzales had to have been brought in on some Bush family secrets. There
were probably nettlesome things in Bush's background that the family
wanted hidden but that they had finally decided to share with Alberto
Gonzales. At the time, Wahlberg didn't know what those secrets were, but
they must have been heavy enough to have caused the general counsel to
the governor of Texas to make his first criminal courtroom appearance. It
was truly like a scene in a movie. For cynics who loved the intrigue in
Austin, it was like a Robert Duvall–as–Tom Hagen scene from *The Godfather*—the discreet "fixer" attorney working backroom deals and banking
on his client's obvious political muscle.

Divorced from the partisan politics—apart from whether someone was pro-Bush, anti-Bush, Democrat, or Republican—it was clear that Gonzales was working on things, doing things for George W. Bush that he had simply never done before in his legal career—it was work he hadn't been taught back at Harvard Law School. Years later he would admit that he had been told about Bush's hidden criminal record. Bush had shared something with him that the Bush family had kept hidden during Bush's 1977 race for Congress in Texas and during Bush's 1994 race for governor.

"I knew about his Operating Under the Influence arrest in Maine beforehand. It was only after we arrived that day at the courthouse that we came to know that it was a DWI case. Anticipating that that might happen, we had thought about what we would do, and obviously the governor was there to serve on jury duty and he was going to answer truthfully any question asked of him. Before the hearing, I went up to the defense lawyer and I mentioned to him that there might be an inherent conflict of interest in having the governor serve. But the defense attorney told me that he had already thought about the possible conflict and that he was going to object to having the governor serve as a juror." [18]

Gonzales had crossed into a zone where the political stakes were ratcheted up to the highest level possible. His loyalty and discretion were being tested with a buried Bush family secret. Gonzales had pondered the implications of his day spent extracting his client from a Texas courtroom, and he had pondered the implications of being entrusted with his client's criminal record. And now Wahlberg wondered, as one attorney weighing another attorney's actions, what it all really meant: "A lawyer has a little bit of a conflict there.... Obviously you have a duty to your client, but you have a duty of truth to the tribunal. You have a responsibility to be truthful with the court. And I think that this was really a subterfuge designed to protect Bush's reputation ... and I have some concerns about that." [19]

However the episode is viewed, Gonzales's work under the cheap fluorescent lights in the Travis County courtroom saved George W. Bush from having to reveal the potentially embarrassing and politically damaging details of his criminal past. Bush's arrest for drunk driving, which might have put him in a unique vantage point as he sat in judgment of someone else charged with the same offense, would remain hidden until just a few days before the 2000 presidential election, when it magically appeared as a so-called October Surprise.

Gonzales had worked legal wizardry to keep his client from having to answer questions in a Texas courtroom and by extension had kept the track to the presidency free from things that Bush's critics could use to their advantage. If Alberto Gonzales hadn't realized how overtly political his job had become, his appearance on behalf of his client in a drunk driving case in 1996 painted it in impossible-to-ignore colors.

There would be even more maneuvers inside the Bush administration that would steer Gonzales down different paths than he had anticipated when he decided to leave the velvet coffin at Vinson & Elkins. The case of a Mexican fisherman sent to death row in Texas put Gonzales into another uncharted, international territory: In June 1997 Gonzales sent a letter to the U.S. secretary of state, essentially arguing that Texas was not bound by certain international rules—specifically, Article 36 of an international treaty known as the Vienna Convention. In 1969 the U.S. Senate had approved the treaty and turned it into law: citizens of foreign countries who were accused of crimes were entitled to contact their consulates and ask for legal advice from someone representing their native land.

In 1985 a Mexican national named Irineo Tristan Montoya was found guilty of stabbing an American citizen twenty-two times in far South Texas, where the Rio Grande spills out to the Gulf of Mexico, after the American had stopped to give the hitchhiking Montoya a ride. The country of Mexico insisted that Texas violated Montoya's rights under the Vienna Convention by not immediately telling the Mexican consulate about his arrest. Montoya's supporters said Texas had simply broken U.S. and international law. Montoya, who didn't understand English, signed a document that he said he thought was an immigration form, but it was actually a confession. He was sent to death row in Texas and his execution was set for the summer of 1997.

Gonzales's letter to the State Department two days before the death date said, "Since the State of Texas is not a signatory to the Vienna Convention on Consular Relations, we believe it is inappropriate to ask Texas to determine whether a breach occurred in connection with the arrest and conviction of a Mexican national." Two days later Montoya was executed while his father watched. Bush's office released a press statement suggest-

LEFT: Alberto Gonzales played on his baseball team at MacArthur Senior High just north of Houston. He struck his teammates as intense and competitive. *(MacArtair, MacArthur High School yearbook)*

BELOW: Gonzales had some minor success as a roving defensive back on his football team; he was singled out as one of the better players in his district. *(MacArtair, MacArthur High School yearbook)*

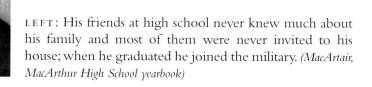

LEFT: His friends at high school never knew much about his family and most of them were never invited to his house; when he graduated he joined the military. *(MacArtair, MacArthur High School yearbook)*

While at Rice I have had much to be thankful for. My parents have stood behind me all the way and for this I am very grateful. I thank Diane whose love and understanding were so helpful in getting me through these four years. God has been too good to me and for this I praise him.

Al Gonzales
(1979 Poli)

I SALUTE USAFA CLASS OF '79

When he graduated Rice, he wrote this letter that was subsequently published in the school yearbook. *(Campanile, Rice University yearbook)*

His father, an alcoholic, died after a violent fall at the rice silo where he had gone to work as part of a maintenance crew; his father was buried alongside his brother Rene, who died in mysterious circumstances in 1980. *(Wendy Grossman)*

Gonzales, pictured with the other members of the Texas Supreme Court, found himself involved in an abortion ruling that would change his life forever. *(Copyright © Anne Butler)*

Some long time observers of the Texas Supreme Court wondered if Gonzales's appointment to the bench was just a political plum from George W. Bush. *(Courtesy of Texas Supreme Court)*

Gonzales's father had a second grade education; his mother had a fifth grade education. He was the first in his family to attend college, and years later he would be honored at his alma mater, Rice University. *(Tommy LaVergne/Rice University)*

Alberto Gonzales's nomination to become the first Latino Attorney General in U.S history was greeted with intense opposition by protestors who saw him as an agent of torture. *(Copyright © KRT)*

After Gonzales was accused of calling the Geneva Convention "quaint," he and his supporters, including Senator John Cornyn from Texas, were forced to explain their position. *(Copyright © KRT)*

Gonzales, with his wife Becky behind him and to his right, prepares to testify to the Senate Judiciary Committee. *(Copyright © KRT)*

His life, and his wife's life, has been intrinsically rooted in almost every phase of George W. Bush's political career. *(Copyright © KRT)*

It is the nature of their relationship—the counselor following the client. *(Copyright © KRT)*

Gonzales had reached a firm crossroads in his life and made a decision to finally leave the easy anonymity that he had enjoyed working behind the scenes. *(Copyright © KRT)*

Gonzales, the son of migrant workers, listens as Justice Sandra Day O'Connor swears him into the office of the Attorney General. *(Copyright © KRT)*

Armchair psychologists said that Bush was the older brother Gonzales never had. Arguably, his mother and Bush have been the two most pivotal figures in his life. *(Copyright © KRT)*

ing that Montoya had gotten a fair trial and the full protections of the Constitution, though Alan Berlow and others would argue that Article 6 of the U.S. Constitution, along with various Supreme Court rulings, clearly bound Texas to follow U.S.-signed treaties as "the supreme law of the land." The people who supported Gonzales's letter simply said that Montoya was given a fair trial, that he had viciously killed an innocent man and went partying after he dumped his victim's body in a grapefruit grove, that he was probably given a better legal shake in the United States than he would have gotten in Mexico. The people who opposed Gonzales's letter said that Montoya might very well have been guilty and that he might very well have gotten a fair trial, but that in Mexico there was no death penalty. It had been outlawed in that country in 1929.

A few months after Montoya's execution, Bush summoned Gonzales to his dark office. Bush sat behind a chunky, masculine wooden desk that once belonged to his father. Behind him, spread out on a low table, was a series of family pictures—pictures of himself with his father, pictures of the Bush family that were just like the ones that Gonzales had chosen to decorate his own office with. From where he sat, Bush could see the glass case containing his 250 autographed baseballs, the Western-style painting of a lone cowboy, the old maps of Texas, and the other painting that cracked him up every time he stared at it: the portrait was rescued from deep inside the bowels of the state archives and it depicted old, grizzled General Sam Houston, the hero of the Texas Republic, dressed in a toga.

Bush told Gonzales that he wanted to appoint him to the position of secretary of state—that it would raise his profile, that it would put another Hispanic in a prominent position, that he could use the mostly benign office to beef up the number of registered voters in Texas, especially Hispanic voters Bush was hoping to lure to the Republican Party.

Rove had become convinced that with the help of a few key appointments Bush could fly in the face of convention and win even more of the Hispanic vote. In speeches, Bush sometimes dropped in a line or two in stilted Spanish, and he was spending a lot of time in El Paso and South Texas, places with heavy Hispanic concentrations. Bush and Rove had talked about the fact that the Democrats tended to take the Hispanic vote for granted, that the media assumed Hispanics voted as one liberal bloc. Rove, particularly, had come to believe that there were a large number of Hispanic voters who were inherently, deeply conservative—deeply opposed to abortion, deeply in favor of the death penalty, pro-military, and ready to introduce religion into schools and state-run programs.

Rove told Bush that the Republican Party had never adequately pitched its socially conservative credentials to Hispanic voters. There were talks in Austin among the GOP insiders about how to get more utility from Alberto Gonzales. How to maximize his presence, how to capitalize on it. That year he had won a presidential citation from the State Bar for staying connected to various lawyers' groups around the state and giving speeches aimed at helping to address the legal needs of indigents—and surely that kind of thing could help with the overall "compassionate conservative" perception of Bush.

Gonzales had "gone in-house" with Bush and had passed several brutal tests, including that loyalty and discretion drunk driving trial in Travis County. Now it was time for Gonzales to go public. The office of the secretary of state was long considered a relatively low-stress, uncomplicated way to get your name in the paper and your face on TV. When Bush had taken office, he had given the job to Tony Garza, the rising Hispanic star from South Texas, as a way to "introduce" Garza. The same rules would apply with Gonzales. The jokesters in Austin would, of course, never let up on that notion of the Bush Dynasty being like the Corleones: the gag in Austin was that Bush had made Alberto Gonzales "an offer he couldn't refuse." Gonzales had only said no to the Bush family once before—when he turned down the old man's invitation to come to Washington. Either way, Rove, Hughes, and the others now knew that Gonzales was one of Bush's closest advisers. When Bush told them that he wanted Gonzales to be the secretary of state, he made it clear that the move didn't mean Gonzales would not be keyed in on all the most important political decisions in the Bush network. "The most important thing is for Al to remain in the inner circle," Bush said.[20]

Gonzales agreed to become the 100th secretary of state in Texas, but during the transition to that job in late 1997 while he served as acting general counsel and secretary of state, there was one more explosive death penalty case to contend with.

The world was waiting, the clock was ticking, and a woman was about to learn if she would live or die. The pope had sent petitions. Thousands of people had sent petitions . . . prime ministers, first-graders in New York City, fiery Baptist preachers in the Deep South. The phone lines were jammed and the fax machine had over a thousand messages stacked up in the little plastic tray. Hundreds of reporters were filing stories. In Washington the Supreme Court was huddling to hear emergency last-minute pleas. While he waited, Gonzales occasionally stared across the room at Bush. Peripatetic and already predisposed to being edgy, Bush was fussing back and forth in his office. Gonzales was like a counterpoint to Bush—patient, still.

There was a perfect storm welling, a convergence of smash-mouth politics and those naked presidential aspirations. A rangy, pleasant-faced woman named Karla Faye Tucker was on death row and scheduled to die on February 3, 1998. She was a former crystal methamphetamine addict convicted for murder after ingesting heroin, cocaine, and pills, going into a nightmarish, bloody rage, and hacking away at two people sleeping in their beds. Tucker was now inching toward becoming the first woman put to death in Texas since the Civil War. Her case was commanding international attention—and not just because of her gender. Her supporters said she had become an ardent born-again Christian and she had issued passionate messages proclaiming her fallibility and her remorse. Wildly disparate forces had lined up to beg Bush to spare her life: Bianca Jagger and Christian evangelists Jerry Falwell and Pat Robertson were among the strange bedfellows demanding that Bush do something to halt her execution.

It was late on a hot Texas afternoon, pushing 5:00 P.M. She was set to die in the next hour. Bush had already conferred about the fallout with Rove. Karen Hughes had come in and jutted her jaw at him, as if she was trying to will him to be strong. Bush heard the same coldly pragmatic political take from them. *Either way—you put her to death or you let her live—the road to the White House suddenly gets very, very treacherous.* Bush, too, was hearing from Bush family friend and loyalist Doug Wead—that former Bush White House staffer, Amway salesman, and evangelical Christian who would grow fond of secretly taping Bush. Now Wead was sending Bush urgent faxed messages telling him to throw the Christian Right a bone and not kill Karla Faye Tucker. Wead was worried, as always, that Bush would lose hold of that thing that Wead liked to call "the move-ment"—the Christian evangelical vote in America.

Bush paced his office and repeated something he had been saying all day: *"Where does Alberto say we stand right now?"*

Gonzales and Bush each considered the other to be a best friend. They were spending time together on the back patio of the stately, almost ghostly Texas governor's mansion—Bush's foot bobbing up and down as he tried to make a point, Gonzales slowly nodding in agreement. The security de-tail would hover nearby, watching as Rove or Garza would join the discus-sion and a small cloud of cigar smoke would come wafting over toward where Bush's Lincoln Town Car was parked.

Now Tucker's execution was less than thirty minutes away. News up-dates flashed across the wires with every sudden twist: The U.S. Supreme Court had rejected the last-second appeals to save her life. Her panicked proponents quickly retreated to lower courts in Texas, trying to file differ-ent state appeals. Those, too, were instantly shot down. Suddenly, as Bush lingered nearby, Gonzales took an emergency call from Tucker's attorney. Gonzales listened closely as the weary defense attorney said he had one final message: *There will be no more challenges. It's over. It's in your hands.*

Gonzales turned to Bush and told him there were no legal obstacles: *There were no more obstacles . . . now the only recourse would be an emergency stay of execution order issued from the governor of Texas.* Now, right now, it was up to Bush and Gonzales to decide if Karla Faye Tucker was to live a little longer—maybe long enough for Bush to use his political muscle, his vast political capital, to push the state boards to reconsider her fate. Alone and together, Gonzales and Bush huddled one last time behind closed doors. Gonzales told Bush he was on high ground. *The law is clear.*

With less than twenty minutes to her execution, Bush finally stepped out of his office. He said he had an announcement: *"The execution of Karla Faye Tucker will proceed."* Gonzales, still taciturn, his broad face revealing nothing, listened as Bush added, *"May God bless Karla Faye Tucker, and may God bless her victims and their families."*

Growing up the way they did in and around Houston, it would have been impossible to foresee Alberto Gonzales and George W. Bush frozen inside the same brutal, defining moment—a woman's life in their hands—and that the decision to let her live or die could possibly tilt the entire direction of their careers. Now Gonzales stood in Bush's office and listened to the phone delivering the news from the death chamber in Texas. The chilling details of the last minutes of a woman's life emerged from the tinny-sounding speakerphone. Gonzales heard the voice on the other end:

"6:26: prisoner strapped to gurney."

And,

"6:28: needle inserted."

And,

"6:35: lethal dose administered."

And, finally,

"6:45: prisoner is pronounced dead."

Gonzales was silent. He and Bush had never wavered. He and the future president of the United States were now bonded by this convergence of politics and death. As he walked out the door of his office, Bush suddenly stopped and turned to look back at Gonzales. He said to Gonzales, *"Thank you. You did a good job."*

The reverberations from that day would linger and sting. Reports would later emerge that Bush had viciously mocked Karla Faye Tucker by imitating her in a sing-song, high-pitched voice desperately begging for her life. Critics would even say that Bush falsely characterized her execution as one of the most difficult decisions of his life—and that the only reason Gonzales and he seemed to deliberate on her case, the only reason that Gonzales prepared a lengthier briefing on her case, was because Karla Faye Tucker was attracting the attention of the Christian conservatives . . . and Karl Rove didn't want to make that voting bloc angry . . . Karl Rove didn't want to upset Jerry Falwell and Pat Robertson and the other evangelicals who had decided that Karla Faye Tucker had authentically been born again and religiously rehabilitated.

In an interview seven years later, Gonzales talked about his career, one where he was accused of easily letting dozens of people die: "You have to be courageous, because you're going to be making some decisions that are going to be unpopular and you have to accept that. . . . I think loyalty is something that's also very, very important, and that's the lesson that I really have learned from our president [George W. Bush]." Gonzales continued: "They want the agenda of our president to succeed because of the tremendous loyalty and affection that we hold for our leader. . . . I don't think I would change anything in my life. . . . Were there mistakes? Yes. Were there things that I wish never happened, people that may have been hurt? Yes, but I have no complaints about my life."[21]

NINE

Supreme Justice

G onzales took advantage of the friendly confines of the state's biggest newspaper—the *Dallas Morning News,* which enjoyed close ties with the Bush family—and began writing the sort of profile-building pieces that budding politicians like to place on welcoming editorial pages. His first one, in early 1998, probably had his real estate and racquetball buddies in Houston smiling when they read his academic and painfully careful column about why trade between Mexico and Europe was a good thing. "As the governor's newly appointed chief adviser on relations with Mexico and border affairs, I believe that Texas need not necessarily fear closer ties between Mexico and Europe....As a general rule, what is good for Mexico is good for Texas. Of course there are some exceptions to that rule." [1]

Gonzales was still juggling some duties as Bush's acting general counsel, but increasingly he was moving from being that purely "in-house" consigliere to making speeches, cutting ribbons, and shaking hands as secretary of state—and he was essentially serving as the Texas ambassador to Mexico. There were more op-ed pieces, written in that same deadpan, earnest tone of someone trying to seek his voice, someone unaccustomed to presenting a vigorous, rousing public campaign: "Why is Mexico so important to Texas? Because we have a special relationship.... Mexico also is important to Texas because of trade.... So, you see, by assisting Mexico in helping itself, we help ourselves as well."[2]

Behind closed doors Gonzales had also quietly agreed to go upriver on another mission for Bush. It was basically a plan to discredit and hopefully dislodge the leading Hispanic Democrat in the state: someone who could pose not just an immediate political threat but could stymie that master plan to permanently attract Hispanic voters to the GOP. Dan Morales was the well-groomed Texas attorney general who was fresh from a huge success—winning the largest legal settlement in history, a $15.3 billion judgment against the tobacco industry. Morales had graduated from Harvard Law in 1981, the year before Gonzales. Now he was anointed by some as the rightful Hispanic heir to Henry Cisneros, the once shining star in Texas who had gone from the mayor's office in San Antonio to the Clinton Cabinet, but then had become a fallen angel whose credibility had been damaged by a scandalous extramarital affair.

Morales was dominating the airwaves with that staggeringly lucrative win against Big Tobacco—and doing it just as Bush was immersing himself in both his gubernatorial reelection and the 2000 presidential campaign. The biggest story line out of Texas, overshadowing Bush, was that early 1998 news about the young, bright Hispanic Democrat who had brought a Goliath to its knees. Betting money even had Morales running for the governor's office sometime in the future. There was already bad blood between Morales and the Bush insiders, in particular Karl Rove. In late 1997 Morales had blasted Rove for working as a paid consultant to Phillip Morris, the largest public tobacco company in the world, for five years—and he alleged that Rove was still working for Phillip Morris while also advising Governor George W. Bush.

The animosity reached a head after that $15.3 billion settlement when Bush and Rove went on the warpath and attacked Morales for approving $2.3 billion in fees for the attorneys who led the lawsuit against the tobacco industry. It appeared that the state of Texas would actually have to pay for some of the attorney's fees—and worse, in Bush's estimation, there was a sense that those plaintiffs' attorneys would chunk millions from their fees back into Democratic war chests. It was a surreal nightmare: the state of Texas paying Democrat lawyers who would take that money and fund Democrat campaigns in Texas.

Bush was livid. And at the quaint old Austin Club on a side street a few blocks from the State Capitol, Republican senators and representatives in Texas had settled in over their power lunches and were gossiping about how Morales was almost like the people on death row in Huntsville— except that he didn't know it. He was marked for execution; he was a dead man walking, someone who would somehow, some way, be thrown under the wheels of the runaway Bush for President campaign. That train, everyone in Austin knew it, was already leaving the station—and for the really politically crass and incorrect souls who washed back their prime rib steaks with tumblers of Jack Daniels, it was going to be a matter of which Latino would survive as the big-time player in Texas: Dan Morales or Alberto Gonzales, the man Bush was clearly positioning for bigger things?

G onzales, for his part, was dutifully tracking and monitoring the huge tobacco settlement as it first unfolded. Early on, when Morales seemed like the Lone Ranger, operating out of a heroic, independent attorney general's office and exacting billion-dollar justice from the tobacco industry, Gonzales had done some digging for Bush. In a definitive article in the *Dallas Observer,* reporter Miriam Rozen says Gonzales knew a huge settlement was coming and that he had been on the phone with New York lawyers representing the tobacco industry, trying to find out from them the status of the negotiations. Bush and Gonzales didn't want to be blind-sided when the largest settlement in the nation's history was announced. It was coming down at about the same time that Karla Faye Tucker was going to be put to death. The stakes were high, and, as Bush constantly drilled into everyone in his office, "perception is everything in politics." He didn't want to be perceived as being eclipsed by an upstart Democratic attorney general—and he didn't want to be perceived as too bloodthirsty, or too soft, by people watching the Karla Faye Tucker case come to its somber conclusion.

Gonzales, of course, was there by his side for both calamitous events in early 1998. In time the outcome of any real or perceived posturing between Gonzales and Morales would become devastatingly clear. Morales was eventually crushed by greed and hubris and perhaps political revenge, eventually succumbing to a complex investigation that led him to a four-year prison term for tax evasion and mail fraud—with all of it tied to allegations that he had tried to steer hundreds of millions of dollars from the tobacco settlement to his own pockets and to a friend. Meanwhile it was understood that Gonzales had helped to make sure that Texas didn't have to pay millions of dollars to Democratic lawyers.

Bush, said people who watched his deepening relationship with his counselor, had come to view Gonzales as someone as politically invaluable as the more noticeable Rove and Hughes. People who knew both Rove and Hughes viewed Gonzales as a loyalist now very willing to do the same intense dirty work on legal issues that Rove and Hughes were doing with the media. There was some suspicion among the politicos in Austin that Gonzales had tripped over into sycophant land, that it had become odd that he was putting so many pictures of the two George Bushes up on his wall. But friends said it was incorrect to suggest that there was some form of hero worship going on or that Gonzales had come to see George W. Bush as the older brother he never had, or had come to see the elder Bush as the father he always wanted. Houston attorney Patrick Oxford says, "No, they didn't have that kind of relationship. Theirs is man-to-man, friend–friend, and lawyer–client. To my knowledge it's very much a respectful and equal relationship. There's not an analogy, at least that I'm aware of, in the family context." [3]

In 1998 Gonzales crisscrossed Texas in regions where the Republican Party was aggressively wooing Hispanic voters. He and Bush both made repeated visits to El Paso—the forgotten, neglected big city of Texas. One of Gonzales's roles as secretary of state was to urge Texans to head to the polls and to issue various statistics on voter registration and turnout. "I think you're going to have politicians paying a lot more attention to El Paso," he said in the summer of 1998, and he instructed people in his department to see if there were ways that voter registration drives in El Paso could be replicated in other cities. [4] He was clearly a point person in getting Hispanics registered and to the polls; Rove was still convinced that if Bush simply appealed to Hispanic voters, if he pitched some socially conservative agendas, they could tap into a resource that previous GOP candidates had ignored. For Gonzales it was as close to outright political campaigning as he had come. At one voter turnout drive in Dallas, Gonzales suddenly found himself in awkward surroundings, making an appearance with quirky popster Lisa Loeb at a Rock the Vote concert.

By that September there was news that both Gonzales and Bush had been anticipating: Justice Raul Gonzalez, one of the two last Democrats on the Texas Supreme Court, announced that he was going to resign. There was going to be a vacancy. (Supreme Court justices are elected in Texas, but a governor can fill a vacancy with a temporary appointee.) The move didn't shock anyone, insiders had seen it coming, and it added fuel to all the hype and speculation about the real reasons why Alberto Gonzales would subject himself to a tedious, pandering kind of position like secretary of state.

Glad-handing with low-level Mexican officials and possessing no legislative clout, appearing at strip shopping centers in Dallas with pop musicians whose concerts he would never dream of attending, issuing big charts showing how many people voted in elections, writing droning editorials that read like the strained compositions of a college history major, touring to eighty far-flung high schools across Texas and trying to deliver a speech that would keep bored teenagers from laughing at him. Now all of it seemed to make sense. Bush and Gonzales knew there was going to be an opening on the Supreme Court, the highest civil court in the state, and having Gonzales tread water in a high-profile but ultimately neutered position like secretary of state would be a small price for him to pay as he waited for that opening on the high court.

The buzz had been building for years that Raul Gonzalez—really a Republican-in-Democrat-clothing who had been the first Hispanic elected to statewide office in 1984—was squarely aiming at quitting after becoming fully vested in the state's retirement program. And a completely Republican-run Texas Supreme Court was an audacious but achievable plan; Rove had long ago mapped out strategy sessions that would result in the Republicans taking every single statewide office in 1998. Well before Raul Gonzalez resigned, a decision had been made to fill the seat with another minority. The positive public relations for appointing a minority to a Supreme Court seat would always be extremely valuable. Picking Alberto Gonzales was really a no-brainer.

Bush won his November reelection bid in a bruising landslide. The hard work he and Gonzales had done to win the Hispanic vote in places like El Paso paid off big time: Bush won 49 percent of the Hispanic vote, a stunning number for a Republican in the Lone Star State. (Bush also took 27 percent of the black vote, an equally unusual number for a Republican.) The race was over before it began. And a week after he won, he announced that he was appointing Gonzales to the Supreme Court in Texas, though Gonzales had never been a judge before and, frankly, had barely been inside a courtroom. Bush, when asked if Gonzales being Hispanic had something to do with his choice, blurted out, *"Of course it mattered what his ethnicity is."* [5]

If Gonzales was the beneficiary of some sort of internal quota, Bush was not letting on. But Gonzales alluded to that possibility: "When I was appointed to the Texas Supreme Court, Gov. Bush was asked whether race was a factor in this decision. He said, of course it was a factor. He said he thought it was important to have at least one person of color on the state's highest court, but it wasn't the most important factor. Competence and character were." [6]

His friends certainly never talked with him about quotas, affirmative action, and whether he felt like he was moved to the head of the line because of the color of his skin. His friends, by and large, were too polite to bring it up and too loyal to him. One political observer in Texas said that by 1998 Gonzales was no longer embarrassed by his background. Now his reasons for avoiding his background were different. Now it was more a matter of his aggressively wanting to avoid any speculation, any hint that he was unqualified for the appointments and jobs he was taking on. Whatever the reason for his continued reticence to talk about his father, his mother, and some of the family members still crammed into that tiny house on Roberta Lane, he was part of a unique minority.

By the end of his first term as governor, 79 percent of Bush's appointments went to Anglos, 12 percent to Hispanics, 8 percent to blacks. (Ann Richards had given 18 percent of her appointments to Hispanics and 16 percent to blacks.) [7] "I think it is going to be a pretty interesting mix to have somebody who may not have been a judge before, on the court. I think the judges, and I think those who argue in front of Al, are going to see that he is a great judge," announced Bush.

Gonzales's appointment to the Supreme Court clearly emboldened Bush and Rove. There were no pushbacks, no stinging rebukes in legal circles or in news accounts. And the fact that Gonzales had zero experience on the bench struck Bush and Rove advisers as not just refreshing but daring, decisive, counterintuitive, and maybe even motivated by some anti-intellectual streak in Bush's and Rove's background. The two had long ago achieved a bond, an instant kinship, when they talked about how both felt disenfranchised during the tumultuous '60s and '70s—how they sometimes felt ostracized by the swirling social events back then, how they loathed the way that time period spawned what they considered to be so much indulgent and pandering legislation. Their mutual heroes were Ronald Reagan and pumped-up gunslingers like Lee Atwater—the people whom they thought had mainlined some dizzying energy back into the Republican Party.

Bush and Rove talked about themselves as edgy outsiders who moved more nimbly than the stuffy GOP masters mired inside the Washington beltway. The younger Bush hated the way the media had once portrayed his father as a fancy-pants anemic. *Newsweek* had struck a death blow to the Bush family when they used the word "wimp" to characterize the old man. The younger Bush desperately wanted to avoid all that. He didn't mind tweaking the nose of the Republican establishment in Texas. He had just won two huge gubernatorial races and entered into a precoronation, pre-presidential march. Naming a judicial neophyte to the Supreme Court, someone who had never tried a criminal or civil case, was easy for Bush— and it was in keeping with the confident, some said recklessly arrogant, approach to appointments that he was developing with Rove. It also was a tactic he'd try to replicate in a few years in Washington with Gonzales's close friend and kindred soul Harriet Miers—but with far more disastrous results.

For his part Gonzales was loathing the fact that it was a trial appointment and that he would eventually have to campaign around the state to keep that seat on the Supreme Court. Campaigning would mean opening his life in a way that he had never done before. For now, with the Gonzales appointment as the cherry on top, Republicans officially held all twenty-nine statewide elected offices in Texas. At the Supreme Court it would be the first time since Reconstruction that Republicans would occupy every one of the nine seats.

Gonzales was delivered to the apex of the legal establishment in Texas. His orchestrated ascension, rise to power, was considered remarkable by both Democrats and Republicans. His circle of influence was growing exponentially, and he finally knew it had something to do with his ethnicity: *"I know that I've been helped because of my ethnicity. But the bottom line . . . is that Hispanics should expect nothing more than an equal opportunity. For us to now say that we should be given an opportunity because of our ethnicity, irrespective of our competence, means that we'll be discriminating against someone else who doesn't happen to be Hispanic, which is the very thing that we've been screaming about for decades. . . . Personally, I'm not offended that race is a factor. But it should never be the overriding factor or the most important factor."* [8]

When Bush was sworn into his second term as governor at the end of January 1999, the national media descended on Texas. It wasn't just a good photo opportunity—getting the younger Bush in the same frame as his father—it was a chronicle of an unannounced campaign for the presidency. It was in full, intense swing from here on, and every public utterance was going to be pored over for the obvious as well as the hidden meanings. That cold day in January, as Bush took the oath of office again, he decided to mention the name of one of his most trusted advisers in his speech. In fact, the first name mentioned in his speech, immediately after Bush thanks God, is Alberto Gonzales:

"I think of my friend Al Gonzales, recently sworn in as a Supreme Court justice. His parents reared eight children in a two-bedroom house in Houston. They worked hard every day. They sacrificed so that their children would have a chance to succeed. Al Gonzales has realized their dream."

Apart from the misstatement that the Gonzales home was in Houston, not Humble, the significance of the reference to Gonzales was immense. National reporters began calling regional journalists to get a read on who Alberto Gonzales was and why Bush had singled him out in such a high-profile speech. Unfortunately, there wasn't much to offer the reporters. The details of Gonzales's work shielding Bush from having to serve on that drunk driving jury were not widely known. His behind-the-scenes work on the death penalty cases was certainly not known. It would be years before his death penalty memos would be unearthed by Alan Berlow or news would emerge about Gonzales even attending an execution.

Gonzales's million-dollar real estate deals and his work for Enron had barely registered in Houston. And, of course, the details of Gonzales's upbringing had never been written about or talked about, including his father's lingering alcoholism; his brother's mysterious death at a young age; his father's fall at the rice silo; his divorce; his ex-wife's tragic death; the possibility that one of his sisters, as neighbor Brenda Pond said, had gotten into some kind of "trouble"; and the possibility that Alberto used to hire his brother Tim to cut his lawn for him.

"Tim was my boss at a plumbing company. He worked at the shop where all the supplies were. He was in charge of signing the paperwork for all the supplies that came in. He had a wife and he had, I don't remember how many kids. Maybe two boys and a girl or three boys and a girl? He played guitar. He loved to play guitar. He played all the time. He was a good boss. I was a punk kid," says Brent Gibson, who worked with Tim Gonzales in Houston. "And he was always having to put me in line. He rode his bicycle to work. He didn't have a vehicle. He told me sometimes he'd go work for his brother. Mowing his lawn. He said he'd go work for him, stay at his house, and get some money working for him. He told me, 'My brother's a big-time lawyer.' He was always talking about how he's up there—up the ladder. I didn't know who he was. I do now, though.

"We used to hide his bike all the time. He's the only person who rode a bike to work. I'd hide it and he'd get all upset. He'd be riding his bike to work and people would act like they were going to run him off the road— they'd honk and he'd go off into the ditch. They'd say, 'Oh, there's Tim.' "[9]

Gonzales's years avoiding his upbringing meshed easily with the general anonymity that protected the now completely Republican Texas Supreme Court. Bruce Davidson at the *San Antonio Express-News,* one of the savviest political reporters in Texas, wrote in early 1999—just after Gonzales put on his judge's robes—that only 1 percent out of six hundred registered voters could tell you that Alberto Gonzales was the newly appointed justice. (Only 2 percent could name Tom Phillips, who had been on the court for years; several other justices didn't even receive enough mentions to register a whole percentage point.)[10] The justices, who certainly wielded plenty of power, were willingly exiled to a realm where they were only really known by a small group of political junkies and academics around the state. It would be a soft landing for Gonzales—a place where he could learn to be a judge, where he could study under seasoned Republican lawyers-turned-judges who had made the leap years ago from various gilded Texas firms similar to Vinson & Elkins.

Half the people on the court owed their presence to Bush. Gonzales, as Bush's chief legal mind and someone with impeccable ties to the State Bar of Texas and its former president Harriet Miers, had been advising Bush on judicial appointments in Texas, anyway. These were people Gonzales knew, had worked with before, had seen at legal conventions, academic settings, and parties all over the state. These were not going to be strangers, and Gonzales was quickly welcomed into a clubby environment that encouraged an exclusive, anonymous culture. For the next twenty-three months he'd serve on the Texas Supreme Court. It would eventually become one of the only heavily scrutinized periods of his life. It would have almost everything to do with whether he would be named to the U.S. Supreme Court. His brief time on the Texas Supreme Court would one day be dissected and gnawed on by everyone from Rush Limbaugh to Ted Kennedy.

Some people were already scrutinizing Gonzales. "It was the first appointment in a long time where no one knew who he was and that he hadn't been a judge before. It truly was unique, and it had people terrified," says Texas attorney David Keltner.[11]

At home there was a change for his wife as well. On January 31, 1999, Rebecca quit her state job at the attorney general's office and moved to a new position at the state comptroller's office in Austin. Critics wondered if her husband had helped her get the job or if her husband's rise to the top court in Texas had inspired her selection.

The Texas Supreme Court swung wildly back and forth through the 1980s and 1990s, gaining a reputation for being extraordinarily sympathetic to trial lawyers and plaintiffs lodging big complaints against big businesses, then swinging hard in the other direction and being seen as boldly pro-business, ready to throw out what Bush and others were aggressively deriding as frivolous lawsuits. (Politicos in Texas said that Bush's attacks on those lawsuits were again based in part on the thought that lawyers would extract a big wad of money from big businesses, then donate plenty of that cash to Democratic legislators.) By the time Gonzales joined the court, it had begun to inch a little bit closer to the middle, but as a court completely dominated by Republicans, it was still seen as one that generally would be expected to lend credence to the business community and not be a knee-jerk, pro-consumer outfit.

At his investiture in Austin, on the House floor at the State Capitol, Bush recited the same speech that he had given before, telling the story about Gonzales selling Cokes at football games at Rice University and dreaming about going to school there someday. Gonzales listened to Bush tell the story again, and when Bush was through, the two men embraced. Gonzales turned to friends from Houston who had traveled to witness and videotape the swearing-in ceremony and he told them that he was grateful to Bush for making him Judge Alberto Gonzales of the Texas Supreme Court. Gonzales's mother was there, and it suddenly looked as if Bush was becoming authentically emotional, his eyes maybe welling up with tears. People who were there said it was odd in the sense that it was clear that Gonzales had come so far beyond everyone else in his family.

With each new and escalating phase of his career, the gaps were widening between the first son of Pablo and Maria Gonzales and everyone else still tethered in one way or another to Roberta Lane in Humble. It was yet another batch of psychobabble perhaps, but his friends really did wonder if Gonzales didn't draw attention to his family because he didn't want to embarrass them with his success. "What's happening in my life is no more important than what's happening in my brother's life. It is difficult in the sense that it makes you painfully aware of the inequities in life. It does make you wonder why a person who has grown up in exactly the same environment is able to succeed," he would say.[12]

One thing was obvious that day as his friends, family, and colleagues from Vinson & Elkins gathered to witness his elevation to the highest court in Texas. There were no clues, no foreshadowing hints that his relatively brief tenure as a judge in Texas would eventually have everything to do with big stabs of American history . . . and very dramatic events swirling around the makeup of the U.S. Supreme Court. Bush, schooled almost from birth to think about long-range political planning, had already talked to Republican leaders in Texas, including Rove, about Gonzales's future. If he didn't go all the way to the U.S. Supreme Court, he would still be positioned to run for some kind of office in Texas. Maybe even governor. A former clerk at the Texas Supreme Court described the milieu Gonzales was about to enter as very insular, very isolated, and it brewed up a sort of prevailing caginess, with the Texas justices instructing their clerks to mingle with the colleagues and see what they could find out about the new judge. The clerk said that several of her fellow clerks had come to the conclusion that "Gonzales really didn't want to be a judge and was only doing it as a favor to Bush."

Bush said he was putting a new generation "in place" in Texas: "None of us will ever forget the emotional moment when I administered the oath of office making Al Gonzales, who started out as my General Counsel, then served as Secretary of State, a justice of the Texas Supreme Court," said Bush. "I believe I have helped put in place a new generation of leaders for my state." [13]

Bush, as he would later infamously suggest about Harriet Miers, felt that he knew what was in Gonzales's heart and soul. Gonzales's lack of experience as a judge really didn't matter. Gonzales was *a good man* who could be expected to vote from the bench in ways that would be solidly aligned with Bush's policies. He certainly wasn't going to flake out and start regularly voting in some harebrained way that ran completely counter to Bush's agenda. Like Clarence Thomas, like Antonin Scalia, he could sometimes be defined—rightly or wrongly—by race and ethnicity. Like Thomas and Scalia, he could almost always be expected to take a heavily conservative posture on the Texas bench. In the end, Bush had no fears that Gonzales would become the David Souter of Texas—the sometimes liberal U.S. Supreme Court justice appointed by elder Bush and the man who had become a hated rallying cry for rankled, betrayed conservatives.

Style-wise, Gonzales entered the Supreme Court doing what he had

always done throughout his legal career: He refrained from taking any sort
of bold, aggressive posture with his fellow justices during their conferences and deliberations. It could have been related to the fact that he was
new to the bench, to any bench. It could have something to do with the
fact that he had told a handful of friends that he was still a bit unsure about
leaving the security of being completely "in-house" and off the radar as
Bush's general counsel. He was quickly accepted into the fold. Gonzales
wasn't a grandstander; he wasn't someone who appeared outwardly in-
toxicated with the thought that he had become one of nine select members of the highest court in Texas.

In almost two years on the court, Gonzales wrote fourteen majority
opinions (along with five concurring opinions and two dissents), and
those opinions proved that Gonzales was no judicial activist. Among the
fourteen opinions, there were a half-dozen that were clearly more important than the others—important in terms of case law, precedent, and providing a window into his judicial style and philosophy. Looking at the
totality of his work, he clearly wasn't interested in legislating from the
bench and he seemed perfectly obsessed with a mostly safe adherence to
the letter of the law. He was in the end a plodding worker bee—a dogged
journeyman who was going to apply law—and not a brilliant visionary or
intensely interpretative scholar on the bench. Years of working with real
estate and energy executives who wanted to know the financial and legal
bottom line—and with Bush, who absolutely insisted on being handed
the bottom-line analysis—had predisposed Gonzales to steer clear of what
proponents would call the artistry of the law and what critics would call
self-indulgent pontification. Gonzales was not going to try to get into the
heads and hearts of the people who put the laws on the books; he was going to apply, enforce, whatever they had come up with. Texas had certainly
seen its share of activist judges in the previous two decades. Gonzales
wasn't one of them.

Instead, he became known as what might best be called a moderate
conservative who sometimes surprised court-watchers by occasionally
voting against corporations and in favor of the little guy. Gonzales was
once described by a watchdog group as being part of a so-called New

Guard—with Justices Greg Abbott, Deborah Hankinson, James Baker, and Harriet O'Neill—that was bringing the court back in from a sometimes too-edgy ride into conservative activism. The New Guard, most of whom were appointed by Bush, was also said to be far more helpful when it came to presidential candidate George W. Bush's wish to be known as a compassionate conservative. They certainly weren't going all the way toward the legal land of liberal William O. Douglas, but they also were not scaring moderates in Texas on a daily basis.

Gonzales wrote a January 1999 opinion in *General Motors Corp and Lawrence Marshall Chevrolet Oldsmobile. v. A. J. Sanchez,* a case involving a Texas cowboy who was found dead by his ranch foreman alongside a corral. Sanchez's 1990 Chevy pickup had rolled backward with the driver's side door open, violently pinning him against the pen gate. He struggled to get free while the pickup idled, severed an artery in his right arm, then helplessly bled to death over the course of the next hour. His wife and family sued the local dealer and GM for product liability and negligence, contending that the truck had a faulty transmission and had "mis-shifted." GM said Sanchez could have simply left the car in reverse or neutral, and if a "mis-shift" had occurred, it was the cowboy's fault, not the vehicle's.

A trial court awarded the Sanchez survivors $8.5 million in actual and punitive damages. Gonzales, only weeks into his new role on the bench, asked very few questions during the oral arguments, then found a middle ground: He reversed the lower court rulings and said the survivors could keep the actual damages but not the punitive damages. Gonzales wrote that "there is some evidence of a product defect." In the end the family was awarded $1.3 million. The lawyers on either side seemed moderately happy with the somewhat Solomon-like decision. One of them simply noted that it could have been much, much worse.

That same January, Gonzales heard arguments in a case pitting Texas Farmer's Insurance against a woman named Daisy Murphy who was seeking a settlement after a house fire. There were allegations that her husband committed arson, and the insurance firm claimed it didn't owe him money; the husband accused the company of breaking his policy contract. In the middle of it all, Daisy Murphy filed her own claim for the policy benefits. The complex case was punctuated by Daisy and her husband getting divorced but agreeing to split any insurance money. The argument revolved around whether Daisy had anything to do with the possible arson or whether she was, in effect, an innocent and unwitting spouse who simply lost her home in a fire.

Gonzales ruled that "Daisy is entitled to recover her share of the policy benefits"—but legal experts have said his opinion is so carefully worded that even though it looks like he was letting an innocent, ordinary woman in Texas earn some monetary relief, Gonzales was straining to make sure his opinion couldn't be used to open the door for a flood of similar cases. Gonzales wanted Daisy Murphy to get some money, but he didn't want her case to set any lingering legal precedent.

Gonzales also reviewed the arguments in a compelling case *(Southwestern Refining v. Bernal)* that touched on the very things that made Texas hum and that Gonzales would certainly be aware of from his days of cooking energy deals at Vinson & Elkins. A group of 904 people in the heavily Hispanic seaside town of Corpus Christi were alleging that they were injured from a toxic cloud that blew over their homes after a storage tank at the Southwestern Refinery exploded in 1994. Lower courts had affirmed their right to file their personal injury claims under the umbrella of a class-action suit. Of course, Southwestern wanted the Supreme Court to rule against the whole notion of a class-action suit, hoping to avoid what could possibly be a huge settlement. Business leaders around Texas watched the case closely; they simply didn't want to see personal injury lawyers being given free license to put together class-action lawsuits.

There were four lead plaintiffs—Hispanic women with the last names of Suarez, De La Garza, Bernal, and Barrera—who were eventually joined by 900 others in the class-action lawsuit. The residents said they were suffering from a wide, debilitating array of ailments brought on by all the toxic chemicals. They complained of breathing problems, eye irritations, headaches, nausea—and that their plants, trees, and pets had already died from the toxic plumes. Critics said some of the claims were bogus and that the only reason all the claimants joined together in a class-action suit was that they thought they could score a much bigger settlement than they would by pursuing the costly process of filing each individual claim one-by-one against Southwestern.

In the end Gonzales broke the back of the entire notion of a class-action lawsuit by writing a majority opinion that damned the lower court rulings as "an abuse of discretion," and "because of this conclusion we need not consider Southwestern's other objections to the class action." In the big picture of things, Gonzales essentially helped throw a lingering monkey wrench into any future attempts by attorneys in Texas to certify class-action lawsuits driven by personal injury claims. The majority opinion was among his most important because it was the most lingering; anyone looking to file a class-action lawsuit in Texas would be looking for clues inside Gonzales's opinion. And anyone looking to take on the oil industry in Texas with a class-action lawsuit would have been well served to look at Gonzales's ruling in favor of the big oil refining firm. Lawyers in the case complained that Gonzales not only shouldn't have been writing the majority opinion, he should have recused himself from the case—he had too many ties to Ken Lay, Enron, the oil industry, and even groups that were going to contribute money to his political campaigns.

The same day that Gonzales wrote that pro-business majority opinion, the Texas Supreme Court also handed down an opinion in *Ford Motor Company v. Sheldon*—again, ruling against plaintiffs who were contending that they were having to shell out up to $2,000 each to fix paint that was peeling just eighteen to thirty-six months after they had bought new Fords (built from 1984 to 1993). As it had done with the case from Corpus Christi, the Texas Supreme Court tossed out the lower court rulings that gave the green light for the car buyers to coalesce in a class-action lawsuit. A watchdog group in Texas said that the Ford ruling, the Southwestern ruling, and one other Gonzales-supported ruling called *Intratex Gas Co. v. Beeson* were a trifecta aimed at limiting class actions and protecting big business in the Lone Star State. That group pointed out that Gonzales had said in April, "The court has said relatively little about class-action cases. We currently have an opportunity to present a much fuller picture in class action in Texas," and that now it was very easy to see what picture Gonzales wanted.

Out on the streets of Austin, Bush-haters reduced it to the nitty-gritty: Bush had declared that one of his four major food groups centered around tort reform and stamping out frivolous lawsuits—and his best friend, his *abogado,* his counselor who had helped Bush cover up his drunk driving arrest, was now doing Bush's bidding on the Texas Supreme Court.

———

Fellow Justice Craig Enoch said Gonzales could be easily summed up: "He would really think through issues and not quickly jump to conclusions. We'd be working on an opinion or some issue on a case and I'd go sit in his office to talk about it with him. There'd be no jumping to conclusions—it would be 'let's explore this, let's explore that.' Pretty soon, Alberto would say, 'This is what I think,' and it would be pretty doggone accurate."

It was surprising then when Enoch would walk into what the judges called the robing room—where the Texas Supreme Court justices would gather before they would go out on the bench to hear arguments. Between cases, Gonzales, Enoch, Nathan Hecht, and the others would retreat to the robing room to have muffins, fruit cups, breakfast tacos, or something to drink. Frequently Enoch would see Justice Tom Phillips and Justice Alberto Gonzales in squatting positions with their backs to the wall. One day Phillips had challenged everyone to a squatting contest to see who could keep their legs at 90-degree angles for the longest period of time. "I challenge anyone to do this with me," said Phillips. "I'll take that challenge," shouted Gonzales. The two men began squatting, trading victories and defeats. "You could see that little competitive flair," says Enoch.[14]

Gonzales also wrote the majority opinion in *City of Fort Worth v. Zimlich,* a case that had been watched closely by whistle-blowers and their advocates in Texas and even around the country. A dogged deputy marshal in Fort Worth named Julius Zimlich had gotten an anonymous tip and come across what he thought were tons of illegal toxins allegedly being dumped at a solid waste site owned by an influential former city councilman. Zimlich, who in the past had regularly gotten stellar reviews at work, embarked on a personal nightmare scenario in which he told supervisors what he knew, wondered why more wasn't being done and why it seemed that a heads-up had been given to the site owner. Zimlich decided to go on TV to talk about the alleged dump site. Months into the evolving mess, he found himself reassigned to what was generally considered a shitty job working the security detail at the local courthouse. The whistle-blower and his allies said he had been targeted for retribution after sticking his nose where he shouldn't have.

Ultimately, a trial court in Texas awarded Zimlich $200 for lost earnings in the past, $300,000 for lost earnings in the future, $300,000 for mental anguish, and $1.5 million for punitive damages. The City of Fort Worth asked the Texas Supreme Court to toss the whole deal out—and with Gonzales writing the opinion, it threw out most of the awards. Gonzales concluded there wasn't any malice and the facts supporting the case were thin. He wrote, "There is no evidence supporting the jury's finding that the City delayed or denied Zimlich's promotions because of his report." And he added, "We reverse the $200 award for lost past earnings and the $300,000 award for lost future earnings," and "we reverse the award of punitive damages." Again critics in Texas said that Gonzales was not just working with Big Business; now he was stepping his foot on courageous whistle-blowers and veering from the intent of the Texas Whistle-blower Act.

In other cases he wrote the majority opinion in favor of the State of Texas in a long-running land battle (*John G. and Marie Stella Kenedy Memorial Foundation v. Dewhurst, Commissioner of the General Land Office and the State of Texas*) with a powerful charitable foundation that had been bankrolled with the fortune accumulated by one of the iconic oil and ranching families in South Texas—the Kenedy family that had lent its name to the town Gonzales's father perhaps was born in—and that sought ownership of several thousand acres on the Gulf Coast. In *Pustejovsky v. Rapid American*, Gonzales also wrote the majority opinion that paved the way for a trial jury to consider the merits of a case in which a metal worker in Rockdale, Texas, claimed he had been exposed to asbestos for twenty-five years. The hang-up in the case came when the worker sued one company in 1982 for his condition and subsequently received a $25,000 out-of-court settlement. Then, as his medical condition worsened in 1994, he sought to sue three other companies, including Owens Corning. The three companies resisted the attempt, basically claiming that the statute of limitations had already run out. Gonzales ruled in favor of the metal worker. Court-watchers said it was another indication that on occasion Gonzales would take the side of the individual against industry.

That fact didn't seem to scare many conservatives in Texas. Again, Gonzales wrote opinions that were so carefully worded that he obviously seemed to be straining to make sure his words, his opinions, couldn't be used as blanket judgments over and over again in other cases—and he seemed to be erring on the side of writing in such a dispassionate, facts-only way that his words also couldn't ever be used against him for political reasons. Of course, there was one case that no matter what he wrote or how he voted, someone was bound to either be scared of him or elated with him. It was one case that divided the court like never before and would linger with him for years, perhaps for the rest of his public life.

The Texas Parental Notification Act, requiring parents to be told by a health care provider when a minor planned to have an abortion, had become a favorite for Bush and conservatives in the state. Some observers predicted things would get tricky with some of the gauzy wording in the new law, particularly the part that allowed a minor to bypass the law and make up her own mind if she was deemed mature and knowledgeable enough to decide on abortion. To bypass the law, judges had to believe the minor had some solid reasons for not wanting her parents to know about her abortion.

What would constitute maturity—what would being "knowledgeable enough" really mean? What were the standards, and what weight should be given to any possible financial, physical, and mental backlashes that the girl might face in the future . . . maybe from her parents? What would be a big enough, solid enough reason for a girl to be afforded the chance to keep her abortion secret from her parents?

Those questions got their first acid test when a pregnant seventeen-year-old in Texas went to lower courts to try to have an abortion without telling her mother and father. The high school senior, who had good grades and a part-time job, got pregnant with her college boyfriend, and it threw her life into chaos. Her parents were extremely pro-life and religious, and the high school senior wasn't even exactly sure if both her parents knew she had been having sex in the first place. The one thing she was sure of was that her parents would be vehemently opposed to her having an abortion and probably would work hard to block it. They might throw some financial roadblocks at her.

With the new law the Supreme Court had been forced down a judicial path without a map. There was simply no precedent, and the nine justices were left to try to make sense of what the Texas legislature really intended when it put together the Parental Notification Act. It was, by default, a case in which politics and personal feelings would rear their heads, and accusations of "judicial activism" would be hurled back and forth by the justices like it was the worst anathema possible. The normally collegial, back-scratching mood at the courthouse gave way to very corrosive arguments about how to define maturity—how to define when someone has a full understanding of what it means to have an abortion. For weeks the arguments continued to simmer at the Supreme Court, and Gonzales admitted that it finally turned into a full-blown "heated debate. Some members accused others of trying to impose their own personal ideology, and I wanted to reassure my colleagues that that was not going on." [15]

When the justices first got the case from a lower Texas court, they studied what other states—including Ohio, Alabama, North Carolina, Nebraska, Massachusetts, and Kansas—had done with relevant laws. Figuring out if someone was even entitled to argue that she was mature enough to have an abortion was difficult. But with Gonzales voting with the 6–3 majority, the Supreme Court agreed that the high school teenager should be allowed to go back to a lower court and argue for a bypass to the Parental Notification Act. She had a right to present a case that she knew enough about abortions and that she was now "mature enough" to have one.

When she went back to the lower court, the young woman came armed with what she thought was strong evidence that she had truly, honestly done her homework on abortion: she claimed to have consulted with high school parenting experts and Planned Parenthood, studied a video of an ultrasound scan of a fetus, talked to a woman who had an abortion, talked to a married teenaged mom, read booklets on abortion, and also said she had become very well aware of the psychological ramifications of abortion as well as adoption. She talked about not being moved by the prospect of offering her baby up for adoption: "Well, personally, I feel if I were to carry this child for nine months that I would grow emotionally attached to this child. And to give it away to another family would not feel right. . . . Plus, I don't know if it would be put in a worse lifestyle than what I could give it or if the parents would care it and love it as actually their own." [16]

The lower court judge threw her case out, she appealed again, and the entire matter went back to Gonzales and his fellow justices. Again Gonzales voted 6–3 with the majority, arguing that the law didn't say that parental rights were "absolute." He and the other majority judges essentially gave the girl and others like her that judicial bypass to the Parental Notification Law. She could have her abortion without letting her parents know. And pro-lifers were instantly stunned and bitterly angry. It wasn't anything that they expected from an all-Republican Supreme Court populated with George W. Bush appointees. Meanwhile, pro-choice advocates waded in, trying to determine which Supreme Court justices had possibly revealed their antiabortion stripes and would be the likely suspects in any future attempts to overturn abortion rights. Both sides began delving into who did what, and everyone found two easily identifiable armies at war with each other: one led by Justice Priscilla Owen and her allies and the other by Justice Alberto Gonzales.

The whispers automatically began to seep out from the courthouse into the backrooms where the political spin doctors do their business in Austin. Gonzales was either a devil or an angel: He might have helped pierce the heart of Bush's plan to monopolize the Christian conservative vote . . . but . . . he had helped make Bush seem like more of a moderate. A Texas Right to Life official said, "We were shocked that a long-term friend and conservative political ally of the Bush family would rule against a law that Bush aggressively pursued. At the time of his appointment, we did not perceive Mr. Gonzales as an abortion-rights advocate; however, we think he interpreted the law in a way that we would call judicial activism and we were very disappointed in his decision." [17] Pro-choice advocates said the real judicial activism came from the minority opinion dissenters, particularly Owen, and that their resistance to Gonzales and the other judges amounted to "posturing by radical political extremes." [18]

Reading the opinions, majority and minority, reveals an increasingly ugly schism that touched on far more than just judicial style: The opinions were so sharp they could only help to do what Bush had religiously advocated against. They would create a "perception," and that perception would mean everything. It would be explored by the media, then it would become indelible. Gonzales had always been more than careful in choosing his words in every phase of his life. It was what had brought him this far.

The dissenting opinions from Owen and her allies were so pointed, so blistering and condemning that maybe this time they shattered his iron-willed reticence. One of Owen's allies on the bench wrote that Gonzales, along with his like-minded justices, "refuses to listen to all reason" and that the majority opinion was an insult "to the office they hold."

Justice Nathan Hecht concluded that "the only plausible explanation" was that Gonzales and the others had "resolved to impair" the original purposes behind the Parental Notification Act, "which were to reduce teenage abortions." Owen added that the decisions by Gonzales and the others "raise disturbing questions" and that the majority group has "acted irresponsibly in this case" and "has disregarded the law."

Gonzales didn't take the insults lightly or idly. He struck directly back with this concurring opinion in which he flatly stated that there might have been some "unconscionable" judicial activists at work on the bench: "To construe the Parental Notification Act so narrowly as to eliminate bypasses, or to create hurdles that simply are not to be found in the words of the statute, would be an unconscionable act of judicial activism. As a judge, I hold the rights of parents to protect and guide the education, safety, health, and development of their children as one of the most impor-tant rights in our society. But I cannot rewrite the statute to make parental rights absolute."

He didn't stop there: "It is my obligation as a judge to impartially apply the laws of this state without imposing my moral view on the decisions of the Legislature. Justice Hecht charges that our decision demonstrates the Court's determination to construe the Parental Notification Act as the Court believes the Act should be construed and not as the Legislature in-tended. I respectfully disagree. This decision demonstrates the Court's de-termination to see to it that we discharge our responsibilities as judges, and that personal ideology is subordinated to the public will."

In the end Gonzales had railed against what some said were the pro-life "judicial activists" on the bench. And in the end it was one of those moments that he had rued, one of those moments when fate and circum-stance had conspired to force him to publicly offer some thoughts on an issue that he had intense personal feelings about. This was the part he hated, having to go public, to reveal any bit of his soul. This was why he didn't write very many internal memos, didn't write very many personal letters, even refused to send e-mails. He had been trained to believe that his clients—the military, Enron, real estate giants, George W. Bush—were paying him for his discretion. Now he had gone public, perhaps in a way that he would later regret. Maybe he had risen to the chum thrown in the water by his angry colleagues on the bench. He revealed something else in his counteropinion ostensibly aimed at the pro-life justices on the bench: "The results of the court's decision here may be personally troubling to me as a parent, [but] it is my obligation as a judge to impartially apply the laws of the state."

That one line was ironically seized upon by pro-choice advocates as a sure sign that Gonzales was actually pro-life—that he was clearly saying he was personally against abortion and that he might actually be a justice to ultimately worry about in the future. Even though he had sided with the teenager who wanted to have an abortion without telling her parents, "personally troubling" could be read to mean that he wouldn't just be worried about his child secretly having an abortion but that he was personally against the whole notion of abortion in the first place and that it was only a matter of time before Bush convinced Gonzales to rule against pro-choice laws.

Gonzales, so careful throughout his life, had dropped two bombs in his opinion in the by-now infamous Texas abortion case. On the one hand he scorched his almost obviously pro-life colleagues on the bench as "unconscionable." On the other hand he said he was "personally" troubled in a case about abortion rights. Which one was it? Where was Gonzales coming from? "I wasn't implying anything," he said several months later. "My moral views on these issues are immaterial."[19] He added, "While I may seem to be neutral, I have very strong convictions about issues. But as a judge, I think it would be inappropriate to apply them."[20]

His behavior in the abortion case led someone to say that his two years on the Supreme Court showed that he "served like a pro-business conservative but not like a wacky social conservative."[21] He had occasionally defended the little guy—in one case he said the state transportation agency couldn't hide behind immunity in a car crash and was liable to being sued. But for sure the abortion case was the defining moment during his tenure as a Texas Supreme Court justice, if only because it led to conflicting perceptions about him that rightly or wrongly would roar to life and hover over him for years.

Bush had told him about it. Bush had a habit of warning all the newbies—all the political newcomers into his orbit—that they would live and die by perceptions. Bush also had another pet phrase that his father had shared with him. He said that people in politics, in high-profile political settings, were like "corks in a raging river," and the river was really a rushing body of perceptions that could carry you forward or take you under. As both Owen and Gonzales moved from the Texas Supreme Court, their battle over the Texas teenager would be constantly referenced and mulled over.

In March 2001, months after considering that abortion case in Texas, Gonzales added this: "My own personal feelings about abortion don't matter. . . . The question is, what is the law, what is the precedent, what is binding in rendering your decision. Sometimes, interpreting a statute, you may have to uphold a statute that you may find personally offensive. But as a judge, that's your job." [22]

One spring weekend Gonzales took a rafting trip with twenty other people, mostly state officials, through the spectacular Big Bend area in far West Texas. Gonzales took his turn setting up camp, steering the rafts. Democratic Texas State Representative Pete Gallego had had some early run-ins with Gonzales, especially about whether the state and the federal government should share jurisdiction over the Big Bend area. Gallego thought that Gonzales was too fastidious, too reluctant to move forward quickly. They locked horns but eventually got to know each other better and count each other as good friends. Gallego watched Gonzales pitching camp, rafting in his T-shirt and cutoffs, as the state officials pushed down the Rio Grande. "Al's not an easy person to get to know for people who are effusive and outgoing. I thought he was shy when I first met him, but he's just very reserved, and he doesn't allow much up front. So it was just awkward for a while, until we got to know each other. Al's a difficult guy to get to know, he really is. He's kind of sparing in his conversation sometimes. When you first meet him, you don't know if he can smile or not." [23]

Some observers said Alberto Gonzales simply sent out mixed messages—that it was impossible to tell what his convictions were. He had grown up in a large Catholic family, and the betting money among friends was that Gonzales was probably just as vehemently antiabortion as Hecht and Owen—but that his personal preference for discretion had led him to put a tight seal on his abortion beliefs and to send that set of jumbled signals from the bench.

The end result was that the evangelical Christian supporters of George W. Bush—and anyone else who demanded an ideological purity in every member of Bush's team—had begun to decide that Gonzales was indeed hard to read. He certainly didn't fly the pro-life flag as clearly as some wanted. But some said he was being faulted for being independent, that he was being unfairly expected to move in lockstep with conservatives, Hispanics, Republicans, moderates, whomever. Attorney David Keltner thought Gonzales ruled the way that U.S. Supreme Court Justice Byron White did. "He was his own man and was deeply respected by everyone on the court. That's Al Gonzales; he's very much his own man. I never saw him bend to pressure." [24] One time Gonzales called up Keltner and said, "What I've found is there's no future in bending to pressure. I've seen others do it, and once you bend, you keep bending." [25]

One thing was clear: The abortion issue really did drive a wedge in the Texas Supreme Court that few people, Gonzales included, had seen in recent memory. It persisted even as Gonzales turned to yet another avenue he had never explored: raising campaign money for the fall reelections to the Supreme Court. The justices grudgingly resumed their work, buried the accusations, and set back to hearing more cases and raising money for their various campaigns. They were all Republicans and they'd all be helping each other at the usual parties, fundraisers, and golf matches around the state.

At the time, Justice Hecht was dating Harriet Miers in Dallas, and Miers was still insisting that despite the schism over abortion, Gonzales was a loyal friend to George W. Bush. The abortion war on the Supreme Court bench was hopefully a snafu, an aberration, caused by a truly imprecise law. Miers told anyone who would listen that Gonzales was truly a deep social conservative and that he shared the same principles and beliefs as Bush.

But it almost appeared that Gonzales was looking back at his decision months later and wondering what it meant for his career—and maybe any chance that he would go all the way to the U.S. Supreme Court. He would tell a *Washington Post* reporter that he had never discussed his view of abortion with Bush, adding that he also believed in *stare decisis,* the legal principle of strictly adhering to established legal precendent when it came to the famous *Roe v. Wade* decision that legalized abortion. Gonzales told the *Post* that *Roe v. Wade* was the law and should be enforced: "You need to be careful about disregarding precedent. There are dangers in doing that," said Gonzales.[26]

At least one Texas justice didn't need to be reminded that Gonzales, even after the conflicting signals on the abortion case, was still solidly in George W. Bush's corner. "I knew about his loyalty and his real fondness for President Bush," says Enoch, who voted with Gonzales on the abortion case.[27] Meanwhile, Hecht, his bench foe on the abortion case, abruptly found himself traveling Texas with Gonzales, and it was a bonding, healing experience as they hit the road to go campaigning to keep their seats: "He is very thoughtful, deliberate, and unflappable. In campaigning around the state together, he was very cordial," offered Hecht in the fall of 2005.[28]

Critics in Texas have yelped about the fact that Supreme Court seats are up for election and that the judiciary is tainted by the stink of fund-raising and campaigning. For Gonzales it was more than odious; it was like chewing glass, and it was one more unexpected twist in the ongoing education of Alberto Gonzales. He hated the idea of having to campaign, to grip and grip, to shake the money tree in Texas. His friends on the bench wondered how someone as careful as Gonzales would do on the road in front of strangers he was supposed to be glad to see. The judges who had been on the bench for a few years knew about campaigning, how it was a bit like coming down from the ivory tower and having to hit the streets and get your hands into the oil and grease of the political machinery. Gonzales's wife knew he hated the whole idea: "He didn't want to know who gave him the money. His campaign staff would come up to him at a reception and say, 'Be nice to so-and-so, he gave a check,' and he'd say, 'I'm going to be nice to everyone.' He hates the money part of it; he hated the idea of judges having to raise money. It sickens him."[29]

As repulsive as it might have been, he raised unusually large sums of money. The watchdog group Texans for Public Justice says that from January 1999 through December 2000, the length of Gonzales's time on the Texas Supreme Court, he received $843,680 in contributions—a very high figure for a race in which he had no Democratic opposition. The bulk of it—$400,527—came from lawyers and lobbyists. The next largest amount, $102,738, came from the contributors affiliated with the energy and natural resources sector. Enron gave Gonzales $6,500, Vinson & Elkins gave him $28,950, the billionaire Bass family from Fort Worth gave him $27,500, and the group Texans for Lawsuit Reform—which was part of the Republican-driven drive to shut down the big-dollar plaintiff's award and personal injury claims—gave him $25,000.

The other high-powered law firms in Texas were contributors: Baker & Botts, Hughes & Luce, Fulbright & Jaworski, Haynes & Boone. Bracewell & Patterson, where his friend Patrick Oxford worked, and various industry groups like the Texas Automobile Dealers Association, Perry Homes, and the Texas Medical Association gave him money. As he steamed toward the Republican primary and election, he was accumulating a bulging war chest. And he was being scrutinized and eventually assailed by groups in Texas and around the country that believed he was inappropriately accepting money from people and companies like Halliburton that were tied to matters before the Supreme Court—and from industry organizations and lobbyists who had a vested interest in tamping down personal injury lawsuits and consumer complaints. At best, those groups said, Gonzales should have declined the contributions to avoid the appearance of a conflict of interest.

One case involved an allegation that he received $2,000 from Texas Farm Bureau Mutual Insurance after the Texas Supreme Court had heard arguments in which a man injured in a car wreck was seeking a higher settlement than the insurer was willing to pay. Gonzales accepted $2,500 before oral arguments from a law firm representing an insurance company that was embroiled in another case in which a plaintiff was seeking a settlement. A detailed piece by Miles Moffeit and Dianna Hunt in the *Fort Worth Star-Telegram* would outline how Gonzales, Hecht, and Owen received campaign contributions from energy giant Halliburton.[30]

In 2000 Gonzales told a reporter that money didn't influence the way he ruled from the bench: "In the whole scheme of things, $2,000 isn't going to have any kind of influence on me."[31] Years later Gonzales would write to the Senate Judiciary Committee that he had done nothing wrong in terms of accepting campaign contributions in Texas: "My contributors, as well as of those of every other justice, are a matter of public record. I am confident that during my service as a justice on the Supreme Court of Texas, I complied with all legal and ethical requirements regarding acceptance of campaign contributions." [32]

One night at an Austin campaign party, Gonzales mingled with high-dollar, high-powered lawyers, lobbyists, and judges who had been invited to show some support and maybe share some cash. Texas attorney Douglas Alexander had argued the Zimlich whistle-blower case before the Texas Supreme Court, the one Gonzales essentially reversed. Now he stood next to Gonzales at Gonzales's party and listened to him say that Bush had insisted he had to "go out, get his name out there."

Gonzales added that Bush had made it clear that if he didn't get "out there," he would "come up short."

Someone else at the party, a Democratic Texas judge who had been swept out of office by the powerful Bush bandwagon, stared at Gonzales and simply said, "The system doesn't work."

Gonzales got a puzzled look on his face, then tried to steer the topic elsewhere. "It was interesting to me to see [how Gonzales reacted]," says Alexander. "The thing I clearly gathered was that Gonzales is really loyal to Bush." [33]

Away from the campaigning, Gonzales would visit with a handful of old Hispanic friends, including Houston attorney Roland Garcia and former Supreme Court justice Raul Gonzalez. Their families had mingled over the years. In Houston they all went to a comedy club one night. Gonzales and Gonzalez traveled to see the Round Rock Express, the minor-league baseball team owned by the family of Nolan Ryan—one of George W. Bush's heroes.

Gonzales's friends congratulated him when he was named the 1999 Latino Lawyer of the Year by the Hispanic National Bar Association. But former Supreme Court justice Raul Gonzalez, who had first met him in the mid-1980s, decided his friend was still "very difficult to read because he plays everything close to the vest." When Gonzalez checked in with his old sources at the courthouse, he heard that Alberto Gonzales hadn't said much in the Supreme Court conferences, hadn't been one to hold the floor, to go on a stream of consciousness observation. Gonzalez decided that he was sure of one thing: "Al's good fortune was that he met the president [George W. Bush] early on, before he was president and before he was governor. Apparently they had good chemistry and good karma between them."[34]

Alexander, who had argued before Gonzales on the Supreme Court and had stood next to him in social settings, also simply knew that Gonzales was forever tied to Bush. "His rise has been . . . meteoric is not at all too strong a word," says Alexander, reflecting back on Gonzales's career arc. "He has been tapped by Bush. He's been kind of amazed himself at how quickly he's risen. He knows it is because of Bush."

As the buildup to the November presidential election marched on, the national media began writing about exactly who Bush would name to any Supreme Court vacancies in case he won. Articles in publications like *USA Today* began to mention that Bush was likely to pick a Hispanic; maybe he would be tempted to roll the dice with someone like a relatively inexperienced justice such as Alberto Gonzales from the Texas Supreme Court. Hispanic leaders around the country also began the pre-presidential speculation, and several simply said their support of Bush was predicated on a firm understanding that he would be naming the first Latino to the U.S. Supreme Court if he got elected.

At the 2000 GOP Convention in Philadelphia, Gonzales and his wife were given seats right behind the former president Bush and the former first lady Barbara Bush. Gonzales, running his campaign in Texas under the watchful eye of Karl Rove and his assistant Libby Camp, hadn't really had time to barnstorm for Bush.

Of course, that year Gonzales went on to best his Republican primary opponent and then the sacrificial lamb Libertarian in the general election. Critics were still beating up on him, saying that right up until the last minute he was taking money from groups like the Texans for Lawsuit Reform, even though he had only paper-thin political opposition. People wondered why he had worked so hard to raise money that he really didn't need. Some said it had everything to do with his innate insecurity that voters in Texas might still not be inclined to send someone with a Latino name to a high statewide office. Even with Bush's endorsement—and even with his time as a justice, as secretary of state, as a State Bar board member and a Vinson & Elkins partner—Gonzales might still be facing the reality of lingering, hidden biases.

"He accumulated something like $850,000 in campaign contributions, and he did not have a Democratic opponent. In those days that was absolutely a huge amount to get in a primary, in a Republican fight. The story I got was that, I believe, it was that a person with a Hispanic name would have trouble winning in a Republican primary. So he had to raise a lot of money ... overwhelmingly from business interests and defense firms. That was a huge war chest," says Tony Champagne, a Texas Supreme Court expert at the University of Texas at Dallas.

Intrigued by the amount of money Gonzales had whipped together, Champagne asked one of Gonzales's big donors why he had written Gonzales a check: "A Hispanic couldn't win without major backing," was the reply.

"It was interesting," says Champagne. "In those days he was 'Al' Gonzales and not 'Alberto' Gonzales." [35] Gonzales had muted his Hispanic heritage a bit and worked overtime to raise money to combat biases against Hispanics. One friend of Gonzales's once stood outside the doors to the Texas Supreme Court on a brisk December day and said it was the exact reason why Gonzales no longer spoke Spanish.

There was another question running through Texas—another question about why he would raise so much money, do things that he hated doing: Why was Gonzales running so hard when anywhere that George W. Bush went, Gonzales was surely going along for the ride? As the country tumbled into the seemingly never-ending trauma of the unsettled 2000 presidential election—an election that featured the last-minute national revelations that George W. Bush had a drunk driving arrest on his criminal record—the political bookies in Austin were taking bets on who would go to Washington with Bush in case he was given the White House.

Alberto Gonzales was on everybody's short list. He and Bush had been inseparable for the last five years. Bush had trusted Gonzales with embarrassing criminal secrets. Bush had plucked him from corporate anonymity and made him general counsel, secretary of state, and a Supreme Court justice. Too much time had been invested by Bush in packaging Alberto Gonzales to leave him behind in Texas—and by now Gonzales owed George W. Bush too much to leave his side and avoid the Sturm und Drang inside the DC beltway.

After the election, when Bush had been awarded the White House by the U.S. Supreme Court, Texas attorney David Keltner ran into Gonzales and told him he had seen the future: "Al, here, I've got your career planned out," said Keltner, outlining a plan that had Gonzales being appointed to a federal judgeship by newly minted President Bush, and then after some seasoning, being appointed to the U.S. Supreme Court.

Gonzales looked back at his friend. "You know it's not going to happen like that. You need to know George Bush better. That's not how it works," said Gonzales, who had just won his own election to the Texas Supreme Court. "I'm going to stay with this job."

Not long afterward, at a December birthday party in Austin for Karl Rove, friends of Gonzales watched him mingle with all the other insiders from the Bush political machine. Bush had finally been declared the presidential winner, and most of the partygoers were still buzzing with the raw, combative energy left over from the edgy days and nights spent in political limbo. Now they were jockeying, angling, and wondering who would be going north, who would be part of Bush's powerful inner circle in Washington. Bush had an air of chinny defiance as he strutted from one room in the house to another, from one friend to another. Suddenly he spotted Gonzales. Bush steered him outside onto the driveway.

The kingmakers, rainmakers, and insider baseball players looked up and watched through the windows as Bush and Gonzales huddled in the cold weather outdoors. One of the onlookers remembered thinking that it was Alberto Gonzales, more than anyone else, whom Bush wanted to talk to. More than Karl Rove, Karen Hughes, and anyone else who was there that night. In the last month the media had dragged Bush through the thorns for hiding his drunk driving arrest, and the articles suggested there was legal skullduggery done by blindly loyal Alberto Gonzales. Their secret was unveiled. The depth of the attorney–client relationship was revealed. Bush, who treasured loyalty above all else, saw that his *abogado* had not, as Gonzales once said about himself, yielded to the pressure . . . he had not bent.

One time, years ago, Bush and his younger brothers had created a militaristic litmus test of that loyalty. *"Are you willing to throw yourself on the grenade for the Bush family?"* is how George W. Bush framed it.

Gonzales said he just had three questions for Bush before he would shake his hand and agree to come to Washington: *"Will we have the same kind of relationship? Will I still be able to walk in and give you advice? Will I have to go through anyone else?"*

Bush told Gonzales the same thing he had said when he wanted Gonzales to be secretary of state in Texas: Gonzales was a good man; he was part of the inner circle. He wanted Gonzales to be the president's counselor.

TEN

At Their Peril

B ush, with a slight smile on his face, glanced for a second at his *abogado,* then announced that Alberto Gonzales was going to be the new White House counsel. It was December 17, 2000, at the governor's mansion in Austin. The old plantation-style mansion was decorated with wreaths and boughs, and it smelled like cedar and melted candle wax. Aides bustled across the well-worn hardwood floors. That same day he announced that Condoleezza Rice would be the national security czar and Karen Hughes would serve as a special adviser to the president. Bush was rocking on his heels, bobbing up and down in an antsy way. He nodded at Gonzales:

"I'm proud to announce that Al Gonzales, Supreme Court justice of Texas, has agreed to become my White House counsel. I understand how important it is to have a person who I can trust and whose judgment I trust to serve as the White House counsel. I know firsthand I can trust Al's judgment, because he was my first counsel as governor," said Bush. *"Al is a distinguished lawyer. Al is a man who has only one standard in mind when it comes to ethics, and that is the highest of standards. So I'm honored you're back with me, Counselor. Look forward to working together."*

Gonzales stepped forward and said in his soft, low voice:

"Mr. President-elect, this is the fourth time in six years that I've had the op-

portunity to say thank you—thank you for giving me another opportunity to serve. I have the great privilege currently of serving on the Texas Supreme Court, and it's been a tremendous honor to serve the citizens of Texas and to work with this particular group of justices. But working with the president-elect for three years as his general counsel gave me the opportunity to get to know the type of man that he is; how he makes decisions, what kind of information is important to him in making those kinds of decisions. And in him I saw a man of unparalleled integrity and judgment and, quite frankly, Mr. President-elect, I could not pass up the opportunity to come serve with you again, and I am very grateful."

A reporter had a question for Bush: *"Mr. President elect, in the last two days you have appointed two women, two African-Americans, a Hispanic-American. Aside from the fact that these are incredibly competent, qualified people, is there another message that you're sending to America with these first choices?"*

Bush replied: *"You bet. That people who work hard and make the right decisions in life can achieve anything they want in America. And I think of my friend Al Gonzales, who is a great lawyer, but his background is such a compelling story. And let me first say that he wouldn't be standing here if I knew he couldn't do the job. But he's a guy who grew up in a two-bedroom house; his mother and daddy working, you know, as hard as they possibly can to bring up—six brothers and sisters?"*

Gonzales chimed in: *"I have seven siblings."*

Bush continued: *"Seven siblings. Eight in the family. And now he's going to be sitting at the right hand of the president of the United States. To me, these appointments—and each—each person has got their own story that is so unique, stories that really explain what America can and should be about. And so I welcome them. I can't tell you how good of folks they are, not only in terms of the jobs they'll have, but just in the quality of character."* [1]

Four times Gonzales had thanked Bush—first, for hiring him as general counsel to the governor of Texas; second, for his job as secretary of state; third, for his appointment to the Texas Supreme Court; fourth, for his new post as White House counsel. Now his newest job for Bush was obviously going to be more acutely political than anything before. His friends in Texas wondered what exactly was making Alberto Gonzales run so hard. "I thought he was comfortable on the court in Texas. You've never seen Al in outright politics. . . . I think he does better when it is not political. I think he's more comfortable when it's not," says attorney David Keltner. He remembered one moment after Gonzales had finished speaking at a continuing legal education panel in Texas. It was a high-powered gig with top-dollar lawyers and heavyweight judges filling up the room. People stood in line to meet Gonzales. Some of the legal wonks congratulated Gonzales on various opinions he had handed down while he was on the Texas Supreme Court. Gonzales shook their hands and replied, "Well, I very much appreciate that. I thought it was the right thing to do."

Keltner heard several other judges standing nearby, hearing the same compliments from lawyers, and how they were boasting about the way they came to their decisions, the legal precedents they had relied on, how they agonized over their cases. And he compared it to what Gonzales was saying. He decided that Gonzales was fairly unflappable, that he didn't linger or worry about things too much. "I think Al sleeps very well at night," thought Keltner.[2]

Gonzales once said essentially the same thing about himself. He had developed a style that excluded melancholy at the workplace—and perhaps on the long drive home from work. In the same way that he rarely revisited his upbringing, friends said he rarely second-guessed or regretted any policy decisions, like prisoner executions, he had weighed in on.

"I think you have to have a sort of maturity and a faith in knowing that you've done the very best you can, and at the end of the day you move on, comfortable in the knowledge that you've done your best," Gonzales said about himself.[3] By the time he was packing and planning to relocate his family from the hills of west Austin to the wooded area around Vienna, Virginia, he had learned how to push on. It was something else he had in common with Bush. People close to both men said that neither wallowed in recriminations, that neither sensed any benefit from ambiguity.

Unlike Bush, Gonzales had the benefit of enormous juxtapositions throughout his life: he grew up poor, then became wealthy; he lived in humid Humble, then served his country near the Arctic Circle; he did legal work for huge corporate clients, then spent hours deliberating from the bench; he was married, then divorced; he grew up devoted to a father who then died at an early age. Gonzales might have had more reasons to suspect that life is less defined by black-and-white colors than by enormous gray zones. Gonzales might have had more reasons than Bush to think that life could be routinely ambiguous, not easily boxed in to definitive answers and solutions.

And in Texas several of Gonzales's friends wondered how easy he really would sleep in Washington. He had sacrificed several times to go to work for the Bush family. He had altered the course of his career, and his critics said he had also willingly corrupted his once-innocent love of the law in ambitious, blind loyalty to the family who was promoting him.

One day when he was still at the Supreme Court in Texas, he ran into a friend, and they talked about Gonzales's new job in Washington. The friend said he was worried that Bush was already revealing a more intense ideological, ultra-conservative bent—different perhaps than what Bush had been promising during his campaign as a "compassionate conservative." Gonzales's friend feared that Bush would be repaying too many favors to the far right. Gonzales said not to worry: "I'm a moderate, and I believe the governor is a moderate." [4]

Obviously Bush was positioning Gonzales as some sort of unassailable, ethical contrast to the Clinton White House. By introducing Gonzales and saying he had "only one standard when it comes to ethics," Bush was taking a blow at the Clinton administration and giving a bit of an early inoculation against anyone in Washington who was preparing to dig more deeply into Gonzales's role in crafting those fifty-seven memos for the doomed convicts in Texas, raising close to a million dollars so that he could be elected a judge, and working with the law firm that was the quintessential Big Oil outfit in Texas.

Bush obviously knew what Gonzales would face, but Bush also told friends that he thought Gonzales would be better able to handle life in the fish bowl than just about any other Texan who Bush was going to bring with him. After watching Gonzales deal with high and low matters—figuring out if there was any legal way Bush's daughters could go swimming at a country club, figuring out why Bush should be excused from jury duty in a drunk driving case, figuring out what to write in a death penalty memo—Bush knew that Gonzales would do exactly what all of his best friends agreed he would do: he had no ambitions other than to protect and serve his client.

Gonzales hadn't exactly forgotten his old clients, the ones from his days as a freshly minted lawyer trained at Harvard Law and vaulted to a power office with Vinson & Elkins. The night before Bush was sworn in as president, Vinson & Elkins hosted a DC dinner party for Gonzales—their man who was going to the White House. V&E had contributed a little over $200,000 to Bush, and the firm was almost electric at the fact that one of its alumni was the White House general counsel—the first Hispanic to ever hold that position.

On inauguration day V&E invited fourteen hundred people to attend their "parade-viewing party from its Pennsylvania Avenue office suite in the elegant Willard Hotel, just two blocks from the White House," and to enjoy some "Vinson & Elkins inaugural barbecue sauce, bottled especially for the occasion."[5] A spokesman for Vinson & Elkins said the firm was more than entitled to some celebrating. "I don't see anything unsavory about celebrating the transfer of power," said V&E's Joe Householder. "We have a lot of people who are involved in government work, and this is a way to celebrate what we do in this country. And that's what we are doing."[6]

In early January Gonzales had set up shop in the Bush–Cheney transition headquarters in a bare-bones second-floor office. He was going to be paid $140,000 a year. Pending approval, there were three prominent Hispanics named by Bush: Linda Chavez as secretary of labor, Mel Martinez as secretary of Housing and Urban Development, Gonzales as White House counsel. Gonzales thought about how he might really be better off if he knew the ropes in DC: "All things being equal, it would probably be helpful. I would probably be able to avoid some of the mistakes I will probably make. But it's not necessary, if you surround yourself with good talent."[7]

Gonzales had already embarked on a series of meetings and calls with old Reagan, Nixon, and Bush hands, seeking the advice, and most important, the names of possible assistant counsels, from the seasoned GOP lawyers who had worked in previous administrations. Above all others, he conferred with C. Boyden Gray, who had essentially been George Herbert Walker Bush's counsel from 1981 to 1993, an extraordinarily long tenure in the hot seat during Bush's vice presidential and presidential years.

Gonzales also conferred with other eminences from the GOP legal firmament, especially Fred Fielding, who worked as an associate counsel to Nixon, served under John Dean (the Nixon counsel who became infamous for his role in the Watergate scandal), then became Reagan's counsel for five years in the mid-1980s. Fielding was so deep inside the political maze, such an insider, that betting money had him being the "Deep Throat" source for the *Washington Post* stories that unraveled the Watergate fiasco (years later it was revealed that former FBI official W. Mark Felt was actually "Deep Throat"). Gonzales, too, spent time talking to A. B. Culvahouse, who also served as counsel to Reagan and helped to steer Reagan through the Iran-Contra—"Irangate"—scandal and the accusations that the United States was selling arms to Iran, then using the money to fund a secret war in Nicaragua.

As he sat in his transitional office, still waiting to find out where he would be sitting in the White House, Gonzales sifted through recommendations on who should be on his general counsel team. He had already asked Stuart Bowen, the deputy counsel in Texas who had helped craft several of those death row clemency memos, to join his staff in Washington and help him pick a round table of assistant White House counsels. Gonzales had called Bowen and offered him the job the same day that Bush had offered the White House counsel job to Gonzales.

Gonzales could have brought more Texans, but in the end he only chose Bowen. The Bush team had dispatched Bowen to help the Bush/Cheney recount team in Florida during the postelection wrangling. Bowen had mingled with and assessed all the other front-line lawyers that the GOP had dispatched to fight for Bush in Florida. Bowen had come up with a list of names for Gonzales. And meanwhile Gonzales also mysteriously told people that "someone who knows someone who knows someone" had recommended other names to him.[8]

Ultimately Gonzales was looking at a crew that would be squarely in that neoconservative world of true believers, men and women who had been cheered and invigorated as much by Bush's victory as by the fact that Bill Clinton and his team were being chased from Washington. In the legal wing of things—particularly inside the Federalist Society, the organization founded in the early 1980s to promote a conservative legal philosophy and to monitor what it considered to be debilitating trends to actively interpret the Constitution as opposed to simply applying it—people were wildly enthused when word hit the street about who Gonzales had been summoning for interviews.

Antonin Scalia, Robert Bork, Clarence Thomas, and Gray were all members of the influential Federalist Society, a haven for conservative intellectual firepower, and Gonzales would unknowingly begin tapping a number of younger, energetic lawyers who also had ties to the society. Some gushing news accounts would eventually call it a "Dream Team" of young, passionate, conservative minds. Other accounts said it was like a "Republican Camelot" and that Gonzales had succeeded in assembling "one of the best law firms in Washington."

Critics wondered if Gonzales had packed his staff with zealots, ideologues, with Hard Right foot soldiers—with thirty-something lawyers who were going to move wickedly and fast to give Bush the legal license to completely, conservatively revamp the nation's judicial system and to give him the legal freedom to do whatever the hell else he wanted to do to promote a truly conservative domestic agenda. At the end of January there was a prescient account by Dana Milbank in the *Washington Post* that foreshadowed the ultimate might and influence of the elite, hungry team that Gonzales had decided to surround himself with. The story seemed to intimate that the people working for Gonzales were so plugged in and so driven that they would have an unusually enormous role in shaping every legal opinion that would leave Gonzales's desk. That article left a sense that these hired hands were like zealous knights bound by some sense of a common cause: there was a clear understanding that many of them had worked for the men who battled and toppled the Clinton administration or had worked for the justices who awarded Bush the presidency, and now they had been empowered with their carpe diem moment, with their chance to seize the day and advance their cause.[9]

Among Gonzales's first hires were Brett Kavanaugh, a Federalist Society member, a senior deputy to Kenneth Starr, and coauthor of the famous Starr Report that examined allegations against Clinton; Bradford Berenson, a Federalist Society member who clerked for Supreme Court Justice Anthony Kennedy and served as a consultant for the Independent Counsel investigation into former Clinton cabinet member Henry Cisneros's extramarital affair; Christopher Bartolomucci, who had served as an associate special counsel to the Senate Whitewater Committee; Courtney Elwood, who had clerked for Supreme Court Justice William Rehnquist and Judge J. Michael Luttig of the U.S. Court of Appeals Fourth Circuit; Noel Francisco, a Federalist Society member who clerked for Antonin Scalia and had gone to Florida to help with the presidential recount litigation; Helgi Walker, who had clerked for Justice Clarence Thomas, served on the Bush squad in Florida, and worked for Senator Strom Thurmond; Rachel Brand, who worked for a law firm, Cooper, Carvin & Rosenthal, which had been described in one news account as having a "well-known conservative ideology." [10]

At the recommendation of members of the previous Bush White House, Gonzales settled on Timothy Flanigan as his deputy counsel. Flanigan, a Mormon and a father of fourteen children, had been a clerk for Chief Justice Warren Burger (a report in the *Chicago Tribune* said he had been paid $800,000 by the Federalist Society to serve as a consultant and write a biography of Burger). His fealty to the Bush family was underscored by the fact that he had served the elder George Bush as head of the Justice Department's Office of Legal Counsel and that he reportedly was once involved in discussions with C. Boyden Gray about whether it was appropriate to tap into Bill Clinton's classified passport records during the 1992 presidential campaign. Flanigan had also been picked to be a key member of the GOP and Bush legal team that descended on Florida to stop the recount of votes and also battle for that state's electoral votes in the bruising conclusion to the 2000 presidential race. In Florida he had met Gonzales's aide, Stuart Bowen, and after the legal mess in Florida was wrapped up, Bowen called Flanigan and asked him if he wanted to interview for a new job as Gonzales's deputy in DC.

Flanigan, like the others, first met Gonzales in the Bush-Cheney transition offices. Disconcertingly Gonzales left the TV news on during the interview. Flanigan thought that Gonzales was very, very careful. A little hesitant. Maybe a little worried about his new role. Still, Flanigan told his wife that Gonzales was someone he could respect and work for. Later that evening there was a phone call from Gonzales offering Flanigan the job as deputy counsel to the president of the United States.

Flanigan knew that Gonzales wanted experienced DC insiders, and he knew that the muscled-up legal community in DC considered Gonzales an outsider: "I think people viewed him, people like the Republican legal establishment—those who had been in positions in past Republican administrations having to do with the law—viewed him as a Texas outsider." [11]

Washington-watchers, especially ardent conservatives, wondered where Gonzales would take the White House counsel's office—and where the young Turks on his staff would take him. Word had already filtered out of Texas that Gonzales could be a moderate and that his decision in the abortion case in Texas had angered the pro-life community. Too, word had already gurgled up that Attorney General John Ashcroft was willing to go to war with Gonzales over who would steer the ship when it came to filling dozens of federal court vacancies around the country. Unspoken by some in Washington was the fear that Gonzales had probably benefited from affirmative action and might be predisposed to look favorably on establishing quotas for minorities. He was simply an unknown quantity for many Beltway insiders, and he moved hard to ameliorate any fears by stocking his staff with true-blood conservative lawyers who had cut their teeth on some of the most intense, high-profile investigations into Bill Clinton, Hillary Clinton, Henry Cisneros, and the Clinton/Gore political machinery in Florida.

Gonzales, born in Kenneth Starr's hometown of San Antonio, had essentially surrounded himself with an intense conservative firewall. With the way he was stacking his staff, insiders said it was only a matter of time before Gonzales's team revealed its full stripes as a feisty, aggressive, neoconservative army that would take an activist approach to shaping Bush's judicial appointments, ethical standards, speeches, and legislation—and one that would simply move out ahead of Attorney General John Ashcroft and the Justice Department's Office of Legal Counsel, the other body that provides the president with legal advice. Gonzales carefully and quickly announced that he didn't plan to run a legal fiefdom from his office and that he was going to work closely with freshly minted Ashcroft and the Office of Legal Counsel, which had been somewhat overshadowed during the Clinton administration's last days.

But insiders in Washington had a hunch that the combustible Ashcroft was already moving to control the playing field, moving to make his wing the powerful legal center of the Bush administration, especially when it came to the closely watched job of picking judicial nominees around the country. That job, the judicial selection process, was considered a huge prize for conservative leaders; it was a way to dig deep across America, to really light a fire under the conservative revolution by putting authentic conservatives on courts from coast to coast.

Gonzales was already talking like he had assembled a tough posse, a machine that was going to go to war for Bush. He knew that the people who had been brought to his attention by Gray and others were already tested veterans who had put the screws to Al Gore's campaign, had come hard for Bill Clinton's White House, and lent their muscle to Kenneth Starr's investigations. Gonzales liked his warriors, and he talked about them as if they were part of a battalion: "If we get into a fight, I need someone who can go into battle with me, and protect this president and protect this White House. That's my job." [12]

The White House counsels who worked for Clinton said the fact that Gonzales had chosen so many Federalist Society lawyers who had once worked for Scalia, Thomas, Starr, and the team that fought to squash Al Gore's election was really more like a partisan Mafia hit team being put together: "It looks like it's very partisan," said Abner Mikva, one of Clinton's counsels. "The White House counsel's not supposed to be a consigliere for some don on the way to war." [13]

Gonzales practically laughed: "I think, generally, this group has beliefs that are fairly consistent with the president's." [14]

But Gonzales also unsubtly let everyone in Washington know that even though he didn't have years of experience in DC and didn't have the persona of a John Ashcroft, he had something even more valuable. He had the ear and the consummate trust of George W. Bush: "Most often, when I have given him legal advice, he has followed that advice," said Gonzales in what was for him a surprisingly cocky moment. "I will be the person in the White House every day. I will be at his side. The attorney general is in another building, running another agency." [15]

Gonzales added one more thing: "What he is asking me to provide is legal advice. He has plenty of advisers who can give him the political landscape. . . . My objective is to be the president's lawyer. My job is to make sure we don't make the same mistakes made by previous administrations." [16]

Culvahouse, one of the veteran Washington insiders, said that everyone understood the new rules. Everyone knew that Gonzales was part of Bush's inner circle and was not to be crossed or undermined: "He has the kind of relationship with the president that people know they are going to have to go around him at their peril." [17]

And it was that relationship that really mattered more than experience. In fact, experience really didn't matter at all as long as Gonzales was surrounding himself with the right people, thought C. Boyden Gray. Gonzales could learn on the fly, and he was going to be advised by old hands from the Nixon, Reagan, and elder Bush days. Old man Bush had told his son that Dick Cheney should be his choice for vice president, and it was for the same reasons—to surround the younger Bush with a Washington veteran.

Gonzales would be fine, thought Gray. And the reason he was so sure was that it was obvious to anyone mired in Washington—all those deeply embedded politicos who didn't get outside DC that often—that the younger Bush and Gonzales were joined at the hip. The younger Bush had a reputation for being harsh on anyone who wasn't overtly loyal. His inner circle was smaller than his father's. The son seemed less trusting and probably more unforgiving. Bush wouldn't give the White House counsel job—a job that was so crucial in the constantly-under-attack Clinton White House—to anyone he didn't trust with his career, his political life.

"It's a job that requires total and complete trust," said Gray. As for experience? "You can get experience from other sources," added Gray. [18]

In Texas some of his Hispanic friends were marveling over his ascension. Gonzales was the counselor to the president, and it ramped up his ranking among acquaintances he had left behind in the state. Some of them breathlessly compared him to other legendary Hispanic leaders: "He is one of the icons of the Hispanic community," says Massey Villareal, the former chairman of the Texas Association of Mexican-American Chambers of Commerce and the former national chairman of the Republican Hispanic National Assembly. [19] Other national Hispanic leaders were more cautious. For many of them, Gonzales was still an unknown commodity, even if he represented a major breakthrough in terms of a Latino presence at the White House. "He seems a thoughtful guy, someone we can work with," said a perhaps careful spokesperson for the National Council of La Raza.[20]

In Washington, Gonzales was attending "educational" seminars with the Judicial Conference and still just trying to get used to the pace and his role among the high-powered egos and forceful personalities surrounding Bush. One day he drove to the White House and was lining up to drive past the massive iron security gates that block off the driveways. He was following another car, preoccupied with something else and not paying close attention, and one of the gates started closing down on his car. Gonzales recoiled as he watched the hood on his BMW being crushed by the thudding, unrelenting security gate. Like eyeballs being squeezed out of a cartoon character's face, the headlights on his car popped right out of their sockets. The security guard realized what was happening and finally stopped the gate. By then it was too late. For the next few days Gonzales drove back and forth from the White House with his headlights duct-taped back into the front of his car. Gonzales told friends in Texas that the gate was unrelenting and unforgiving—unlike the stupid security gates back at the Texas Supreme Court. People, including Gonzales, were always driving into those Texas security gates as they closed on their cars—but those gates were weak, they always broke on contact, they never left a scratch on the car.

Something else was different in Washington. At the recommendation of Republican friends, Gonzales eventually decided to attend Falls Church Episcopal in Falls Church, Virginia. Sometimes described as an evangelical Episcopal congregation, the church was well known by political watchers as a place where powerful Republicans and conservatives liked to worship then and in years to come: Fred Barnes from the *Weekly Standard,* writer and TV commentator Tucker Carlson, CIA director and former congressman Porter Goss, Bush speechwriter Michael Gerson (a theology student–turned–evangelical Christian who once worked for the Prison Fellowship Ministries run by Watergate felon Charles Colson), Georgia congressman Jack Kingston, Alabama congressman Robert Aderholt, and GOP pollster Ed Goeas. The parish traces back to the early 1700s. George Washington, Robert E. Lee, and Francis Scott Key have all prayed at Falls Church—and Washington once served as a church warden. Legends emerged that the Declaration of Independence was read to rebellious colonists from the church steps. Today it is a conservative-leaning house of worship, clearly aligned with the wing of the Episcopal faith that is against same-sex marriage and the consecration of gay clergy—matters that would deeply divide Episcopal leaders.

Rector John Yates, who has overseen the church since 1979, is a father of five who is well known for his strong opposition inside the Episcopal General Convention to the consecration of a gay bishop. He sent an open letter to his congregation in which he wrote, "This is an endorsement of the lifestyle of this man who divorced his wife and has been living with another man in an openly sexual relationship. We want you to know we reject and repudiate this action in the strongest terms. When the scripture speaks, I try to speak." Yates has also tended to blur the lines between politics and religion by suggesting that lawmakers should vote against legislation that they think would result in "sin." The church services offered to the thirty-five hundred parishioners also blur the lines between old and new forms of worship: Parishioners have a choice of attending a kind of pop-rock service with louder music, hand clapping, and arm waving or the older-style mass dominated by traditional hymns and a more somber atmosphere. The 6:00 A.M. prayer services are often populated by well-groomed GOP and even some Democratic politicos who are trying to get a little religion in their lives before heading into the trenches in DC.[21]

The church makes its doctrines on abortion, marriage, and other issues very clear on its web site: "All human life is a sacred gift from God and is to be protected and defended from conception to natural death. We will uphold the sanctity of life and bring the grace of and compassion of Christ to those who face the realities of previous abortion, unwanted pregnancy and end-of-life illness." And the church seems to suggest that religion should play a very important role in public policy: "We are committed to seek ways to express these commandments and principles in all spheres of life, including the public life of the nation." Rector Yates has said that he would certainly welcome George W. Bush to the congregation; Bush had grown up attending Episcopal church services, worshipped at Presbyterian churches for a while in Midland, Texas, then began attending Methodist services after marrying Laura Welch in 1977.

Bush, who once announced that he did not know the exact doctrinal differences between the Episcopal and Methodist churches, had adopted a sort of adaptive conservative Christianity, and he had mingled with a wide variety of religious leaders and advisers over the years, including Billy Graham; Assemblies of God minister and high-ranking Amway salesman Doug Wead; and Houston Methodist Reverend Kirbyjohn Caldwell. And to some extent Marvin Olasky, a former communist who became an elder in his Christian church and an editor of a Christian-flavored magazine, and who also wound up teaching journalism at the University of Texas at Austin while penning controversial articles that said "a lot of liberal journalists have holes in their souls," that some of those journalists "don't want to repent," that "it's sad that leading journalists are acting as proselytes in the religion of Zeus,"[22] and that "any particular woman should be able to compete for any job and should receive equal pay for the job, but in practice the jobs that require greater aggressiveness and single-minded pursuit will be held disproportionately by men."[23]

Throughout his encounters with religion and his religious advisers, Bush has consistently made it clear that anyone in his inner circle is welcome to join him in religious worship. Bush, according to his close friends, is also a devotee of the "One-Minute Bible"—an easy-to-digest collection of theological highlights presumably fashioned for people who have neither the time nor the personal inclination to linger for a lengthy period with the Bible. In the end Gonzales and Bush would be on the same religious page—men who grew up in a business and political culture in Texas in which a particular brand of brisk, conservative Christianity was not just encouraged, it was almost mandated in certain circles in Houston and Dallas. The churches where Bush and Gonzales wound up worshipping would attract a generally affluent and influential congregation. Congregants would hear a certain kind of Christian noblesse oblige at the services, a sense that when powerful Christians enter public service, they are not just expected to reach out to help others behind them, but they are supposed to do it through some stringently Christian guiding principles.

Leavened into the sermons, seminars, and prayer services was often also a sense that God had "rewarded" the attendees with their obvious political and financial success, and that almost as repayment and acknowledgment that God had singled them out, God now expected those recipients to spread the holy word to others.

Gonzales and other White House staffers were officially sworn in January 22 by Vice President Dick Cheney in the East Room at the White House. After the ceremony Bush made a short speech, and again Gonzales was the only person he mentioned by full name: "I expect every member of this administration to stay well within the boundaries that define legal and ethical conduct. This means avoiding even the appearance of problems. This means checking and, if need be, double-checking that the rules have been obeyed. This means never compromising those rules. No one in the White House should be afraid to confront the people they work for, for ethical concerns, and no one should hesitate to confront me as well. We're all accountable to one another, and above all, we are all accountable to the law and the American people. My White House counsel, Al Gonzales, is my point man on these issues. If you have even a hint of ethical doubt, I urge you to talk to Al." [24]

Gonzales took a second-floor corner office in the West Wing of the White House, not far from Karl Rove, Karen Hughes, Clay Johnson (Bush's roommate from Phillips Academy and Yale, and his appointments adviser in Texas and again at the White House), Nicholas Calio (legislative director), Margaret Tutwiler (communications director), Lawrence Lindsey (economic policy adviser), and Margaret La Montagne (domestic policy adviser). He was in the same office occupied by the men who served Clinton during the various tumultuous investigations that consumed the former president.

Gonzales decided to decorate his room with pictures of his family, pictures of himself in the air force, and some of his awards from Texas. And he hung up a poster-sized framed picture taken inside the Oval Office that showed the elder George Bush standing alongside the younger George Bush, who is seated at the "*Resolute* desk" made from the timbers of the abandoned British vessel HMS *Resolute*. Visitors to Gonzales's office would remember that shot, taken on Inauguration Day, being displayed more prominently than any of the other bits of memorabilia. "I love that picture," Gonzales would tell people. [25]

Flanigan's office, smaller and less grand, was next to his room. Their four-person secretarial–clerical–executive assistant staff sat outside in a larger reception area. Rove's office was the next one over, down the hall, and it was very common for Gonzales and his staffers to run into Rove on a daily basis. Within days of settling in, Gonzales's aides were leaving articles on his desk with circles drawn around his name—articles suggesting that Alberto Gonzales was on the extremely short list of candidates for the U.S. Supreme Court.

For the next five years he would repeat variations of the same refrain—that he wasn't looking for a job back on a bench, that he was dedicated to doing what he had always done best: serving the needs of his client. "That was kind of the elephant in the room. It was very rarely discussed. There might be some occasional joking reference. But everybody knew that the talk about him as a potential Supreme Court justice had begun right away," says Bradford Berenson, one of his White House counsels.[26]

When the *Washington Post* ran its end-of-January story describing his staff as "an influx of talent," a "new generation of conservative intellectuals," and an "elite band," it mentioned almost in passing that "many of them are members of the Federalist Society, a haven for intellectual movement conservatives."[27] Gonzales read the piece, and that Tuesday morning, sitting in his wingback chair, he stared at the group of associate and assistant counsels surrounding him.

"Are you guys members of the Federalist Society?" asked Gonzales.

The fact that he didn't know—and the obvious fact that he didn't know much about the Federalist Society—struck some people as a clue to how much of an outsider Gonzales still really was.

Around the room his lawyers raised their hands. Gonzales was, said someone who was there, "very surprised" to see how many members of his staff were Federalist Society stalwarts. "I think he was kind of shocked to find out that these guys were all members of the Federalist Society—card-carrying members of some organization that he didn't understand," said one of the attorneys.

It was early February, and his wife and the children still had not made it to their new home. Gonzales was up before dawn, the same routine as in

Texas, and in the office to meet with Flanigan at 6:15 or 6:30. They reviewed the *New York Times, Washington Post,* and *Wall Street Journal,* getting Gonzales ready for meetings with the associate counsels and the White House senior staff. Bush was partially right: Gonzales was able to see him virtually anytime he wanted, but he still had to sail his memos and requests through another old friend from Texas. Harriet Miers had quietly moved to Washington as well. Amid all the attention paid to Colin Powell, Rice, Rove, Hughes, and even Gonzales, her appointment to the job of staff secretary went virtually unnoticed. She was the woman who had singled Gonzales out years ago when she was president of the State Bar, the woman who had recommended that Bush pick Gonzales as his general counsel in Texas, the woman who constantly crossed paths with Gonzales during the various Bush family political campaigns. She was the woman who owed the last several years of her career to George W. Bush, in many of the same ways that Alberto Gonzales had—and she was a friendly, familiar presence for Gonzales.

While waiting for his wife and the children to close out the school year and finally arrive from Texas, Gonzales lived temporarily with Stuart Bowen and then found an apartment. He worked until 7:00 or 7:30 P.M., then would peek in on Flanigan and simply say, "Let's go home, Timmy." For the first few weeks he was absorbed with reviewing judicial appointments around the country—there were ninety-four seats to be filled on district and circuit courts. Gonzales's team would have a direct hand in what some legal scholars said was a hugely substantive impact on the nation's legal system. Most insiders expected bloody battles over the nominations, with suspicious Democrats already weighing the possibility that Bush's conservative counsel from Texas, along with any input from Ashcroft, would try to ram home dozens of archconservative candidates. "I can't control the politics of it," said Gonzales.[28]

He couldn't control the politics, but he was well aware from the moment he took his seat in the White House that politics was going to inform almost all of his decisions and his advice to Bush. Working so closely with a man who was by nature a political creature—and who had officially and unofficially been running for the presidency for the last eight years—had obviously attuned Gonzales to begin to see politics around every corner. Coming to Washington, he knew he'd be riding a razor's edge while big-time political stakes were almost always on the table:

"There's an ethical component to what I have to do. There will be some instances where something is very important to the president's agenda, and my job is to try to find a way to do it in a way that's legal." [29]

Gonzales took control of the process as head of a fifteen-member administration team that would handle the reviews, interviews, and selection of those federal judges. (At the White House, at Federalist Society functions, some staffers and members had taken to calling him Judge Gonzales in deference to his twenty-three months on the bench in Texas.) By early March he already had worked late into the night to help interview more than fifty possible candidates. Some legal analysts said that the judicial selection process was like a holy grail for Gonzales's team—that the young, hungry attorneys on his staff saw the opportunity to pick such a large number of judges as a once-in-a-lifetime chance to transfer the strict constitutional aims of the Federalist Society to benches across America.

Gonzales sent out an early warning missile in March when word leaked out that he wasn't going to be relying on the fifty-year-old tradition of having the American Bar Association do early evaluations of nominees to the federal bench. The ABA's detractors said that the association had tilted the nation's courts away from conservatives during the Clinton years and that a lukewarm analysis of Robert Bork by the ABA had sabotaged Reagan's attempt to put Bork on the Supreme Court. The ABA quickly announced that their recommendations were never slanted by partisanship or ideologies. Some legal scholars railed that the whole maneuver was a "right-wing takeover" [30] and a bald attempt to completely reshape the nation's courts in a quick, conservative way. The White House very publicly released a letter that Gonzales wrote to the ABA president (Martha Barnett was the ABA president; she had been offered a job on the Al Gore legal team in Florida during the election debacle) in March saying "the Administration will not notify the ABA" of judicial nominees before their names are submitted to the Senate or released to the public. For good measure, Gonzales sent a letter to leading Democrats telling them the same thing. California Senator Barbara Boxer's response to Gonzales's decision was simple: "It's war." [31]

In one rare, insightful interview with Irvine Senior Fellow Gregory Rodriguez in the pages of the *Los Angeles Times,* Gonzales opened up about his philosophy on judicial appointments and his own philosophy on what being a judge really means:"Oftentimes, I had to interpret statutes in Texas that I felt were terrible public policy, but that is immaterial. If I want to change that policy, I need to hang up my robe and go run for the Texas legislature." He said that now in Washington he wanted people who would approach the bench the same way. There were standards he had in his selections: "The first is character. The second is competence. In terms of character: Is this a person of integrity? Fundamentally, is this a good person? I realize this is fairly subjective, but that is what I'm looking for. . . . In terms of competence: What I look for is intellect. Does this person have the intellect to do a good job?"[32]

The bold, controversial move to oust the ABA and hopefully thwart Democrats helped set a tone for how people would perceive Gonzales in DC. His signature was on the Bush administration's aggressive declaration of war against fifty years of tradition. Conservative commentators crowed about how wrong the Gonzales-doubters were, that this was surely a sign he was as ideologically committed as anyone else in the upper level of the administration.

Meanwhile, back inside the White House, Gonzales was eventually entrusted with another behind-the-scenes task squarely aimed at the legacy of the Clinton White House. He was put in charge of keeping an eye on accusations that the departing Clinton staffers had acted like drunken fraternity rats on their way out of the White House and scrawled nasty messages on walls, pulled phones out of the jacks, and plucked the letter "w" off of computer keyboards. True or not, it was eventually going to be a delicious story for the media to feast on. Gonzales began putting together a heavily detailed, multiappendix, 160-page guide to the General Accounting Office outlining what he would call "vandalism, damage, and pranks." Political baseball players said this one had to be a Karl Rove Special—only he was cunning enough to try to use the White House counsel to continue to bury the Clintons and Gore, to erode any lingering feelings that "nice guy Gore" had been cheated out of the presidency.

The report that Gonzales would finally release should be required reading for its bipartisan hilarity—it's hard to tell who comes off as more unhinged, Gonzales or Clinton staffers. Gonzales harrumphs throughout his report with the same pious, stiff-backed righteousness that critics saw in Kenneth Starr; the Clinton staffers look like chucklehead whiners whose humor level hadn't moved far beyond the *Three Stooges, Animal House,* and *MAD* magazine. Page after page, Gonzales presents an indignant inventory of perceived political Scud missiles that the Clintonistas had left behind for the incoming administration to see: "T-shirt with tongue sticking out draped over chair";"picture of former First Lady taped to inside of cabinet"; "sign reading 'VP's cardiac unit' ";"sign comparing President Bush to a chimpanzee found in a number of printers"; "sign taped to a desk of a mock MasterCard ad that includes a picture of President Bush and reads, 'New Bong: $50, Cocaine Habit: $300, Finding Out That the Good-Old-Boy Network Can Still Rig an Election in the Deep South: Priceless. For the rest of us there's honesty.' " [33]

Gonzales wrote a memo on White House letterhead insisting that any final General Accounting Office report on the affair include some curse words that Bush staffers said they saw scrawled on signs. In particular, Gonzales wanted the exact language from a mock *Time* magazine cover that had the headline "We're Fucked." Gonzales told the head of the GAO that he wanted the bad word put in the final report, even if some people thought it was offensive:

"While we agree that the statement itself is not 'appropriate,' particularly when affixed to government property, and while we certainly do not wish to propagate such statements, those considerations are outweighed here by the clear relevance of the content of the statement to the objective of the GAO's inquiry. . . . The content of a message can—and often does—indicate who wrote the message and when. We think it unlikely that a reader would attribute the message in question to members of the incoming Administration, for example." [34]

Noel Francisco, a White House counsel, remembers an orderly but slightly uncertain first few weeks and months:

"What stands out to me is that when we all arrived there—and this is how it is with every new administration—the file cabinets are empty, the prior administration was kind enough to leave a transition book where they explained a lot of the basic issues with us. And they were readily available to us when we had questions. But we were pretty much walking into a blank state and trying to figure out how things went, starting essentially from scratch. The one guideline he gave was that our main charge was to steer the White House far well into the ethical line so that we weren't skating at the edge, even remotely at the edge. But beyond that, none of us had been there before and we were feeling our way through, and he was leading us through it." [35]

In Washington, Gonzales still demurred from talking about his upbringing with the people surrounding him. What people knew about him, most of all, was that he was usually the first one in and one of the last people out of the office. No matter how early anyone would arrive, his BMW, still with its Texas government license plates, was parked on Executive Avenue near the White House.

"He did not talk about it much at all. He would refer to his parents once in a while. I remember him referring to his father and how his father was just a very quiet, humble man. But I think some people in his position might want to say, 'Look where I came from and look how I climbed out of this,' but he was so far away from ever tooting his own horn or puffing himself up that I think he would have felt he was doing that if he had talked more about the background that he came from. I do remember his mother and sister came to visit once. You could just see the pride in their eyes—it was something to behold. I remember they came and I remember the president ended up spending I think a couple of hours with them. He took them around the White House, showed them everything, brought them into the Oval Office—it was just amazing," says Francisco. [36]

Francisco watched Gonzales lead morning staff meetings at 7:10 A.M. along with Flanigan, the assistant counsels, and sometimes visitors such as David Addington, Vice President Cheney's counsel. Gonzales's executive assistant, Libby Camp, would sometimes be there. According to Gonzales family friends, Camp had worked with Karl Rove in Texas and had also coordinated Gonzales's campaign for the Texas Supreme Court. Like several of the White House counsels, she had also been dispatched to Florida to serve as one of the "Republican observers."

Sometimes Gonzales, just like Bush, wearing black cowboy boots with his dark suits, would sit in his wingback chair at the front of the wood-paneled room and get updates from the dozen or so lawyers who would come in. The office had almost a nautical look, like something you'd find in the captain's quarters on a ship, with the paneling, the dark look, and the built-in desk. He had put a souvenir oversized gavel on the wall—maybe four feet long. His award from the National Hispanic Bar Association. Photos of his wife. He hung a drawing on the wall done by one of his sons, with the words "Daddy, when are you coming home?" written on it. His family was still in Texas and wouldn't be coming to Washington until June or July. He was only seeing them every third or fourth weekend.

Gonzales's lawyers went down a daily laundry list of legal issues they were facing—the ABA unhappiness with being excluded from vetting federal judges, the pace of interviews with possible judicial nominees, what White House staffers needed to do to make sure they were avoiding any perceived conflicts of interest with companies they might have represented or owned shares in—and congressional investigations, white-collar crimes, executive branch law, and the inner workings of the various judicial bodies, committees, and organizations around the city and really the nation.

On an arching level there was a literal, much-talked-about drive to restore power and authority to what some of Gonzales's inner circle felt was a diminished Office of the Presidency. Whether it stemmed from their collective loathing for Clinton or it was actually an honest evaluation of Clinton's eroding influence on the power of the presidency, several members of Gonzales's inner circle vowed to give Bush the single-minded presidential muscle and executive privilege that they felt Clinton had squandered. There was even high-concept talk about how Gonzales and his team could move the new Bush presidency back to a time several decades ago when the executive branch was simply a more brawny, some would say imperious, entity—moving with uncompromising confidence apart from congressional subpoenas and maybe the Supreme Court.

There were mundane things, too—what the legal and financial boundaries were when it came to paying for Laura Bush's makeup and hair styling for all the social events she was going to be attending. Francisco found himself sending letters asking people to stop using the White House image or Bush's name in advertisements. Sometimes Gonzales would reach into his small office refrigerator and grab a Diet Coke as they mulled who was out there using White House logos, seals, symbols.

Unspoken was the sense that everyone in this room had an aura of visibility in the White House courtesy of Gonzales's intimate relationship with Bush. Many of the lawyers in the room were younger than Gonzales but more seasoned in the way power ebbs and flows in Washington. After work, out of earshot, other White House staffers talked about how there had obviously been an early, raw test of wills between Ashcroft and Gonzales over who would be the quarterback picking judicial appointments—and that Gonzales had won because Bush had been through the judicial selection process before with Gonzales and, well, because Bush liked Gonzales more.

A high-ranking White House staffer said the "center of gravity" was established at the White House and Ashcroft was forced to defer to Gonzales, literally, by sometimes having to attend meetings run by Gonzales at the White House. For people in Washington who saw the dynamic between the two men, it was easy to read Ashcroft's body language: he was pissed at having to yield the judicial selection powers to Gonzales. It was also clear right away that whatever the co-counsels conveyed to Gonzales—if it was important enough—it would go right into Bush's ear.

"It gave the office and hence the attorneys a certain level of visibility within the White House, because they knew that if we were advising on an issue, you were advising on behalf of Judge Gonzales, and Judge Gonzales was somebody the president was going to give a lot of deference to on legal issues. I think that within the White House and within the government generally, people understood that you couldn't just ignore what the White House Counsel's Office was doing," says Francisco.[37]

One of the other lawyers in the room, Bradford Berenson, looked around and knew that most of these young conservative guns were still pretty much unfamiliar to Gonzales. There was a high likelihood that Gonzales was also being judged every step of the way—for his knowledge of the law, maybe even for his ideological purity. Berenson says, "I think he made a very, very difficult and gutsy decision to surround himself with a group of people that he did not know personally, just as he was embarking on a very difficult, high-profile mission."[38]

And again it might have been gutsy but not foolhardy, according to Berenson:

"I mean, one thing was clear early on—that his relationship with the president was very close, very confidential, and very valuable to the office. My sense was that quite apart from formally scheduled meetings in the

Oval Office, he had pretty regular communication with the president in-
formally on the telephone or in other settings where he could brief the
president confidentially on something, get some informal guidance, and
make sure that our office was doing what the president wanted done without having to tee up formal decisions and go through the process of sched-
uling a meeting and preparing briefing memos and the like. That kind of
informal back-and-forth between the president and his counsel was very,
very helpful for the Counsel's Office and for the work of the lawyers in it.
You know, when people in the White House and the rest of the government have the sense that the counsel is close to the president, then everything that the counsel and the people who work with him do is taken
more seriously and has greater impact. It also helps avoid mistakes.

"I mean, if you know that you are, in fact, speaking for the president . . . if you know that you are, in fact, carrying out his wishes, it is a lot
easier to avoid misunderstandings or mistakes. So one thing that was apparent early on . . . you know, you'd be sitting there in his office talking to
him about something and the phone would ring and it would be the
president and, you know, most of the time he would sort of excuse you
from the office because he was going to speak directly to the president.
But that kind of access to and relationship with the president was a very
important, a very important thing.

"He relayed to us that the president had two early and overriding priorities for our office: one was judicial appointments; the president wanted
to move very, very quickly to begin to fill the almost record number of
vacancies in the federal judiciary with top-quality people of the kind that
the president favored; and the other overriding priority was to try to
strengthen the institutional prerogatives of the presidency, to try to
strengthen the office and reclaim some of the ground that had been lost
during the Clinton years. So executive power issues were very important
and judicial appointments issues were very important early on. And that
was guidance given to us by Judge Gonzales, you know, relaying the president's wishes."[39]

The associate counsels were obviously not privy to the private conversations between Bush and Gonzales. Most of them had worked for people
who were quite unlike either Bush or Gonzales personality-wise. Bush's
disarming wisecracks were far removed from anything Ken Starr, Scalia, or

Thomas were prone to utter. Berenson heard Bush calling Gonzales "Fredo" and wondered *where* that came from. There was some instant ease between Bush and Gonzales, something almost familial that imbued their working relationship. Nobody was psychobabbling in the background as they watched the easy camaraderie, the way Gonzales willingly suffered the abuse when Bush was breaking his balls in front of a room full of Harvard- and Yale-educated lawyers. Bush didn't care—and Gonzales didn't *seem* to care.

Berenson says, "Fredo was the nickname. In the interactions I saw between the two of them, there was almost a big brother/little brother feeling there. The president is kind of the confident big brother giving a bit of the business to the little brother, who saw it as his job to kind of smile, quietly take it, and enjoy it."[40]

ELEVEN

Just a Staffer

An early image of Gonzales was emerging for the people deep inside the White House hierarchy. He was a reserved presence at the staff meetings, oftentimes one of the last people to weigh in, not openly ideological, certainly not prone to engage anyone in a line-in-the-sand debate or eloquent speechifying. He had begun a process of delegating more and more work to his associate counsels; most people began to build an intuitive sense of when to barge in on him. Some staffers thought Gonzales oozed a mortician's calm, an at-first disconcerting placidity that they eventually decided could be helpful when it came to keeping the peace with the disparate tendencies among the pumped-up, true-believer co-counsels. He didn't possess a gravitas, a sagelike bearing, and he didn't come frontloaded with a red-hot reputation as a profound legal heavy-weight emerging from Texas—but he did have a soothing manner, a lack of pretension, and his style seemed to nourish the egos in the office while keeping them from running amok.

Most people working for him came to like him, in just the way Stuart Bowen had almost instantly enjoyed working for Gonzales in Texas. There was a bit of banter but always an extremely low level of volatility with Gonzales. One time, as the lawyers working for him tried to prod a bit, he opened up for a second about the fact that he had been stationed in a place called Fort Yukon, Alaska.

"I was protecting Alaska from the communists," he joked.

To Flanigan and some others, he behaved a bit like how they suspected a judge in Texas might behave—someone who wanted to be briefed on a matter, handed some analysis, offered some opinions. In the first few weeks in his office he clearly was not being proactive, not defining a "Gonzales agenda"—he was receiving the issues, reacting to them. For some of his associate counsels, he would always remain hard to read. But as time went on, that fact didn't seem to matter. Gonzales seemed comfortable where he was; he didn't seem to be jockeying for anything else in the administration, in Washington. He was working closely with Flanigan, with Cheney's intimidating and ballsy counsel David Addington, and with Defense Department General Counsel William Haynes III. If he struck people in the White House as inscrutable, it didn't look like it was because he had some secret personal agenda.

Of course, for the politicos, hobnobbers, and chess players around the city, Gonzales was still an almost universally unknown quantity. He was a Republican businessman, really, not a heady ideologue: He had come of age in corporate Republican circles in an almost incestuous zone of like-minded power players in Houston. In Texas he didn't have to don conservative armor and fight ideological battles. He was not pushing change, he wasn't a foot soldier in the movement, he wasn't a passionate activist out to change the world. In a sense, Gonzales *embodied* change. He was the new face of the Republican Party, and his ideological goals, if there were any, were to serve as a role model for other Latinos and to recruit even more Latinos to the GOP.

In Washington, like Karen Hughes, Gonzales abhorred that kind of schmoozy, off-the-record contact with the media—and most reporters who tried to cultivate some sort of ongoing relationship with him found that Gonzales either didn't grant very telling interviews about his personal philosophies or he simply spoke in extreme generalities with clipped, simple responses. A short while into his time in DC, he said the single thing that had surprised him the most was that "you can't keep a secret. Things are said and you figure they're said in confidence and the next thing you know, you read about them in the papers."[1]

A few of those news stories that had tossed his name into the hat as a possible Supreme Court candidate mentioned that he was a "stealth" candidate because he had very little of a paper trail and hadn't rocked any boats back in Texas. The stories coolly speculated that the fact that he had left no public DNA, no political baggage, might be the very reason he'd vault onto the court. White House watchers said they couldn't get close to Gonzales and when they did he was extremely hard to read.

"I've only met him a few times, and when I met him, he was just kind of a nobody. Really. I didn't really come away from it with strong feelings one way or another. It could be him or it could be just me, but people in politics usually have strong personalities," says Norm Orenstein at the American Enterprise Institute for Public Policy Research think tank.[2]

The political education of Gonzales, and the education of people in Washington about Gonzales, was well underway in his first several months in office. Senate Democrats had sent him a stinging letter demanding more participation in picking federal judges. Gonzales met with Senators Paul Sarbanes and Barbara Mikulski to review their complaints. Gonzales was figuring out who the power players were, who he needed to respond to, how he needed to respond. Flanigan, for one, knew his role with Gonzales: "He is a very skilled fellow at analyzing problems whether they are a political or a legal problem. He was the counsel to the president. I helped him, to a very limited extent, find the levers and talk through issues and personalities in Washington."[3]

By spring it was almost a routine—every other story that mentioned his name suggested that he was probably going to the Supreme Court. He was Hispanic; he was loyal to Bush. He came from Texas and was always going to be predisposed to push for states' rights—he didn't have a particular history of judicial activism; he most likely would turn out to be a reliable conservative vote on the highest court. And that sense that he was weak-kneed on the abortion issue? That again was explained away as an aberration—an outgrowth of his having to interpret on the fly a new, confusing law in Texas.

Court watchers kept quietly coming back to one thing: it would be politically risky for the Democrats to come hard for Alberto Gonzales. He had grown up poor and would be the first Latino nominated to the highest court in the land. Those facts would make him almost bulletproof. There was behind-the-scenes talk about how Antonin Scalia had become the first Italian-American on the court, that no one would really vote against him, that the Senate voted 98–0 to put him on the bench. Gonzales, unless there was some massive screw-up during his tenure as White House counsel—some guilt-by-association disaster in the Bush White House or some skeleton in Gonzales's closet—would be a very handy candidate for the bench. It seemed, for some, like a strong possibility, except for the fact that there didn't seem to be too much of a résumé, some written evidence of his true conservative credentials. The little bit that was there, the paperwork that the media kept circling back to, was his ruling in the abortion case—and that didn't help allay any fears that he was the Latino David Souter.

For some conservatives, Souter had simply become known as old man Bush's worst mistake. There were few clues that Souter would eventually rule in ways that would drive conservatives crazy. In Washington, as the political bookmakers placed their bets, people wondered if the real Alberto Gonzales, maybe a liberal Alberto Gonzales, would suddenly appear the instant he donned his Supreme Court robes.

In May, Bush introduced eleven judicial appointees who Gonzales and his team had recommended for positions on the circuit courts of appeal. For Gonzales-watchers, there were three notable picks: Miguel Estrada, a native of Honduras and a former assistant solicitor general in the Clinton years who also had made fifteen arguments before the Supreme Court; John Roberts, the former deputy solicitor general under Kenneth Starr and a veteran of the Justice Department and the Office of White House Counsel; Priscilla Owen, Gonzales's colleague on the Texas Supreme Court and the one who vehemently, controversially tried to block Gonzales and others from allowing a Texas teenager to have an abortion without telling her parents.

Estrada, like Gonzales, might be seen as the right Latino candidate for Bush; Roberts was seen as the soaring legal mind who would no doubt satisfy the academic-intellectual wing of the Federalist Society; Owen would probably be very palatable to evangelical Christians who hated abortion. All three candidates would reflect very well on Gonzales with hard-edged conservatives—the choices, perhaps, could even serve to "rehabilitate" his image among the people who thought he lacked ideological purity. The Owen pick, of course, might even show that Gonzales knew she was right all along when it came to abortion—it might be a coded message that next time, if there was a next time for Gonzales, he would rule against abortion.

In June, Gonzales continued his negotiations with Democrats who saw his judicial selections, the way he was conducting the search, as a bit of wild-eyed zealotry aimed at creating some sort of states' rights, second Reagan Revolution in the nation's courts. Ironically he also lingered with his attempt to block the release of sixty-eight thousand pages of confidential Reagan White House memos that were scheduled for release to historians and the public in 2001. Critics said Gonzales was covering up something that could be embarrassing for elder George Bush, Colin Powell, White House Chief of Staff Andrew Card, and anyone else in the new Bush administration who had once worked in the Reagan White House; White House spokesmen said it was just a matter of being careful and reviewing what was going to be released and how it was going to be released. That same month Gonzales joined Ashcroft in interviewing candidates to take FBI Director Louis Freeh's place. And in mid-June he was forced into some high-stakes political poker when he had to handle Democrat accusations that senior adviser Rove hadn't moved fast enough to unload $2 million in stock in Enron, Intel, Pfizer, Johnson & Johnson, and other megafirms that might be influenced by White House policy.

The blasts centered on reports that Rove, who owned more than $100,000 in Intel, had met with top Intel executives about federal approval for a merger and whether Rove had had several conversations about federal energy policy with Enron officials when he also owned more than $100,000 in the Houston energy giant that was represented by Gonzales's old law firm, Vinson & Elkins. The Democrats, led by Henry Waxman from California, pushed Gonzales to consider whether Rove was "involved in shaping the Administration's policy on a patient's bill of rights" while he owned more than $200,000 in Pfizer and whether Rove had done something wrong by talking about federal nuclear energy policy while owning stock in General Electric, which has a nuclear power division. In a letter to Gonzales, Waxman decided to take a hard punch at the very thing Bush had promised Gonzales would bring to the White House: "These allegations appear to be at odds with President Bush's statements about the importance of maintaining a high standard of ethics in the White House."[4]

If there had been an early honeymoon for Gonzales, some sort of free pass because he was seen as part of a refreshing new minority vanguard in the Bush White House, it was over.

By the end of the month Rove had divested himself of all the stocks. "Due to the enormous volume of clearance work and other difficulties attendant upon the beginning of a new Administration, combined with an abbreviated transition period, this process took longer than either Mr. Rove or I would have wished, or than it would have taken at other times during a presidential term," Gonzales wrote back to Waxman. He added that Rove and other White House staffers had taken ethics classes put together by Gonzales. His carefully worded three-page letter cites various guidelines in the Code of Federal Regulations and says: "With respect to your questions concerning Mr. Rove's holding in Enron, Mr. Rove was not a member of the National Energy Policy Development Group, and he did not attend any of its meetings. He did participate in a number of other meetings at which the contours of the Administration's energy policy were discussed. . . . In summary, in connection with the matters raised in your letter to Mr. Rove, Mr. Rove either had passing, inconsequential contacts or participated in broad policy discussions, neither of which presents an ethical problem under applicable regulations."[5] Reports would later emerge that Enron chief Ken Lay met with Rove early in the Bush administration and that Lay offered names of various individuals whom he thought should be appointed to the Federal Energy Regulatory Commission.[6]

Waxman wasn't going to let up. He kept the barrage going by sending a nine-page letter to Gonzales that called for a Department of Justice investigation into Rove. His bullet-point missive was filled with allegations that Lay, the CEO of Enron, had played an active role in the Bush administration's energy policies and that, in addition to being a major fund-raiser for Bush, Lay was friendly with various cabinet members and had routinely talked with Enron shareholder Rove. Waxman accused Gonzales of a "flawed reading of the law" and that "the cumulative effect of your reinterpretation of the ethics laws would make a mockery of the President's pledge" to maintain integrity at the White House.

If Waxman knew that the White House counsel he was sending a letter to had once worked for Enron, had once worked with Ken Lay, he didn't mention it. The same day Gonzales got his stinging letter denouncing his legal skills and calling for a federal investigation into Karl Rove's finances, news reports said that White House lawyers were pushing to keep the details of Rove's stock holdings private.

By the summer, in the weeks building up to the nightmare of September 11, Gonzales had moved his family to their comfortable home not far from the Wolf Trap performing arts complex in Vienna, Virginia. The day before the Fourth of July and three days before Bush's fifty-fifth birthday, Gonzales, Bush, and presidential personnel director Clay Johnson went golfing at Andrews Air Force Base. It was the first time Bush and Gonzales had hit the links since they moved to Washington. Bush liked to play golf with people he *really* liked—and with people who could put up with his smart-ass commentary, his penchant for "aerobic golf," his distaste for losing.

Gonzales had been picked to play golf with the president of the United States, had been picked to tag along on one of the few recreational pleasures that Bush exulted in. People who knew that Bush had flattered Gonzales by bringing him along were thrown for a huge loop a few days later when a Robert Novak column contained some whispers from deep inside the House of Bush.

Novak, who some journalists and politicos contended had a long, mutually beneficial relationship with Karl Rove, began his nationally syndicated column this way: "President George W. Bush's aides are telling worried conservatives that moderate White House counsel Alberto Gonzales will not be Bush's first or second selection for the Supreme Court, though he may end up there after two new justices have been seated."

Novak reported: "Privately, Gonzales won't hint where he stands on contentious issues. That might ease his confirmation, but it plants fears among conservatives that Gonzales will be 'another Souter.' " [7]

There it was. Novak had neatly outlined in a few brutal sentences why some people thought Gonzales would never wind up on the Supreme Court. It was as if Novak threw some Gonzales chum on the water and was waiting for the true believers to rise to it—and in the backrooms all over DC, speculation perked up about what the hell was exactly going on at the White House. Novak was presumed by many to have a nicely flow-ing pipeline of information for years and years from Rove. Was it Rove who was really bashing Gonzales? Was it someone else, maybe even Ashcroft, who was already resenting the influence and power that Gonza-les wielded in the judicial selection process? People knew that Rove had handled political campaign work for Ashcroft's Senate race in 1994. Were they involved in some sort of unfathomable alliance? Was it Rove pander-ing to the hard right base? Did Bush endorse or even know what Rove was doing?

Reports were already surfacing that Gonzales was dropping in on peo-ple at the White House or piping up more regularly at those morning se-nior staff meetings and telling the inner circle that the Bush White House was being watched like never before. He could see it in the letters he was getting from Waxman and in the visits he was getting from pissed-off sen-ators. White House staffers assumed that Gonzales had to have singled out Rove and told him what Bush had always been repeating: *"Perception is everything in politics."* Gonzales might have even decided to issue some lawyerly "behavior modification" to Rove—acting like he was delivering some tough love and telling Rove that questions about his stock holdings were raising serious ethics questions, bubbling up in the media, and turn-ing into one big pain in the ass for Bush. That theory was backed up when Gonzales told people he had gotten into the habit of "reminding folks" that "anything you do here at the White House you need to be very mind-ful of, because appearances can cause problems." [8]

The conspiracy theorists and the people who knew that Rove was hardly ever one to be admonished or lectured, speculated that Rove re-sented being cautioned by Gonzales. Maybe he had told Novak that Gon-zales wasn't at the top of the list to go to the Supreme Court. If he did, maybe it was more than just a move to soothe conservatives convinced that Gonzales was the Second Coming of Souter. Maybe Rove didn't want Bush blinded by loyalty to Gonzales—blinded to the point of anger-ing Bush's political base.

By July, his wife and the children were settled in but still not sure about the social pecking order in DC. Things were easier, more contained, more predictable in Texas. Gonzales knew the faces, the power players, and at some point the same faces were at the same parties in Texas year after year after year. Like he had done in the past, he was going to rely on Rebecca to make friends, invite the right people to their home, decide what social functions they needed to be at together. His wife was miffed to learn that her husband had received several invitations to the White House Correspondent's Dinner but that none of them had included her. It was not something that would have happened in Texas. Gonzales turned down all three invites. On the home front he was exceedingly glad to have his wife and children with him. In one of those rare, private admissions, he had told Flanigan that he had been truly lonely, that he had missed Texas and his wife and kids. At the White House, people could sense a difference in him now that his family had moved east.

Rebecca Gonzales would eventually land a job as a development director with the National Endowment for the Arts. They began preparing their kids for their new schools and were cheered by the fact that they were on the same school "pyramid" as Flanigan's children—they would follow each other to the same schools as they got older. People who hadn't seen them together in Washington were struck by how different Gonzales and his wife looked, acted. To his new friends in DC, Gonzales and Rebecca were moving on different tracks when it came to their respective personalities. Flanigan says, "From a personality standpoint, she is either a kick in the pants or a breath of fresh air, depending on your point of view. She's a wonderful lady. Being in their home is very pleasant. With the Gonzales couple, it is friendly and informal, and there is a little sort of push back and forth between the two in a jocular way. You know there are some married couples that you can tell they get along well and some married couples you can tell don't get along well—and they are definitely in the first category." [9]

Rebecca had gotten closer to Laura Bush during the Texas years, and when the Bush campaign decided to push hard for the Hispanic vote, the two women sometimes wound up appearing together in different parts of the state. Rebecca was disarming to some people. Once, Rebecca was on the phone with a friend who the Gonzaleses and the Bushes had in common, Kenna Ramirez, the wife of El Paso mayor Carlos Ramirez, the man who helped steer many former Democratic Hispanics to the Bush camp. As Rebecca talked to Ramirez, Rebecca heard another call coming in.

She put Ramirez on hold, then came back a few second later: "Oh, it was the president. He is looking for Al."

The women resumed their conversation, talking about the fact that the upcoming Texas lottery featured a fat, multi-million-dollar payout and talking about cruises and things they'd spend the money on if one of them would win. Rebecca interrupted the conversation again:

"There it is again," she said, referring to another call coming in. "I've got to take it."

After a few more seconds, she came back on the line with Ramirez: "It's the president again."

Ramirez replied, "Tell the president to get a life."

Rebecca said, "He's looking for Al. But Al took the boys to the movies and he took the phone off the hook."

The women started laughing. And Ramirez knew that there was an ease between Rebecca Gonzales and George and Laura Bush, a sense that they were bound by being from Texas. Rebecca's exuberance worked well with the president, and her disinterest in taking the limelight from her husband also made her a comfortable partner for the first lady.

One day Rebecca—her best friends call her Becky—shared something with Kenna Ramirez: "There is no one who can tell who President Bush is—and talk about his agenda, and talk about what he does—better than Al can . . . because he is so close to him." It was the kind of brash statement some people associated with Gonzales's wife. "She's a very strong personality. She's unlike him. She's more outgoing than he is. She's always prepared to speak her mind," says Stuart Bowen. "She's no shrinking violet." [10] Some of their friends would even surprise people by saying that they had talked to "Al's boss"—and people assumed that meant President Bush. In fact, those friends were referring to his wife.

When the Ramirez family would visit their friends in Washington they toted tamales made in Texas, and the two political spouses would cook enchiladas while their husbands watched TV with the boys. One time Rebecca's family was visiting Virginia and Gonzales suggested that everyone go eat at the food court in Union Station. They arrived separately, and as they were standing on line to get their hot dogs, Carlos Ramirez wanted to know why Gonzales didn't have a security detail. Gonzales looked at his Texas friend: *"Come on, Carlos. I'm just a staffer."* [11]

Kenna Ramirez believed that Gonzales and his wife would not get caught up in any personal Potomac power trips. Others said the same thing—people like Gonzales, Harriet Miers, and even Karen Hughes had simply moved to some level of unobstructed, unquestioning fidelity to Bush. Hughes practically tackled reporters who had given Bush bad press. Miers gushed in private about Bush's brilliance. Gonzales never turned down an assignment from Bush and was willing to reinvent himself to adapt to each new mission Bush had given him. People who knew them, who saw them in Texas, said that they certainly weren't driven by much of a personal agenda and that perhaps their devotion to Bush was spurred along by each of them being seduced by the proximity to power, the way the Bushes kept their friends very close.

In the end it also wasn't surprising that in the heat of the long political game, all of them moved more closely to religion: Gonzales, Miers, and Hughes began to talk more openly about God the longer they worked for Bush. Ardent Christian Marvin Olasky, who had influenced Bush and Rove back in Texas, had once strangely waxed on about the religion of "Zeus"—and now it was clear that Bush administration stalwarts like Gonzales, Miers, and Hughes were openly professing their eager Christianity to a degree that they might not have done before. Kenna Ramirez certainly saw it with Gonzales and his wife, Rebecca. Religion defined the Gonzales family in many ways that even some of their friends might not adequately understand. Scratch the surface, thought Ramirez, and you would find very devout Christians: "You will find their faith. It is God. It is their faith in God. They are very God-oriented people."[12]

A few days after Novak's plainly stated column denouncing his chances to be an early nominee to the U.S. Supreme Court, Gonzales didn't help his standing in conservative circles by some comments he offered at a DC Bar Association luncheon. The room was packed, filled to overflowing with anxious lawyers angling to see and hear the president's new counselor—and to take the measure of the outsider who had just stepped on the American Bar Association's neck by ruling out the ABA's longstanding role in picking federal judges. People wanted a look at him. Maybe he was reaching out to the people in the audience who were predisposed to dislike him because he had disrespected the ABA, but whatever the reason,

Gonzales caused more than a few jaws to drop when he announced: "We look for people who believe in judicial restraint. If they use the right process, we don't care if the outcome is liberal." [13]

He left the meeting with more questions than answers trailing after him. Back at the White House, the war with Waxman was dragging on into the dog days of summer. Bush was going to his Crawford ranch for a month, until September 3 at least. With Bush in Texas, Gonzales sent a note from the White House to Waxman saying he was "disappointed" in Waxman and that his last letter to Gonzales "contains a series of factual and legal inaccuracies." Gonzales said he wasn't going to furnish a list of meetings or phone calls Rove might have had. Gonzales finished his note by saying, "Mr. Rove actually suffered considerable financial losses because of his inability to sell his stockholdings at the beginning of the Administration, as he had wished. We understand your role as a member of Congress and we hope that any further pursuit of this matter is motivated solely by a reasonable concern over Mr. Rove's conduct." [14]

Even if the dark seers were right in seeing Karl Rove's fingerprints on the damning evaluation of Alberto Gonzales that appeared in Novak's column, it didn't appear to matter to the White House counselor. With almost everyone fleeing Washington, Gonzales was staying the course for both Bush and Rove. Given the fact that Rove and his associate Libby Camp had orchestrated his winning bid for the Texas Supreme Court, Gonzales certainly owed Rove more than a little loyalty. He was really just being careful. Bowen knew that was the watchword with Gonzales, that was the one word to describe his legal style: "Careful. He's by nature very careful about what he says and is certainly not the first to speak, usually the last to speak in a room when an issue is being discussed. He wants to hear all other aspects, and then if he is going to offer an opinion, he will offer it—sometimes he won't. He's very circumspect about offering up his own opinions." [15]

Also, by the end of the month, Gonzales was still resisting any release of the Reagan presidential memos. Several conservative and liberal scholars were coalescing to suggest that history demanded the release of the papers from the National Archives. Freedom of information advocates said it was one thing for Gonzales to protect Rove, to punish the ABA, but it was another thing to stop the release of papers that even some die-hard Reaganites wanted to see. Why was Gonzales pushing back so hard? Why was he risking a reputation as the White House counsel who stood in the way of any historical assessments of the Reagan legacy? Bush-watchers said it actually had everything to do with precedent—something Gonzales knew quite a bit about when he was making his rulings on the Texas Supreme Court. Gonzales, ever discreet, didn't want the Reagan presidential memos released because that would mean . . . the Bush family's presidential memos would also have to eventually be released.

Gonzales had studied the long-range ramifications. If he released the Reagan papers, it would set a precedent, and the confidential, controversial memos for either Bush administration would have to be opened to the public one day. Gonzales was protecting the legacy of his best friend's father—and ultimately the legacy of his best friend. He had masked Bush's criminal record; blocking the release of Bush's memos, any memos from deep inside the White House, would perhaps be even more important.

TWELVE

Swift Justice

At his ranch Bush had been handed an August 6 intelligence memo: *"Bin Ladin Determined to Strike in US."* The two-page memo concluded by saying: *"FBI information since that time indicates patterns of suspicious activity in this country consistent with preparations for hijackings or other types of attacks, including surveillance of federal buildings in New York."* Exactly a month later Bush was back in Washington donning a tuxedo for a state dinner that he had long been looking forward to. Bush had invited Mexican President Vicente Fox to the White House for an evening that was uncorked with a receiving line and drinks in the East Room. Gonzales was there with Rebecca, as were their old friends from Texas, Kenna and Carlos Ramirez. Various luminaries were also in attendance: Secretary of Commerce Don Evans, Clint Eastwood, football star Anthony Muñoz, Jeb Bush, Alan Greenspan, Colin Powell, William Rehnquist, Placido Domingo, HUD Secretary Mel Martinez, John McCain, Tom Daschle, Joe Biden, Dick Gephardt, and Trent Lott.

Bush, wearing his black handmade cowboy boots, toasted his visitors, welcomed them to the "Casa Blanca," and said this was like a "family gathering." His wife was wearing a red and hot pink Arnold Scaasi gown with a diamond necklace borrowed from the designer, and she led the 136 guests into the State Dining Room where she took a seat between Eastwood and the Mexican president. Waiters brought out gold-embossed menus, then Maryland crab and chorizo pozole appetizers. Then, a favorite of Bush's—Colorado bison crusted with pumpkin seeds, something Bush had personally chosen—was served. To finish the meal, there was a mango ice cream "dome" perched on a nougat base surrounded by circles of fresh strawberries, peaches—with sugar hummingbirds and hibiscus flowers for edible decoration, and a red chili pepper sauce and a tequila sabayon. After the meal there was dancing and singing in the East Room. Finally guests were invited to step onto a Blue Room balcony to enjoy an elaborate twenty-minute fireworks display.[1]

Kenna Ramirez thought it was one of the most magical evenings of her life. Laura Bush had elbowed President Bush and pointed to Ramirez sitting close to Alberto Gonzales and Rebecca Gonzales. President Bush grinned. He blew Kenna a kiss, grabbed her hand, and took her to meet the president of Mexico. Laura Bush decided to kiss Kenna's husband on the cheek. Gonzales and his wife were hugging each other. They all stood on the White House balcony and watched the sky light up over and over again with pyrotechnic starbursts. Kenna suddenly shouted at her friends: "Hey guys, this is the life!"[2]

Five days later, on the morning of September 11, Gonzales had just finished breakfast at the Waterside Marriott Hotel in Norfolk, Virginia. He was in a waiting room, preparing to give a speech at the Annual Government Ethics Conference hosted by the federal Office of Government Ethics. Gonzales had traveled to Norfolk with Robert "Moose" Cobb, his on-staff ethics counsel. Following a Tuesday morning breakfast, there would be two days of speeches, seminars, conferences, and presentations on the rules and regulations for government employees accepting gifts, traveling, writing books, using the Internet, avoiding conflicts of interest, and filing financial disclosures. After several months of defending Karl Rove from ethics accusations, Gonzales was deemed to be the perfect person for the conference.

Gonzales had left Flanigan in charge while he was away. Back at the White House counsel's office, Flanigan had just wrapped up the morning staff meeting. As everyone walked out, Flanigan glanced at the TV in the anteroom. The breaking news reports were being aired about the first plane hitting one of the World Trade Center towers. Flanigan stared at the TV. He had a scheduled meeting coming up with Clay Johnson, Bush's old high school and college roommate who was now overseeing presidential personnel matters, and Johnson was already waiting in Flanigan's office. Flanigan quickly called Gonzales.

At the Marriott, just before he was going to give his speech, Gonzales answered his cell phone. Flanigan told him the World Trade Center had been struck.

"Well, keep me informed. Call me if there is anything else," replied Gonzales.

Flanigan and the others in the White House turned back to the TV. When the second plane roared into the second tower, Flanigan quickly dialed Gonzales's number again. Gonzales had already stepped up to the podium at the conference and was giving his opening remarks, plowing into his speech. Gonzales paused, reached for his ringing cell phone, and saw that it was an unidentified number, which meant that it was the White House calling. With everyone watching him, he answered and heard Flanigan urgently telling him there had been a second plane slamming into the WTC.

"I should get back, shouldn't I?" asked Gonzales.

"Yeah, you should," answered Flanigan.

Flanigan hung up and found Gonzales's executive assistant, Libby Camp, and ordered her to make sure that Gonzales got instant transportation back from Norfolk to DC. Meanwhile Gonzales excused himself from the ethics conference and waited while Camp worked the phones to see how Gonzales could get back to Washington. Arrangements were made for Gonzales to head for the Norfolk Naval Station. Military bases in the country were moving into high alert, and it wasn't easy for Gonzales to even get on the base. Finally he was allowed to enter and special arrangements were made to scramble a Navy helicopter. Confusion was epidemic. No one was even sure where the hell Gonzales was going to fly to—and he was asked if he wanted to land on the south lawn of the White House. Gonzales said no. It was decided that the military copter would fly him to Andrews Air Force Base, then a security detail would bring him back into the heart of the city.

As Gonzales sat inside the helicopter, there was an overpowering mechanical fuel or diesel-like smell, some sort of intense stench. It was right where he was sitting; it was all around him and seemingly in the body of the helicopter. It was dizzying, nauseating, and it was a bumpy, thundering ride for the next sixty minutes. Gonzales stared at the ground and thought hard about what his role was likely to be. After his helicopter landed, he was raced away by security details. Gonzales was going to join Dick Cheney; the vice president had been literally hoisted by his pants and carried out of his White House office into the bunker known as the Presidential Emergency Operations Center.

In the minutes and hours after the attacks, National Security Council adviser Richard Clarke had frantically arranged videoconferences for key administration officials. Flanigan went to the White House Situation Room to represent the counsel's office. When Flanigan looked up at one of those videoconference images, he finally saw Gonzales standing behind Cheney—that's when Flanigan knew the White House counsel had somehow gotten back to DC from his speech in Norfolk.

Later in the day Gonzales and Flanigan were reunited in Gonzales's office. The rest of the counsel staff had evacuated and set up a sort of makeshift operation in some nearby offices belonging to carmaker DaimlerChrysler; a staffer had a spouse who worked for the company, which had agreed to make its offices available to the displaced associate counsels. No one really knew what to do. Calls would occasionally come in from Flanigan, telling everyone to stand by. Finally, toward early evening, a message was relayed that everyone was to report back to their regular stations Wednesday morning.

Back at the White House, Gonzales and Flanigan scrambled to think about priorities. The conversation was electric, wide-ranging: What were Bush's emergency authorities? Would a federal disaster area be declared? Who would draft any emergency proclamations? Were there any—any—legal precedents to think about for anything that had just happened that morning? Surely Bush was going to strike back. What war powers did he have? Bradford Berenson and Brett Kavanaugh, two of the associate counsels, would go that night to the American University Law School library and research emergency powers and war powers.

Flanigan watched Gonzales. He seemed calm amid the chaos. They had decided to form an emergency interagency legal task force, drawing in Cheney's lawyer, David Addington, and select Defense Department and Office of Legal Counsel lawyers.

"It was as if everything was thrown into fast forward, high gear. The volume and velocity of issues picked up tremendously," remembers Flanigan.[3]

Gonzales didn't share anything specific about his deep inner feelings toward the events of 9/11. There were few outward signs that might tell Flanigan or other people around him how he was reacting: "Only in the most nuanced way, where we were talking about the disaster generally, and there would be a shake of a head, a lowering of the eyes . . . the facial, the body expressions, would express what a profound tragedy this was and how significant it was."[4]

Gonzales and members of his team were involved in all of the top-level legal issues that arose after 9/11. The counsel's office was represented in the temporary "domestic consequences group" chaired by the White House deputy chief of staff Josh Bolten. Gonzales was attending the regular national security briefings. He was spending time with Bush and the other senior advisers at the Camp David meetings. In the hours building up to the virtually unanimous September 14 joint congressional authorization for Bush to respond with military might to the attacks, it was becoming increasingly clear that Gonzales's work for the next several months, maybe years, was almost always going to circle back to 9/11.

In the first frantic hours and days after 9/11, Gonzales, Flanigan, and the other attorneys in the White House counsel's office and the Justice Department's Office of Legal Counsel raced to finish that sweeping September 14 resolution that would authorize the president to fight back against the terrorists. Too, they were increasingly guided by parallel, long-running attempts to fast-track presidential authority, to streamline presidential authority, to broaden presidential authority. That expansion was considered not just a political necessity, from the first day of the Bush administration it was considered a way to render Bush and the White House crisp and decisive. Now it was also simply considered a way to give Bush the muscle to fight the war by any means necessary. In principle, it obviously wasn't a novel concept; earlier administrations had wrestled with how to invest the Oval Office with even more authority, with how to move beyond what in-house counsels felt was the cumbersome, foot-dragging, partisan politics that would stymie quick, decisive action. But in reality, Gonzales and the other counsels were embarking on a clandestine and extraordinarily controversial path.

In those first few days after the terrorist attacks, and with massive uncertainty still swirling, "gathering information" became an oft-repeated mantra among the White House counsels—snaring any intelligence, information, that would either extract justice or bolster national security. If America was now fighting a war against twenty-first-century terrorists who relied on the Internet and cell phones to stay threaded together, then—Gonzales argued in-house—the president needed the authority to move quickly to prosecute terrorists and extract all conceivable information from them or about them. And, increasingly, the sense in the White House was that the lawyers needed to be "forward leaning"— to test the boundaries, to reinterpret, to provide a means not only for waging the new war on terror but for gathering every shred of intelligence possible.

Some critics suspect that sometime after that brash September 14 anti-terrorism resolution was being set in motion, Gonzales kept circling back to the Foreign Intelligence Surveillance Act of 1978. Congress had created FISA in the post-Watergate environment as a way of monitoring and authorizing warrants for wiretaps. That act and the various limitations on domestic surveillance, installed to corral any runaway tendencies by local and national law entities, were perhaps later combed over by Gonzales—as were all other Fourth Amendment–related provisions and regulations tied to "unreasonable searches and seizures." Gonzales would perhaps eventually come to the conclusion that the key questions centered on whether Bush, as commander in chief, could be empowered by the September 14 emergency anti-terrorism authorization to also order use of covert domestic surveillance techniques.

If an anti-terrorism resolution could be drafted with broad enough language—and if Congress would pass it—then might the government be able to begin monitoring calls between people overseas and people in the United States, and to embark on a spying program without warrants and without congressional oversight or permission? The stumbling block was FISA itself. That law was always designed to rein in and oversee any use of domestic wiretaps, but as well to provide a "secret court" that could quickly hear and perhaps approve warrants in which permission was sought to eavesdrop. Critics allege Gonzales finally felt that he had found the key in a section of the September 14 resolution. It granted Bush the authority "to use all necessary and appropriate force against those nations, organizations or persons he determines planned, authorized, committed or aided the terrorist attacks that occurred on September 11, 2001, or harbored such organizations or persons, in order to prevent any future acts of international terrorism against the United States."

That phrase, that language about "all necessary and appropriate force," was the solution, the guiding principle. It could be what Gonzales and anyone else would return to if and when the Bush White House were ever attacked for creating a domestic spying program. The wording, of course, never spelled out eavesdropping, domestic spying, or wiretaps—but some could argue that those tools, those weapons, could fall under the umbrella framework of the September 14 resolution. When Congress and Bush finally passed that resolution, there might have been a sense that the legal means were suddenly available to roll the domestic spying program forward. Gonzales could perhaps simply maintain that Congress had given the president those expanded powers to fight the new enemy, that Congress had literally signed off on broadening the powers of the presidency—and had, in effect, given the president license to fight the war on terror in any way possible, including by monitoring phone calls and e-mails without warrants. Gonzales might have felt it would be easy to argue that the president needed the authority to move far beyond the so-called constraints of securing warrants for eavesdropping, of working within the frameworks of FISA, of going to Congress and suffering through long, frustrating, and dangerously open discussions about who would be spied upon—and how they would be spied upon.

Meanwhile inside the White House counsel's office, there was almost a sputtering, frustrated reaction to what some of the attorneys saw as the anemic illogic of other older, codified limitations. For many of the true believers on Gonzales's team, parts of the internationally recognized Geneva Convention on the treatment of captured combatants were ridiculously obsolete or inapplicable where al Qaeda was concerned. This was a new war, a new enemy, and Gonzales and the attorneys working under him—or filtering their opinions to him from the Department of Justice's Office of Legal Counsel—would push vigorously, seemingly almost frantically, to interpret existing international laws in a way that they felt fit the times. Months later, of course, after allegations of so-called torture memos were ultimately revealed, people who knew Gonzales would suggest that he was simply doing what any loyal attorney does for his client—he had identified an outcome and then worked ceaselessly to achieve it.

He had been abjectly loyal to Bush, and few people in Washington truly appreciated that Gonzales and Bush had literally grown up together, politically speaking, at a time in Texas when Bush had his way on almost every issue or agenda item he addressed. Bush didn't have strict constitutional clout in Texas, but he got his way on almost every legislative and political issue that emerged. Gonzales was raised in a political environment where he was accustomed to seeing his client invested with nearly unlimited political freedom—as an outgrowth of the fear Bush instilled in Texas Democrats, the sheer might of his network, and Bush's absurdly high approval ratings.

That prehistory, coupled with Gonzales's predisposition to always protect, promote, and serve his client, fed a confident, uncomplicated decision-making process to secure that expansion of presidential powers—even if it meant going into usually inviolable, almost sacred, areas of civil liberties in the United States. And now, with the urgencies of the post-9/11 environment suggesting that decisive action by Bush was the only course, Gonzales was ever more inclined to do what he had always done for his client. He would find the way, find the nuances within the existing laws that would free Bush as much as possible. It was, really, not much different from when Gonzales was preparing those boiled-down death row clemency memos for Bush. He wrote them, said his foes, to free Bush to allow the executions. This time he would be "forward leaning" on matters of national security, on matters related to domestic spying, on matters related to the interrogation of enemy combatants and terrorists. And maybe now he had identified the outcome and then worked backward to find the means to achieve that outcome.

The twin pillars of the post-9/11 blueprint for the war on terror emerging from Gonzales's office—how to detain and prosecute prisoners—were now inexorably moving ahead. And they were still proceeding in secret, as if the buttoned-down counsels, the ones who would normally be spending bits and pieces of their time on far more mundane matters (like deciding who could use the White House logo in their advertising), had deliberately embarked on their own war on terror. If there was a sense that the new rules were being drawn inside a rogue legal environment, it was either selectively forgotten or overshadowed by each news byte about the terrorists and their plots. If there was any sense of setting out on a legal and constitutional "slippery slope," as some in Congress would later allege heatedly, it was set aside in the name of a higher mission. Expanding presidential powers was essential to the task.

Besides it was what Bush wanted—it played to his inclination to be viewed as a black-and-white, quick-acting president. As a personality, he was hardly ever enormously, endlessly contemplative; as a political creature, he was driven by his Reaganesque philosophy that "perception is everything in politics." For years he had told Gonzales that he wanted to be known as an unambiguous, bold leader. This new drive to expand Bush's presidential powers—and the specific attempts to give him wartime powers, to give him sway over military tribunals—was predicated somewhat on serving Bush's political personality and his presidential style at a time when urgency had been ratcheted up to the perhaps most intense level in recent modern history. It was, in the end, very easy for Gonzales to plot the controversial courses he designed inside the White House counsel's office. It was, in the end, the only thing he could think of doing in order to serve the needs of the one client he had personally served for his entire public life.

The people in the White House counsel's office, the men like Flanigan and Berenson who were working the twelve- and fourteen-hour days with Gonzales, were still wondering what was really deeply inside Gonzales's soul, in his heart, during the immediate days after 9/11. He had remained almost perfectly enigmatic, as if he were a ceaselessly working machine. Now, that almost emotionally flatlined precision was both unsettling and soothing at the same time. At staff meetings, he still adopted the air of a deliberative judge jotting down notes, peering over his eyeglasses while sipping yet another Diet Coke. He would let the more energized, caffeinated attorneys argue about exactly how "forward leaning" they should go with the law. And if he had any long-range concerns that all of it—the discussions about the Geneva Convention, about torture—might lead to the most criticized moments of the Bush administration, he apparently never expressed those concerns in any forceful terms.

The dynamic in these historic White House meetings was still defined by the same principles that have prevailed since day one: Alberto Gonzales was Bush's most trusted legal adviser, and Gonzales would do anything he could to empower his most important client. Gonzales was ultimately going to endorse anything that would aid Bush either politically or policy-wise. Unspoken, but also clearly understood, was the fact that if there was ever any push back, any heated indictments, then Gonzales would be the one to stare it all down. He would be the public face to handle it, to give an accounting, an apology, an explanation—and, if it came to it, he would be the one who would have to testify, under oath. He would eventually have to do the lawyering, the defense work, to explain how the September 14 resolution could be read to mean that a domestic spying program was not just legal but vital—even if the words "eavesdropping" and "wiretapping" weren't there.

Not many people knew for sure if Gonzales would ultimately have the stomach for this, if he really had once gone to some proverbial political crossroads and made a pact with the devil to forever protect his client at the expense of his own personal legacy. Not many knew for sure, but several people close to Gonzales had a feeling he would go all the way—that he would find any means necessary for Bush to expand his presidential powers, and that he would ultimately do what he had always done: Protect Bush to the bitter end.

It was, after all, what he had done in Texas over and over again.

Two weeks after the attacks Gonzales and Flanigan were sent a secret memo from John Yoo, who was helping run the Justice Department's Office of Legal Counsel. Yoo, in many ways, was another one of the confident, conservative Federalist Society attorneys who were bonding in the Bush administration. People who knew him said he packed an academic, highly conservative and intellectual muscle and that he had the will to back up anything he argued. Gonzales liked Yoo and had wanted him to work on his staff, and had heartily approved the decision to put Yoo partly in charge of the Justice Department's legal office.[5] In the immediate aftermath of 9/11, the mood among some of the White House counsels and their counterparts at the Office of Legal Counsel had shifted quickly to outright anger and even a sense of unabashed retribution against the terrorists—and there was intense discussion about what the legal boundaries were for declaring war on shadowy, underground enemies and the sympathetic nations suspected of supporting them. Yoo's fifteen-page memo was titled "The President's Constitutional Authority to Conduct Military Operations Against Terrorists and Nations Supporting Them." When Gonzales pored over it, he came across this line: "The President may deploy military force preemptively against terrorist organizations or the States that harbor or support them, whether or not they can be linked to the specific terrorist incidents of Sept. 11."[6]

As Gonzales met with the president, Cheney, and Ashcroft, he was increasingly armed with those so-called forward-leaning memos and briefs from his own counsels, from Cheney's forceful lawyer, David Addington, and from the insistent attorneys, like Yoo, operating inside the Office of Legal Counsel. In particular, the memos being whipped together in the days after 9/11 touched on what to do with any terrorists who were taken prisoner—how to detain them and prosecute them, what rights they had under American law and international law, and, increasingly, what was the best way to use the prisoners to aid the war on terrorism. In other words, what would be the best way to extract information from captured terrorists? Immediately after 9/11, arguments were raging at the White House, inside the Pentagon, at the CIA, and at the FBI about whether the U.S. intelligence gathering apparatus had simply broken down—if our intelligence community hadn't done enough, hadn't been proactive enough, hadn't been skilled enough to extract leads about al Qaeda's structure and operations. The buzzwords were still *information* and *reconnaissance*—and how to fill in the blanks on the al Qaeda chain of command, the infrastructure, its funding, and its international scope.[7]

It was now taken as a given that Bush needed an expansive legal framework; he needed his lawyers to be thinking of ways that would "liberate" him to both respond immediately and to gather information in the "best way" possible. In the White House, word had spread quickly that Bush had literally said, "We're going to find out who did this and kick their ass." There was a sense that he was waiting impatiently for his lawyers to come up with the "creative" legal boundaries to unleash a counterattack, to capture terrorists and extract that precious reconnaissance and information.

It was in the end a clarion call to that small handful of feisty lawyers from different wings of the administration who were now urgently coalescing into a group that simply said it was time to seize the moment, time to react swiftly and forcefully with controversial legal interpretations . . . it was time to give Bush the legal options he wanted, needed, to wage war and ferret out justice and answers from the terrorists who had attacked the United States and anyone who might be suspected of supporting them. In the Office of the White House Counsel there was perhaps a palpable sense that Gonzales's team desperately wanted to convert their anger, their frustration over the 9/11 attacks. That they wanted to find the means to wage their own war against the terrorists. That the administration lawyers wanted to turn their personal revulsion into a search for any legal interpretation that could empower Bush and that could cripple the terrorists. It was in a sense a form of judicial activism—and on a personal level it was a way to turn revulsion into retribution.

It would, of course, eventually lead to enormous, howling debate about how far the American government would go to fight the ongoing war on terror. Years later, as the scope of his memos and initiatives emerged, Gonzales would ultimately be accused of arrogantly abusing American civil liberties—and essentially lying to or misleading Congress and the nation about the existence and scope of the programs being crafted by the administration. Years later, his secret legal work as White House counsel would become the focus of the most heatedly disputed moments for the second Bush administration. Civil libertarians would say Gonzales had thudded with jackboots across inalienable human rights and American principles—and then misled Congress when he was quizzed about how far the government might go to prosecute people. They would point to the fact that Gonzales would one day appear before the Senate Judiciary Committee, where he was quizzed about possible wiretapping—and where, under oath, he described that form of domestic spying as "hypothetical" when in fact it was occurring at that exact moment in the United States.

Gonzales, in Washington for only eight months and only a few years removed from handling real estate deals for a Texas law firm, was certainly not an expert when it came to emergency war powers, military commissions, war crimes, the Geneva Convention, and tribunals. But Flanigan had somewhat been there before, in the aftermath of Desert Storm, when he served the previous Bush administration. And some observers wondered if Flanigan, more than Gonzales, was doing hard legwork for the post-9/11 legal recommendations being sponsored through the White House counsel's office.

Flanigan, Addington, and the other hidden, anonymous lawyers, such as Yoo in the Office of Legal Counsel, had forged an alliance across agency boundaries and were zeroing in on the same exact blueprint for the treatment of any prisoners and detainees. They were emboldened by two facts: They had the full and direct support of both Dick Cheney and Alberto Gonzales. And they simply moved into high, urgent gear, maybe moving faster than the usual lawyers who might be called on to shape legal policy in the new war against terrorism, including federal prosecutors who had already spent years taking some terrorists to criminal trials and military lawyers who specialized in interpreting emergency war powers, military history, court-martials, the rights of prisoners-of-war, the rights of detainees, and any international treaties that touched on wartime codes of conduct. "And then Al and David and I were frequently discussing issues as they came up. It was a pretty closely coordinated relationship between the vice president's counsel and our offices," says Flanigan.[8]

As 2001 wound down, some of those outside federal and military lawyers slowly became aware that there was a tight, unyielding alliance forming in the Bush administration, and it was beginning to ram forward its urgent analysis for the White House. Some of those prosecutors and military lawyers felt deliberately excluded; some felt they were being outpaced, outmaneuvered by a band of lawyers who had something they couldn't dream of in the weeks immediately after 9/11—access, through Gonzales and Cheney, to the Oval Office. There was sporadic opposition from a few of those excluded lawyers to that impromptu—some would say brazen—legal alliance, but going public, forming a counterbalancing alliance, was politically foolhardy.

No one wanted to be painted as anemic, a wimp in the war on terror. Some of the excluded lawyers—the ones who might have argued that the new drafts, opinions, and memos were giving Bush, and any president, far too much leeway—held their tongues. The post-9/11 mood at the White House was too intense, too combative, to go public and say that the administration needed to take a breath before it decided to race after the terrorists, to empower the president to declare war where he wanted to administer justice to suspected terrorists in ways that were not the norm for American citizens.

"Prosecutors . . . wanted to take what some called a 'cops and robbers' approach to terrorism, which was, you conduct a criminal investigation, you make a case, you bring them up before a grand jury or you convene a grand jury, you investigate it, you return an indictment, and then you try them and they go to jail—that's the 'cops and robbers' approach. In contrast to that was sort of the 'war powers model,' where this is not just a criminal incident, this is an act of war, therefore the president has certain powers as commander in chief under the Constitution and the laws of the United States—which allow him to do things which he could not do in a normal criminal setting," said someone who was very close to the whole process at the White House. "For example, he has the power to hold people subject only to the writ of habeas corpus. He has the power to authorize military commanders to take certain actions, which, if they were done by the FBI, would be illegal searches and seizures—I'm speaking of actions outside the United States at this point. Gonzales was not one who said, 'Wow, the president's commander in chief power authorizes him to do absolutely everything.' But he did say, 'Look, the president's role here as a wartime leader needs to be respected in this process.'"

And if that meant Bush didn't want to go through the usually lengthy "cops and robbers" kind of prosecution, then that was his right, argued Gonzales. Ignoring any faint complaints, Gonzales shared several emergency drafts in the weeks and months after 9/11, and it almost appeared that each one was bolder, more expansive, when it came to what Gonzales would eventually recommend to the president. And as always, that part—

the persuasion of the president—would be left almost exclusively to Gonzales. He would drive the train home; he'd present the new legal package of post-9/11, war-on-terrorism recommendations to Bush. Flanigan, Addington, and just about everyone in the Office of Legal Counsel knew that there was probably no one in the White House whom Bush trusted more. When Gonzales walked into the urgent post-9/11 meetings with the president's inner circle of advisers, it was understood that Bush was almost always predisposed to follow what Gonzales recommended. It led in the end to a mutually agreed upon decision for Gonzales to perhaps move quickly, cleanly, and apart from anyone who might slow the directives down, including Rice and her senior staff, lower-rung military lawyers, Powell, Ashcroft, and the assistant attorney general Michael Chertoff.

The almost familial bond between Bush and Gonzales was the key to anything flowing out of the White House counsel's office, said several staffers. It was the thing that would always give him a leg up. That personal bond between Bush and Gonzales had been drilled home over the last eight months for anyone to see. Gonzales was loyal, and Bush had inherent trust in every bit of Gonzales's legal advice. The aggressive, risk-taking lawyers who were pushing and prodding and exploring the most dramatic elements in this country's reaction to 9/11 certainly knew that Gonzales could go right to Bush anytime he wanted. And they had to know that Bush would listen to whatever Gonzales recommended. More than once, people close to Gonzales referenced the fact that he had once been entrusted with Bush's hidden criminal past.

History has proved that key portions of America's post-9/11 behavior—from how and why it conducted its wars on terrorism, the Taliban, and Iraq, to how it decided to treat the prisoners from those wars, to how it decided to extract that precious intelligence information—were shaped in no small part by a platoon of government counsels who most Americans would be hard-pressed to name. Their insistent and ultimately controversial recommendations were marched down a furtive funnel by White House Counsel Alberto Gonzales—and he was the calm, trusted messenger who then walked into the Oval Office and delivered some of the nation's most important and ultimately divisive wartime directives straight to the president of the United States.

Gonzales, for one, did not look back as he crafted his memos and recommendations: "I wish I'd get more sleep in the job than I do, but to be able to, you know, to walk in the Oval Office and brief the most powerful person in the world on a Supreme Court vacancy, or to be in the Situation Room when the president orders our young men and women into battle, or to walk into the residence and give the president a piece of paper that you drafted for him to sign—a piece of paper you know is going to be analyzed and reviewed by historians for years to come—that's some pretty good stuff, and so I've got no complaints." [9]

E verybody who was involved in this process had, in my mind, a white hat on," said Flanigan, defending the post-9/11 work flowing out of Gonzales's office. "They were not out to be cowboys or create a radical new legal regime. What they wanted to do was to use existing legal models to assist in the process of saving lives, to get information. And the war on terror is all about information." [10]

The scope was expanding: Gonzales and the others were looking at, processing, and creating memos that suggested the president could go to war against Iraq or any nation it suspected of supporting terrorists. And now, operating under the assumption that the United States and its allies were going to be scooping up terrorists around the world, there were memos about exactly what to do with those prisoners and how to get something useful out of them. *Information* was absolutely the electric by-word—how to get it, how to use it to the advantage of the United States. Maybe it wasn't a "radical new legal regime," maybe it was. One thing was clear: They all thought it was time for a new paradigm. "Legally, the watch-word became 'forward-leaning,' by which everybody meant: 'We want to be aggressive. We want to take risks,' " said Bradford Berenson. [11]

Gonzales pushed other initiatives. He and his lawyers helped craft the September 24 initial "asset freeze" orders aimed at twenty-seven people and organizations suspected of having ties to terrorism. The same day that those asset freeze memos were being adopted, Ashcroft was at a House Judiciary Committee pushing hard for controversial things that would dominate headlines and op-ed pages: holding suspects indefinitely and expanding the use of wiretaps and Internet monitoring. Ashcroft, in the wake of 9/11, increasingly became a person both loved and hated: He was a polarizing figure who, depending on your viewpoint, was the point person for unleashing some new rules in the hunt for terrorists, or was a scary Big Brother hell-bent on trampling basic civil liberties. Gonzales was involved in the same controversial work but he remained hidden, off the radar—for a while at least.

He or his assistant counsels would confer with other administration officials in the Situation Room or in so-called Sensitive Compartmented Information Facilities (SCIFs), heavily secured rooms where top-secret classified information is usually stored. There are several SCIFs scattered around Congress and the White House. At most of them it's impossible to use a phone, and documents are not allowed to be taken out. At one of the emergency interagency meetings run by Gonzales several days after 9/11, he put together a working task force of lawyers and criminal prosecutors from the Justice Department, the State Department, the Office of Legal Counsel, the military, and his own office. The task force's mission was to come up with one clear recommendation on exactly how to prosecute any captured terrorists.

The prosecutors from the Department of Justice pushed for criminal trials like the ones that resulted in a life sentence for the Muslim cleric accused of conspiring to blow up several New York landmarks in 1993. There was serious pushback from Gonzales and his team—their argument revolved around the thought that a criminal trial was too tedious, too dangerous, and it certainly wouldn't serve the higher purpose of extracting quick, hard information that would keep the country safe and the terrorists on the run.

By October there was clearly a sense of impatience with the pace of the task force. It was disbanded, and the White House counsel's office—with the help of hardliners from the Office of Legal Counsel—simply took charge of any planning for the prosecution of foreign prisoners captured during the new war on terror. By the end of October and into early November, Gonzales's team had formulated a proposal that would pave the way for the most aggressive military tribunals since World War II—ones that would suspend the kinds of rights normally afforded Americans in the U.S. judicial system. These formulations were more than just notable for the fact that they were crafted and designed in remarkable isolation—in secret and divorced from Condoleezza Rice and influential members of the State Department. They were emblematic, some would later say, of a systematic culture that was emerging in some wings of the Bush administration—a culture that was theorizing about rewriting the rules of engagement, civil liberties, prosecution, presidential power, imprisonment, and interrogation. The harshest critics would say they were emblematic of a sad drift away from the very humane principles and morals that set the United States apart from its bloodthirsty, unconscionable enemies. Supporters would say they were simply opening up every avenue of intelligence-gathering imaginable, leaving no stone unturned.

On the first day in November and in the name of national security, Bush signed an executive order prepared by Gonzales that gave U.S. presidents expanded powers to keep their White House papers sealed after they left office. Lost amid the post-9/11 furor, that act would eventually lead to a federal lawsuit claiming that valuable American history was being hidden. It was an additional, unabashed move to expand the executive privilege of the presidency—it was yet another of Gonzales's attempts to give Bush expanded authorities, powers. On November 13 Bush signed another directive—a three-page order authorizing "full and fair" trials through the use of military tribunals to prosecute non-U.S. citizens accused of terrorism. The order created a singular emergency legal system—one in which the normal rules of due process in the United States were suspended.

The order, prepared in part by Gonzales, permitted the detention of detainees for an indefinite period of time. It gave the president the right to create a tribunal wherever terrorists were captured or detained and to designate the people he wanted to stand trial at those tribunals. The trials would be before military judges hand-picked by the secretary of defense. The proceedings would be conducted in secrecy, with an eye toward keeping any antiterrorism intelligence emerging from the tribunals under wraps, toward preventing any would-be-terrorists from picking up sensitive information. The normal rules of "proof beyond a reasonable doubt" would be suspended. The right to remain silent would not be applicable. There would be no appeals. There would be no presumption of innocence. And if a death sentence was handed down, only two-thirds of the military tribunal would need to agree—there didn't need to be a unanimous verdict. The president could at his discretion decide who would be brought to trial before any military tribunal.

The framework for the order that Gonzales wanted Bush to sign came from a case in 1942 in which eight Nazi saboteurs secretly arrived in the United States by U-boats, aiming to blow up targets in New York, Chicago, and Detroit. The plot was broken up with the help of the Coast Guard and the FBI. President Franklin Delano Roosevelt signed his own order creating emergency military tribunals; lawyers for the captured Germans said the men had a right to be tried like any other American, in an open, ordinary court. The Supreme Court unanimously ruled against the Nazis and simply said they were not entitled to the same judicial rights as Americans because they were foreign "belligerents."

Seven weeks after a secret military tribunal, six of the men were executed. Former attorney general William Barr was the one who brought the idea to Gonzales's office. Years earlier he had been walking by a historical memorial outside his office that referenced the 1942 military tribunal and the thought lodged in his head that it was a rarely used option that could be used in emergency wartime situations. After 9/11 Barr called Flanigan and relayed his theories. Flanigan was intrigued and went to Gonzales. The counsels went to work, digging into the 1942 case and finding what they needed to draft the military tribunal order that they put on Bush's desk.[12]

When Bush signed the controversial decree, it was a victory for Gonzales, a heady and empowering moment that he and his underlings relished—and something they had done without input from National Security Adviser Condoleezza Rice or Secretary of State Colin Powell, the two people whose international reputations could be directly affected by any fallout from the decree.

If Gonzales had learned anything in his legal career, it was not to second-guess himself. He had been acutely, personally involved in reviewing the desperate last-minute pleas from almost sixty men and women in Texas who were destined to be executed. He was the last person to review their claims before they would be put to death—and he had done his work seemingly unemotionally, without regret. From the beginning of his service to Bush, he knew what it might mean to be "forward-leaning"—

to push hard to find the laws, the legal groundwork that would give Bush the freedom he needed. And people who knew both Bush and Gonzales had come to the belief that the two men were more alike than anyone had ever realized—and that Gonzales's unperturbed demeanor, the way he seemed to have a nailed-down lid on his emotions, the way he seemed so quietly affable, was the only thing that made him different from Bush. When it came to his policies and politics, he had everything in common with Bush—and, as Bush would always say about people like Gonzales and his other lawyer, Harriet Miers, he knew what was in their hearts. For good measure, as if to reinforce his conservative credentials, that month Gonzales decided to don formal wear and make an appearance at the Federalist Society's twentieth anniversary celebration; he would be invited back as a guest speaker.

In exactly sixty days Gonzales had perhaps given the president of the United States the means to conduct war against terrorists, the Taliban, and maybe even Iraq. He perhaps had also given him the means to bring captured foreign citizens to justice by, as some observers said, "any means necessary."

"We push the envelope, but never beyond what the Constitution permits, in my judgment," said Gonzales.[13]

When Gonzales's work was revealed, when news first emerged about the military tribunals, there was a slow but insistent opposition. Congress initially refused to openly attack Bush—it would have been political suicide just two months after 9/11. But some academics, military lawyers, historians, and constitutional experts began to raise objections. As the scope of the post-9/11 directives from Gonzales's office—and the scope of the anti-terrorism Patriot Act—began to become more clear, there were more voices of dissent.

Finally at a Senate Judiciary Committee hearing there were blunt complaints that lawmakers were being excluded from shaping the war on terror, being shut out of the constitutional interpretations on how to prosecute both the war and the prisoners captured in that war—and that they had simply not been informed about the fact that the president was going to be overseeing secret military tribunals. Senator Patrick Leahy, loathed by Cheney and others in the administration, had flatly stated that no one had even remotely mentioned the idea of military tribunals to ranking members of Congress. Constitutional experts were giving interviews suggesting that Gonzales's order gave Bush unlimited power to put anybody before the secret tribunals; it was something you might see in a monarchy, not a democracy. Various law enforcement officials and community leaders around the country were also raising objections to the Patriot Act net being cast in the search for terrorists on U.S. soil, complaining that ethnic groups, Muslims, and immigrants were being unfairly targeted, detained, and interviewed, and that civil liberties were being threatened like never before. A professor from Harvard Law, Gonzales's old school, talked to one Senate hearing about fears that the United States would be "inadvertently succumbing to our own reign of terror... the tyranny and terror of oppressive government no less than the tyranny of terrorism." [14]

Ashcroft and the assistant attorney general Michael Chertoff went public, defending the Patriot Act as well as the military tribunal order, and suggested that the Department of Justice leaders had decided public criminal trials would not just destroy the chances to net some valuable antiterrorist information but could actually put courthouses, communities, and whole cities in danger. Meanwhile Gonzales was also dispatched on a flurry of media missions, meant in part to defend the work he had done on the Patriot Act and the other post-9/11 policies. He broke his personal protocol by inviting reporters to his office to talk about administration policy, he arranged to write an op-ed piece for the *New York Times,* he spoke to the American Bar Association, and he quickly scheduled some rare TV appearances. He conducted one interview with Bush family favorite Brit Hume on FOX at the end of November. Hume, who liked to call him Judge Gonzales, asked why these orders were so quickly put together and whether Democrats were lodging complaints solely for political reasons:

"Well, of course, we are in extraordinary times, Brit. The United States has never seen an enemy like this. And the president felt it important to have all available tools to deter and disrupt and to, in any way, respond to terrorist attacks, further terrorist attacks against this country. The order was not something that was entered into lightly. This was a decision that took some time to make. There were many lawyers in the administration that worked on this, that looked at this

issue. And finally, when it was ready to go, the president felt it was then the appro-
priate time to sign the order. . . . I think Congress has an appropriate oversight role,
in looking at what the president of the United States has done here . . . and so
I would say that I don't want to attribute any political motives in what's going
on here."

Just a few years removed from his airy commentaries in the *Dallas Morning News* about how much Texas and Mexico had in common, Gonzales wrote an end-of-November op-ed piece in the *New York Times,* arguing, "In appropriate circumstances, these commissions provide important advantages over civilian trials. They spare American jurors, judges and courts the grave risks associated with terrorist trials. They allow the government to use classified information as evidence without compromising intelligence or military efforts. They can dispense justice swiftly, close to where our forces may be fighting, without years of pretrial proceedings or post-trial appeals." He added that the order he had given Bush to sign did not undermine the "constitutional value of civil liberties." [15]

He and Bush had been down this road together in the past. When Bush put a check mark in the box marked "Deny" on the clemency petitions in Texas, he frequently told reporters that the men and women who were about to be executed had been given "full and fair trials." For months Gonzales would come back to the same refrain: "What has been done here is not unusual in a time of war. . . . The decisions here haven't been based upon how we are going to look in history. My job as a lawyer is to provide legal advice to the president of the United States, to tell him whether or not this is an option that is in fact lawful or unconstitutional. So the president's place in history would not be my No. 1 priority." [16]

Gonzales had only been in Washington for ten months and he had fought to keep an intentionally low personal profile. Some senators and congressmen had dueled with him, visited him, bartering about Karl Rove's stock holdings and the selection of judges to federal benches. But very few of the power brokers outside the White House inner circle truly understood the relationship between Bush and Gonzales or truly understood Gonzales's ranking inside the administration. But by the end of 2001 it was becoming increasingly clear that Gonzales was as plugged in, as influential, as men such as C. Boyden Gray and the other powerful counsels who had served the Bush family in the past.

Given the fact that it was becoming increasingly clear that Gonzales was intimately involved in the most intense decisions emerging at one of the most intense times in American history, some began to believe that Gonzales was even more influential than his predecessors. Everyone knew that Bush liked to delegate, but he only had deep, infinite trust in a small number of advisers. Gonzales's friendship with Bush, their bond, and the fact that he was clearly the point person on extraordinary pieces of the terrorism battle plan, made his status more clear. An aide to a Democratic senator simply said Gonzales was "the White House's eyes, ears, and hands in developing the administration's initiatives." [17] And some people said that was exactly the problem. That Gonzales now had an inordinate hand in the dramatic post-9/11 decisions—decisions that would affect all Americans, including the possibilities that the president could pick any foreign citizen he wanted to be tried in a hidden tribunal, that innocent people would be caught up in some plague of racial and ethnic profiling, that the accepted rules for protecting attorney–client privileges would be tossed out the window, that presidential powers would be expanded without congressional oversight. Gonzales didn't have the years of training in criminal justice, military justice, civil liberties, and international law to be contributing wholesale chunks of America's blueprint for the war on terror. He certainly didn't have the diplomatic portfolio to adequately measure what the creation of an all-encompassing tribunal aimed at citizens of other countries might mean for relations between the United States and its allies. He had been a "dirt and deals" real estate lawyer in Texas, gone on to hold a window-dressing job as Texas secretary of state, then weighed in on fourteen civil cases in Texas, most of which had to do with insurance and business deals.

Gonzales, blasted one legal scholar in Washington, was "in over his head . . . you're dealing with someone who's gone from being a state court judge in Texas to being thrown into this." [18] In Washington other people simply said that he was being used—that Addington, Yoo, Flanigan, Berenson, and the other aggressive lawyers with lower profiles were the ones doing the gritty, controversial work crafting the memos Gonzales was delivering to Bush. There was a prevailing theory emerging that Gonzales's name was on the memos—he signed off on them, but he didn't actually write them—the legal firepower came from somewhere else.

There were other whispers in Washington that Gonzales's role in the controversial post-9/11 orders would personally backfire on him. If there was some thunderous movement in the United States and abroad, some boomeranging backlash that the nation was behaving barbarically and not democratically—that Gonzales had just given Bush free reign to have the military detain and put before a secret tribunal any foreign citizen suspected of aiding or abetting terrorism—some insiders said that it would be Gonzales who would be left out to dry. The cutthroat game would leave Gonzales exposed and mortally wounded. He would have to take the blame for promulgating bad policy. He had been told by Bush that perception was everything in politics, and if there ever was a negative public relations fiasco over the tribunals and the antiterrorism program, then it could only come back to directly haunt the president's counselor.

By December Rove had a sense that Gonzales had so far done very well with the media, and the backlash might really be confined to a narrow group. CNN's Wolf Blitzer, in particular, had raked "Judge Gonzales" over the coals, but Gonzales seemed to hold his own. That same small smile creased his face as Blitzer pressed him on the legality of the tribunals, and Gonzales appeared inherently unflustered. The people watching Gonzales at the end of 2001 said he had somehow survived the allegations, the accusations, the quick firestorm—and that really only a handful of policy wonks, reporters, and politicians even understood the full importance of Gonzales's memos to Bush. Perception is everything in politics, and there were some who thought Gonzales *looked* like an unthreatening, informed bureaucrat on national TV.

On the last day of 2001 the pundits gathered on ABC to talk about their political predictions for 2002. George Stephanopoulos offered his forecast: "And the Supreme Court will get an Hispanic person. Alberto Gonzales, President Bush's counsel right now, will be the next choice for Supreme Court when there are resignations."

For the people who had raged at Gonzales's inexperience in criminal, military, and international law, the suggestion that he was at the top of the list to go to the U.S. Supreme Court were almost too much to bear. His friends, his supporters, had gone to a far different place—they had vaulted Gonzales into the pantheon of prominent American leaders: "The Hispanic community talks about Cesar Chavez. He was a great leader for Hispanics. Al is a professional version of Cesar Chavez. You can speak their names in the same sentence as being examples of ascending in this community to a better life," says Massey Villareal, who had served as national chairman of the Republican Hispanic National Assembly.[19]

THIRTEEN

Torture

Three weeks into the New Year, Gonzales put his signature on another classified memo for the president of the United States;
he had no idea that it would turn into political plutonium. He
had just gone on a secret flight to examine Guantánamo Bay and the
first batch of prisoners who had been brought in. On the way back to
Washington, Gonzales was mulling over the fact that Secretary of State
Colin Powell had pushed back on Bush, had said he loathed the idea of
the United States antagonizing allies by seeming to flaunt international
treaties and protocol. Powell was worried what the world would say about
the way America was warehousing, interrogating, the detainees. Bush
had asked Gonzales for a reading on Powell's fears. Gonzales usually spent
some time condensing drafts of his memos for Bush. He would rewrite them, revise them, over and over again. His final, concise, plainly
stated memos were a distillation of his years grooming them for his client
George W. Bush. His assistant, Stuart Bowen, thought that Gonzales was a
persuasive writer when he needed to be. "He is a very good writer, a *very*
good writer," Bowen once said, putting some extra emphasis on the word
very.[1]

The new memo signed by Gonzales would be crafted on the heels of those other quick, stunning, secret legal victories steered by Gonzales and his team in the White House. They had set the parameters for war, for gathering intelligence and how to treat suspected terrorists, and they had done it without consulting Congress or the other foot-dragging bodies in Washington. They had done their work with Cheney, and they had virtually excluded Rice and Powell. It was, as one staffer said, no time for statesmanship—at least the traditional, slow-moving kind. It was beyond the point of painstaking deliberation.

It was really an extraordinary turning point for Gonzales. He rarely moved this fast, especially in legal arenas that were outside his usual ken and that were so drenched with the twin possibilities of precedent and enormous controversy. The education of Alberto Gonzales—bumped along in life by the changing attitudes toward the treatment of minorities, gusted forward by his proximity to the Bush family and by being "tapped" by the Bushes—had lurched to a new phase in 2001. No one had dealt with anything like 9/11 before, but for a lawyer whose roots were in a crowded bungalow in Humble, Texas, it was especially like being rocketed into a distant orbit. In six quick years he had gone from the zoning committee hearings in Houston to secretly crafting and publicly selling the nation's plans to prosecute the war on terror.

When he committed his thoughts to paper in the abortion debate in Texas, it floated into a metaphorical file available to anyone who wanted to try to gauge his heart and his mind. The new memo he signed for President Bush on January 25, 2002, would just as quickly and just as irreversibly join that abortion memo. Some would say that it was a cleaner window into what was really inside Alberto Gonzales's soul. Or, at least, as some would add, it was a window into the evolution of how his heart, mind, and soul were now working in Washington in service to his president. There would be allegations that he simply never wrote the draft—that it was probably done by Addington or one of the other uncompromising attorneys hidden in the White House. It was, some would say, almost as if he was acting just like George Bush did when he was handed Gonzales's death penalty memos back in Texas—it was as if Gonzales was briskly signing off on intense and grave memos that touched on the most profound life-and-death matters known to man.

Memorandum For The President
From: Alberto R. Gonzales
Subject: Decision Re Application Of The Geneva Convention On Prisoners
        of War To The Conflict With Al Qaeda And The Taliban

Purpose
    On January 18, I advised you that the Department of Justice had issued
a formal legal opinion concluding that the Geneva Convention III on the
Treatment of Prisoners of War (GPW) does not apply to the conflict with al
Qaeda. I also advised you that DOJ's opinion concludes that there are rea-
sonable grounds for you to conclude that GPW does not apply with respect to
the conflict with the Taliban. I understand that you decided that GPW does
not apply and, accordingly, that al Qaeda and Taliban detainees are not pris-
oners of war under the GPW.
    The Secretary of State has requested that you reconsider that decision.
Specifically, he has requested that you conclude the GPW does apply to both
al Qaeda and the Taliban.²

Gonzales goes on to state that the president has the constitutional authority to say that the Geneva Convention—the agreement signed by
most countries in the world that outlines the international codes for treatment of prisoners of war—does or does not apply. Among a few of the
Geneva Convention's tenets: Prisoners of war are to be treated humanely,
and torture and cruelty are forbidden; while detained, prisoners of war
shall be paid their usual salary; if they were put to work as prisoners, they
were to receive a fair pay rate; prisoners of war must not be subject to vio-
lence, intimidation, insults, and public curiosity; prisoners of war are entitled to the same treatment given to a country's own forces, including being
housed in rooms that have the same amounts of space, lighting, and heating; prisoners of war must be served the same kinds of foods they would
normally eat; prisoners of war must receive due process and fair trials; every prisoner of war, when questioned on the subject, is bound to give only
his surname, first name and rank, date of birth, and army, regimental, personal, or serial number, or failing that, equivalent information; no physical
or mental torture, nor any other form of coercion, may be inflicted on

prisoners of war to secure from them information of any kind whatsoever; prisoners of war who refuse to answer may not be threatened, insulted, or exposed to unpleasant or disadvantageous treatment of any kind. There were other matters in the conventions: prisoners of war were entitled to sporting equipment, kitchen utensils, musical instruments, and even scientific equipment.[3]

Gonzales and his team had scoffed at some of the details in the Geneva Convention. "The notion of paying nine Swiss francs a day to Osama bin Laden's bodyguard and inviting him to visit the Guantánamo Canteen to purchase sundries is quaint and a little silly," says Bradford Berenson. "You know, the Geneva Convention also require you to supply prisoners with utensils to prepare their own food. So we're going to put knives in the hands of al Qaeda at these prison camps. You know that stuff was designed for a different kind of soldier and a different kind of war. . . . You know, when you are talking about people like those who flew the planes into the World Trade Centers, who are religiously inspired fascists, unbelievably bloodthirsty and unbelievably fanatical, who don't respect any of the customary laws of war, the kind of treatment that the Geneva Convention mandates just can't be afforded."[4]

And Gonzales's January 2002 memo to Bush continued this way:

As you have said, the war against terrorism is a new kind of war. It is not the traditional clash between nations adhering to the laws of war that formed the backdrop for GPW. The nature of the new war places a high premium on other factors, such as the ability to quickly obtain information from captured terrorists and their sponsors in order to avoid further atrocities against American civilians, and the need to try terrorists for war crimes such as wantonly killing civilians. In my judgment, this new paradigm renders obsolete Geneva's strict limitations on questioning of enemy prisoners and renders quaint some of its provisions requiring that captured enemy be afforded such things as commissary privileges, scrip (i.e., advances of monthly pay), athletic uniforms and scientific instruments.[5]

Gonzales's memo urged Bush to stick to his guns and insist that the Geneva Convention did not apply to al Qaeda and the Taliban. He said that Bush should be prepared for some pushback from allies and even the U.S. military:

> *Since the Geneva Convention were concluded in 1949, the United States has never denied their applicability to either U.S. or opposing forces engaged in armed conflict, despite several opportunities to do so. During the last Bush Administration, the United States stated that it "has a policy of applying the Geneva Convention of 1949 whenever armed hostilities occur with regular foreign armed forces, even if arguments could be made that the threshold standards for the applicability of the Convention . . . are not met." . . . Our position would likely provoke widespread condemnation among our allies and in some domestic quarters, even if we make clear that we will comply with the core humanitarian principles of the treaty as a matter of policy. Concluding that the Geneva Convention does not apply may encourage other countries to look for technical "loopholes" in future conflicts to conclude that they are not bound by GPW either. Other countries may be less inclined to turn over terrorists or provide legal assistance to us if we do not recognize a legal obligation to comply with the GPW. A determination that GPW does not apply to al Qaeda and the Taliban could undermine U.S. military culture which emphasizes maintaining the highest standards of conduct in combat, and could introduce an element of uncertainty in status of adversaries. . . . The statement that other nations would criticize the U.S. because we have determined that GPW does not apply is undoubtedly true. It is even possible that some nations would point to that determination as a basis for failing to cooperate with us on specific matters in the war against terrorism.*[6]

Gonzales instantly laid bare a schism among Bush's advisers: Colin Powell digested Gonzales's memo and immediately went to Bush, demanding that the Geneva Convention had to be applied in the new war—otherwise, international relations could be thrown into an impossible tangle. The Pentagon's military lawyers loathed the draft, too. The way the military lawyers saw it, they would be put in the untenable position of having to conduct prosecutions in military tribunals that they had no hand in crafting or that they simply might not have wanted—and they were going to be prosecuting detainees, perhaps overseas, without those prisoners being granted international Geneva Convention rights.

The military lawyers had no hand in Gonzales's memos, but they were the ones who were going to do the controversial, dangerous work that his memos could unleash. Through Gonzales's directives, the officers at Guantánamo were told to fill out one-page forms that would attest to the president's "reason to believe" the detainees were tied to terrorism—and that would speed up their prosecution in the secret tribunals. But when the officers reported that several of the detainees appeared to be peripheral players in the shadowy world of terrorism and that there really was very little evidence against them, a decision was made to simply hold the detainees indefinitely, to put them into a boundless legal netherworld with no lawyers and no real sense of what to do with them.[7]

Gonzales was plodding deeper into a bloody political minefield with Powell hovering nearby. He was signing off on incendiary memos that would eventually turn into heavy ammunition for newspaper editorials, human rights groups, career military officers, constitutional scholars, academics, and an endless number of Democrats and even Republicans. Something he could never have foreseen when he was at Vinson & Elkins was now moving with blinding speed. Gonzales was emerging from his treasured anonymity—by his volition when he did a full-scale public relations push at the end of 2001, and by dint of a curious national and international community.

His international exposure before he came to Washington was limited to some light interaction with Mexico. Now Bush was reading Gonzales's recommendations to set aside some provisions of the Geneva Convention, to hold foreign citizens indefinitely and prepare for secret military tribunals—all while the Bush administration was moving away from other famous international treaties, from the Kyoto Protocols on the environment, to the Anti-Ballistic Missile Treaty, to the Rome Treaty that created an international criminal court. As the world watched Bush lead the United States from various avenues of international consensus, attention shifted to the unassuming man providing the president with legal advice.

The lawyer from Humble, Texas, was appearing on the international radar, and he would remain there as the United States began its convoluted

but insistent march to war in Iraq, the Abu Ghraib scandal and the revelations about domestic spying programs. Critical Gonzales-watchers were
firmly emerging around the nation, around the globe, and they were beginning to assemble some threads, beginning with his moves in Texas as
the general counsel to then governor George W. Bush. Back then he had
once quietly suggested that the Vienna Conventions didn't apply to
Texas—that foreign prisoners in Texas weren't entitled to the international
legal rights outlined in those conventions. The threads would accumulate.
For the next three years his critics would increasingly work harder and
harder to weave them together—from his challenging the Vienna Convention, to his brisk memos that paved the way to executions in Texas, to
creating secret tribunals, to discarding provisions in the Geneva Convention.

The people who worked in the counsel's office were well aware of
Gonzales's emerging public image. They told each other that he was increasingly being judged by people who had none of the context, background, and experience that Gonzales was privy to. They said he was
actually authentically patriotic, because he really did believe he was the
embodiment of the American Dream, because he was always fully aware
that he had gone to work as the president's counselor after growing up in
a house with no hot running water and no telephone. Bradford Berenson
says: "You know, I suspect he is an intensely patriotic person. We never
talked about it in those terms, but my hunch is that, like many American
success stories, he probably has a deep, deep love of his country, which
animates him—and is coupled with a gratitude and humility for some of
the amazing opportunities he's had. . . . I suspect that commitment comes
from kind of a deep and patriotic place."[8]

Some people who had worked closely with him said that Gonzales
was authentically interested in the American Dream insofar as it meant
accumulating personal wealth. One time he told a close colleague that
when he worked in corporate law, he made money for his clients: "My job
was to make the rich richer." He didn't say it in a derogatory way or a self-
disparaging way. His colleague believed that Gonzales was always interested in making money, in using his public career stops as preparation for
a financially satisfying endgame. His colleague felt that Gonzales—who
liked fine suits, who enjoyed golf at private resorts—was probably partially

in the game for the big payoff that would surely arrive after he left his high-profile government jobs. He was in government out of a mixture of things, said another observer—a sense of public service, of competition, of abject loyalty to Bush. That latter part was, for Gonzales, like some ultimate rung on the ladder out of Humble. People who knew the Bush family had seen it happen before to people like Karen Hughes and others. The proximity to power, the way the Bushes seamlessly drew people into their inner circle as if those people were being invited to join some sort of exclusive, burnished club, some kind of history-laden fraternity that they knew existed but could never figure out how to access.

It wasn't so much that Gonzales was being seduced by the Bushes, said people, as it was more a matter of the Bushes being a goal for Gonzales. He has always been intensely competitive; he had rolled the dice and left for Fort Yukon; he took advantage of the opportunities to get into the Air Force Academy, Rice, and Harvard. People who knew him well in Texas and Washington said that it was a mistake to see his quiet style as a form of meekness; people who worked directly with him said that quiet style was simply the outer layer on a man who remained extremely competitive, calculating.

One time Gonzales talked to a friend about something he rarely shared with others. He said he couldn't sleep at night unless he heard the noise of a crappy little plastic fan blowing on him; it was a link, a reminder, to when he was dirt-poor and there was no air conditioning in 100-degree Humble, Texas. The people who worked with Gonzales were taken aback to hear him talk about it, about how a grown man with a six-figure income and powerful jobs and friends couldn't get a good night's sleep unless he had that cheap plastic reminder of how far he had come in life. There was a sense among some of his friends that Gonzales felt that no one—absolutely no one—he worked with could ever even remotely relate to the way he grew up. They were born into wealth, like Bush, or they had straighter, easier paths to good schools, good careers. He had to scramble, to push to invent himself, to move, to gamble. There was a sense that Gonzales felt he would always be misunderstood but that he would also never regret his decisions and his compromises.

———

In Washington, Gonzales privately told his best friends in the counsel's office that he hated the way the media was misinterpreting his role as the president's counselor, how they didn't really examine the specifics and the context of the advice he was giving Bush. He was frustrated by the politics. He had only been in Washington one year and already he was locked in a perpetually wary chess match with Ashcroft and now the reporters, especially Michael Isikoff at *Newsweek,* who were beginning to dig deeper into his role in the White House. Through Bush's first four years as president, there were two names that people learned not to mention in glowing terms around Gonzales: Ashcroft and Isikoff. As Gonzales was hashed over in editorials, cover stories, and on the cable and network news shows, he told others that he now knew what Bush had meant when he told him that entering politics was like being a cork in a raging river—and the media was the river. The reaction to his draft memo on the Geneva Convention, he would later say, was typical of reporters picking and choosing from his legal decisions until they found exactly the word or two that they wanted to pull out of context.

He especially felt that way two years later when the draft memo was eventually leaked to the media. (People watching the agitated jockeying between Gonzales and Ashcroft wondered if the attorney general knew who had released the explosive memo.) Instantly, there were two words— "obsolete" and "quaint"—in the memo that became blazing lightning rods for his critics, for Bush's critics: *"In my judgment, this new paradigm renders obsolete Geneva's strict limitations on questioning of enemy prisoners and renders quaint some of its provisions."*

"Quaint" and "obsolete" would enter into that Gonzales file being kept by reporters and administration foes. Those words would become the defining parenthetical that followed Gonzales's name. His January 2002 memo and another one later in the year that he endorsed but didn't write would be collectively known as the Gonzales Torture Memos. And ultimately the use of the words "quaint" and "obsolete" in reference to provisions in the Geneva Convention were singled out as proof that Gonzales had lost his soul and surrendered to that same fanatical disregard for humanity that America's enemies sometimes exhibited. By calling portions of the heralded, internationally recognized standard for moral codes of conduct "quaint" and "obsolete," Gonzales was going to be accused of merely doing with a pen what some people did with a sword . . . or a gun or a suicide bomb . . . or a plane that was hijacked and aimed at innocent lives.

All the scrutiny would eventually shake him, anger him. He was following Bush's lead, Karen Hughes's instructions, and never going off the record with reporters—never really trusting them with some extra bit of insight that would put things back in the right context or allow him to get control of the public perception. It was the price, the downside perhaps, of a life predicated on discretion. If he finally felt maligned in the media as an architect of torture, as the Antichrist of civil liberties, it might have had something to do with the fact that he had deliberately been an enigma—to his staffers working sixteen-hour days alongside him and to almost every member of the media who had to cover him. Six straight years of avoiding the media—and after years of hearing Bush supporters laughing at what they said were the free passes given by the *Dallas Morning News*—had instilled in Gonzales a sense of distrust and disrespect for them. Anyway he looked at it, the media would never do the right job covering the Bush administration. Being an enigma was still better than doing what other people in the White House were beginning to do. Leave it to others in the White House to try to coax and coach the media—leave it to Rove, to Lewis Libby, and to the others in the Bush administration who were feeding the media, planting stories with the media, beginning the buildup to the invasion of Iraq.

Later Gonzales would think that he was hired, first and foremost, for his discretion. There were always better legal minds around him—even he knew it—but no one was more discreet. No one was more trusted by Bush. Discretion is what he did. And now he was signing some of the most classified memos surrounding an intentionally hidden agenda to fight terrorism—a war that he and others believed needed to be fought without ever tipping your hand to the enemy. By design, by job definition, by the new post-9/11 rules, and by personal inclination, Gonzales was bound in tight, overlapping layers of secrecy and discretion. He said that the media—and really very few people—would ever truly understand it: "I have learned that the media oftentimes writes things that are incorrect because they don't have all the information, and so you learn to live with it. I mean that's just the way it is. There's some information that cannot be shared, should not be shared, and so you don't share it."[9]

At the end of the month Gonzales received a Department of Justice order instructing everyone in the White House to keep any e-mails, computer entries, or notes they had that involved contact or conversations with Enron executives about Enron's sorry financial affairs. Gonzales, well aware of the widening probe into his old corporate client, ordered an "administrative alert" in an interoffice memo, telling White House staffers to comply with the Justice Department order, including ordering agencies to keep any records having to do with Cheney's energy task force. It's unclear when Alberto Gonzales ceased sending e-mails, but he would later announce that he simply did not compose e-mails on any topic anymore.

He had to weigh what his role might be in any internal White House investigation into Enron, and he decided that he had come clean years ago to the Texas Ethics Commission about his Enron contributions, that he had last worked for them as a partner at Vinson & Elkins in 1994. He told people at the White House that he had no legal liabilities. It was another matter for Cheney. The General Accounting Office was filing a suit against Cheney to force him to announce the names of any oil executives who might have helped the Bush White House craft its energy policy.

Gonzales, as he had done at Bush's drunk driving trial in Texas, invoked some statutory defense, suggesting that the GAO didn't have the authority to launch its investigation. The investigation into Bush administration ties to Enron would occupy Gonzales for several more months, with Waxman issuing a report citing 112 contacts between Enron and White House or other administration officials (including Treasury Secretary Paul O'Neill and Commerce Secretary Don Evans) over the course of 2001 and Senator Joseph Lieberman telling Gonzales he was "deeply disappointed" with Gonzales's "inadequate" response to the investigation.

Meanwhile Powell was still clearly unhappy about Gonzales's Geneva Convention draft. He had Pentagon officers telling him that disregarding the Geneva Convention would forever put any captured American troops in harm's way. There were citizens of twenty-five different countries being held at Guantánamo, and State Department officials were hearing from foreign dignitaries who were already upset that they were being denied what they considered their international rights. Word was filtering out that Gonzales's memo had shined the light on those welling divisions in the cabinet. Bush tried to hit it down the middle between Gonzales and Powell, and he announced on February 7 that the United States was always intending to comply with the "spirit" of the Geneva Convention, that everyone on his senior staff was on the same page, and that he had now decided that the conventions would apply to captured Taliban fighters but not to al Qaeda detainees. At the White House, most people said that Gonzales had really won, that Powell had wanted Bush to go all the way and tear up any hint of a turning away from the Geneva accords.

The last several months had been both rocky and secretive. Addington, Flanigan, and a handful of others were meeting in Gonzales's office in the West Wing and plunging deeper and deeper into things that Gonzales had never dreamed of back in the softly humming corporate confines of Houston. At the meetings there was still the ever-increasing sense that everyone needed to think far outside the box, to work harder, smarter and, more aggressively than ever before to come up with the means to win the war. When Addington, Flanigan, Berenson, and the others went into Gonzales's wood-paneled "captain's quarters" office and sat underneath the pictures of Gonzales in his air force uniform, it was almost as if they had formed their own frontline squad. Beginning in March and through the summer of 2002, Gonzales and various attorneys and advisers with ties to the CIA, the Department of Defense, traded memos or attended meetings in Gonzales's office to talk about where interrogation ended and torture began—what it really means to torture another human being. The discussions, conducted at the request of some CIA officials, touched on the graphic details of the CIA's interrogation training and techniques: open, hard slaps to the face and stomach; handcuffing detainees and forcing them to stand for almost two straight days without sleep; dripping cold water on naked detainees who are forced to stand in cells that are 10 to 20 degrees above freezing; having prisoners move from one extreme temperature to another; forcefully, abruptly grabbing prisoners and shaking them. The discussion moved into the general productivity of the various methods, which ones had historically proven to yield accurate information—not hysterical information that was the product of a pliant, degraded, and whimpering prisoner who was apt to say whatever he thought his captors wanted to hear.

There was talk about a centuries-old technique called "water board-ing," which has many variations. In one form, a prisoner has his eyes cov-ered, his mouth gagged, and he is strapped to a board with his feet elevated while water is dripped on him until he thinks he's drowning and reaches a frantic panic attack. In other forms that date back to the Inquisition, a prisoner could be dunked in a vat of putrid water for increasingly longer amounts of time. A prisoner could also have his head wrapped in see-through plastic and be subject to the same drowning sensation.[10]

The surreal nature of the discussions taking place that spring and sum-mer in the West Wing of the White House was underscored by the fact that they were overseen by a former real estate lawyer from Texas—and by the fact that the lawyers in the room who had been picking federal judges and studying Karl Rove's stock holdings were now having very specific, literal debates about the instruments of torture and how torturers applied them.

The war on terror had yielded several suspected al Qaeda leaders. Bush, Rumsfeld, Cheney, and others wanted information and intelligence im-mediately—before America was attacked again, before more American lives were lost. They wanted to hear about the asset and liability assess-ments of how the United States would look to its allies if and when any of the harsh "interrogation techniques" were employed. In Gonzales's office a consensus was clearly building as he and the others weighed the inter-rogation techniques—methods that touched on the history of how the CIA was training its interrogators, how water boarding had been used in Central and South America in the 1970s and 1980s, how the Israelis pre-ferred to interrogate Islamic prisoners, how captors tried to extract infor-mation by burying people alive. Just like Gonzales's earlier memo that said a "new paradigm" rendered portions of the Geneva Convention quaint and obsolete, the international codes for interrogation needed to be re-examined. The endgame, everyone told each other, was a just cause; it was all predicted on intelligence gathering that would ultimately save Ameri-can lives.

The meetings and discussions were held without the direct input of the senior international statespeople Rice and Powell. And they were intense, to say the least. In the end the by-product of those discussions would touch on the most harsh accusations ever leveled at the Bush administration—that it endorsed torture, that it had gotten so "forward-leaning" in its hunger to squeeze information out of its prisoners, that a culture of permissiveness had welled up inside the West Wing . . . and flowed straight to Abu Ghraib, straight to the heart of secret prisons run by the CIA, straight to a corruption of America's standing as a bastion of humane conduct and civil liberties.

Gonzales had to know that the politics were spiraling to some dizzying level. The round of secret meetings were juxtaposed with the way people handicapping the Supreme Court seat were still writing about Gonzales on a regular basis. Each new story that landed on his desk was addressing in bullet-point fashion the things that would make him an easy, perfect, and welcomed high court justice. But those stories were also filled with bullet points that said he had serious baggage. They were repeated over and over again in print and on the air: his abortion ruling in Texas, his work for Enron, his fight to keep presidential records sealed, his achingly slow release of White House papers, his race to fill federal benches with strong conservatives . . . and in time the stories would mention his draft memos about secret tribunals and the Geneva Convention.

In May, Gonzales agreed to talk to a reporter from San Antonio, the city where he had been born. Their conversation seemed almost wistful, with Gonzales talking about something he had not revealed to any other reporter or anyone else he had ever worked with—that he had labored in the hot and dusty cotton fields, just like his parents, when he was a little boy. He talked about the fact that two of his sons were still quite young—one was just ten, the other was seven—and that they really were not impressed that he worked in the White House. For a second he mentioned something that he had only very occasionally brought up with his wife and his closest friends and colleagues: He missed Texas. Things seemed easier in Texas than in Washington.

"The atmosphere is different. Doing what is right seemed easier to define and easier to accomplish in Texas." [11]

In Texas, Gonzales had no media scrutiny. And in Texas, his boss once had Democrats eating out of his hand or too scared to speak up. Bush, even before he became governor, had spent considerable time, along with his father, cultivating the support and endorsement of the powerful Democratic lieutenant governor. The alcoholic Bob Bullock was literally nearing the end of his life, and he had found a second son in the younger Bush. Truth be told, by the end of Bullock's life, his politics had veered to some sort of flinty, pragmatic place that made it very easy for him to ignore any entreaties from die-hard Democrats. The conversion of Bullock, borne out of a convergence of acutely personal moments and sheer pragmatic politics, was an exceedingly easy thing—and when it happened, Bush and Gonzales had very little partisan politics to contend with in Texas. Gonzales and everyone else who worked with him had grown accustomed to easy victories. It was no wonder if he wanted to leave Washington and go back to Texas.

Not long after his wistful interview with a reporter from his native city, Gonzales was reminded of how he seemed to be trapped inside a never-ending political game. No doubt under the direction of Karl Rove, he accepted an invitation to speak at a meeting of the Council for National Policy, an ultraconservative organization that forbids media coverage and has included among its members several influential Christian right leaders such as Reverend Jerry Falwell, the Eagle Forum's Phyllis Schlafly, Reverend Tim LaHaye, and Paul Weyrich. The council, which quietly meets three times a year, had become a favored destination for Republicans seeking to win or solidify the Christian conservative base. If Gonzales was being prepared for a Supreme Court nomination, he needed to have the support of hardliner conservatives, and he needed to be sent out to allay their fears.

The conference, held at a Ritz-Carlton in Virginia, was filled with curious conservatives who wanted to know if Gonzales had the toughened-up ideology they were looking for—or whether Robert Novak was right when he published that column saying Gonzales was scaring red-blooded conservatives. Gonzales, whose speaking style is studied, simple, and muted, didn't have people shouting his name. He came across as measured, careful, and hard to read. It was like the dilemma he found himself in when he served on the bench in Texas; he wasn't going to be a judicial activist, but some die-hard conservatives were demanding to know where he really came from.

His work on the abortion case was a classic example to the Christian conservatives who had him under a microscope. Back in Texas he almost seemed to suggest that he was against abortion, that as a parent he found it abhorrent, but at the same time he didn't do a damned thing about it. He had a chance to attack *Roe v. Wade* but he chose not to join sides with his then fellow justice Priscilla Owen. Either Gonzales blinked or he simply didn't agree that abortion was bad enough to be outlawed. Either way, he was still not convincing true believer conservatives that he was one of them on every social issue. People who were at the conference in Virginia essentially walked away with more questions than answers about Gonzales's socially conservative credentials.

Some of it had to do with something gauzier, trickier, and politically incorrect that no one would really ever come forward and talk about. It was like the invisible 800-pound gorilla in the room: Gonzales had alluded here and there to how he might have been afforded some help in his career because he was Hispanic—and Bush, too, had blurted out Gonzales's ethnicity mattered to him when he made personnel decisions. No one would dare go on the record, no one would ever flatly state that Alberto Gonzales was the beneficiary of quotas, affirmative action, special help— and, of course, none of his critics would publicly announce that he had sold his Hispanic soul and that he really had become a "coconut". . . brown on the outside and white in his soul. His ethnicity had always been a squishy, hot potato topic—impossible to get a handle on and something no one wanted to touch.

Gonzales's friends literally said that he had once been "tapped" by Bush, which struck some Bush-watchers as a deliciously ironic way to frame it: Bush had famously been "tapped" at college to join the ultraselective, secret society known as Skull & Bones. It was part of his legacy, his heritage, and Bush was going to be joining a social and business network that his father had joined, his grandfather had joined, and dozens of other family members and friends had joined. And when anyone joined, it was said that they had been "tapped" for entry into the exclusive club. Years later Bush "tapped" Gonzales for admission into his family, network, inner circle.

Loyalty was a two-way street. Gonzales was bound to Bush for the rest of his public life. And when Bush decided—for political reasons or for more enlightened reasons—to advance some minorities, Gonzales was one of his most prominent and important choices. And now, no one in conservative circles—in any circle, for that matter—wanted to flatly suggest there were hundreds of more qualified people than Gonzales. No one wanted to argue that the reason critics said he was in over his head on any number of things—negotiating with powerful Democrats, massaging the media, writing the memos for how we would prosecute the post-9/11 war—was because he had been a "token" minority appointee.

If Gonzales knew it or not, he never mentioned it to many of his friends, but there were whispers all over Washington that if there was a cohesive and ardently conservative legal strategy emerging out of the Office of the White House Counsel, it was coming from those other adrenaline-laced conservative lawyers who had seized the opportunity to push their Federalist Society inclinations, their neoconservative inclinations, their Reagan–Scalia–Thomas–Starr inclinations in ways that they could never have dreamed. It was Flanigan and Addington and Yoo running the show, said some insiders. They were the lawyers who had gone belowdeck to tinker with the big machinery, to change the course of U.S. wartime policy, and to figure out ways to get precious intelligence out of captured al Qaeda terrorists. The whispers went on: If some of Gonzales's allies affectionately thought he was authentically aggressive, was a true hard-liner, was really a quiet assassin—someone able to pinpoint problems and destroy them—they were all wrong. Gonzales's calm demeanor capped an inherent placidity. He might have been from Texas, but he was no edgy gunslinger.

If he heard any of those doubters, he didn't tell very many people. And if he did, he might also have chalked it up to something Bush often called "the soft bigotry of low expectations." If people thought that it was Gonzales's underlings who were really running the show, it might have been because they secretly, automatically fell for the stereotype that Alberto Gonzales was an underqualified minority figure who had simply been kicked upstairs. They were guilty of abject racism. They *assumed* he was put in charge because his skin was brown. His friends at work in Texas and in

Washington simply refused to talk about his ethnicity and whether it was something that had opened doors for him.

Many of them have come to realize that Gonzales's quiet demeanor masked a methodical shrewdness: he was still measuring, analyzing you even when you didn't know it. He was one of those people, his coworkers said, who would let uneasy silences well up in a conversation, and it would throw you off guard, it would give him the upper hand. For clues, one lawyer who worked for him said that all you needed to do was look at the way he painstakingly, fastidiously addressed every single comma, every bit of grammar, in every document that he lingered with. When his lawyers got back the drafts they had sent him, it looked like he had put them under a microscope—every nuance, detail, and tidbit had been combed over.

A few days after his less-than-inspiring appearance at the conservative conference in Virginia, Gonzales elected to escape Washington and take a plane back home to Texas. He was happily headed to what had turned into an annual homecoming party for him. When he got to Houston, he seemed at ease as he joked and mingled with old friends at the local Hispanic Bar Association's President's Day party. He had also come to the fete the year before, and now it was almost like he was a member of visiting royalty, with people lining up to shake his hand, women kissing him on the cheek, and people he used to do business with asking to take his picture. As he worked the joyous room—far from the nagging questions about him in Washington, far from the powerful doubters who thought he only seemed conservative because he was surrounded by conservatives—his friends in Houston were gushing and excitedly asking if he was really going to become the first Hispanic on the U.S. Supreme Court.

"I have the best job in the world because I have the best client in the world," he told his admirers.[12]

Most people in the room *assumed* he really did think he had the best job in the world.

No one in the room knew—how could they?—that their nattily dressed old friend Alberto Gonzales, from Humble, Texas, had spent time in extremely "forward-leaning" discussions about burying people alive and the various ways that people can be interrogated and whether those forms of interrogation were actually torture—and whether they were legal and necessary in the new war on terrorism.

W hen he finally came back to DC, there were subpoenas being issued to the Bush White House, seeking papers, documents, proof that there were contacts between Bush's staff and Enron. Within hours of getting the subpoena, Gonzales released a prepared list of contacts and said there was no proof that anyone on Bush's or Cheney's staff had been approached by Enron to bail them out of their welling billion-dollar debacle. By June he had overseen the White House's release of twenty-one hundred pages of subpoenaed documents to Lieberman's investigation, and he had taken a break to fly to Massachusetts and deliver a commencement address at Harvard Law School. Some of the young law students were less than pleased to have Gonzales; there were debates about whether he was manipulating the law, finding the legal means to enforce a political agenda in the middle of a war.

Gonzales stared out over the graduating third-year law students assembled in front of Langdell Hall and said, "We've already discovered that this type of conflict doesn't always fit neatly within traditional theories of civil liberties."

It was hard to tell if Gonzales was weary or even more muted than usual.

"I can assure you," said Gonzales, "that public service will make you a better person."

For most of the summer Gonzales had to wonder whether public service also meant a never-ending series of twisted compromises and oily sales jobs. Bush, frustrated at the pace of approval for his conservative judicial nominees, ordered Gonzales and leading Republicans to put on a united front and get Priscilla Owen—Gonzales's former Supreme Court colleague and his opponent in the fractious abortion debate in Texas—approved for the Fifth Circuit Court of Appeals.

Gonzales watched as one old powerful friend after another from Texas flew to Washington to testify to Owen's brilliance. And all summer, as the Senate conducted hearings into Owen, he had to hear his name mentioned over and over again as someone who had once accused Owen of the dreaded "judicial activism." The Owen hearings became in many ways a subhearing about Gonzales. When Senator Ted Kennedy began throwing Gonzales's own words back at Owen, it was like acid on the wound. Ted Kennedy was quoting Gonzales in an attack against a federal court candidate with unassailably tough conservative credentials.

In early August, as Bush was preparing to settle in at his ranch in Texas, Gonzales delivered an answer that Bush was looking for. The drumbeats of war had gotten louder, and the pace of the convoluted and Machiavellian dance toward an invasion of Iraq was quickening. The jumbled, contradictory, and slippery bits of "proof" that Iraq had weapons of mass destruction or was planning to build them—and all the other bits of intrigue, coercion, political posturing, international dictates, rivalries between cabinet members, off-the-record leaks, counterleaks, and backroom discussions with a handful of willing media members—were all rolling forward like some giant, ill-defined but unyielding amoeba. In the White House, in Alberto Gonzales's office, one thing was manifestly clear. He knew it and so did the eager members of his legal team: George W. Bush loathed Saddam Hussein.

In August, with Bush headed to Crawford, Texas, Gonzales advised the president that he didn't have to get an okay from Congress for an invasion of Iraq. Flanigan had researched it and told Gonzales that the Constitution was quite clear that the commander in chief had the war powers authority to order troops into combat. As a failsafe, as a backdrop, Bush could rely on the Persian Gulf resolutions from Desert Storm in 1991: The president could simply argue that Iraq still had not lived up to those international resolutions from a decade ago and that it was still refusing to let weapons inspectors examine whatever was in Iraq's arsenal.[13] A decision was made to have Gonzales compose a letter to Bush, then have it released publicly. The letter, of course, thrust Gonzales into headlines and critical editorial pages as the "architect" of Bush's imperious attempt to interpret the Constitution for his own plots and ambitions.

What very few people knew was that there were two other guarded documents trading among White House lawyers in August—documents created in response to nagging questions from the CIA about how far its people could go in prying information from anyone they were holding in Guantánamo or in secret prisons around the world. Gonzales waited while the lawyers cobbled together some answers. The first week of August, he received a six-page personal letter sent from Yoo, the lawyer in the Office of Legal Counsel who had crafted that foreshadowing memo saying Bush could declare war on any nation suspected of having terrorist ties. The same day Gonzales also received a fifty-page memo from Jay Bybee, a like-minded colleague of Yoo's in the Office of Legal Counsel—and someone who had gone to college with Tim Flanigan. Read together, the documents suggest another new paradigm in the post-9/11 policies of the United States. Those new documents were the end product of those dispassionate meetings to talk about all the ways in which the CIA knew how to extract information—about water boarding, about striking prisoners, about pretending to drown prisoners, about threatening to bury prisoners alive.

The Yoo letter began by saying, "Dear Judge Gonzales: You have requested the views of our Office concerning the legality, under international law, of interrogation methods to be used during the current war on terrorism." It went on to say that the al Qaeda terrorists were illegal combatants "who are not entitled to the protections of any of the Geneva Convention" and that "interrogation of al Qaeda members, therefore, cannot constitute a war crime." Yoo added that the United States had nothing to fear from international courts in case a "rogue prosecutor" tried to level charges against the United States about its interrogation techniques.[14]

The Bybee memo is a dissection of "title 18 of the United States Code, section 2340-2340A" about the U.S. codes of conduct related to torture. The memo argues that only intense and "extreme" acts constitute torture: "physical pain amounting to torture must be equivalent in intensity to the pain accompanying serious physical injury, such as organ failure, impairment of bodily function, or even death."[15] The memo suggests that the European Court of Human Rights decided that a combination of interrogation techniques applied for hours at a time was "inhuman and degrading" but did not amount to torture: forcing prisoners to wear a black hood during interrogation; forcing prisoners to be locked in a room with loud and continuously hissing noises; depriving prisoners of sleep, food, and drink; forcing prisoners to stand spread-eagled against a wall with their fingers high over their head and feet back so that they are standing on their toes and forcing all their weight onto their fingers. The memo adds that "there is a significant range of acts that though they might constitute cruel, inhuman or degrading treatment or punishment, fail to rise to the level of torture." [16]

The memo that Gonzales had been given by Bybee also maintained that Bush had absolute authority over the way prisoners held by the United States were treated and interrogated: "As Commander-in-Chief, the President has the constitutional authority to order interrogations of enemy combatants to gain intelligence information concerning the military plans of the enemy. The demands of the Commander-in-Chief are especially pronounced in the middle of a war in which the nation has already suffered a direct attack. In such a case, the information gained from interrogations may prevent future attacks by foreign enemies. . . . Congress may no more regulate the President's ability to detain and interrogate enemy combatants than it may regulate his ability to direct troop movements on the battlefield." [17] Finally, if there were problems, if there were accusations lodged against U.S. interrogators—or if someone was harmed by a U.S. interrogator—there were standard arguments that could be used as a defense. They were, the memo said, the same strategies that a criminal defense attorney would wage: If a prisoner was harmed during an interrogation, the incident could be defended as an act of "self-defense" or "necessity" and "could justify interrogation techniques needed to elicit information." [18]

Along with his work on disavowing provisions in the Geneva Convention, these two new documents would bind an image that he would never shake—one that suggested Alberto Gonzales endorsed very specific acts of unspeakable torture and that he had laid the poisoned groundwork for the events surrounding the Abu Ghraib prison scandal. He would continue to tell friends that he had been misunderstood before but never like this. And in Humble, Texas, where his mother had entered her septuagenarian years, he knew that Maria Gonzales would eventually read the stories.

She would grow weary of it, the way reporters would knock on her door, call her, or wait for her on the street. One time a reporter called her from Dallas and spoke to her in Spanish. Maria listened, patiently and quietly, as the woman said she would like to visit Maria and talk to her about her son. Maria said the stories about her son were wrong. It's like what she would say to her parish priest one day: *"He is a good boy. . . . I hate to see him go through that."*

In the fall of 2002, Gonzales, uncomfortable as always with any media attention, was dealt a blow when the Senate Judiciary Committee—with Ted Kennedy using Gonzales's own words as evidence—rejected Texas Supreme Court Justice Priscilla Owen's nomination to a federal court. It was an enormous defeat for Bush, and any of his smash-mouth political handlers, the unforgiving sorts who worked in sync with Karl Rove, had to have wondered what it all meant for Gonzales's future. Bush had "tapped" him, Bush had promoted him, and everyone knew it. But was Bush blinded by loyalty and was Gonzales more of a liability than an asset? Would Bush still continue to stake major pieces of his legacy on his *abogado* from Texas?

Bush was going to keep Owen's name in play, and she would probably eventually get appointed. There were more important issues, bigger issues, including having Gonzales's office draft the resolution that would pave the way for an invasion of Iraq. He told Gonzales to meet with congressional leaders to hammer out any differences on the resolution. Gonzales paid an early October call on the reluctant Republican senator Richard Lugar, convincing Lugar that Bush's war resolution was the right option.

From the fall until the end of the year, war was an inevitability in Gonzales's mind. It was a matter of when, not if, there would be an invasion of Iraq. He was mostly divorced from the CIA and State Department intrigues over the search for weapons of mass destruction, and he was dedicated to reviewing, expanding, and protecting Bush's war powers. "It's a moot point," said Gonzales when someone in Texas asked him if he thought Bush needed congressional approval to invade Iraq. "He's decided he's going to get it. He's going to go to Congress and get authorization. We think there are legal arguments to make that it's not necessary to do this and that he can rely on the powers of the Constitution. But, again, I think the focus should be on the fact that he decided to go to Congress and seek authorization." [19]

Gonzales, contradicting other comments about whether he was concerned about Bush's place in history, said he worried about Bush's legacy—but he could also have been talking about himself: "I do worry, as do many of the other advisers, about his legacy. And the fact that something may be lawful doesn't mean you ought to do it. How will he be judged fifty years from now? I do think about that. I worry about that."[20]

Tim Flanigan, the father of fourteen who had been Gonzales's coarchitect in the counsel's office, had decided to accept a high-paying job as one of the lead in-house counsels for troubled Tyco International. Flanigan endorsed David Leitch as Gonzales's new right-hand man. Leitch had worked for Flanigan in the first Bush administration and he had the same sort of impeccable conservative credentials. Leitch served alongside then attorney general William Barr, he had put in a year as the head lawyer at the Federal Aviation Administration, and he had helped on the strategy sessions for building the Department of Homeland Security.

He came aboard just as Gonzales was having to face a new domestic firestorm that would strike close to home: The Supreme Court was gearing up to hear arguments in an affirmative action case in which the University of Michigan was resisting challenges from white students to its policy of using race to determine admissions to its college and law school. People on either side of the affirmative action fence were watching to see what Bush—and Gonzales—would do. There was a prevailing assumption that Gonzales was leaning toward supporting the University of Michigan, not so much because he might have benefited from any similar official or unofficial policies, but because any Bush administration opposition would damage chances to recruit more black and Hispanic voters. Gonzales had once said he knew he had been helped because he was Hispanic and that it didn't bother him.

People studied his words again for clues on where he was coming from on affirmative action: "I know that I've been helped because of my ethnicity. But the bottom line . . . is that Hispanics should expect nothing more than an equal opportunity. For us to now say that we should be given an opportunity because of our ethnicity, irrespective of our competence, means that we'll be discriminating against someone else who doesn't happen to be Hispanic, which is the very thing that we've been screaming about for decades. . . . Personally, I'm not offended that race is a factor. But it should never be the overriding factor or the most important factor."[21]

In Washington people wondered if Gonzales had become so intensely political that he wasn't just worried about upsetting minority voters who might support affirmative action—he was worried about upsetting anyone, including Democrats, who might be voting on whether he should be sent to the Supreme Court. If Gonzales had learned anything from years spent alongside Bush and Rove, it was to move and think strategically, to think long-range.

And the year ended just like the one before—with outsized expectations and money being bet on where Gonzales was headed. On December 30, *Newsweek*—just like George Stephanopoulos had done the previous December—said Gonzales was on its very short list of people to watch in 2003: "There's White House counsel Alberto Gonzales, whom President Bush may nominate to become the first Hispanic justice on the Supreme Court."[22]

FOURTEEN

Where He Was Taking Me

The increasingly coordinated infighting to either send Gonzales to the Supreme Court or stop him in his tracks was in full gear in early 2003. Any one of three justices would probably leave in the near future: William Rehnquist, Sandra Day O'Connor, or John Paul Stevens. Meanwhile, Bush saved Gonzales from having to take the lead on any White House news about affirmative action by holding a hasty Roosevelt Room conference in which he very gingerly announced that he was opposed in principle to the University of Michigan's "quota system" but that more needed to be done to protect diversity.

Bush's decision didn't deliver the intense repudiation of Michigan's policies that some of his aides, including the solicitor general Ted Olson and John Ashcroft, wanted—they were looking for free rein to attack Michigan hard and fast in the Supreme Court. The in-house White House debates finally cracked open and the rejected hard-liners said that it was all because of Gonzales, that he must have convinced Bush to take a weaker, softer approach. There was White House chatter that at one point Olson had called Gonzales and yelled at him, suggesting that if Gonzales wanted Olson's job, he could take it.

Gonzales, one of the leading minority figures in the administration, was sent to do a flurry of interviews. Ashcroft, who had battled with Gonzales on and off since the administration was formed, was still not pleased with the affirmative action outcome—and he couldn't have been pleased to see Gonzales on the road, acting as an apologist for something he and Olson had fought hard against.

"What the president is urging is that colleges and universities employ race-neutral means. . . . We need to work with colleges and universities to look at other admissions criteria," said Gonzales. "It is wrong to assume simply because a decision may be made by this court that initially race cannot be used as a factor in admissions decisions that the number of minorities is going to decrease. We cannot let that happen." [1]

An official with the National Council of La Raza, the biggest Latino civil rights association in the nation, said the association was "surprised and disappointed" with the way Bush and Gonzales were weighing in. "I can't imagine a better warrior for the Hispanic community than this president," responded Gonzales. [2]

If Gonzales was losing the luster that he might have enjoyed among some Latino leaders, the erosion from pro-life groups was beginning to mount as well. An official with the American Life League said it would be a "tragedy" if Gonzales was nominated, and a spokesman for the Family Research Council called Gonzales a "nonstarter." It all culminated yet again in another attack from conservative bellwether Robert Novak, whose nationally syndicated column at the end of January 2003 painted Gonzales as someone who had "succeeded in weakening" attempts to roll back racial preferences, as someone who "had increased the difficulty for his friend and patron, George W. Bush," as someone who "had pulled the Texas court leftward," as someone who "led prominent Catholic conservatives and other foes to inform the White House that Gonzales is unacceptable for the high court." For good measure, Novak reprised the Souter Prediction—that Alberto Gonzales was a David Souter waiting in the wings. He was going to become the same "grave political blunder" for the younger George Bush as David Souter had become for the elder George Bush. [3]

The whisper campaign had become like an unrelenting, painful drone. There was an assumption that there was more bad blood flowing between Gonzales and Ashcroft—and that that duel would leave one of the two men exiled outside the administration. "In my 15 years of watching the nomination process, I have never seen something so dramatic happen so early. This is a very aggressive campaign by legal conservatives to hurt his chances for the high court," said Washington attorney Ronald Klain, who had helped advise Clinton on Supreme Court selections.[4]

There was a joke making the rounds in DC: *"How do you say 'Souter' in Spanish?"*

The answer: *"Gonzales."*

There was, too, a reverse whisper campaign—one that would eventually become more public. It had everything to do with race, affirmative action, ethnicity, and whether Alberto Gonzales was being victimized by extremists who were holding his race against him—and whether he was being held to a different standard because he was Hispanic. Gonzales had to contend with conservatives saying he was too liberal and liberals saying he was too conservative. And he had to contend with Republicans who said his nomination was really all about whether it could help win minority votes for Bush and anybody else in the GOP.

Most of the work he had done that would cheer conservatives was either hidden or overlooked: the grinding work to consolidate power in the office of the presidency, the way he had shielded investigations into Cheney's energy connections, the way he had protected Karl Rove from questions about his stock holdings, the work he had done in giving Bush the license to prosecute wars and terrorists. In the end, they were "process" things—activist "lawyering" to get Bush and the White House the protection and answers they wanted. Added up, they might leave someone with the impression that Gonzales was a hard-liner conservative, but the hard-liners wanted more clear ideological proof that Gonzales was one of them. They wanted a paper trail, a thundering speech, some clearly stated passion for conservative values. Some decided that either he didn't have it or that he was too discreet, too judicious, to ever reveal it.

It was, after all, his discretion that led Bush to hire him.

Through the first few months of 2003 Gonzales found himself in the awkward position of having to make the rounds on Capitol Hill and in the media, pushing hard for Senate approval of Miguel Estrada to a federal appeals court. Estrada, a native of Honduras, had powerful conservative credentials and the kind of American Dream story that appealed to Bush and his supporters. His name had also popped up on the short lists for the Supreme Court. Senate Democrats were stonewalling, filibustering, and it was decided that Gonzales would talk Estrada up. For weeks he traded meetings and letters with senators and talking heads. In several encounters he openly wondered, almost as if he was talking about his own career, if Estrada was being "held to a different kind of standard."

Bush loyalist C. Boyden Gray—*a good man*—decided to enter the fray as he watched Gonzales being whipsawed. Gray had talked to old man Bush and his son and endorsed Gonzales. He and some of the other "old heads" in Washington, like Fred Fielding, were always there to help Gonzales, even to introduce him to the Federalist Society regulars. In the span of a few months he had gone from being the presumed Supreme Court nominee to being a liberal David Souter hidden inside the West Wing of the White House. The fact that Gray went public to defend Gonzales— and the way Gray decided to do it—was a stunning barometer of how suspect Gonzales had become to the gatekeepers of Bush's hard right conservative base: "I don't regard him as an unreliable conservative. You can never precisely predict one's degree of conservatism, but I am confident that Gonzales is not a liberal."[5]

On March 18 Saddam Hussein rejected Bush's ultimatum to flee Iraq. The next day Bush ordered the launch of cruise missiles. Gonzales was in the room when Bush issued his command. Bush had looked around and asked if everyone was ready. Bush gave the order and said, "And may God bless the troops." In the silent room, Gonzales stared straight ahead until a thought popped into his head: "I had just witnessed history."[6]

Ten days later, while war raged, the now-Republican-controlled Judiciary Committee voted in favor of putting Priscilla Owen on a federal appeals court. In ways that few people really knew, Gonzales—through circumstance, fate, and a convergence of wildly disparate forces—had become completely interwoven with both of these dramatically different developments in March.

He knew things, had been witness to the backroom deals, bartering, and highly classified memos. He had seen the strategies being played out and had come to realize the need for extreme political circumspection. When the 9/11 Commission was finally formed to investigate the attacks on America, Gonzales knew that the inquiries would have to snake toward his office. He'd have to decide which presidential memos and papers would be held back from the commission, and he'd have to decide which memos with his own signature would also have to be kept hidden.

His office had already routinely invoked executive privilege as a course of action over the last several months, and when the commission began asking for White House input, there were going to be tests of will between Gonzales and the commission. Invoking executive privilege with the commission would be a political gamble. With the nation clamoring for insights into what unfolded on 9/11, it could turn into a perception fiasco if Bush and the White House appeared to be keeping secrets from the American people. Gonzales knew it could quickly spiral out of control. If he stonewalled the commission with executive privilege, then people would wonder what the White House was hiding: Did the White House know that there were going to be attacks? Did the White House put innocent Americans at risk by not taking terrorist intelligence seriously? Executive privilege seemed to work when the White House wanted to hold on to Cheney's energy task force paperwork, but this was another political beast.

In May, Gonzales decided to do something different—something Rove thought was a good way to make the White House seem less like an exclusive bastion and was a good way to reach younger votes. Gonzales took part in a heavily screened "interactive forum" in which people could submit online questions to various White House officials.

He told Rebecca in Ohio, "The president is a remarkable person. It is hard to be around the president and not learn just by watching and listening." He told Lori from Texas, "Although we love Washington, we look forward to the day we can return to my beloved state." When Rich from New York asked if Gonzales could team up with Miguel Estrada and take Senators Charles Schumer and Ted Kennedy in a tag-team wrestling match, he responded, "Oops, got to go!"

A few days later he and Rebecca were headed home to Texas again and a party in his honor at his old friend Roland Garcia's house. There was guacamole, beef fajitas, and refried beans—the good stuff that he missed when he was in Washington. He was at ease again, on familiar turf, and he seemed unusually expansive—until it happened again, until people started asking him about the Supreme Court. It was clear that he didn't want to talk about it at all.

On the last Friday in May he had the first of two encounters in 2003 with J. C. Willke, the head of the Life Issues Institute and the former president of the National Right to Life Foundation. Willke asked Gonzales at a meeting of conservative Christians how he felt about *Roe v. Wade* and whether *stare decisis* applied in that famous case—whether courts should "stand on the decisions" made by the Supreme Court and refrain from overruling or reconsidering those decisions. When Gonzales answered in the affirmative, some of those conservatives in the audience began to boo. Several weeks later Willke was at the White House along with several other conservative business leaders. Gonzales left some people with the impression that he believed the Constitution is what the Supreme Court says it is.

As the summer of 2003 moved forward, as Washington began to empty, there were questions left behind about where Gonzales fit into the Supreme Court nomination process. "We are absolutely opposed to Alberto Gonzales. He is soft on the constitutional issues we care most about," said an official with the Christian conservative Focus on Family organization.[7] "There is a long list of qualified candidates who would uphold laws defending the sanctity of human life. It's not clear that Al Gonzales is one of them," added an official with the Family Research Council.[8]

Gonzales was in the middle of a bumpy ride with an uncertain destination. He had talked with Bush about the Supreme Court, about his future. The friction with Ashcroft seemed to be growing, according to people who saw the strained relationship at the White House. Gonzales, some suspected, thought that Ashcroft was grandstanding, was too bombastic, simply wasn't discreet enough. Ashcroft, some suspected, resented the way John Yoo and some people who worked for the Justice Department had been so clearly aligned with Gonzales and his team—and they said that

Ashcroft had tried to block Yoo from taking over the Office of Legal Counsel even though Gonzales wanted his ally promoted.

Meanwhile the political swipes were coming from both directions. When his name was mentioned, Bush foes increasingly said Gonzales was an enabler of torture, of an unforgiving right-wing ultraconservative military policy that marched America to war and discarded both domestic civil liberties and the international codes of humane behavior. Some Bush supporters said Gonzales was the president's Achilles' heel, the weak point in the administration, not strong enough to seize a chance to squash affirmative action and abortion rights. The staffers in the White House counsel's office said that he talked a lot about Texas, about how much he missed it, how he'd like to live there again. But he wouldn't leave Washington as long as Bush was there—even though there were rumblings about who would stay and who would go if Bush was reelected in 2004. The list was growing—and the list of inner circle advisers from the Texas days was especially growing. Joe Allbaugh at FEMA. Karen Hughes. Commerce Secretary Don Evans. Many of these hard-core inner circle members were leaving or planning to leave. Rove, of course, would stay. But what about Gonzales?

"In the years that I've known the president, I've never doubted where he was taking me," Gonzales told people.[9]

In the summer of 2003 Gonzales was receiving increasingly frantic calls from his friend Kenna Ramirez in El Paso. Her husband, Carlos, the former mayor of El Paso and a star of the 2000 GOP convention, was acting erratically, not talking, not recognizing people, and sometimes just repeating the same words over and over again. He had been such a Bush stalwart, a turncoat Democrat who had campaigned hard for Bush and helped sway Latino voters to Bush's camp. After he left the mayor's office, Bush had named him commissioner of the International Boundary and Water Commission. Gonzales put the Ramirez family in touch with a neurologist he knew in Austin; the physician sent her findings to the National Institutes of Health. It looked like Ramirez had a rapidly advancing degenerative brain disease known as frontotemporal dementia, and it could lead to speech, memory, motivation, and eating problems.

Gonzales took charge of Ramirez's leave of absence and later the plans on how to announce his resignation. He told Kenna Ramirez that the "less you tell" the press the better. She warned him that her husband was not aware of his sliding mental state and that he wasn't going to want to resign. "No, no, no. I'll know how to handle it," Gonzales told her. "I know how to handle it." Several minutes later, Gonzales called her back.

"I had to tell him, 'The president is giving an order, Carlos.'"

Ramirez was confused, but he insisted that there was nothing wrong.

"Carlos, you don't understand. I am calling on behalf of the president of the United States."

When the Ramirezes flew to Bethesda Hospital for Carlos's examination, the couple took time to attend the National Book Festival. Kenna's cell phone rang and it was Gonzales calling from the White House. "You are not alone," said Gonzales. He and Kenna finalized arrangements for the Ramirezes to meet with Gonzales in his West Wing office the following Monday. When they arrived, Gonzales told Carlos Ramirez to stay in his office. Kenna gave her husband some chewing gum because she knew that something as simple as that would keep him happy and occupied. Gonzales escorted Kenna Ramirez to the Oval Office. When they arrived, Bush and Laura Bush were already there.

"Al," said Bush, turning to Gonzales, "anything she needs, make sure of that, that we can facilitate her."

Carlos was eventually brought to the Oval Office, and he didn't recognize Laura Bush. It was an impossibly bittersweet, awkward moment for people who had campaigned so closely together. As Gonzales watched, Bush told the former mayor of El Paso that he should relocate to Washington where people could help him. Ramirez simply replied, "No, I want to go home."

Later Gonzales told Kenna Ramirez, "You always remember wherever I am, whoever I am, I will always be your friend. Don't ever forget that." She began crying, and she began thinking about how she and her husband, and Alberto Gonzales and his wife, Rebecca, had watched the fireworks one night from a White House balcony—and how that night almost exactly two years ago had been one of the greatest nights of her life.

––––––

In September Miguel Estrada, the other rising Latino judicial star and presumed rival of Gonzales's for a Supreme Court seat, withdrew his nomination to the circuit court of appeals. He had gone to Gonzales and they had talked about giving up the bid. Gonzales had been absorbed in Estrada's exile in limbo: Estrada had been nominated twenty-eight months earlier and had never been able to inch forward against Democratic resistance. Republicans had the rare chance to claim that one of their candidates had been a victim of racism. Gonzales told Estrada to stay the course, but Estrada insisted he had to drop out. He had, said some Democrats, a million-dollar income at a law firm to fall back on.

On the last day of the month Gonzales conferred with Bush just as he was arriving at the Oval Office at 7:00 A.M. He told Bush that he had been contacted at 8:30 P.M. the night before by Justice Department officials and that they were going to launch a full-scale criminal investigation into who at the White House might have leaked CIA agent Valerie Plame's name to the media, that they wanted the White House staff to preserve all materials that could be related to the investigation, but that Gonzales did not have to issue a notice to anyone else at that exact moment—it could wait until morning.

After finally telling Bush at 7:00 A.M., Gonzales made the same announcement to the senior advisers at their 7:30 A.M. meeting. He said that Bush had just told him that everyone in the White House was to give their full cooperation to the investigation, and Gonzales then instructed the senior advisers to order any of their White House staffers to preserve their documents, e-mails, and notes. Gonzales quickly wrote a memo and had it shipped throughout the White House.

Hours later, aboard Air Force One en route to Chicago, White House Press Secretary Scott McClellan was peppered with questions about why the president hadn't been told right away by Gonzales, why Gonzales hadn't sent out a memo right away, why hours elapsed before anyone was instructed by the White House lawyer not to destroy any important material. McClellan said that the Justice officials had told Gonzales it could wait until morning.

One of the trickiest politics and media mysteries in twenty-first-century America was just being revealed: Who committed a possible felony by leaking Valerie Plame's name to the media, and was it a move to attack her husband, Ambassador Joseph Wilson, who had criticized the Bush administration's very reasons for going to war in Iraq? The investigation would, of course, touch on the role of the media, the way leaks emerge from the White House, the way the White House can view the media as a willing tool—as something to be shaped, cajoled, and seduced.

A handful of reporters had perhaps slipped too far into a dangerous world of bartering and trading for information. They lived by the leaks they were being given from a parsimonious administration that had built up a firewall blocking the press—and perhaps some of them ran so hard with their bits and pieces, with their presumed proximity to power, that they would write ill-advised stories that, intentionally or not, served the military ambitions of the Bush White House. Some cynics in DC said that a new version of the groundbreaking book that had helped usher in a new age of White House coverage—Bob Woodward's and Carl Bernstein's classic *All the President's Men*—should be published. This one should be devoted to any journalists who had tripped over the line, and the book should be called *All the President's Stenographers*.

As White House staffers trooped into work on September 30, 2003, they were greeted with this first memo from Gonzales:

We were informed last evening by the Department of Justice that it has opened an investigation into possible unauthorized disclosures concerning the identity of an undercover CIA employee. The Department advised us that it will be sending a letter today instructing us to preserve all materials that might be relevant to its investigation. Its letter will provide more specific instructions on the materials in which it is interested, and we will communicate those instructions directly to you. In the meantime, you must preserve all materials that might in any way be related to the Department's investigation. Any questions concerning this request should be directed to Associate Counsels Ted Ullyot or Raul Yanes in the Counsel to the President's office. The President has directed full cooperation with this investigation. [10]

Gonzales sent out a second memo later on Tuesday, saying he needed White House staffers to pull any phone logs, computer records, diary and calendar entries, notes, memoranda, correspondence of any kind. Two days later he sent out a third memo with specific instructions and a deadline for compliance:

To ensure compliance with the time deadlines imposed by the Department of Justice, you are directed to provide to the Counsel's Office, by no later than 5 P.M. on October 7, 2003, copies of the following documents, created during the time period February 1, 2002, through September 30, 2003, inclusive:

1. *All documents that relate in any way to former U.S. Ambassador Joseph C. Wilson, his trip to Niger in February 2002, or his wife's purported relationship with the Central Intelligence Agency; and*
2. *All documents that relate in any way to a contact with any member or representative of the news media about Joseph C. Wilson, his trip to Niger in February 2002, or his wife's purported relationship with the Central Intelligence Agency; and*
3. *All documents that relate in any way to a contact with any or all of the following: reporters Knut Royce, Timothy M. Phelps, or Robert D. Novak, or any individual(s) acting directly or indirectly on behalf of them.*

For purposes of this memorandum, the term "documents" includes "without limitation all electronic records, telephone records of any kind (including but not limited to any documents that memorialize telephone calls having been made), correspondence, computer records, storage devices, notes, memoranda, and diary and calendar entries" in the possession of the Executive Office of the President, its staff, or its employees, wherever located, including any documents that may have been archived in Records Management. However, at this time, you do not need to provide to Counsel's Office copies of the following, provided that they have not been marked upon in any way and are not accompanied by any notes or other commentary: (a) press clips or articles, whether in hard copy or e-mail or electronic form, or (b) either of the two memoranda I sent on September 30, 2003, regarding document preservation.

You are also directed to complete and return the attached Certification by 5 P.M. on October 7, 2003. Note that you must complete the Certification

*whether or not you have responsive documents. All documents and Certifica-
tions should be hand-delivered to EEOB Room 214. Room 214 will be
staffed from 2 P.M. to 8 P.M. today; from 9 A.M. to 6 P.M. on Saturday
October 4 and Sunday October 5; from 8 A.M. to 11 P.M. on Monday
October 6; and from 8 A.M. to 5 P.M. on Tuesday October 7. Appropriate
procedures will be in place to handle classified documents. If you have any
questions, please call Associate Counsels Ted Ullyot or Raul Yanes in the
Counsel's Office.*

> *Alberto R. Gonzales*
> *Counsel to the President* [11]

Bush took time out from a presidential campaign fund-raiser to say, "If
there is a leak out of my administration, I want to know who it is. And
if the person has violated the law, the person will be taken care of." This
time the betting money was all over the map, but there was always one
name on everyone's tout sheet: Karl Rove. He had talked to columnist
Robert Novak in the past; there were always suspicions that Novak was
fed news by Rove. Rove, his foes said, possessed a streak of political retribution that would make him a likely suspect to try to harm Wilson and his
wife. Wilson was going public with accusations that the invasion of Iraq
was built on sham evidence. But Karl Rove, his friends said, was simply too
smart to do something so stupid and so felonious—and McClellan, speaking for the president of the United States, would specifically insist that
Rove, Cheney's chief of staff, Lewis Libby, and Elliott Abrams, a senior
director at the National Security Council, were not involved. McClellan
would say that he had talked to them, personally and individually, and that
they were simply "not involved."

What no one seemed to remember was that Alberto Gonzales had
once been put in the position of possessing a client's criminal resume—a
resume that he helped to keep from the public. When confronted with the
fact that he was going to have to serve on a jury in Texas and that he was
probably going to have to reveal his criminal record, Bush finally decided
to entrust Gonzales with the truth. Bush had decided Gonzales was loyal—
loyal enough to be trusted with something that Bush kept secret for de-

cades, through a race for Congress, two gubernatorial races, and finally a run for the presidency. There may be little comparison between a client owning up to a drunk driving arrest and a White House official talking about CIA agents to the media, except for the fact that some legal experts said it had a lot to do with the same arching attorney–client conundrums.

If Gonzales knew—or *learned*—who had leaked the information about Valerie Plame, what would it mean to his role as White House counsel? Where would his obligations to his clients at the White House end, and when would his obligations to the criminal investigation begin? How far could he invoke the executive privilege that he had relied on over and over again during his tenure serving the president? He was going to be in possession of significant information. Before he turned anything over to the FBI, Gonzales's office was going to review any possible evidence submitted by almost two thousand staffers; Gonzales would have first look at the possible evidence that could solve the entire investigation.

In the middle of the same week that the Valerie Plame incident erupted and oozed over Washington, Bush and Gonzales worked their way through several hundred people jammed into the East Room to celebrate Hispanic Heritage Month. Gonzales was always a standard fixture at any Latino-related event at the White House. Bush listened as someone sang a version of "Girl from Ipanema," then he introduced Gonzales to the audience and said something that struck people at the party as beyond ironic, especially considering the fact that someone in the White House was suspected of committing a felony and could go to jail for an entire decade:

"Everybody needs to have a good *abogado* . . . I've got a really good one." [12]

At the end of October 2003, Thomas Kean, the head of the 9/11 Commission and the former Republican governor of New Jersey, testily announced that he was considering issuing a subpoena to force Gonzales to release White House documents that would show what the Bush administration did or did not know about any possible attacks on America. He had been calling Gonzales and negotiating for the remaining paperwork. The tug of war would last into the new year, with Gonzales telling his staff that they risked setting a dangerous precedent. Releasing the "holy of the holies"—the President's Daily Briefs, the PDBs that are his top secret intelligence briefings—would soil any of the executive privilege luster that Gonzales had fought so hard to win.

He had started out his tenure with Bush trying to block the release of Reagan's papers and had spent the last three years arguing that the presidency was going to be perpetually undermined if it was forced to hand over its classified memos. The debate became a kind of insider baseball sticking point for some members of the media when it was suggested that someone had given Bob Woodward access to the PDBs for a book he was writing—and it became part of a broader question of why Gonzales would hold them back from the 9/11 Commission, but perhaps somehow, someone might have let a reporter look at them.

Gonzales, as always, was moving closer to some objectified status that he neither sought nor enjoyed. He was, to put it bluntly, becoming the poster boy for Bush foes who saw an administration that was stonewalling and promoting an illegitimate legal agenda. In the modern pantheon of White House counsels, his critics accorded him his own distinct legacy of infamy: the coursing, pulsing hum of "instant media" described him as the mastermind of torture, the most anti–civil liberties counsel to ever serve a president, a singular threat to human rights. Into 2004 fate and circumstance had conspired to trap him in a public relations box. With so many provocative developments being touched on by Gonzales's office—the 9/11 Commission, the attack on Iraq, the Valerie Plame incident, the release of presidential papers, the treatment of enemy combatants—he was increasingly singled out.

As 2004 rolled on, it simply would not stop: Gonzales was caught up in the glare and the politics. Civil liberties organizations especially targeted Gonzales when Bush decided to hold two U.S. citizens as enemy combatants in the war on terror and to deny them lawyers and courts and the usual legal avenues that all Americans have available when they are detained or arrested. The more famous of the two detainees, a Chicago gang member and Muslim convert named Jose Padilla, had been shipped to a naval brig in Charleston, South Carolina, after first being arrested in 2002 at O'Hare Airport under suspicion of being an al Qaeda associate and participating in discussions to build so-called dirty bombs. Under the wartime rules that Gonzales had interpreted for the president, Padilla had been held for close to twenty-one months before he was allowed to have a lawyer. "The United States must use every tool and weapon to win the war against al Qaeda. We believe strongly in access to counsel, but we will not put American lives at risk by recognizing a nonexistent right for enemy combatants to obtain a lawyer," said Gonzales when he delivered a lengthy, dramatic defense of the detention policies at an American Bar Association breakfast meeting.[13]

It was the kind of brash proposition that reinforced his image as the face of human rights excesses in the Bush administration. When Ashcroft had been out pushing the Patriot Act, he seemed to be the lightning rod for civil libertarians and other critics who said the administration was marching down a path littered with basic human freedoms. Now Gonzales had gone public and said that "enemy combatants" needed to be isolated—in Guantánamo or in navy brigs—and not allowed contact with outsiders, all as a matter of national security. Human rights advocates said it was all too dangerous—that no one would ever really know what was being done to the hundreds and hundreds of people being detained in secret locations.

As the secret memos sent through Gonzales's office began to filter into the public domain, as he gave speeches like the one at the ABA, as six hundred fifty "enemy combatants" sat for as much as two years in legal limbo at Guantánamo, as he took the lead in trying to save Condoleezza Rice from having to testify to the 9/11 Commission, Gonzales had replaced Ashcroft as the whipping boy for the Bush White House. In the West Wing people said that it was something Gonzales took to heart, that he swung from confusion to bitterness over being labeled a torturer and someone who was obstructing the truth. The Padilla case, and all that it entailed, would follow him for months.

Jenny Martinez, a law professor at Stanford who was finally allowed to take on Padilla's case, had once served as a lawyer with the United Nations war crimes court in the Hague. She believed that Gonzales hadn't written the memos that critics claimed had opened the door to the United States denying detainees basic legal rights and possibly allowing them to be tortured. But she felt that "there is a high degree of endorsement of lawlessness"—to the degree that there was a "breaking of laws passed by Congress and of treaties ratified by the Senate." She measured it against her experience working on war crimes cases overseas:

"I had worked on war crimes in The Hague. In Bosnia you could see the breakdown of the rule of law and the human rights violations that come from that. I'm not saying we will go down that road, but they've opened the door for that to happen in our country. And it is absolutely providing a justification for people in other, less scrupulous countries who can say, well, I can do that, too. While some people might trust the U.S. government to pick the right people to detain and interrogate, there is no way to trust other countries. It is breaking down the absolute prohibition on torture and it becomes open to other countries. It has cut the legs out from under a lot of human rights activists around the world." [14]

Mariano-Florentino Cuellar, another Stanford law professor and an expert in international human rights issues, was equally troubled by Gonzales's role on the geopolitical stage. As he pored over the decisions coming from the White House counsel's office, he decided that no one really trains to be White House counsel—it is usually thrust on them—and that Gonzales was no doubt under enormous pressure at one of the most critical moments in American history.

"Alberto Gonzales was in the White House, presiding over a staff and making legal decisions in a time of peril and of difficulty for this country. So it is easy to understand that it was a difficult time to be there, developing policies on counterterrorism that meant changes in criminal law and in the framework of international law. And you can't expect people to get every technical aspect of the law right, but you can expect him to be intellectually honest in the way he presents his arguments. First, he was commissioning and disseminating a memo that watered down the prohibition on torture, putting forth a definition of torture as 'causing organ failure or death.' This is not a position that is consistent with the way we've interpreted the law before," said Cuellar. "He basically gave advice to the president—this bothered me the most—that the provisions of the Geneva Convention were obsolete. Those principles are bedrock principles of American law, it is doctrine. So I have serious questions about how intellectually honest he could be." [15]

Cuellar wondered what had happened to Gonzales on his journey from the migrant farms in Texas to the West Wing in the White House. Cuellar had been born in the Mexican city of Matamoros, along the Texas–Mexico border, and he grew up in Brownsville in a Deep South Texas world filled with migrant workers. Cuellar felt that he knew about the roadblocks faced by Latinos in Texas; he felt that he knew how far Gonzales had come. He seemingly wondered if Gonzales lost part of himself on the trip:

"I think there are different aspects of lawyerly virtue. There is fidelity to the legal text and arguing about, and developing positions on, the legal text, and I think that with respect to fidelity the memos and thinking were not especially well crafted. Do I think it would be possible to do a worse job? It could be worse. I have not reviewed his opinions from when he served as a Texas judge and I have not reviewed the work he did in the private sector, so I entertain the possibility that he is a spectacular lawyer and that there was a combination of pressures he was under as White House counsel . . . encountering different and novel aspects of the law that he wasn't familiar with.

"He's a remarkable individual, and I really am impressed with and am admiring of his story. I am also one who traces his roots back to south Texas and northern Mexico. I was born in Matamoros and lived in Brownsville. He is a shining example of what makes this country truly extraordinary. But what also makes this country truly extraordinary is a version of law that is fairly stated. Look, if you don't like the Geneva Convention, you can get out of it. That would bring a torrent of criticism from the world—a flood much like what Hurricane Katrina brought—but that would at least be intellectually honest." [16]

In Texas, the brilliant writer, historian, and cultural analyst Rolando Hinojosa-Smith had also measured where Gonzales was coming from. Hinojosa-Smith had grown up in South Texas, too. He knew more about where Alberto Gonzales's roots were buried than probably any of the people who worked round-the-clock with the White House counselor. He felt that Gonzales moved on his own—but always moved knowing that he served at the pleasure of the man who appointed him. Why would anyone expect Alberto Gonzales to do anything other than what the man who appointed him wanted him to do? His life was dedicated to finding the answers Bush wanted.

"Alberto Gonzales's appointment may please those Hispanics who aren't self-actualized, who see any appointment as a winner. Hispanics, as a minority, should focus on Hispanics who are elected to office. Elected officials, if they care to be effective, carry more weight than appointed ones. He's a friend of the president. That's what he was in Austin and that's what he is in Washington. He will toe the party line. The Republicans are wise in appointing minorities; that's known as laying the groundwork for future goodwill come elections. But I speak as a minority of one. What my fellow Democrats may see is something else. What they don't see is that Hispanics are, for the most part, no different from their fellow citizens: they are and always have been conservative," said Hinojosa-Smith. "What influence he will exercise will depend on what comes out of the White House—since he will not contravene the directives from that quarter. To expect otherwise—some course of progressive, affirmative action, say—is a waste of time and betrays the naïveté of those Hispanics who expect independence on his part. To repeat, it's an appointed office and he is an appointee who serves at the pleasure of the president." [17]

Washington was fixated on the inquiries and wranglings at the 9/11 Commission and whether Rice and other administration officials would appear and be forthcoming about the terrorist attacks. The White House wanted her there to refute anti-terrorism adviser Richard Clarke's damning accusations that the Bush administration had failed to prepare for terrorist attacks. And in the middle of it all, several relatives of 9/11 victims were creating a public relations nightmare. They were converging on Washington, taking the White House to task, pushing for cooperation with the commission. At the end of March, Gonzales was told to meet with some of the families. Before the families came in, he said he was hoping to "educate" them on the fact that he was negotiating with the commission for "access" to the classified information that the White House had in its possession. He was asked if he sometimes viewed the families of the 9/11 tragedy as being his clients: "I serve the president, quite frankly. . . . I view my responsibility as representing the president and negotiating with the commission." [18]

A few days later, March 20, he wrote a letter to Thomas Kean, the chairman of the 9/11 Commission:

"As we discussed last night, the President is prepared, subject to conditions set forth below, to agree to the request of the National Commission on Terrorist Attacks Upon the United States for public testimony, under oath, by the Assistant to the President for National Security Affairs, Dr. Condoleezza Rice....The Commission must agree in writing that it will not request additional public testimony from any White House official, including Dr. Rice.... I would also like to take this occasion to offer an accommodation on another issue on which we have not yet reached an agreement—Commission access to the President and Vice President. I am authorized to advise you that the President and Vice President have agreed to one joint private session with all 10 Commissioners, with one Commission staff member present to take notes of the session."

The next day Richard Clarke appeared on National Public Radio and said that it was the 9/11 families who had put the heat on Gonzales and the White House and that he felt sorry for Rice because he knew that she wanted to testify all along to the 9/11 Commission but that Gonzales kept blocking her. And reports suddenly surfaced that just before Clarke delivered his own bombshells to the commission, Gonzales had called his old friend Fred Fielding—one of the ten commission members.[19] It raised eyebrows, especially when later in the day Fielding questioned Clarke's credibility and integrity during his testimony to the commission.[20]

In April the Abu Ghraib scandal shoved Gonzales to yet another public relations nadir. As people scrambled to make sense of the senseless acts at the Iraqi prison, the expanding reports, rumors, and allegations seemed like something so impossibly dark but so insistent—Iraqi prisoners raped, smeared with feces, tortured, and murdered. The images of naked prisoners, hooded prisoners, beaten prisoners, prisoners with wires dangling from their penises, were numbing, and they were beamed globally—and as they were, Gonzales was sucked into the deep end of the nightmare. With each horrific tale of degradation emerging from Abu Ghraib, national and international human rights activists argued that there had to be a thread, a tie that went straight to Alberto Gonzales.

That same spring the details of his Geneva Convention draft memo came to light in damning news accounts and it reached critical mass. There were stunning arguments that suggested the United States, through Alberto Gonzales, really had built a secret but unyielding legal foundation for what happened in Abu Ghraib: He had put his name to a memo that was part of the cultural blueprint for war crimes. His describing certain provisions in the Geneva Convention as "quaint" and "obsolete" had fed a runaway military culture; his memo to Bush deriding sections of the internationally recognized code for the treatment of prisoners of war was the ideological starting point for a poisoning of American principles. The palpable mixture of hatred directed at Gonzales from some of his critics was not to be underestimated. They simply were accusing him of giving the president the license to invade Iraq, of putting American citizens in secret prisons without access to lawyers, of abandoning the Geneva Convention, of endorsing the vilest forms of degradation, humiliation, and torture. Abu Ghraib, critics said, was a very public bookend for events that Gonzales actively participated in beginning in the first few days after the planes roared into the World Trade Center.

It was easier than ever before for some people to say that he was the author of torture—and the odds makers in Washington obviously moved him down the tote board for the Supreme Court. In the twisted, counterintuitive way his career seemed to be unfolding, Gonzales had had the backing of Democrats who hoped he'd go to the court and support abortion rights and affirmative action. The Republicans and the conservatives were the doubters when it came to Gonzales: They thought he was ideologically impure. Now any Democratic backing he might have had was seriously eroding as people raced to identify the man who might have laid the bricks in that legal foundation that led to Abu Ghraib. And just like that, there was a sense that maybe . . . now . . . there would be a conservative boomerang; maybe now conservatives would understand that Gonzales was as intense, as pugnacious, and as *forward-leaning* as they were.

Gonzales, said friends, was more bitter and confused than ever before. He told friends that he was a lawyer who was indulging in legal theorizing, creating hypothetical scenarios, writing exploratory memos that were never meant to be solid policy. He was being faulted for being a lawyer, for looking at a hundred different scenarios. He was a serious lawyer, not some pumped-up, blinded-by-ideology zealot who secretly knew that the spirit of his draft memo would one day be used as the legal inspiration for loathsome American soldiers to brutalize prisoners in some shitty prison in Iraq:

"He felt it was unfair. The quote was always used as if the prohibitions of the Geneva Convention against torturing people were 'quaint.' But that's not what he said at all. What he said was that there were certain provisions in the Geneva Convention—specific provisions which he named—which are, I think everybody would acknowledge, not in current use. So I think his reaction was a little bit of unfairness. And he tended to personalize that reaction, too," says Flanigan. "He feels as if the press treatment has been unfair, that the press treatment has missed . . . has tended to gloss over the nuances of his role as counsel or the specifics of the advice he gave." [21]

On the last Thursday in April, Gonzales accompanied Bush and Cheney into a White House meeting with the 9/11 Commission members. Bush had been prepping with Gonzales for the last few days. The meeting in the Oval Office lasted three hours. Bush and Cheney sat in blue-striped, high-backed chairs in front of the fireplace. Commissioners spread out on two couches and wooden chairs arranged in a semicircle. And as Gonzales had insisted, there were no cameras, no stenographers, and no tape recorders to preserve the comments of his client. Gonzales never advised Bush to refrain from answering a question.

A week later Gonzales wrote to the *Washington Post:* "In recent days, horrific abuses have come to light, but there should be no doubt that the United States fully recognizes its obligations under the Geneva Convention. . . . With respect to the war on terror, the president determined in February 2002—with the advice of the attorney general, the secretary of state, the secretary of defense and others—that the Geneva Convention does not apply to al Qaeda and that, under the Third Geneva Convention, Taliban detainees are not entitled to prisoner of war status. At the same time, the president ordered that U.S. armed forces treat detainees humanely." [22]

The same day his comments appeared in the *Post,* Gonzales had flown to Houston and back to the school where he had sold Cokes and popcorn as a kid—and where he had once dreamed of moving into the wealthy,

gilded circles that were always outside his grasp. Rice University had
drawn up a list of possible commencement speakers. Rice, Gonzales, and
the Dalai Lama were on it—and Gonzales was the only one who came to
Houston, to his old school. There was absolutely no mention of Iraq, of
Abu Ghraib, of the Geneva Convention, of the fact that people were saying that Bush had accused Hussein of being a "torturer"—and now people
were using the same word to talk about Americans and about a White
House counsel's office that would not state in commanding terms that
torture of any kind was forever forbidden by U.S. forces.

In the audience at his alma mater, a student had put "No War" on some
tape and affixed it to his mortarboard; other Rice graduates put peace
symbols on their clothing. Gonzales delivered his speech:

*"How would you live your life differently, starting today, this very moment, if
you knew that one day you would befriend a president? If I only knew that another
George W. Bush would come along, I would prepare myself in every way that I
could—through education and training—to take advantage of an opportunity that
comes along only once in a lifetime. If I only knew . . .*

*"The average tenure for assistance to the president, such as myself, is eighteen to
twenty-four months. This is hard stuff that we deal with in Washington—because
political opponents constantly criticize our decisions, the national media is ever-
present to criticize every action; and the stakes can have enormous domestic and
international consequences. . . .*

*"In time, you'll be concerned with inventions and discoveries and trials and
deals. The climb to partnerships and titles and awards will dominate your ambitions.
It did for me. So moving forward, it will be important to find the right balance between your responsibilities to your family and to your profession."*[23]

While Gonzales was giving his speech at one university, his name was
being harshly debated at another college 70 miles outside of Washington. Faculty and students at Mount St. Mary's College, a Catholic
school in Maryland, had coalesced to protest Gonzales's being invited to
accept an honorary degree and to deliver a commencement address. Sixty-
one teachers and students signed a petition saying that Gonzales was unwelcome because of his work on the death row cases in Texas. The petition
said that his "public record is glaringly incompatible" with the mission of

the school and its teachers. Meanwhile reports were emerging that perhaps as many as thirty-seven detainees in Afghanistan and Iraq had died while being held by the United States and that maybe some of those detainees had been brutally hit and had been suffocated. At Mount St. Mary's, the school president announced the honorary degree was being withdrawn but that Gonzales could still come and speak.

He had other awards in his West Wing office. There were several plaques that he never had time to hang up. There were those "partnerships and titles and awards" that were testimony to his own climb—to the way that climb used to "dominate" his own "ambitions."

Gonzales was exasperated. How could he be blamed for Abu Ghraib?

"If you were to ask soldiers in the field if they ever heard of my draft memo, they would have said, 'What?' " [24]

By June, Bush, Rove, and Gonzales had talked about the political necessity of confronting the torture debacle. White House staffers knew that Gonzales was being pressed to be the point person; there was literal discussion about the fact that Gonzales, imperturbable and with a rounded, cherubic face, would be the best apologist and defender. He moved with a compact solidity, and he wasn't going to take the bait and bark back like Ashcroft, Rumsfeld, or Cheney. Gonzales would, in effect, go public and present the prosecution's case for its policies aimed at cracking al Qaeda, the Taliban, and Iraq—and extracting from them whatever useful information it could. On Tuesday, June 22, Gonzales presided over what was an unparalleled occasion for an administration that—following Gonzales's legal directives—had consistently refused to release documents, memos, and records, including ones that dated back a decade or more.

At 3:12 in the afternoon, at the Eisenhower Executive Building, Gonzales announced that he would be releasing hundreds of pages of previously hidden memos. Gonzales called it "an extraordinary set of documents," including various drafts and documents prepared by Jay Bybee, John Yoo, Donald Rumsfeld, and President Bush. Each of them was related to the Geneva Convention, torture, interrogation, detention, and war crimes. As a package, they were designed to mute the very thing that had swirled over Gonzales's head for several simmering weeks—the release of so many pages was meant to suggest how deliberate, careful, wide-ranging, and thoughtful the discussions at the White House had been. There had been no legally loose sprint toward endorsing torture as part of U.S. policy. There was disavowal of Bybee's fifty-page memo and the release of all the papers was pushback against the nagging theory that had taken root around the world—that people inside the White House had crafted memos and policies that tacitly or directly encouraged a culture of torture in the American military.

Gonzales didn't like to release documents, and releasing hundreds of sensitive pages, including several with his name on them, ran completely counter to the executive privilege he had been using over and over again to cloak and empower the White House. This was different. This had to be done. People who worked with Gonzales said that it had truly gotten personal. He talked about his children to them, about the fact that he still had two little kids, about the fact that he missed Texas more than ever. In his West Wing office he had brought in some doodles and drawings that his kids had done. He wasn't a torturer; he wasn't a cold-blooded draftsman who talked about waterboarding in a casual fashion. Rove must have said that the release of the documents, putting on a united front, was more than necessary to stem any more bleeding by the White House. Some staffers wondered if it really meant the bleeding by Gonzales. Gonzales offered some comments as he released the memos:

"These are tough issues, and some of the conclusions by the lawyers you may find controversial. . . . I want to reaffirm yet again that the United States has very high values. We do not engage in torture. We are bound by the convention against torture, as ratified by the United States. . . . All interrogation techniques authorized for use against the Taliban and al Qaeda and in Iraq have been carefully vetted and determined to not constitute torture. . . . We are a nation of rules and values. It's as simple as that. And we are fighting the war accordingly. . . . The president said we don't commit torture, we don't condone torture." [25]

Staffers knew that Gonzales hated every bit of it: having to release the papers, having to lay bare the way the legal process worked in his office, having to repudiate one of Bybee's memos, having to come out and almost issue an apology for something that he thought was incredibly misunderstood. Gonzales told people that all of it—the memos, the discussions, the drafts—was what lawyers do. It wasn't really different from what he had done his entire career. They were briefs, possibilities, theories that were being kicked around—not law. It really was what he had done back in Texas: there would be meetings, more meetings, briefs, memos at V&E, the governor of Texas's office, the Texas Supreme Court. He had moved from one cloistered culture to another, fully expecting that the memos, the brainstorming sessions, the paperwork, and the discussions were not privy to the public.

Now maybe he finally realized it didn't work that way in Washington. And now, friends said, he was faulting himself for not having the political vision, the arching ability, to see that all the post-9/11 memos churning into and out of his West Wing office were really incendiary. Things were moving so fast, there were so many insistent voices coming at him—Bush, Yoo, Flanigan—that he must have wondered if he could have done more to slow the whole process down. To not have been so *forward-leaning*—maybe he had been too forward-leaning, and it had become a political and personal nightmare for him . . . and for Bush. In retrospect, some administration staffers must have felt it was also only a matter of time before attention would shift to the secret domestic spying program. For now, only the so-called torture memos were being touched upon, revealed, debated. The spying program, gusted along by the same urgencies and the same forward-leaning legal interpretations, was more hidden but it had certainly emerged from the same mind-set. And, in the end, it would prove to be as intensely damaging politically as anything Gonzales had ever seen.

At the Republican National Convention at the end of the summer, a decision had been made to open up with a video saluting Latinos in America. The video featured a tribute to Gonzales and other Latinos appointed by Bush. Cynics who saw the video said that Gonzales was the living embodiment of Bush's campaign slogan about education—aimed in large part at minorities—to "leave no child behind." The joke went that Bush would "never leave Gonzales behind." He had brought him this far and he would continue to carry him.

There were over thirty-five million Latinos in the United States, the largest minority group in the country, and political insiders in Texas said that Bush and Rove wanted to get the most utility out of Gonzales—and that there was a tug of war going on between the two of them about where Gonzales should be steered. Bush trusted Gonzales enough to have once thought about putting him on the Supreme Court. But Rove no doubt told Bush there was now an enormous political liability, that Bush's conservative base would still be furious. It would be better if Gonzales, who seemed weary of Washington, went to a job in which he could begin to rehabilitate his image with hard-liner conservatives and even begin to sculpt some sort of statesmanlike image that would soften the Democratic and liberal views of him as the proponent of torture. Gonzales, some in the White House and Texas said, had had his eyes on becoming the first Latino attorney general.

Word had already filtered that the man who might be Bush's best friend in life, Secretary of Commerce, Don Evans, was going to leave for the private sector. He was one of the inner circle Texans—with Gonzales, Hughes, Allbaugh, and Clay Johnson—who had gone to high-ranking positions in DC. One by one, they all had decided to leave the administration. But friends of Gonzales said he was very well aware that he was still a valuable political chip and that he would stay in Washington and see if he was offered the attorney general job. One friend in Texas was quite sure that, from talking with Gonzales, he didn't ever really have his heart set on a nomination to the Supreme Court. He would accept it, of course, if Bush asked him. The temptation to cap his legal career would be immense, but it wasn't something that he was obsessed with. The fact that he would have to basically campaign for the job, he'd have to open the books on his life, personal feelings, memos, and court rulings, was almost unbearable. He would accept a nomination to the Supreme Court if Bush wanted, but he would loathe the final, grinding political steps he'd have to take.

Gonzales didn't have to worry. Rove surely had decided that Gonzales would not be Bush's first choice for any open seat. Instead Gonzales would be nominated to replace Ashcroft. In the months building to the 2004 election, it was clear that Ashcroft was on the way out. His bluster at the 9/11 Commission hearing, the belief that he had too often acted like a free radical in the administration, and the battles with Bush's personal friend Alberto Gonzales were adding up to a crystallizing notion that he was one of the cabinet members who would not be returning if Bush was reelected. He was either going on his own or being steered to the door, and if the outwardly subdued, media-averse Gonzales replaced him, it would be like introducing a polar opposite personality. Supporters of Rudolph Giuliani thought he would be an ideal candidate to replace Ashcroft, but there was always a sense that the former prosecutor and New York mayor had his eyes on bigger elected offices, maybe even the presidency at some point.

In Texas a friend of Gonzales assumed that he was tired of the way the White House counsel job had transmogrified during his watch into a repetitively public position. If it was going to be that way, then he wanted out, too, just like Evans—or he wanted to go to a place like the attorney general's office where he would have more autonomy. The fact that he would be replacing Ashcroft, the man he had fought with for control of the White House's legal pecking order, would also have to be supremely satisfying. In the fall Gonzales did a modest amount of campaigning for Bush's reelection. And he talked with Bush, Rove, and his friends about whether to take the job as attorney general.

Ashcroft had made the job easier for him. Ashcroft had succeeded in alienating the media, and he had become the very thing that Bush loathed. Ashcroft had become a perception problem. If whoever followed Ashcroft didn't make the same kind of waves, the battle would be half won. Bush and Rove suspected that if Gonzales was put in a more public posture, with a chance to display his imperturbably calm demeanor, he could help rehabilitate the harsh image of the attorney general's office. Gonzales could also use the high-profile position to counter critics who saw him as the behind-the-scenes destroyer of civil liberties; at the very least, by being more public, he would start to move away from a reputation for being the shadowy White House counsel who crafted dark, almost immoral memos. It was long-range planning: put Gonzales in the attorney general's office for a year or two and then he'd be in a position to run for office—or finally to win approval for a Supreme Court seat.

There was, of course, the immense political utility of naming the first Hispanic to the office of attorney general—to an office that for many minorities over the years had come to symbolize a law enforcement culture in the United States that routinely, unfairly targeted minorities. Gonzales was arguably the most influential Latino in the Bush administration, and now he was going to be given what was arguably the most influential cabinet position ever held by a Latino. Rove wanted Gonzales positioned for other things than the first Supreme Court opening that might come up. Gonzales's options were to go home to Texas or take the attorney general nomination.

FIFTEEN

Old Buddy

In late October, Gonzales was in Philadelphia, telling a luncheon audience that both John Kerry and George Bush had believed there were weapons of mass destruction in Iraq. He talked, too, about how he had scrambled to get back to the White House on 9/11. "I want to try to force you to remember your sorrow and your sadness and your anger," Gonzales told his listeners.[1] By then he had made his choice to accept a position on Bush's cabinet. If he still harbored any ambitions to move to the Supreme Court, the move to the attorney general's office would only help flesh out his resume, and he could spend time erasing any lingering fears that conservatives had about his ideological purity.

His brother Tony, the Houston cop, watched from a distance. His older brother was probably going to be the nation's top cop; he was on his way to the top of the Department of Justice. If he was confirmed, Gonzales would not only be the first Hispanic attorney general in U.S. history—he would allay the cries of Hispanic leaders who wondered when Bush would add someone Hispanic to the cabinet in the wake of the departure of HUD secretary Mel Martinez.

On election night Gonzales chose to be at Clay Johnson's house. Being around the easygoing, tall former high school pal and college roommate of George W. Bush was almost like being back in Texas. Johnson's roots ran deep in Texas, and Gonzales liked being around him. It was a Texas-centric party, with thirty guests, including Margaret Spellings, who had worked as a senior adviser to Bush back in the governor's office and was headed to the cabinet as secretary of education; Texas senator John Cornyn; HUD secretary Alphonso Jackson from Dallas; Dina Powell, who had now taken over the White House personnel duties from Johnson. When the news reports announced that Bush had won, Gonzales had an ear-to-ear grin as he headed out of the party and to the White House to see his chief client. Bush appeared to have won 41 percent of the Hispanic vote.

Three days later Gonzales was in Houston to visit his mother, his six living siblings, and his old friends. They had read the reports, the specula-tion about where he was headed. He refused to give any hints to anyone, even though people at the White House already knew that Ashcroft had submitted his resignation and that Gonzales was going to be the new at-torney general nominee. As a treat, Gonzales took his younger brother Tony golfing. Tony pressed him for news. Gonzales wouldn't budge. "He wouldn't give an inch," said his brother. Being in Houston had to be a reminder of how much money he had given up. The AG's office paid $175,700—a fifth of what he might be making at Vinson & Elkins by now.

A week after the election, Bush walked into the Roosevelt Room at 3:40 on a Wednesday afternoon. Gonzales stood to one side. Rebecca and two of their three children, Graham and Gabriel, looked on:

THE PRESIDENT: *"Good afternoon. I'm pleased to announce my nomi-nation of Judge Al Gonzales to be the attorney general of the United States. This is the fifth time I have asked Judge Gonzales to serve his fel-low citizens, and I am very grateful he keeps saying yes. A decade ago, when I was elected governor of Texas, I asked Al to be my general coun-sel. He went on to distinguished service as Texas's secretary of state and as a justice of the Texas Supreme Court. Since I arrived in Washington four years ago, he has served with skill and integrity in the White House as counsel to the president. I have counted on Al Gonzales to help select the best nominees for the federal courts, one of the president's most important responsibilities. His sharp intellect and sound judgment have helped shape our policies in the war on terror—policies designed to protect the* security of all Americans, while protecting the rights of all Americans. As the top legal official on the White House staff, he has led a superb team of lawyers and has upheld the highest standards of government ethics. My confidence in Al was high to begin with; it has only grown with time.

"Over the past decade I've also come to know the character of this man. He always gives me his frank opinion. He is a calm and steady voice in times of crisis. He has an unwavering principle, a respect for the law, and he and Becky are dear friends of Laura and my—of me, and I'm also very friendly with Graham and Gabriel Gonzales. My newest cabinet nominee grew up in a two-bedroom house in Texas with his parents and seven siblings. Al's mother and dad, Pablo and Maria, were migrant workers who never finished elementary school, but they worked hard to educate their children and to instill the values of reverence and integrity and personal responsibility. These good people lived to see their son, Al, study at Rice University and Harvard Law School. Maria still lives in Humble, Texas, in the house her husband built, and I can only imagine how proud she is today of her son, Al. Serving as attorney general is one of the most challenging duties in our government. As the nation's chief law enforcement officer, Al will continue our administration's great progress in fighting crime, in strengthening the FBI, in improving our domestic efforts in the war on terror. As a steward of civil rights laws, he will ensure that Americans are protected from discrimination so that each person has the opportunity to live the American dream, as Al himself has done.

"With the Senate's approval, Judge Gonzales will succeed another superb public servant, Attorney General John Ashcroft. Attorney General Ashcroft has served with excellence during a demanding time. In four years he's reorganized the Department of Justice to meet the new threat of terrorism. He's fairly and forcefully applied the Patriot Act and helped to dismantle terror cells inside the United States. During his watch, violent crime has dropped to a thirty-year low, and prosecutions of crimes committed with guns have reached an all-time high. Drug use amongst our students is down. Confidence in the financial markets has been restored because the attorney general aggressively prosecuted corporate fraud. And thanks to John Ashcroft's leadership, America has stepped up its efforts to prosecute the cruel exploitation of children by Internet pornographers. The

*nation is safer and more just today because John Ashcroft has served our
country so well.*

*"I'm committed to strong, principled leadership at the Department of
Justice, and Judge Al Gonzales will be that kind of leader as America's
eightieth attorney general. I urge the Senate to act promptly on this important nomination. I look forward to welcoming my great friend to the
cabinet. Congratulations."*

Gonzales smiled and stepped forward.

*"Thank you, Mr. President. I am joined today, as the president said,
by my beautiful wife, Rebecca, and two of our three sons, Graham and
Gabriel. And on behalf of my family, including my mom, Maria, and our
other son, Jared, thank you, Mr. President, for this extraordinary opportunity. This has been a day of conflicting emotions for me—obviously, great
humility and gratitude, but also some sadness, that, if confirmed, I will no
longer drive to work every day to the White House, nor interact as closely
with this remarkable White House staff, including my great team in the
Counsel's Office, all led ably by my friend and inspiration, Chief of Staff
Andy Card. But I do look forward, if confirmed, to continuing to work
with my friends and colleagues in the White House in a different capacity
on behalf of our president, as we move forward to make America better,
safer, and stronger. As a former judge, I know well that some government
positions require a special level of trust and integrity. The American people
expect and deserve a Department of Justice guided by the rule of law, and
there should be no question regarding the department's commitment to
justice for every American. On this principle, there can be no compromise.*

*"I am indebted to General Ashcroft, who, as the president just ac-
knowledged, has served well during an historic time for our country. I appreciate John Ashcroft's courage and friendship, and I will work hard to
build upon his record. Finally, to our president, when I talk to people
around the country, I sometimes tell them that within the Hispanic community there is a shared hope for an opportunity to succeed. 'Just give me
a chance to prove myself'—that is a common prayer for those in my community. Mr. President, thank you for that chance. With the consent of the
Senate, God's help, and the support of my family, I will do my best to
fulfill the confidence and trust reflected in this nomination. Thank
you, sir."* [2]

L ost amid all the picture taking, hugs, and handshakes was the fact that Harriet Miers—the woman who endorsed Gonzales for his first job with Bush back in Texas—was being moved from her virtually anonymous position as deputy White House chief of staff to take over as White House counsel. If there was anyone who was more loyal to Bush left in the White House—now that Hughes, Gonzales, and Clay Johnson were leaving—it was Miers. She and Gonzales had been sycophantically bound to Bush for years in many of the exact same ways. Bush had tapped both of them, and both of them had traded jobs back and forth and followed Bush to Washington. Gonzales had no idea that Miers would probably be the one person who would throw his chances for a seat on the Supreme Court into cold, staggering disarray.

T he eight weeks building up to his Senate confirmation hearings exposed every twist and turn in his life—and how his nomination was chosen by the Democrats as a place to make a stand, as a place to summon up some brio after the deflating Kerry defeat. Every day leading up to his January hearings before the Senate Judiciary Committee, Gonzales was both praised and damned.

He was lauded by the National Council of La Raza executive director Janet Murguia: "We are very encouraged by the Gonzales nomination. . . . Gonzales is a thoughtful, reasonable public servant, a man of his word, and we have every expectation that his nomination will be very well received in the Latino community."[3] "It has yet to be seen whether or not Gonzales would be the best fit for our community, but we are encouraged by this development," added an official with the Mexican-American Legal Defense Fund.

Some Democratic senators even sounded mildly conciliatory, vaguely pleased. Patrick Leahy from Vermont, the ranking Democrat on the Senate committee that would conduct hearings on Gonzales, said he personally liked Gonzales and that Gonzales would probably get an easy approval. Charles Schumer from New York announced that Gonzales was certainly "less confrontational" than Ashcroft and "he at least tries to reach out."

The Christian Coalition said he was a "great example of the American success story." Meanwhile Ted Kennedy said he had concerns about whether Gonzales was committed to the rule of law.[4] And, Michael Ratner with the Center for Constitutional Rights was mobilizing resistance to his nomination, calling it a "travesty" and saying that Gonzales was more "dangerous" than Ashcroft.

Ratner embodied a welling movement of human rights activists, civil libertarians, academics, and former military officers who would coalesce around their opposition to Gonzales. Most of them, like Ratner, would hone in on the so-called Gonzales Torture Memos. "We were completely outraged. He was creating a third nonlaw to do what they wanted: It was not criminal law, it was not military law. They were misleading us," says Ratner.[5] One Latino observer simply said Gonzales had surely lost his way: "While his class origins were humble, now he has adopted the class of those people in power, which is not uncommon," says Nativo Lopez with the Mexican-American Political Association.[6]

But meanwhile some of his friends in Texas—the ones who thought he had already ranked as high as Cesar Chavez in the pantheon of Latino Americans—said that Gonzales was a role model for every young Latino in the land. The National Hispanic Bar Association announced it was happy with his selection. On the other side of the spectrum, Abu Ghraib would not go away: "By nominating the champion of Abu Ghraib as his attorney general, Bush disgraces far more than himself. He shames America," said Jesse Jackson.[7] The U.S. Hispanic Chamber of Commerce said Gonzales was an "inspirational example" and an "exemplary public servant." The League of United Latin-American Citizens said it was "delighted" that Bush had picked "one of our best and brightest," but in California some dissident LULAC members said they were vehemently opposed to Gonzales's nomination because of his march away from civil and human rights.

The divisions were wide, the debates free-ranging. Gonzales, even before he had been measured at Senate hearings, was a polarizing figure.

A t the DC Bar Association annual banquet the first weekend in December, Gonzales arrived early at the Italian embassy, at 7:00 P.M., ready to offer his salute to honoree Fred Fielding, the beefy insider who had worked for Nixon, Reagan, and John Dean. Fielding had been one of the spirit guides who had taken Gonzales through Washington, speaking up for Gonzales when the Beltway true believers wanted to know what the real estate attorney from Texas was made of. Fielding, C. Boyden Gray, and some others had helped Gonzales in ways that he was probably not even aware of. At the Bar Association fete, Gonzales spotted Fielding and hugged him. "This is the man. He's the only thing that got me out tonight," said Gonzales, mysteriously adding that he and Fielding had met "through the secret club." People at the party wondered what the hell he meant. Maybe it was Gonzales's reference to the Federalist Society and that so many things in Washington seemed foreign to him when he first arrived.[8]

The education of Alberto Gonzales had rolled on in DC. His wife who had felt excluded from early soirees, was invited to a campy "Power Chick" holiday bash with 100 of the city's powerful women. And meanwhile, quietly, Texas Senator John Cornyn—another member of the Senate Judiciary Committee that would conduct hearings on Gonzales—was meeting with Gonzales to talk strategy about how to secure his bid to take over the 100,000-employee Justice Department and become the nation's top law enforcement officer. Several things were obvious—some of them had already been forecast by Democratic senators in statements and letters to Gonzales.

He was going to be asked about the Geneva Convention, he was going to be asked about his review of the clemency petitions in Texas, and he was going to be asked about Abu Ghraib. He was also warned that in the weeks building up to the January 2005 hearings, people would claw and scratch for personal dirt on the prospective top law enforcer in America. If Gonzales needed any more warnings on what kind of climate awaited him, it came in the form of sticky news reports that his stepson, Jared, Rebecca's son from her previous marriage, had once worked as a web site and broadcasting consultant for *Hustler* magazine founder Larry Flynt. He was also warned that he'd be attacked for having no law enforcement pedigree to entitle him to the top job at the Department of Justice. When it was revealed that Bernard Kerik, the former New York City police commissioner who was Bush's choice to head the Department of Homeland

Security, had some legal baggage in his background, people blamed Gonzales for not investigating it. As White House counsel it was his job to vet Kerik, and Gonzales hadn't dug deep enough to find the flaws in Kerik's history. What kind of Attorney General could he be?

Before Christmas he also had the big picture spelled out for him in the form of a letter sent to the Senate Judiciary Committee from nine human rights organizations—Amnesty International, Human Rights First, the Human Rights Watch, Global Rights, Minnesota Advocates for Human Rights, Physicians for Human Rights, the Robert F. Kennedy Memorial Center for Human Rights, the International League for Human Rights, and the Carter Center: "It is now widely known that Judge Gonzales was actively involved as counsel to the president in providing guidance on several of the most important questions decided by the Bush administration concerning human rights and the laws of war" and that the controversial discussion about not applying some Geneva Convention provisions had fed the "illegal and abusive methods" that were used against detainees and prisoners.

In some ways Gonzales expected all that. Hearing from Amnesty International was almost a given. What was going to be far more problematic was the fact that several military lawyers, career soldiers, and JAG (Judge Advocate General's Corp) men and women, who had spent their careers mulling court-martials, the Geneva Convention, and war crimes, were assembling as well. So much had been revealed in the last three years about how the United States had launched its counteroffensive against terrorism and what it thought about doing to the men it had captured. Some of the career lawyers in the military looked for signs that they had been deliberately excluded from the policies, the memos, the discussions and more than a few were personally offended. A former real estate lawyer from Texas was in their domain—and, worse, he was threatening decades of careful interpretation and enforcement of those recognized international legal standards.

The Pentagon lawyers were accustomed to civilians sometimes wading in. They didn't like it, but that was the way the cards were stacked. What they really abhorred was a sense that they were completely excluded—

maybe intentionally excluded. Many of them actually believed part of what Gonzales had once said in his 2002 draft memo—that there was a need for a "new paradigm" after 9/11. There really was, but many of the military lawyers simply felt that Gonzales had pursued that new paradigm without them, without knowing the right way to do it, without the experience that comes from the JAG. Many of them were planning to testify against Gonzales; many of them assumed they would be summoned to testify:

"This is not an insignificant issue. These are profound issues that will affect the reputation of the United States for years," says retired admiral John Hutson, former navy judge advocate general who had become president and dean of the Franklin Pierce Law Center. "I've been a lawyer since 1972, and I have come to realize for the first time that the law is not as important as I thought it was, and the lawyer is more important than I thought it was. Alberto Gonzales is a lawyer, and if lawyers can manipulate the law to what they think is to their advantage that easily, then the law isn't as heavily important as I thought it would be.

"I thought long and hard about whether I wanted to testify, because unless something else came out—like a girlfriend on the side, something really crippling—he's going to be confirmed. I figured I risked being included on no-fly lists and tax audits for years to come for what would ultimately be a futile effort. I knew or suspected that he would be confirmed, but I decided that there were things that needed to be said."[9]

Don Evans, Bush's commerce secretary in the first term, had come to think that everyone had it all terribly wrong about his friend from Texas: "The years of my dealing with him, he is a world-class guy, he is very, very bright, very thoughtful, very thorough, and he cares about what you are saying. He is a good listener. He will give you his best, unvarnished advice ... which is the kind of advice you want to hear. He has solid-core beliefs, solid values, cares deeply about his country. He has made great sacrifices with his whole family—they were uprooted and moved to Washington," says Evans.

And, of course, Gonzales was George W. Bush's lawyer for several of the most crucial years in Bush's life. He had literally gone to criminal court for Bush in Texas. He had been with Bush in the minutes before another inmate was put to death in Texas. He had put his name and work to all of

the touchstones of the Bush presidency: the counterattacks against terrorists, the invasion of Iraq, the Patriot Act, the creation of the Homeland
Security Department, the Valerie Plame investigation.

"There is a great deal of mutual trust between the two; there is a great
deal of mutual respect between the two. The president, when he selected
him, he viewed him as a young, rising star attorney that had great potential
to be an extraordinary public servant—and he wanted to give him that
opportunity. I know, I can't help but think that Al is extraordinary grateful
by the then-governor making a bet on him, to take a chance on him that
had no previous track record in the public arena. He is totally loyal to the
president," offers Evans.[10]

A week before Gonzales's Senate hearings, the Justice Department that
he hoped to take command of released a seventeen-page legal memo.
It was a pullback, a retraction of the earlier memos suggesting that the
president's constitutional authority gave him free reign to have wartime
detainees or prisoners treated in ways that moved beyond the Geneva
Convention and that there were easily pursued legal defenses that would
protect any U.S. interrogators or soldiers if they were ever accused of torture.

As he sequestered himself at home and at his office preparing for his
testimony to the Senate committee, people wondered which Alberto
Gonzales would show up: the seemingly moderate Gonzales who helped
protect a breakup of affirmative action policies in Michigan, the moderate
Gonzales who refused to lash out at abortion rights in Texas, the Texas
judge who sometimes took the side of the little guy, or the hard-right
Gonzales who sealed White House papers, who defended Rove and
Cheney from inquiries into their business ties, who helped create the
tough-handed Patriot Act, who was so forward-leaning in figuring out
ways to prosecute the war on terrorism?

Who would show up—and who would become attorney general? The
Alberto Gonzales who some said was like a Stepford wife, a perfect robot,
a highly trained quarterback—you told him what the endgame was supposed to be, you told him what legal outcome you were looking for . . . and
he would figure out the way to get there, by any legal loopholes necessary?

The fiercely intelligent Alberto Gonzales who was slavishly addicted to the exact letter of the law—nothing more, nothing less, and never one to impose his personal ideology or viewpoints on the Constitution and the stated legal principles that guide the country?

Gonzales, up to the end, had remained an enigma who was tugged by fate, expectations, compromises, luck, George W. Bush, 9/11, and his up-bringing in Humble, Texas. He had really only worked for three or four people or places in his life: Bush, the air force, Vinson & Elkins. He had never really worked for the American people at the White House. He had said it himself—he worked for his client, the president of the United States. He no longer spoke Spanish, said his best friends. He didn't seem to drift into that zone that a lot of people do when they reach middle age—when they stop running away from their roots, when they stop running away from their upbringing—and start to reconnect on an extremely deep level with their family's history. If it was happening, if he was working backward and tracing lines through several generations on his family tree, if he was trying hard to keep a passionate ethnic fire burning at home, in his heart, it wasn't apparent to his friends. That said, he still connected with his His-panic friends in Texas, maybe connected with them at some level that no one else would understand. And even the people in Texas who might have hated the policies of his client had come to view him through the prism of his race. Like him or not, like his client or not, Alberto Gonzales had made an unlikely rise to enormous power in America.

The day before Gonzales was set to testify before the Senate Judiciary Committee, Henry Cisneros wrote an op-ed in the *Wall Street Journal* that stunned Latino leaders around the nation. Cisneros—who some said had all the bearing, intelligence, and talent to become the first Latino president of the United States—had long ago succumbed to some personal weak-nesses and then been hounded for years by a relentless Republican-endorsed investigation into his personal life and his finances. He left Washington as a shattered public figure—and, said some, as a symbol of what can happen when Latinos become too successful. They crash and burn—or they are shoved into the fire. Cisneros, back in Texas, was a sort of doomed Hamlet on the prairie. He was in a bittersweet political exile but still a living reminder of what could have been. If he had been elected, his supporters said, it would have been like a Latino Camelot. Now he was endorsing Alberto Gonzales to take a seat on the cabinet, just like Cisneros had once done. Cisneros said he had only voted for one Republican in his life and that was when Gonzales ran for the Supreme Court in Texas. Cisneros said that having a Latino in such a high office was good for America.

Texas Senator Cornyn opened up with an introduction:

> CORNYN: *"Judge Gonzales is truly an inspiration to everyone who still believes in the American dream . . . only in Washington would this good man get raked over the coals for simply doing his job. . . . President Bush and Judge Gonzales have both unequivocally, clearly, and repeatedly rejected the use of torture. . . . I imagine that we're going to hear a lot about Abu Ghraib today. . . . Yet some people actually want to exploit that tragedy to score political points. . . . If there is no evidence whatsoever that Judge Gonzales was in any way responsible for this, why are we talking about this at Judge Gonzales's confirmation hearing?"*

There was a second introduction and endorsement from Senator Ken Salazar from Colorado, a strong supporter of Gonzales. Senator Arlen Specter then swore Gonzales in, asking him to stand and raise his right hand. He asked Gonzales to introduce his family and Gonzales didn't seem to hear him. Specter interrupted him and told him that there was a pending request for him to introduce his family. Gonzales began introducing his wife and three sons, Jared, Gabriel, and Graham; his mother, Maria; and his brother Tony. They were sitting just over his right shoulder, along with his mother-in-law, Lorinda Turner, in the first row of seats. Specter insisted that they stand as they were introduced.

Gonzales finally settled into his seat in a thick, high-backed black leather chair with chunky wooden arms. He leaned forward to the edge of the seat, resting his elbows on a desk covered with maroon cloth. In the back of the hearing room were a small clutch of protesters with shirts saying "Investigate Gonzales." His family members might have seen the other small group of protesters with homemade signs: "Ship Gonzo to Gitmo" and "Bush and Gonzales Are Responsible for Death and Torture." He tilted forward and spoke into the black microphone:

GONZALES: *"If confirmed as attorney general, I will no longer represent the White House; I will represent the United States of America and its people. I understand the differences between the two roles. . . . Wherever we pursue justice—from the war on terror to corporate fraud to civil rights— we must always be faithful to the rule of law. . . . These obligations include, of course, honoring the Geneva Convention whenever it applies. Honoring our Geneva obligations provides critical protection for our fighting men and women and advances norms for the community of nations to follow in times of conflict. Contrary to reports, I consider the Geneva Convention neither obsolete nor quaint. After the attacks of 9/11, our government had fundamental decisions to make concerning how to apply treaties and U.S. law to an enemy that does not wear a uniform, owes no allegiance to any country, is not party to any treaties, and—most importantly—does not fight according to the laws of war. As we have debated these questions, the president has made clear that he is prepared to protect and defend the United States and its citizens, and will do so vigorously, but always in a manner consistent with our nation's values and applicable law, including our treaty obligations. . . .*

"The photos from Abu Ghraib sickened and outraged me, and left a stain on our nation's reputation. And the president has made clear that he condemns this conduct and that these activities are inconsistent with his policies. He has also made it clear that America stands against and will not tolerate torture under any circumstances."

Pennsylvania Republican Senator Specter, the chairman of the committee, wasted no time: *"Do you approve of torture?"*

GONZALES: *"Absolutely not, Senator."*
SPECTER: *"Do you condemn the interrogators—you already answered this in part—at Abu Ghraib and Guantánamo? But again, for the record, do you condemn the interrogators, techniques at Abu Ghraib shown on the widely publicized photographs?"*
GONZALES: *"Let me say, Senator, that as a human being, I am sickened and outraged by those photos. But as someone who may be head of the department, I obviously don't want to provide any kind of legal opinion as to whether or not that conduct may be criminal. And obviously anyone*

that is involved in any kind of conduct that he is subject to prosecution, I would not want to do anything today to prejudge that prosecution and jeopardize that prosecution. But obviously if that conduct falls in the jurisdiction of the Department of Justice, I will pursue it aggressively, and you have my word on that."

Specter seemed concerned with Gonzales's answer: *"Well. . . . having some experience in the prosecution of criminal cases, I don't believe the condemnation of that conduct would impact on what happens at a later date."*

Gonzales was questioned by Vermont Democratic Senator Patrick Leahy. He quoted from the memo that Jay Bybee sent to Gonzales in August 2002: *" 'For an act to violate the torture statute, it must be equivalent in intensity to the pain accompanying serious physical injury, such as organ failure, impairment of bodily function, or even death.' In August 2002 did you agree with that conclusion?"*

GONZALES: *"Senator, in connection with that opinion, I did my job as counsel to the president of the United States to ask the question."*

LEAHY: *"No, no. I just want to know, did you agree—I mean, we can spend an hour with that answer. But my—I'm trying to keep it very simple. Did you agree with that interpretation of the torture statute back in 2002?"*

GONZALES: *"If I may sir, let me try to—I'll try to—I'm going to give you a very quick answer. But I'd like to put a little bit of context. . . . There was discussion between the White House and the Department of Justice, as well as other agencies, about what does this statute mean. It was very, very difficult. I don't recall today whether or not I was in agreement with all the analysis. But I don't have a disagreement with the conclusions then reached by the department."*

Later Leahy asked: *"Now, as attorney general, would you believe the president has the authority to exercise a commander-in-chief override and immunize acts of torture?"*

GONZALES: *"First of all, Senator, the president has said we're not going to engage in torture under any circumstances. And so you're asking me to answer a hypothetical that is never going to occur. The president has said we're not going to engage in torture under any circumstances, and therefore that portion of the opinion was unnecessary and was the reason that we asked that that portion be withdrawn."*

LEAHY: *"But I'm trying to think what type of opinions you might give as attorney general. Do you agree with that conclusion?"*

GONZALES: *"Sir, again . . ."*

LEAHY: *"You're a lawyer, and you've held a position as a justice of the Texas Supreme Court. You've been the president's counsel. You've studied this issue deeply. Do you agree with that conclusion?"*

GONZALES: *"Senator, I do believe there may come an occasion when the Congress might pass a statute that the president may view as unconstitutional. And that is a position and a view not just of this president but many, many presidents from both sides of the aisle. Obviously a decision as to whether or not to ignore a statute passed by Congress is a very, very serious one, and it would be one that I would spend a great deal of time and attention before arriving at a conclusion that, in fact, a president had the authority under the Constitution to . . ."*

LEAHY: *"Mr. Gonzales, I'd almost think that you'd served in the Senate you've learned how to filibuster so well. Because I asked a specific question: Does the president have the authority, in your judgment, to exercise a commander-in-chief override and immunize acts of torture?"*

GONZALES: *"With all due respect, Senator, the president said we're not going to engage in torture. That is a hypothetical question that would involve an analysis of a great number of factors. And the president . . ."*

LEAHY: *"How about this way: Do you think that other world leaders would have authority to authorize the torture of U.S. citizens if they deemed it necessary for their national security?"*

GONZALES: *"Senator, I don't know what laws other world leaders would be bound by. And I think it would—I'm not in a position to answer that question."*

LEAHY: *"Well, the only reason I ask this is this was the—this memo was DOJ (Department of Justice) policy for a couple years. And, you know, it sat there from some time in 2002 and then just a couple weeks before 2005, late on a Thursday afternoon, it seems to be somewhat overwritten. Of course, that may be coincidentally because your confirmation hearing*

*was coming up. Do you think if the Bybee memo had not been leaked to
the press—because it had never been shown to Congress, even though
we'd asked for it—do you think it would still be the overriding legal
opinion?"*

GONZALES: *"Sir, that I do not know. I do know that when it became—it
was leaked, we had concern about the fact that people were assumed that
the president was somehow exercising that authority to engage in torture.
And we wanted to clarify the record that the president had not authorized or condoned torture, nor had directed any actions or excused any
actions under the commander-in-chief override that might otherwise constitute torture."*

The interrogation by Leahy went on for a few more minutes. He
pressed Gonzales on whether there was any connection between what
happened at Abu Ghraib and any of the memos or policies that were flowing from Gonzales's desk:

LEAHY: *"Well, do you think there's any connection whatsoever between the
policies which actually you helped to formulate regarding the treatment,
interrogation of prisoners, policies that were sent out, Department of Defense and elsewhere, and the widespread abuses that have occurred? Do
you acknowledge any accountability for such things, any connection?"*

GONZALES: *"Senator, as I said in my remarks, I categorically condemn the
conduct that we see reflected in these pictures at Abu Ghraib."*

The floor was turned over to a Gonzales ally, Utah Republican Senator
Orrin Hatch:

HATCH: *"Welcome to the committee, Judge Gonzales and your family. We
welcome your family, your wonderful wife, your tremendous mother,
brother, mother-in-law. We're really happy to have all of you here. And I
hope that this will not be too unpleasant a hearing for you. You've acted,
I think, with the highest honor as the White House counsel. I know that
because I've worked very, very closely with you all these years. And I
have tremendous respect for you, not only as a human being and for your
ethics and high standards, but also as an attorney and as someone who I*

THE PRESIDENT'S COUNSELOR

believe has tried to give the president the best advice you and your staff have been able to give. You know, this is one of the highest positions in our country's cabinet—in the president's cabinet. It does require a person of deep commitment to the principle of equal justice under the law, and I know that you have that commitment and you'll make it. I've worked so closely with you, I know firsthand the competency of Judge Gonzales and that he does believe in equal justice for all. I also know that you have the ability to make a very outstanding attorney general of the United States. Your whole life has been a success story. You've already had a distinguished career as an attorney, judge, and civil servant. You made much of the opportunities that you've had by your education at Rice University and, of course, the Harvard Law School."

Hatch asked at one point: *"Am I correct in my understanding that at no time did the president authorize the use of torture against detainees, regardless of any of the legal memoranda produced by various entities of the U.S. government, including the August 2002 Department of Justice memo, the so-called Bybee memo?"*

GONZALES: *"Senator, the position of the president on torture is very, very clear, and there is a clear record of this. He does not believe in torture, condone torture; has never ordered torture. And anyone engaged in conduct that constitutes torture is going to be held accountable."*

HATCH: *"So that's never been a problem with regard to the president or you as his adviser."*

GONZALES: *"Absolutely not, Senator."*

Hatch turned the floor over to Massachusetts Democratic Senator Ted Kennedy:

"So there's a certain kind of sense by many of us here that the administration—and you're the point person on the administration—has not been forthcoming on the whole issues of torture, which not just was committed at Abu Ghraib but is happening today—today. Now, the Bybee torture memoranda, written at your request—and I'd be interested in your reactions to this—made abuse of interrogation easier; it sharply narrowed the definition of torture and recognized this new defense for offi-

cials who commit torture. For two years—for two years—from August 2002 to June 2004, you never repudiated it. That's the record. You never repudiated it. It was written at the CIA's bidding, and you can clarify that if that's false. We can all assume it was promptly provided to the CIA as written. . . .

"You've never repudiated the Bybee memo assertion that presidential power overrides all the prohibitions against torture, enacted and ratified. The president's directive to act humanely was hollow. It was vague. It allowed for military necessity exception and didn't even apply to the CIA—didn't even apply to the CIA. Abuses are still being reported. And you were warned by Secretary Powell—Secretary Powell—and other top military leaders that ignoring our longstanding traditions and rules would lead to abuse and undermine military culture, and that is what has happened. Now, I'm going to get to how the Bybee amendment was first written. As I understand, there is the report in the Washington Post that the CIA asked you for legal opinion about how much pain and suffering an intelligence officer could inflict on a detainee without violating the '94 antitorture statute, which I might point out was strongly supported by Ronald Reagan and Bush 1, and passed the Foreign Relations Committee unanimously.

"Republicans have been concerned about torture as have Democrats, and we can get on—we'll get into the various statutes that have been passed in recent times which would indicate that. Now, the Post article states you chaired several meetings at which various interrogation techniques were discussed. These techniques included the threat of live burial and waterboarding, whereby the detainee is strapped to a board, forcibly pushed under water, wrapped in a wet towel, and made to believe he might drown. The article states that you raised no objections. Now, without consulting military and State Department experts—they were not consulted. They were not invited to important meetings that might have been important to some. . . . Experts in laws of torture in war proved the resulting memo gave CIA interrogators the legal blessings they sought. Now, was it the CIA that asked you?"

GONZALES: *"Sir, I don't have specific recollection—I read the same article. I don't know whether or not it was the CIA. What I can say is that after this war began against this new kind of threat, this new kind of enemy, we realized that there was a premium on receiving information. In many ways, this war on terrorism is a war about information. If we have information, we can defeat the enemy. We had captured some really bad people who we were concerned had information that might prevent the loss of American lives in the future. It was important to receive that information. And people in the agencies wanted to be sure that they would not do anything that would violate our legal obligations. And so they did the right thing. They asked questions. What is lawful conduct because we don't want to do anything that violates the law?"*

Later, Kennedy asked: *". . . did you ever talk to any members of the OLC [Office of Legal Counsel] while they were drafting the memoranda? Did you ever suggest to them that they ought to lean forward on this issue about supporting the extreme uses of torture? Did you ever, as reported in the newspaper?"*

GONZALES: *"Sir, I don't recall ever using the term, sort of, 'leaning forward' in terms of . . . the law."*

KENNEDY: *"Did you talk to the OLC during the drafting of it?"*

GONZALES: *"There are always discussions—not always discussion—but there is often discussions between the Department of Justice and OLC and the counsel's office regarding legal issues. I think that's perfectly appropriate. This was an issue that the White House cared very much about, to ensure that the agencies were not engaged in conduct . . ."*

KENNEDY: *"What were you urging them? What were you urging? They are, as I understand, charged to interpret the law. We have the series of different—six or seven of the laws on the conventions on torture and the rest of that. They are charged to develop and say what the statute is. Now, what did you believe your role was in talking with the OLC and recommending . . ."*

GONZALES: *"To understand their views about the interpretation . . ."*

KENNEDY: *"Weren't you going to get the document? Weren't you going to get their document? Why did you have to talk to them during the time of the drafting? It suggests in here that you were urging them to go as far as they possibly could. That's what the newspaper reports. Your testimony is that you did talk to them, but you can't remember what you told them."*

GONZALES: *"Sir, I'm sure there was discussion about the analysis about a very tough statute, a new statute, as I've said repeatedly, that had never been interpreted by our courts. And we wanted to make sure that we got it right. So we were engaged in interpreting a very tough statute. And I think it is perfectly reasonable and customary for lawyers at the Department of Justice to talk with lawyers at the White House. Again, it was not my role to direct that we should use certain kinds of methods of receiving information from terrorists. That was a decision made by the operational agencies, and they said, 'We need to try to get this information. What is lawful?' And we looked to the Department of Justice to tell us what would, in fact, be within the law."*

Other senators took their turn with Gonzales, including Wisconsin Democrat Russ Feingold, who pressed Gonzales on a matter that would turn into a raging source of debate once Gonzales had become attorney general. He inadvertently broached the topic of the clandestine domestic spying program. It would, of course, engulf the Bush administration a year later—at a time when the White House thought it had finally escaped scrutiny for the "torture" and "Geneva Convention" portions of its post-9/11 blueprint for the war on terror. Almost exactly a year later, after Gonzales ceased being the president's counselor and had moved on to become attorney general, his answers to Feingold at the confirmation hearing would turn into brutal ammunition for critics who said he was misleading, maybe lying, to the Senate committee about wiretapping— especially when he used the word "hypothetical" to describe a spying program that was very real. Feingold stared hard at Gonzales and said he wanted to know something:

FEINGOLD: *"The question here is what is your view regarding the president's constitutional authority to authorize violations of the criminal law, duly enacted statutes that may have been on the books for many years, when acting as commander in chief? Does he have such authority? The question you have been asked is not about a hypothetical statute in the future that the president might think is unconstitutional. It's about our laws and international treaty obligations concerning torture. The torture memo answered that question in the affirmative, and my colleagues and I would like your answer on that today. And I also would like you to answer this: Does the president, in your opinion, have the authority acting*

as commander in chief to authorize warrantless searches of Americans'
homes and wiretaps of their conversations in violation of the criminal and
foreign intelligence surveillance statutes of this country?"

GONZALES: *"Senator, the August 30th memo has been withdrawn. It has*
been rejected, including that section regarding the commander in chief's
authority to ignore the criminal statutes. So it's been rejected by the exec-
utive branch. I categorically reject it. And in addition to that, as I've said
repeatedly today, this administration does not engage in torture and will
not condone torture. And so, what you really are—what we're really dis-
cussing is a hypothetical situation that . . ."

Feingold interrupted: *"I—Judge Gonzales, let me ask a broader question.*
I'm asking you whether in general the president has the constitutional
authority, does he at least in theory have the authority to authorize viola-
tions of the criminal law under duly enacted statutes simply because he's
commander in chief? Does he—does he have that power?"

GONZALES: *"Senator, I—you—in my judgment, you phrase it sort of a*
hypothetical situation. I would have to know what—what is the—what
is the national interest that the president may have to consider. What I'm
saying is, it is impossible to me, based upon the question as you've pre-
sented it to me, to answer that question. What I can say, is that there is a
presumption of constitutionality with respect to any statute passed by
Congress. I will take an oath to defend the statutes. And to the extent
that there is a decision made to ignore a statute, I consider that a very sig-
nificant decision, and one that I would personally be involved with, I
commit to you on that, and one we will take with a great deal of care and
seriousness."

FEINGOLD: *"Well, that sounds to me like the president still remains above*
the law."

GONZALES: *"No, sir."*

FEINGOLD: *"Again, you know, if this is something where—where it—you*
take a good look at it, you give a presumption that the president ought to
follow the law, that—you know, that's—to me, that's not good enough
under our system of government."

GONZALES: *"Senator, if I might respond to that, the president is not above*
the law. Of course he's not above the law. But he has an obligation, too.
He takes an oath as well. And if Congress passes a law that is unconsti-

tutional, there is a practice and a tradition recognized by presidents of both parties that he may elect to decide not to enforce that law. Now, I think that that would be . . ."

FEINGOLD: *"I recognize that, and I tried to make that distinction, Judge, between electing not to enforce as opposed to affirmatively telling people they can do certain things in contravention of the law."*

GONZALES: *"Senator, this president is not—I—it is not the policy or the agenda of this president to authorize actions that would be in contravention of our criminal statutes."*

FEINGOLD: *"Finally, will you commit to notify Congress if the president makes this type of decision and not wait two years until a memo is leaked about it?"*

GONZALES: *"I will advise the Congress as soon as I reasonably can, yes, sir."*

FEINGOLD: *"Well, I hope that would be a very brief period of time."*

O hio Republican Senator Mike DeWine, who was followed by Delaware Democratic Senator Joseph Biden:

BIDEN: *"I don't know of anybody who's announced they're against your being the next attorney general. Even those who have doubts about you say you're going to be confirmed. And so this is not about the president and his judgment. It is appropriate for us to understand the president is not a lawyer. He doesn't know from shinola about the treaty. By the way, nor do previous presidents. Nor do previous presidents. That's why they have legal advisers. That's why they hire brilliant graduates from Harvard Law School and former judges to advise them. I'm being deadly earnest here. It's not a joke. So I don't judge the president on whether or not he supports or didn't support torture. He signed off on a memo that may, in fact, in the minds of many, in fact, constitute torture. And he says he doesn't. That's irrelevant here. And, Judge, this is not about your intelligence. This hearing's not about your competence. It's not about your integrity. It's about your judgment, your candor. Because you're going to be making some very difficult decisions as attorney general, as every attorney general has, decisions on matters we can't even contemplate now. . . .*

"So I want to know about your judgment. It's your judgment. And we're going to—you're going to be the AG. You're not going to be legal counsel anymore. You are no longer the president's lawyer. You are the people's lawyer. Your oath is to the people of the United States. I know you know that."

GONZALES: *"Yes, sir."*

BIDEN: *"And therefore—and this is not a Supreme Court hearing, although some suggest it foreshadows that. As a Supreme Court nominee, you could sit there and say, 'I don't want to comment on that law or interpret it because I may have to judge it.' As the attorney general, you're responsible to tell us now what your judgment is on what the law means. It is your obligation now for us to be able to assess your judgment—your legal judgment. You're in no way—as you implied to two of the questioners, you're in no way jeopardizing a future case. That's malarkey, pure malarkey. So we're looking for candor, old buddy. We're looking for you when we ask you a question to give us an answer, which you haven't done yet. I love you, but you're not very candid so far. And so please do not use the straw man, 'Well, as the future attorney general, I may not be able to comment on what that law means.' You are obliged to comment. It's your job to make a judgment before a case is taken. That's your judgment we're looking at. . . .*

"And so when I get to ask my questions, I hope you'll be candid about it. Because—not that it's relevant—I like you. I like you. You're the real deal."

Before Biden could ask any questions, Specter interrupted him and told him his time was up. Alabama Senator Jeff Sessions was next and then Wisconsin Senator Herb Kohl.

KOHL: *"Attorney General Ashcroft said that he doesn't really believe in torture in the sense that it doesn't produce anything of value. He has said that on the record. Do you agree with that?"*

GONZALES: *"Sir, I don't have a way of reaching a conclusion on that. All I know is that the president has said we're not going to torture under any circumstances."*

KOHL: *"Well, do you believe that the policy is a correct one, that we never*

should have had any torture at Guantánamo or at Abu Ghraib, among
other reasons because it really doesn't produce anything of value?"
GONZALES: *"Sir, the United States has never had a policy of torture."*

South Carolina Republican Senator Lindsay Graham, a military veteran, came next.

GRAHAM: *"I think we've dramatically undermined the war effort by getting*
on a slippery slope in terms of playing cute with the law, because it's come
back to bite us. Abu Ghraib has hurt us in many ways. I travel through-
out the world like the rest of the members of Senate, and I can tell you it
is a club that our enemies use, and we need to take that club out of their
hands. Guantánamo Bay—the way it's been run has hurt the war effort.
So if we're going to win this war, Judge Gonzales, we need friends and
we need to recapture the moral high ground. And my questions are along
that line. To those who think that you can't win a war without—with the
Geneva Convention applying—I have another role in life. I'm a judge
advocate, I'm a reserve judge in the air force. I've never been in combat. I
had some clients that probably wanted to kill me, but I've never been shot
at. But part of my job for the last twenty years, along with other judge
advocates, is to advise commanders about the law of armed conflict. And
I've never had a more willing group of people to listen to the law. Because
every air force wing commander lives in fear of an air crew being shot
down and falling into enemy hands. And we instill in our people as
much as possible that you're to follow the law of armed conflict, because
that's what your nation stands for, that's what you're fighting for, and
you're to follow it because it's there to protect you.

". . . I agree with you, Judge Gonzales, to give Geneva Convention
protection to al Qaeda and other people like al Qaeda would in the long
run undermine the purpose of the Geneva Convention. You would be
giving a status in the law to people who do not deserve it, which would
erode the convention. . . . And I think you weaken yourself as a nation
when you try to play cute and become more like your enemy instead of
like who you want to be . . . those memos talk about that if you go the
road suggested, you're making a U-turn as a nation; that you're going to

lose the moral high ground, but more importantly, that some of the techniques and legal reasoning being employed into what torture is—which is an honest thing to talk about, it's okay to ask for legal advice. You should ask for legal advice. But this legal memo, I think, put our troops at jeopardy because the Uniform Code of Military Justice specifically makes it a crime for a member of our uniform forces to abuse a detainee. It is a specific article of the Uniform Code of Military Justice for a purpose: because we want to show our troops not just in words but in deeds that you have an obligation to follow the law. And I would like for you to comment if you could. And I would like you to reject, if you would, the reasoning in that memo when it came time to give a torturous view of torture. Will you be willing to do that here today?"

GONZALES: "Senator, there is a lot to respond to in your statement. I would respectfully disagree with your statement that we're becoming more like our enemy. We are nothing like our enemy, Senator. While we are struggling mightily, trying to find out what happened at Abu Ghraib, they are beheading people like Danny Pearl and Nick Berg. We are nothing like our enemies, Senator."

In the end human rights activists charged that Gonzales's answers were incomplete and evasive—and that he simply hadn't repudiated the memos that had his name on them, or the memos that he had commissioned or reviewed. His nomination had been sharply criticized by a group of influential, retired military commanders including Army General John Shalikashvili, the former Chairman of the Joint Chiefs of Staff. The hearing ultimately did very little to satisfy either the foes or the friends of Gonzales. Listening to the hearings, there were moments when Kennedy, Leahy, Graham, and Biden bore in on him several times, but they seemed to either retreat or offer their objections with added dollops of encomium.

Longtime observers of the Senate Committee said that there was a very real sense of fait accompli in the air, that these sessions were obligatory but not insurmountable roadblocks to a confirmation. There was a feeling in the room that the senators were screwing up some energy and emotion but almost doing it in a vaguely obligatory way—like they were on cruise control, going through some fake puffery because they had resigned themselves to Gonzales winning the nomination. The feeling was that the Republican-controlled committee and full Senate would never vote against the first Hispanic man headed for the attorney general's office.

His friends said he had acquitted himself admirably, that Gonzales described a deliberate, measured process of review, speculation, and legal investigation that spawned all the memos—and that he had made it quite clear that many of the memos were not law, were never meant to be law, and that the president did not endorse torture in any shape or form. His critics said Gonzales had stonewalled, hadn't wanted to even entertain the possibility that the memos could have been an inspiring, influencing force that trickled down out of the White House and onto Guantánamo Bay and Abu Ghraib.

Gonzales, added his opponents, wasn't sophisticated enough to understand how easily the White House can set the tone for the military, for the way justice is meted out. And beyond all that, they argued that Gonzales simply still seemed to be defending the content and existence of the memos—and the meetings—that talked about torture, water boarding, and burying people alive. He called them discussions, position papers, not statute or law, but human rights activists said that those positions, those explorations, those discussions should probably have never been entertained in the first place and certainly not committed to paper. The very act of entertaining them, the very act of questioning the Geneva Convention, the very act of looking for some way to interpret the standing definition of torture—and looking for ways the president can expand his powers and order interrogations, and looking for ways to reduce any criminal liability for interrogators—all added up to something far less than honorable, far less than humane, far less than American.

Finally, of course, critics would review his testimony a year later when each thread of the domestic spying and eavesdropping program was uncovered. Again, Gonzales had said it was all hypothetical when it was all very real. The elaborate program had, in fact, already been set in motion. He surely knew details for the domestic spying program, but he did not address any of it in his remarks to the Judiciary Committee. The program, he had decided, didn't need to be detailed, let alone apologized for. It was, he would later maintain, more than legal—it was necessary.

As expected, there was that condemning testimony from human rights experts, officials, and advocates. John Huston, the retired admiral, presented his argument that Gonzales had simply showed skewed legal reasoning. His presence served as a reminder that a coalition of a dozen high-ranking military men—including Shalikashvili—had also sent a letter to the Senate committee saying they had "deep concern" with Gonzales's nomination. Douglas Johnson, executive director of the Center for Victims of Torture, testified, "After the Bybee definition was solicited, accepted, and circulated by Gonzales, hundreds of detainees under U.S. control have suffered from torture and inhumane and degrading treatment."

Harold Koh, the dean of the Yale School of Law, offered a thunderclap condemnation of Gonzales for producing "dangerous reasoning." Koh's statement sounded as if he was summarizing the feelings of all of Gonzales's critics; he seemed to suggest that there was one Gonzales memo that should have been written but never was—the one in which Gonzales, as the most important legal adviser to the president of the United States, might have repudiated all the other "forward-leaning" memos that had been produced in the maddening heat and swirl and edgy weeks after 9/11:

"For if U.S. and international law do not forbid cruel, inhuman, and degrading treatment, then lower executive officials would have a license to degrade and dehumanize detainees in their custody, without regard to whether those detainees hold any information of value in the war against terror. The August 1 OLC memorandum cannot be justified as a case of lawyers doing their job and setting out options for their client. If a client asks a lawyer how to break the law and escape liability, the lawyer's ethical duty is to say no. A lawyer has no obligation to aid, support, or justify the commission of an illegal act. In sum, the August 1, 2002, OLC memorandum is a stain upon our law and our national reputation. A legal opinion that is so lacking in historical context, that offers a definition of torture so narrow that it would have exculpated Saddam Hussein, that reads the commander-in-chief power so as to remove Congress as a check against torture, that turns Nuremberg on its head, and that gives government officials a license for cruelty can only be described— as my predecessor Eugene Rostow described the Japanese internment cases—as a 'disaster.' One would have expected the counsel to the president to have immediately repudiated such an opinion. Mr. Gonzales did not."[11]

Afterword

In the end, Biden's prediction was right. Gonzales was approved by the Senate Committee, along straight party lines, by a 10–8 vote. Most people who were there that day thought that some of the Democrats would surely be swayed by Gonzales's personal history—the way he had been the only one of eight brothers and sisters to go to college, the only one to move so far from that tiny two-bedroom bungalow with no hot running water, no telephone, with ten people jammed inside.

His mother, Maria, was there, just over his right shoulder, silent and unmoving, watching her son and watching the somber, carefully groomed senators press her son. By the end of the committee hearings, the Democrats were united in their resistance to Gonzales. Biden may have "loved," him but he was going to vote against Gonzales. Democratic New York Senator Charles Schumer said he was planning to vote for Gonzales until he heard him testify. Herb Kohl, who had said at the outset of the hearings that he thought Gonzales would "do a good job" as attorney general, simply said that as the hearings went on, Gonzales lost his "luster." Leahy, who still liked Gonzales, had called him before the vote and told him that he was voting against him because he thought the White House had one policy in its war on terrorism and that that policy hadn't really changed until the pictures from Abu Ghraib emerged—until the policies became public. Gonzales said that he hoped he could prove Leahy wrong. Leahy told him that he'd be the first to admit he was wrong if Gonzales could do that.

Arlen Specter, the committee chairman, announced that he had voted for Gonzales because he was taken by the "Horatio Alger" story of Gonzales's life. Ted Kennedy simply said, "I wish we could vote for the story and not the individual."

There was grousing about a possible filibuster, but just like the committee hearings, there seemed to be little stomach for any lingering resistance to the Gonzales nomination. There were three days of debate on the Senate floor, and it was again an inevitability just waiting to happen. Hatch, the austere Mormon from Utah, offered a rousing defense of Gonzales, and he drew attention to the political elephant in the room—the color of Alberto Gonzales's skin.

It had been, really, the unspoken thing for so much of his life. The questions had never left him—why the Bush family selected him, what doors were ever opened for him, what his ethnic heritage had to do with his winning positions at the highest levels of government. Now it was almost as if Hatch was accusing Gonzales's foes of bigotry:

"I know that every Hispanic in America is watching how this man is being treated today as we debate his nomination. It is just that important." Hatch then referenced Henry Cisneros's stunning endorsement of Gonzales. He also noted that the president of the National Council of La Raza had supported Gonzales. And finally he said that Gonzales held no unholy allegiances to the man who carried him forward in life:

"There have also been allegations that Judge Gonzales, because he has worked closely with President Bush for several years, is somehow incapable of having his own opinions and will be unable to give frank legal advice. I recall that similar accusations were made over forty years ago with respect to the nomination of Robert F. Kennedy to be attorney general. As many Americans know, Robert Kennedy was President John F. Kennedy's brother. . . . Robert Kennedy went on to become a great attorney general, one that was and still is much admired by many here in this country. I believe Judge Gonzales, too, can exercise that same independence. . . . He is no yes-man."

On Thursday, February 3, 2005, the Senate voted 60–36 to confirm him as the new attorney general of the United States. It was the smallest winning margin for a Bush appointee. Bush immediately called Gonzales to congratulate him. At 5:40 P.M. in a private ceremony in the Roosevelt Room, Cheney administered the oath of office. Alberto Gonzales became the eightieth attorney general and the first Hispanic attorney general in the history of the United States.

In 2005 the speculation would never cease—nor would the controversies. They were really the same things that had chased him since he first decided to become George W. Bush's *abogado*. He was put on, and then off, and then on again—and finally off once more—the short lists for a Supreme Court seat. He was gusted forward by the possibility of being the first Hispanic named to the court; he was shunted by those whipsawing arguments over whether he had a liberal streak, a moderate streak. He was thrust back into the tornado of conflicting opinions, arguments, and news reports about what exactly the nation's stance on domestic spying and torture had been—and would be. With each new revelation of a clandestine domestic program to eavesdrop and spy on people, of secret prisons and of human rights violations—with each new discussion about wiretapping and waterboarding and whether torture was sanctioned as part of America's arsenal—it would circle straight back to him.

For someone who prided himself on his discretion, it was perhaps a perfect irony that Gonzales's legal opinions—the ones he wrote and reviewed . . . and the ones people felt he should have wrote but never did—came to define his public existence. He defended them as the products of a curious mind, as the end result of an ongoing intellectual process that he had embarked upon in service to his client. And yet his foes said that wasn't enough . . . that he needed to move beyond his lawyerly discretion, that he needed to eloquently, passionately, firmly repudiate things so inherently anti-American, so wickedly inhumane.

Of course he had succeeded in life by serving his client. His father was a desperately poor, alcoholic migrant worker; his client was born into the most powerful political dynasty in modern American history.

Now on Roberta Lane the planes thundering in and out of the Bush airport still seem just beyond someone's fingertips. And one day in the winter of 2005 five men are huddled together across the street from where Gonzales grew up. They are construction workers, taking a break from laboring on a small, wooden house. They speak in Spanish and dig their hands into their brown lunch bags.

Big Houston, like it was when Gonzales grew up on Roberta Lane, is still off in the distance. And in Houston, that same day, preparations are under way for a trial in the deadliest human smuggling case ever recorded in the United States. Nineteen Hispanic immigrants had succumbed to a horrific death after they were jammed inside a dark, superheated trailer. As the air ran out and the temperature in the trailer soared to 173 degrees, the doomed passengers tried vainly to claw their way out until their finger-nails turned raw and bloody.

They were immigrants aiming for glittering Houston from south Texas. They were following the same path to the big city that Gonzales and his family had taken decades before. Maybe they were aiming for con-struction jobs, work that would take them to places like the block Gonza-les grew up on.

Gonzales had been gusted forward by the specific circumstances of his background. He was defined by those circumstances, but he never really wanted to draw attention to them. Gonzales never let people inside his house when he was growing up. He spent a lifetime moving beyond Humble. And his father always did what he had to do, what he needed to do. There were, had to be compromises.

"Sometimes when I get tired and discouraged, I think about my father and the burdens he had to carry," he once said.[1]

Acknowledgments

This book could not have been completed without the continued, deep, excellent efforts of several veteran journalists who assisted in doing reporting and research. In particular, Alicia Dennis, Jordan Smith, and Anne Lang are miracle workers, and I'm lucky to know them and to have had them lending their years of experience. They displayed their usual lack of bias and their usual line of profound inquiry—they are friends, good souls, and people truly worth knowing. Wendy Grossman, another friend in Houston, was invaluable and solved several riddles related to the Gonzales family. Anna Macias jumped in to help on acutely Latino-themed reporting. A special thank-you to Becky Chavarría-Cháirez, who volunteered endless hours of reporting, document digging, good cheer, and Latino cultural analysis. Becky's many friends in Texas know her to be a consummate journalist as well as a truly generous human being—her personal interest in this project shed light on many biographical threads that heretofore had remained hidden.

I owe a debt of gratitude and admiration for the brilliant reporting done by a variety of nationally recognized journalists: Michael Isikoff at *Newsweek;* Tim Golden at the *New York Times* (his two-part series in October 2004 on the inner workings of the White House counsel's office is a definitive and authoritative look at how lawyers in the Bush administration coalesced to create the many controversial, post-9/11 blueprints for the war on terror—and his work was vital to several key sections of this book); R. Jeffrey Smith and Dan Eggers at the *Washington Post.* (Their profound, precisely detailed reporting on the role Gonzales played in the post-9/11 decisions, along with that of John Yoo and others, was invaluable in my research. In particular, their work on the behind-the-scenes movements to debate, discuss, and codify torture is required reading for anyone attempting to understand the policies of the Bush administration.) Lois Romano of the *Washington Post* did an early, insightful piece on Gonzales; Dana Milbank and many others at the *Washington Post* have done extraordinary work in describing the machinations and behind-the-scenes movements at the White House. The Academy of Achievement was able to coax many extraordinarily important observations from Gonzales, and the academy must be saluted for its role in understanding him; its conversation with Gonzales remains among the most telling and compelling accounts of his life.

Sincere thanks to Sylvia Moreno with the *Washington Post* and to Dave Montgomery with the *Fort Worth Star-Telegram*. Both personally took the time to share with me their thoughts, resources, contacts, and experiences in doing their excellent reporting on Alberto Gonzales. They were kind to offer their special wisdom and counsel—and to do it without hesitation. They and so many other good-hearted colleagues in the journalism world are living proof that some reporters, editors, and bureau chiefs can be singularly lacking in jealousy, insecurities, and self-loathing. As always, these truth-seekers stand in contrast to the grinning and preening types whose contributions to journalism are simply slated to wane in importance.

Thank you to my colleagues in the Texas Institute of Letters and to the supremely talented Texas-based journalists who have provided advice, friendship, and a kind word. For example, Alan Peppard, the keen social observer for the *Dallas Morning News;* if you want to know what's going on in Texas, if you really want to know what makes Texas tick, you would be well served by reading Peppard's insightful column. (While you are in Dallas, you would also be well served to visit Louie Canelakes at his restaurant Louie's. Mr. Canelakes offers the most brilliant take on everything in Texas.) Also to be noted are: Richard Oppel Sr., Patrick Beach, and Jeff Salomon at the *Austin American-Statesman.* Laura Tolley and John Wilburn at the *Houston Chronicle.* John Branch of the *San Antonio Express-News.*

Very special thanks to the many journalists, authors, and essayists who have been exceedingly generous to me in many different ways over the years: Sir Harold Evans, David Maraniss, Martha Nelson, Larry Hackett,

Richard Sanders, Moira Bailey, Michael Haederle, Shannon Richardson, Gabrielle Cosgriff, Sophia Nelson, Tina Brown, James Lee Burke, Buzz Bissinger, Gail Sheehy, Chris Matthews, Ellen Kampinsky, Don Graham, Bill Crawford, Bill Lodge, Laura Jacobus, Michelle Stanush, Tom Watson, Laura Castro, and Bob Compton.

Aldine Independent School District officials were very kind. Thank you to Bill Miller, who knows everything about Austin. At Rice University, David Medina not only provided his wonderful help—we also shared a laugh about one of the truly nauseating stews in the Dallas newspaper world. Thank you to the officials at the Texas State Archives for quickly processing my many Texas Open Records Act requests. Through their efforts, and with the assistance of Jordan Smith, I was able to obtain thousands of documents—including correspondence, clemency memos, and government records.

Obvious and special appreciation to Rene Alegria, my editor at Harper-Collins, for his trust and faith in me—and for allowing me to benefit from his editorial wizardry. I have been fortunate to work with many fine people in publishing, and Rene is one of the best, one of the most sincere, one of the most elegant. He is a treasure. Melinda Moore, Tim Brazier, and Jill Bernstein at HarperCollins are all very talented and generous. Senior production editor Cecilia Molinari and copy editor Mary Dorian must be thanked for saving me and for working so diligently, so patiently, and with such great care and precision. Thanks to Kyran Cassidy for lending his expert legal eye to this work—and for being an extremely insightful observer of life and politics. My agent David Hale Smith has been a friend and stalwart; no one works harder for his clients. Thanks to James Risen and Eric Lichtbau from the *New York Times* for their superior reporting on the domestic spying program; key sections of this book were heavily informed by their masterful work. And thanks to Kate Pruss for her wonderful work on publicity.

My family's roots run deep in Italy and America and my cherished mother, Tess, will always be my inspiration. Thanks to my brothers Tom, Robert, Frank, John, and their families. Thanks to my extended family, including Linda Smeltzer, Martha Williams, Tom Sheehy, Emily Williams, and Molly Williams.

My wife, Holly, and my children, Nicholas Xavier and Rose Angelina, are, without question, my life.

Notes

CHAPTER 2

1. Alberto Gonzales, commencement address at Rice University, May 8, 2004.
2. Academy of Achievement online interview with Alberto Gonzales, June 3, 2005.
3. Sigman Byrd, *Sig Byrd's Houston* (New York: Viking Press, 1955), pp. 1–2.
4. Academy of Achievement interview.
5. Author's Note: An article in the Spring 2003 *Harvard Law Bulletin* refers to Alberto's parents as "natives of Mexico." The Department of Justice indicates his parents were born in Texas and his grandparents were born in Mexico.
6. Alberto Gonzales, commencement address at Houston Community College, May 7, 2005.
7. "From Cotton Fields to the White House," *San Antonio Express-News,* May 5, 2002.
8. Academy of Achievement interview.
9. Joan Moore and Raquel Pinderhughes, *In the Barrios, Latinos and the Underclass Debate* (New York: Russell Sage Foundation, 1993), pp. 101–106.
10. Houston Hispanic Forum, *Hispanics in Houston and Harris County 1519–1986,* Dorothy Caram, Anthony Dworkin, and Nestor Rodriguez (eds.), p. 50.
11. Alberto Gonzales, commencement address at Rice University, May 8, 2004.
12. "Loyalty May Pay Off," *Houston Chronicle,* Jan. 21, 2003. One report ("Bush Picks a Loyalist to Replace a Politician," *Washington Post,* Nov. 11, 2004) said he grew up "in a home without running water," but that appears to be incorrect.
13. Sigman Byrd, *Sig Byrd's Houston* (New York: Viking Press, 1955), pp. 8–10.
14. Interview with Jacob Valerio, Oct. 5, 2005.
15. Academy of Achievement interview.
16. Ibid.
17. "Positioned for a Call to Justice," *Washington Post,* July 10, 2001.
18. "The White House Counsel Who Potential U.S. Judges Must Please," *Los Angeles Times,* March 25, 2001.
19. Interview with Jacob Valerio, Oct. 5, 2005.
20. Academy of Achievement interview.

CHAPTER 3

1. Academy of Achievement online interview with Alberto Gonzales, June 3, 2005.
2. Ibid.
3. "From Humble Roots, Gonzales Reached New Heights," *Dallas Morning News,* Nov. 12, 2004.

4. "Positioned for a Call to Justice," *Washington Post,* July 10, 2001.
5. Interview with Monsignor Paul Procella, Oct. 7, 2005.
6. "Positioned for a Call to Justice," *Washington Post,* July 10, 2001.
7. Alberto Gonzales, commencement address at Rice University, May 8, 2004.
8. Interview with Marine Jones, Aug. 18, 2005.
9. Interview with Jody Hernandez, Oct. 22, 2005.
10. Interview with Marine Jones, Aug. 18, 2005.
11. Interview with Jody Hernandez, Oct. 29, 2005.
12. Interview with Brenda Pond, Sept. 2005.
13. Interview with Liz Lara, Oct. 29, 2005.
14. Interview with Jody Hernandez, Oct. 22, 2005.
15. Ibid.
16. Interview with Liz Lara, Oct. 29, 2005.
17. Interview with Marine Jones, Aug. 18, 2005.
18. "From Humble Roots, Gonzales Reaches Great Heights," *Dallas Morning News,* Nov. 13, 2004.
19. Interview with Alma Villareal Cox, Aug. 28, 2005.
20. Alberto Gonzales, address at Rice University, May 8, 2004.
21. Interview with Robert Trapp, Oct. 11, 2005.
22. Interview with Arthur Paul, Oct. 11, 2005.
23. Interview with Jon Winfield, Oct. 11, 2005.
24. Academy of Achievement interview.
25. "Positioned for a Call to Justice," *Washington Post,* July 10, 2001.
26. Interview with Marine Jones, Aug. 18, 2005.
27. Interview with Jody Hernandez, Oct. 22, 2005.
28. "Bush's Legal Eagle, Rising with the Son," *U.S. News & World Report,* Mar. 12, 2001.
29. "Is 'Al Gonzales' Spanish for 'Stealth Liberal'?" *Texas Monthly,* June 2003.
30. "Loyalty May Pay Off," *Houston Chronicle,* Jan. 21, 2003.
31. "Positioned for a Call to Justice," *Washington Post,* July 10, 2001.
32. Janet Woitiz, *Adult Children of Alcoholics* (Florida: HCI, 1990).
33. "Is 'Al Gonzales' Spanish for 'Stealth Liberal'?" *Texas Monthly,* June 2003.
34. "Gonzales Gains Clout, Savvy at Bush's Side," *Austin American-Statesman,* Mar. 18, 2001.
35. "Rights Groups Seek Scrutiny of Nominee for Top Justice Job," *Fort Worth Star-Telegram,* Dec. 19, 2004.
36. "From Humble Roots, Gonzales Reached New Heights," *Dallas Morning News,* Nov. 13, 2004.
37. Interview with Liz Lara, Oct. 29, 2005.

CHAPTER 4
1. Academy of Achievement online interview with Alberto Gonzales, June 3, 2005.
2. Rick Bass, *Caribou Rising* (San Francisco: Sierra Club Books, 2004), pp. 6–7.
3. "Alum Named Attorney General," *Harvard Crimson,* Nov. 12, 2004.
4. Academy of Achievement interview.
5. Bass, *Caribou Rising,* p. 135.
6. "Alum Named Attorney General," *Harvard Crimson,* Nov. 12, 2004.
7. Interview with Paul Karch, Sept. 20, 2005.
8. Alberto Gonzales, commencement address at Rice University, May 8, 2004.
9. "Positioned for a Call to Justice," *Washington Post,* July 10, 2001.
10. Alberto Gonzales, commencement address at Rice University, May 8, 2004.
11. "Recruitment of Minority Students at the United States Air Force Academy," *Air University Review,* May–June 1974. This excellent article by Capt. Rolf Trautsch is the best outline of minority placement.
12. Ibid.
13. Ibid.
14. Ibid.

15. "Is 'Al Gonzales' Spanish for 'Stealth Liberal'?" *Texas Monthly,* June 2003.

16. Academy of Achievement interview.

17. Freedom of Information Act Request Number 1-958144482, released October 17, 2005.

18. Alberto Gonzales, commencement address at Rice University, May 8, 2004.

19. Academy of Achievement interview.

20. Alberto Gonzales, commencement address at Rice University, May 8, 2004.

21. Freedom of Information Act Request. Author's Note: A resume prepared by Gonzales during his tenure as secretary of state in Texas contains no mention of attendance at the USAF Preparatory School.

22. "Recruitment of Minority Students at the United States Air Force Academy," *Air University Review,* May–June 1974.

23. Ibid.

24. "Positioned for a Call to Justice," *Washington Post,* July 10, 2001.

25. "Rights Groups Seek Scrutiny of Nominee for Top Justice Job," *Fort Worth Star-Telegram,* Dec. 19, 2004.

26. Academy of Achievement interview.

27. Alberto Gonzales, commencement address at Rice University, May 8, 2004.

28. Ibid.

29. Interview with David Abbott, October 6, 2005.

30. Interview with Paul Karch, Sept. 20, 2005.

31. Interview with Gilbert Cuthbertson, Aug. 25, 2005.

32. "Positioned for a Call to Justice," *Washington Post,* July 10, 2001.

33. Interview with Gilbert Cuthbertson, Aug. 25, 2005.

34. Interview with Mark Scheevel, Oct. 27, 2005.

35. Ibid.

36. Ibid.

37. Ibid.

38. Ibid.

39. Interview with Gilbert Cuthbertson, Aug. 25, 2005.

40. Ibid.

41. Ibid.

42. Ibid.

43. Ibid.

44. Ibid.

45. *Campanile,* Rice University, 1979, courtesy of Mark Scheevel.

46. Alberto Gonzales, commencement address at Rice University, May 8, 2004.

47. Interview with Gilbert Cuthbertson, Aug. 25, 2005.

CHAPTER 5

1. "Gonzales's Journey: From the Stands to the Heights," *Washington Post,* Dec. 28, 2004.

2. Interview with Howell Jackson, Oct. 4, 2005.

3. "Alum Named Attorney General," *Harvard Crimson,* Nov. 12, 2004.

4. Interview with Howell Jackson, Oct. 4, 2005.

5. Interview with David Abbott, Oct. 6, 2005.

6. Ibid.

7. Interview with Paul Fishman, Nov. 4, 2005.

8. Interview with David Abbott, Oct. 6, 2005. (Author's Note: Brackets indicate author's own words.)

9. Interview with Paul Fishman, Nov. 4, 2005.

10. Ibid.

11. Interview with Brenda Pond, Oct. 11, 2005. Repeated request to the Department of Justice for clarification were not answered.

12. Academy of Achievement online interview with Alberto Gonzales, June 3, 2005.

13. Interview with Paul Karch, Sept. 20, 2005.

14. "Positioned for a Call to Justice," *Washington Post,* July 10, 2001.

15. Interview with Paul Karch, Sept. 20, 2005.

16. Ibid.

17. "The Loyalist," *Harvard Law Bulletin,* Spring 2003.

18. "Alum Named Attorney General," *Harvard Crimson,* Nov. 12, 2004.

19. Interview with Paul Karch, Sept. 20, 2005.

20. Ibid.

21. "Loyalty May Pay Off," *Houston Chronicle,* Jan. 21, 2003.

22. Obituaries, *Houston Post,* Jan. 24, 1982.

23. "From Humble roots, Gonzales Reached Great Heights," *Dallas Morning News,* Nov. 13, 2004.

24. Alberto Gonzales, commencement address at Rice University, May 8, 2004.

25. Harold Hyman, *Craftsmanship and Character, a History of the Vinson & Elkins Law Firm of Houston 1917–1997* (Athens and London: University of Georgia Press, 1998), pp. 415–416.

26. "The Gonzales Appointment," *Houston Chronicle,* Nov. 11, 2004.

27. "Rights Groups Seek Scrutiny of Nominee for Top Justice Job," *Fort Worth Star-Telegram,* Dec. 19, 2004.

28. "Storied Law Firm in New Media Spotlight," *Fort Worth Star-Telegram,* Dec. 18, 2004.

29. "The Loyalist," *Harvard Law Bulletin,* Spring 2003.

30. "Is 'Al Gonzales' Spanish for 'Stealth Liberal'?" *Texas Monthly,* June 2003.

31. Interview with Barry Hunsaker Jr., Aug. 25, 2005.

32. Ibid.

33. Ibid.

34. Ibid.

35. Interview with Larry Dreyfuss, Oct. 11, 2005.

36. Interview with Jim McCartney, Nov. 7, 2005.

CHAPTER 6

1. Interview with Bill Sweeney, Dec. 2, 2005.

2. "Ties to Power Put AG Pick on a Fast Track," *Boston Globe,* Jan. 6, 2005.

3. "One Big Client, One Big Hassle," *Business Week,* Jan. 28, 2002.

4. "Storied Law Firm in New Media Spotlight," *Fort Worth Star-Telegram,* Dec. 19, 2004.

5. Ibid.

6. "Is 'Al Gonzales' Spanish for 'Stealth Liberal'?" *Texas Monthly,* June 2003.

7. "Loyalty May Pay Off," *Houston Chronicle,* Jan. 21, 2003.

8. "The Enigmatic Counsel," *Financial Times,* Nov. 13, 2004.

9. Academy of Achievement online interview with Alberto Gonzales, June 3, 2005.

10. "Loyalty May Pay Off," *Houston Chronicle,* Jan. 21, 2003.

11. Ibid.

12. "President George W. Bush: 'My Record Stands,'" *Hispanic,* Oct. 31, 2004.

13. Interview with Lynn Liberato, Nov. 11, 2005.

14. Ibid.

15. Interview with David Medina, Nov. 8, 2005.

16. Interview with Massey Villareal, Oct. 6, 2005.

17. Interview with Tanny Berg, Oct. 6, 2005.

18. Interview with Neftali Partida, Oct. 10, 2005.

19. "Auditor Worked Closely with Enron Chief," *Fort Worth Star-Telegram,* Jan. 17, 2002.

20. Interview with Patrick Oxford, Nov. 7, 2005.

21. Interview with Larry Dreyfuss, Oct. 10, 2005.

22. Interview with George Donnelly, Oct. 12, 2005.

23. Interview with Kenna Ramirez, Oct. 6, 2005.

24. Interview with Marc Campos, Aug. 24, 2005.

25. Interview with Patrick Oxford, Nov. 7, 2005.

26. "GOP Reaps Pre-Convention Pro Bono," *Houston Chronicle,* Aug. 17, 1992.

27. "Zoning Nominees Win Council Approval," *Houston Chronicle,* Nov. 5, 1992.

CHAPTER 7

1. "Gonzales's Journey: From the Stands to the Heights," *Washington Post,* Dec. 28, 2004.
2. Academy of Achievement online interview with Alberto Gonzales, June 3, 2005.
3. Interview with Patrick Oxford, Nov. 7, 2005.
4. "Gonzales' Journey: From the Stands to the Heights," *Washington Post,* Dec. 28, 2004.
5. "An Interview with White House Counsel Alberto R. Gonzales," *The Third Branch,* May 2002.
6. Author's Note: One of Bush's advisers told this author that George Bush had given a nickname to Bill Minutaglio: "Mononucleosis." It was, said Doug Wead, a reflection of the fact that Bush had a hard time pronouncing the name Minutaglio.
7. Interview with Clay Johnson, Nov. 8, 2005.
8. "Gonzales Gains Clout, Savvy at Bush's Side," *Austin American-Statesman,* Mar. 18, 2001.
9. "Positioned for a Call to Justice," *Washington Post,* July 10, 2001.
10. Interview with Karen Greene, Nov. 10, 2005.
11. Ibid.
12. "Is 'Al Gonzales' Spanish for 'Stealth Liberal'?" *Texas Monthly,* June 2003.
13. Ibid.
14. Ibid.
15. Interview with Craig Enoch, former Texas Supreme Court justice, Oct. 21, 2005.
16. From the holdings of the Texas State Archives, obtained under the Texas Open Records Act.
17. Ibid.
18. Ibid.
19. Ibid.
20. Interview with Karen Greene, Nov. 10, 2005.

CHAPTER 8

1. Interview with Stuart Bowen, Oct. 19, 2005.
2. Ibid.
3. Interview with Karen Greene, Nov. 10, 2005.
4. "Loyalty May Pay Off," *Houston Chronicle,* Jan. 21, 2003.
5. Texas State Archives.
6. Interview with Alan Berlow, Aug. 18, 2005. (Author's Note: Berlow's reporting on Gonzales and the death penalty in Texas is outlined in extensive pieces he did for the *Atlantic Monthly* in 2003.)
7. *Talk of the Nation,* Jan. 6, 2005.
8. Interview with Alan Berlow, Aug. 18, 2005.
9. Interview with Sister Helen Prejean, Sept. 23, 2005.
10. Academy of Achievement online interview with Alberto Gonzales, June 3, 2005.
11. "Flawed Trials Lead to Death Chamber," *Chicago Tribune,* June 11, 2000.
12. "A Hearing of the Senate Judiciary Committee: The Nomination of Alberto Gonzales to be Attorney General," Jan. 6, 2005.
13. Interview with David Wahlberg, Aug. 17, 2005.
14. "Bush Silent on DUI When He Got 1996 Jury Summons," *Atlanta Constitution,* Nov. 4, 2000.
15. "Gonzales: Did He Help Bush Keep His DUI Quiet?" *Newsweek,* Jan. 31, 2005.
16. Ibid.
17. Ibid.
18. "Is 'Al Gonzales' Spanish for 'Stealth Liberal'?" *Texas Monthly,* June 2003.
19. Interview with David Wahlberg, Aug. 17, 2005.
20. "For Gonzales, Modest Start Led to Inner Circle," *Washington Post,* Dec. 20, 2000.
21. Academy of Achievement interview.

CHAPTER 9

1. "Mexico–Europe Trade Is No Threat to Texas," *Dallas Morning News,* Jan. 18, 1998.
2. "Mexico's Health Is Important to Texas," *Dallas Morning News,* June 25, 1998.
3. Interview with Patrick Oxford, Nov. 7, 2005.
4. "Pledge May Boost El Paso's Political Punch," *Austin American-Statesman,* July 26, 1998.

5. "Gonzales Named to Supreme Court," *Austin American-Statesman,* Nov. 13, 1998.
6. "Alberto Gonzales: The White House Counsel Who Potential U.S. Judges Must Please," *Los Angeles Times,* Mar. 25, 2001.
7. "Gonzales Named to Supreme Court," *Austin American-Statesman,* Nov. 13, 1998.
8. "Alberto Gonzales: The White House Counsel Who Potential U.S. Judges Must Please," *Los Angeles Times,* Mar. 25, 2001.
9. Interview with Brent Gibson, Dec. 2, 2005.
10. "Poll Another Argument for Appointed Judges," *San Antonio Express-News,* Feb. 13, 1999.
11. Interview with David Keltner, Oct. 24, 2005.
12. "Positioned for a Call to Justice," *Washington Post,* July 10, 2001.
13. George W. Bush, *A Charge to Keep* (New York: William Morrow and Company, 1999), pp. 108–109.
14. Interview with Craig Enoch, Oct. 21, 2005.
15. "Is 'Al Gonzales' Spanish for 'Stealth Liberal'?" *Texas Monthly,* June 2003.
16. "Texan Known in D.C. for One Thing," *San Antonio Express-News,* May 15, 2005. Author's Note: This excellent article by Maro Robbins is the most comprehensive overview available on the abortion issue that swirled around Alberto Gonzales and Priscilla Owen during their tenure on the Texas Supreme Court.
17. "Is 'Al Gonzales' Spanish for 'Stealth Liberal'?" *Texas Monthly,* June 2003.
18. "Abortion Law Again Splits State Court," *Dallas Morning News,* Mar. 23, 2000.
19. "Positioned for a Call to Justice," *Washington Post,* July 10, 2001.
20. Ibid.
21. Interview with Andrew Wheat of Texans for Public Justice, Aug. 24, 2005.
22. "The White House Counsel Who Potential U.S. Judges Must Please," *Los Angeles Times,* Mar. 25, 2001.
23. Interview with Texas State Rep. Pete Gallego, Nov. 15, 2005.
24. Interview with David Keltner, Oct. 24, 2005.
25. Ibid.
26. "Positioned for a Call to Justice," *Washington Post,* July 10, 2005.
27. Interview with Craig Enoch, Oct. 21, 2005.
28. Interview with Nathan Hecht, Oct. 18, 2005.
29. "Positioned for a Call to Justice," *Washington Post,* July 10, 2001.
30. "Halliburton Gifts Target Areas Where It Has Stake," *Fort Worth Star-Telegram,* July 28, 2000.
31. "High Court Rules Liability Must Precede Insurance Awards," *Lubbock Avalanche-Journal,* Apr. 14, 2000.
32. "As Texas Judge, Gonzales Heard Donor's Cases," *Boston Globe,* Jan. 27, 2005.
33. Interview with Douglas Alexander, Oct. 19, 2005.
34. Interview with Raul Gonzalez, Nov. 29, 2005.
35. Interview with Tony Champagne, Oct. 19, 2005.

CHAPTER 10
1. Remarks by George W. Bush, Alberto Gonzales, Dec. 17, 2000.
2. Interview with David Keltner, Oct. 24, 2005.
3. Academy of Achievement online interview with Alberto Gonzales, June 3, 2005.
4. "Friend of the Court," *The New Republic,* May 27, 2002.
5. "The Ultimate in Party Politics," *Dallas Morning News,* Jan. 19, 2001.
6. Ibid.
7. "Learning Curve," *Legal Times,* Jan. 15, 2001.
8. Ibid.
9. "White House Counsel Office Now Full of Clinton Legal Foes," *Washington Post,* Jan. 30, 2001.
10. Ibid.
11. Interview with Timothy Flanigan, Dec. 2, 2005.
12. "Bush's Legal Eagle, Rising with the Son," *U.S. News & World Report,* Mar. 12, 2001.
13. "Gonzales Gains Clout, Savvy at Bush's Side," *Austin American-Statesman,* Mar. 18, 2001.

14. Ibid.
15. "Bush's Legal Eagle, Rising with the Son," *U.S. News & World Report,* Mar. 12, 2001.
16. Ibid.
17. Ibid.
18. Ibid.
19. Interview with Massey Villareal, Sept. 19, 2005
20. "From Rags to Riches," *Hispanic,* Mar. 2001.
21. "Church Attracts Conservatives to Congregation," *Palm Peach Post,* Feb. 14, 2005.
22. "McCain and the religion of Zeus," *Austin American-Statesman,* Feb. 16, 2000.
23. "As They Say, and Now the Rest of the Story," *Austin American-Statesman,* April 13, 2000.
24. Remarks by George W. Bush, Jan. 21, 2001.
25. "Bush's Judge Picker Could Be Picked," *Christian Science Monitor,* July 10, 2001.
26. Interview with Bradford Berenson, Nov. 18, 2005.
27. "White House Counsel Office Now Full of Clinton Legal Foes," *Washington Post,* Jan. 30, 2001.
28. "White House Begins Work on Filling Judgeships," *St. Louis Post-Dispatch,* Mar. 4, 2001.
29. "The White House Counsel Who Potential U.S. Judges Must Please," *Los Angeles Times,* Mar. 25, 2001.
30. "Bush Set to Grant Courts a Conservative Tilt," *USA Today,* Mar. 23, 2001.
31. "ABA Ouster Sets Stage for Bench Battles," *Legal Times,* Mar. 26, 2001.
32. "The White House Counsel Who Potential U.S. Judges Must Please," *Los Angeles Times,* Mar. 25, 2001.
33. General Accounting Office, "Allegations of Damage During the 2001 Presidential Transition."
34. Ibid.
35. Interview with Noel Francisco, Nov. 20, 2005.
36. Ibid.
37. Ibid.
38. Interview with Bradford Berenson, Nov. 18, 2005.
39. Ibid.
40. Ibid.

CHAPTER 11
1. "Positioned for a Call to Justice," *Washington Post,* July 10, 2001.
2. Interview with Norm Orenstein, Nov. 22, 2005.
3. Interview with Timothy Flanigan, Dec. 5, 2005.
4. Letter to Alberto Gonzales from Henry Waxman, June 25, 2001.
5. Letter from Alberto Gonzales to Henry Waxman, June 29, 2001.
6. "White House Told to Save Enron Records," *Saint Paul Pioneer Press,* Feb. 2, 2002.
7. "Conservatives Wary of Possible Nominee," *Augusta Chronicle,* July 7, 2001.
8. "Can Bush Keep a 'Clean' White House?" *Christian Science Monitor,* July 16, 2001.
9. Interview with Timothy Flanigan, Dec. 5, 2005.
10. Interview with Stuart Bowen, Oct. 19, 2005.
11. Interview with Kenna Ramirez, Oct. 6, 2005.
12. Ibid.
13. "Inadmissible," *Legal Times,* July 16, 2001.
14. Letter from Alberto Gonzales to Henry Waxman, Aug. 10, 2001.
15. Interview with Stuart Bowen, Oct. 19, 2005.

CHAPTER 12
1. "The State Dinner That Ended with a Bang," *Washington Post,* Sept. 6, 2001.
2. Interview with Kenna Ramirez, Oct. 6, 2005.
3. Interview with Timothy Flanigan, Dec. 2, 2005.
4. Ibid.
5. "Gonzales Helped Set the Course for Detainees," *Washington Post,* Jan. 5, 2005.

6. "2001 Memo Reveals Push for Broader Presidential Powers," *Newsweek,* Dec. 18, 2004.
7. "After Terror, a Secret Rewriting of Military Law," *New York Times,* Oct. 24, 2005. Author's Note: This extraordinary story, along with a second installment the next day, constitutes the definitive look at how a hidden, bold alliance took shape in Washington in the days and weeks after 9/11.
8. Interview with Timothy Flanigan, Dec. 2, 2005.
9. Academy of Achievement interview online with Alberto Gonzales, June 3, 2005.
10. "After Terror, a Secret Rewriting of Military Law," *New York Times,* Oct. 24, 2005.
11. Ibid.
12. Author's Note: Several excellent articles in the *New York Times* and *Washington Post* explored these developments and laid the groundwork for this section of my book. Among these authoritative articles are two by Tim Golden of the *New York Times* that ran October 24, 2004 and October 25, 2004.
13. "Counsel to Assertive Presidency," *Washington Post,* May 19, 2003.
14. "Prepared Statement of Laurence H. Tribe Before Senate Committee on the Judiciary Subcommittee on Administrative Oversight and the Courts," Dec. 4, 2001.
15. "Martial Justice Full and Fair," *New York Times,* November 30, 2001.
16. "Critics Urged to Hold Off Until Tribunal Rules Are Set," *Houston Chronicle,* Dec. 1, 2001.
17. "White House Counsel Emerges from Shadows," *Dallas Morning News,* Dec. 1, 2001.
18. Ibid.
19. Interview with Massey Villareal, Sept. 19, 2005.

CHAPTER 13
1. Interview with Stuart Bowen, Oct. 19, 2005.
2. Memorandum from Alberto Gonzales to President George W. Bush, Jan. 25, 2002.
3. Convention III, Relative to the Treatment of Prisoners of War, Geneva, Aug. 12, 1949.
4. Interview with Bradford Berenson, Nov. 18, 2005.
5. Memorandum from Alberto Gonzales to President George W. Bush, Jan. 25, 2002.
6. Ibid.
7. "Administration Officials Split Over Stalled Military Tribunals," *New York Times,* Oct. 25, 2004.
8. Interview with Bradford Berenson, Nov. 18, 2005.
9. Academy of Achievement online interview with Alberto Gonzales, June 3, 2005.
10. "Gonzales Helped Set the Course for Detainees," *Washington Post,* January 5, 2005.
11. "From Cotton Fields to the White House," *San Antonio Express-News,* May 5, 2002.
12. "Gonzales Draws a Bright Spotlight," *Houston Chronicle,* May 13, 2002.
13. "Bush Aides Say Iraq War Needs No Hill Vote," *Washington Post,* Aug. 26, 2002.
14. Letter for Alberto R. Gonzales, August 1, 2002.
15. Memorandum for Alberto R. Gonzales, counsel to the president, Aug. 1, 2002.
16. Ibid.
17. Ibid.
18. Ibid.
19. "White House Counsel Talks About Advising Bush," *Texas Lawyer,* Oct. 11, 2002.
20. Ibid.
21. "The White House Counsel Who Potential U.S. Judges Must Please," *Los Angeles Times,* Mar. 25, 2001.
22. "The Editors' Desk," *Newsweek,* Dec. 30, 2002.

CHAPTER 14
1. Alberto Gonzales interview with Wolf Blitzer, CNN, Jan. 16, 2003.
2. "Aide Insists Bush Is Friend of Minority Groups," *Fort Worth Star-Telegram,* Jan. 18, 2003.
3. "Hispanic Republican May Have Blown Shot at High Court," *Chicago Sun-Times,* Jan. 23, 2003.
4. "Conservatives Want Bush Aide Kept Off Court," *USA Today,* Jan. 27, 2003.
5. "A Washington Education," *Texas Lawyer,* Mar. 3, 2003.
6. "Gonzales Tells White House Tales," *Fort Worth Star-Telegram,* July 20, 2003.

7. "Right Wing Objects to Bush Aide as a Justice," *Los Angeles Times,* June 23, 2003.
8. "Abortion Foes Poised for Court Vacancy," *Washington Times,* June 26, 2003.
9. "Democrats, GOP Face Off at Latino Leaders Conference," *Houston Chronicle,* June 28, 2003.
10. Memo from White House Counsel Alberto Gonzales, Sept. 30, 2003.
11. Memo from Alberto Gonzales to White House Staff, Oct. 3, 2003.
12. "President Has a Good 'Abogado,'" *Houston Chronicle,* Oct. 5, 2003.
13. Remarks by Alberto Gonzales to American Bar Association Standing Committee on Law and National Security, Feb. 24, 2004.
14. Interview with Jenny Martinez, Sept. 12, 2005.
15. Interview with Mariano-Florentino Cuellar, Sept. 21, 2005.
16. Ibid.
17. Interview with Rolando Hinojosa-Smith, Aug. 28, 2005.
18. "Inside Washington," *National Journal,* Mar. 27, 2004.
19. "Bush Counsel Called 9/11 Panelist Before Clarke Testified," *Washington Post,* April 5, 2004.
20. Testimony of Richard Clarke to 9/11 Commission, March 24, 2004.
21. Interview with Timothy Flanigan, Dec. 2, 2005.
22. "Abuse of Prisoners in Iraq," *Washington Post,* May 8, 2004.
23. Alberto Gonzales, commencement address, Rice University, May 8, 2004.
24. "White House Memo Criticized," *USA Today,* May 26, 2004.
25. "Press Briefing by Alberto Gonzales," June 22, 2004.

CHAPTER 15
1. "Surrogates Stand in for Bush," *Philadelphia Daily News,* Oct. 28, 2004.
2. Nomination by President Bush of Alberto Gonzales, Nov. 10, 2004.
3. News release, National Council of La Raza, Nov. 10, 2004.
4. "Bush Quickly Picks Chief Counsel as Nominee for Attorney General," *New York Times,* Nov. 11, 2004.
5. Interview with Michael Ratner, Aug. 19, 2005.
6. Interview with Nativo Lopez, Aug. 30, 2005.
7. "It's Hard to Imagine Anyone Less Suited to Be Attorney General," *Chicago Sun-Times,* Nov. 16, 2004.
8. "Out & About," *Washington Post,* Dec. 6, 2004.
9. Interview with John Hutson, Aug. 18, 2005.
10. Interview with former Secretary of Commerce Donald Evans, Dec. 1, 2005.
11. Testimony of Harold Koh, Senate Judiciary Committee, Jan. 7, 2005.

AFTERWORD
1. "Bush's Man from Humble," *Time,* November 22, 2004.

Index